The Transformation of Spain

The Transformation of Spain tells the remarkable story of how a country, which for almost four decades had endured the dictatorship of General Franco, changed its regime radically, rapidly, and without a violent upheaval. Within forty months of Franco's death, Spain had become a constitutional monarchy: sovereignty had been restored to the people, political parties and trade unions had been legalized, and the new constitution recognized human freedoms and the rights of regional minorities.

The stages of the transformation between 1975 and 1979, and the historical background to the events of this period, are closely analysed by David Gilmour. He examines the structure of Franco's dictatorship and traces the socio-economic changes the country underwent during his lengthy rule. He describes the return of the monarchy, the crucial role played by King Juan Carlos during the period, the dismantlement of the old institutions and their replacement by democratic ones. He also looks at those other factors, such as the regional question and the Spanish military tradition, which have hindered and at times endangered the transition to democracy.

David Gilmour

David Gilmour, born in 1952, was educated at Eton and Balliol College, Oxford, where he read Modern History. He is an author and journalist, whose articles and book reviews appear in a number of magazines including the *New Statesman*, *New Society* and the *London Review of Books*. His previous books include *Lebanon: The Fractured Country* (1983), a highly acclaimed analysis of the origins and events of the Lebanese civil war. He is married with four children and lives in Scotland.

The Transformation of Spain

From Franco to the Constitutional Monarchy

David Gilmour

Quartet Books
London Melbourne New York

The author would like to acknowledge the kind permission of Stanford University Press to reproduce extracts from Stanley Payne, *Falange: A History of Spanish Fascism*, 1961.

First published by Quartet Books Limited 1985
A member of the Namara Group 27/29 Goodge Street,
London W1P 1FD

Paperback edition published by Quartet Books Limited 1986

British Library Cataloguing in Publication Data

Gilmour, David
    The transformation of Spain: from Franco to the constitutional
    monarchy.
    1. Spain — Politics and government — 1939-1975
    2. Spain — Politics and government — 1975-
    I. Title
    946.082   DP270

    ISBN 0-7043-0028-1

Reproduced, printed and bound in Great Britain by Nene Litho and
Woolnough Bookbinding, both of Wellingborough, Northants.

To Ignacio de Medina and Alfonso de Otazu

It is quite certain that the essential substance of Spain can embody itself in the form of modern institutions. It will do this beyond a doubt. But this process, if it runs its course undisturbed, will take place as a differentiation and a shaping of what is eternally the same, and *not* as a changing of form.

Count Keyserling
Europe, 1928

I am speaking of Spain's liberal and humanitarian tradition, because this tradition exists, despite those who have long tried to conceal it from you. Spain has not always been an inquisitorial country, nor an intolerant and bigoted one; it has not always been drawn to madness, a madness that might sometimes seem sublime.

Manuel Azaña
Speech in Bilbao 1933

The philosophical affirmation that there is some truth in all ideas has a long history . . . Perhaps in Spain we have not examined with serenity our respective ideologies in order to discover the coincidences, which were perhaps fundamental, and measure the divergences, probably secondary, in order to determine if the latter were worth being aired on the battlefield.

Indalecio Prieto
Palabras de ayer y hoy, 1938

For a century and a half Spaniards . . . have practised the strangest kind of historical behaviour: consumed today by messianic expectation and tomorrow by passive fatalism; one day handed over to frenetic struggle, the next to resignation or cynicism. Yet in spite of all, Spain has not ceased to be a people . . . A people which, more frequently than it may seem, is capable of expressing itself in terms of profound wisdom, but which, from time to time, is captured and undone by despair. A people which, when the time comes, will consign its destiny – for good or bad – to every one of its members, so that none of us can predict its conduct at that crucial hour . . . I know nothing of what time . . . will do to us in the end. But I do believe that the Spanish people will finally decide to make their own history and not to wait for it. And to do so not through impulse, but through reason.

Dionisio Ridruejo
Escrito en España, 1962

Contents

Foreword

General Franco's dictatorship, one of the longest personal rules in modern history, was based on a series of myths: myths about Spain, about Spanish history, about Spanish values, even about the Spaniards themselves. The most persistent of these was the myth that Spaniards are not by nature suited to representative government. The claim is still often repeated by Franco's supporters, but it is not true. Anyone who knows contemporary Spain and can talk to its people will not doubt the widespread support for the present regime. Military officers and their civilian followers who still dream of a return to the obscurantism of past centuries will receive little popular backing for their schemes.

When I first travelled in Spain in 1978, between the first and second elections of the constitutional monarchy, the events of the previous three years still appeared as a sort of accumulating miracle: the peaceful transition from repressive dictatorship to parliamentary government, the dismantling of old institutions and the establishment of new ones, the making of a constitution which enjoyed massive popular support.

I still believe that Spain's transformation was a remarkable achievement in spite of mistakes which were made during those years. But it should not be seen merely as a political process carried out over an astonishingly short period by a few clever politicians. The crucial changes in Spain's society and economy – changes which made the transition possible – had already taken place under the previous regime. The greatest irony of Franco's dictatorship is that his government, which promised to return Spain to the past, should have been responsible for its modernization. The changes brought about by industrialization and the huge exodus from the countryside were of revolutionary proportions. They also made Spaniards realize what an anachronism their regime had become. By 1975 democratic government was no longer simply a remote aspiration for Franco's veteran opponents: it was both the natural development for the country, and the one demanded by a large majority of the Spanish people.

I travelled in Spain many times between 1978 and 1983, usually by train. My main axis was the rapid *talgo* routes between San Sebastian and Madrid, and between Madrid and Seville. From San Sebastian I went by much slower trains through the mountains of Asturias and Galicia, or through the beautiful gorge at Pancorbo to the northern provinces of Castile. From Madrid I travelled across the rest of the *meseta*, and to Aragon and Catalonia; and from Seville I explored the south.

Wherever I went, I was almost always received with kindness by people who did not know me and had no idea what I wanted. I was constantly impressed by the hospitality of people – a trade unionist in Andalusia, a village mayor in Asturias, the director of a cultural institute in La Coruña – who, on the strength of my telephone call from the local railway station, were prepared to spend so much of their time patiently answering my questions.

It is obviously impossible to thank individually all those who, consciously or not, have helped me write this book. But I would like to mention those who have been particularly generous with their help and hospitality: Pilar and Javier Garrigues, Ignacio Medina, Alfonso de Otazu, Antonio Burgos, Beatriz Borrero, Pedro and Ana Schwartz, Gabriel Tortella, Gregorio Marañón, Ramón Bergareche, Pierre and Caroline de Cabarrus, Jorge and Rosario Villavecchia, José María Laso, Luis Rodríguez Ovejero, Pedro Gamero and Fernando Salinas.

My father Ian Gilmour once again read a manuscript of mine and suggested a large number of important changes. The book was also read by Pilar Garrigues, who checked the references and translations, and by Antonio Burgos, Alfonso de Otazu and Ignacio Medina. I am grateful to all of them for their help and suggestions.

I would also like to thank the librarian and staff at both Chatham House and the Spanish Institute in London who were unfailingly helpful in providing me with material for research, and the directors of the newspaper libraries in Seville and San

Sebastian for allowing me to work in their reading rooms. Finally I should thank Zelfa Hourani of Quartet Books for her patience and efficiency, and my wife and children for putting up with such a lengthy project.

Twickenham August 1984

ATLANTIC OCEAN

PORTUGAL

GALICIA
Santiago de Compostela ● Lugo
● Orense

Huelva ●
Cádiz ●

ANDALUSIA
Seville ●

EXTREMADURA
Badajoz ●

Córdoba ●
Málaga ●
Granada ●
Almería ●

Salamanca ●

El Escorial ● MADRID ■
Toledo ●

Segovia ●
Guadalajara ●

Ciudad Real ●

NEW CASTILE

LEVANTE

VALENCIA
Albacete ●
Murcia ●
Cartagena ●
Alicante ●

Valencia ●
Castellón ●

OLD CASTILE

ASTURIAS
Oviedo ●

Valladol'd ●
Burgos ●

Soria ●

ARAGON

Zaragoza ●
Tarragona ●

Santander ●
BASQUE COUNTRY
Bilbao ● Vitoria ● San Sebastián
Pamplona ●

NAVARRE

CATALONIA
Barcelona ●

BAY OF BISCAY

FRANCE

MEDITERRANEAN SEA

BALEARIC ISLANDS

PART ONE

Spain in the Last Years of General Franco

1
In Search of *Franquismo*

The regime of General Franco was conceived by general officers, delivered by the armed forces, and nurtured on aid from Hitler's Germany and the Italy of Benito Mussolini. In its infancy it was sustained by the Falangist Party and by the conservative forces of twentieth-century Spain. Yet the alliance which set out to overthrow the republican government possessed neither ideological coherence nor common objectives beyond the immediate aim of victory. It included conservatives anxious to preserve the old order, falangists intent on carrying out a national-syndicalist revolution and traditionalists determined to go back a hundred years to the era of Don Carlos and renew the struggle for an intolerant church and an absolute monarchy.

Allies and opponents alike have tried to define the regime with a few easy labels, but the very diversity of its components makes such a definition impossible. Writing in 1937, George Orwell argued that 'the military mutiny . . . was an attempt not so much to impose fascism as to restore feudalism'.[1] A few years later, in the aftermath of the Second World War, the United Nations General Assembly recommended the ostracism of Spain on the grounds that it had 'a Fascist regime patterned on . . . Hitler's Nazi Germany and Mussolini's Fascist Italy'.[2] Had Hitler been still alive, he would have laughed at the description. Spain, he had complained, was not run by the fascist Falangist Party but by what he called 'the clerico-monarchical muck',[3] a view echoed many years later by the secretary-general of the party who claimed that the falangists had been 'cast aside by the priests and the military, who are the ones who have governed from the very beginning'.[4] Most of these and other definitions contained much that was true

3

but they cannot by themselves give even an adequate idea of the nature of the regime. *Franquista* Spain was built of so many different materials and was so divided by its own contradictions that it is fruitless to try to explain it as the product of a particular ideological or political movement. Any analysis should begin instead with a look at its leading figure, because in Spain, as with many other dictatorships, the nature of the regime owed more to the character and ideas of its dictator than it did to its official, self-proclaimed ideology.

Francisco Franco Bahamonde was before all else a soldier. According to a veteran falangist minister, 'in his private life he was straightforward, good-natured and austere. He lived and died as a soldier.'[5] A brave and enterprising officer in his youth, a cautious and unimaginative general in middle age, his attitude to life was essentially military. He believed that some areas of civilian life would benefit from military discipline and in old age declared that hospitals and universities ought to be organized along military lines.[6] Throughout his life he remained emotionally tied to the army and its traditions. In his eighties he listened to military marches every day and paced up and down his study in time to them. His doctor was convinced that the activity did much to restore his health and morale after a nearly fatal illness in 1974.[7]

Franco's critics and his supporters agree about many sides of his character, although they use different adjectives to describe them. He was a puritanical man, both in his own habits and in his attitude to other people's, he seldom drank and he does not appear to have been interested in any woman other than his wife, Doña Carmen. He was not noticeably religious as a young man but became so after his marriage, and in later life he appears to have thought highly of the powers of the saints. Beside his bed he kept the mummified hand of St Teresa of Avila and took it around with him when he travelled.[8] Our Lady of the Fuencisla, the patron saint of Segovia, received even more exalted treatment, being appointed a field marshal for her role in the city's defence in 1936.[9]

Almost everyone who met Franco was impressed by his patience and lack of irritability. His ministers have recorded the astonishing calmness and serenity with which he presided over cabinet meetings, never becoming angry, rarely interrupting, yet remaining fully in control of the proceedings. His critics have employed other words to describe these same qualities, comment-

ing on his smugness, his self-satisfaction, his 'overwhelming sense
of self-righteousness'.[10] Sir Samuel Hoare, Britain's ambassador
to Spain during the Second World War, seldom mentioned
Franco's name in his book without remarking on the man's
'amazing complacency'.[11] Hoare regarded his career as 'a series of
unexpected successes over both his friends and enemies' and
refused to ascribe them to anything more than luck, 'his Gallego
cunning' and the weakness of his rivals,[12] but most other
commentators have agreed that he was able and above all
competent. He was a methodical and meticulous man in private
life as well as in government. He counted the number of
partridges he shot and told one American journalist that he had
bagged 8,240 in a single year.[13] Although he read a good deal of
history, he had a hatred for philosophy and intellectual debate. He
despised intellectuals as people who 'consider that they live in a
different world, very superior to the rest of us, and who therefore
think that society is obliged to serve them and to forgive their
faults and errors.'[14]

Franco's main interest outside government was field sports and
he spent much of his time fishing in Galicia or shooting in Castile.
General Franco Salgado-Araujo, his cousin and head of his
military secretariat, complained that Franco went shooting three
days a week and thus had no time to study the nation's
problems.[15] According to one cabinet minister, it was not possible
to discuss politics seriously until the end of February, when the
shooting season ended.[16] Even when he was not pursuing
partridges, Franco liked to live with the atmosphere of 'the chase',
surrounding himself with stuffed pheasants and pictures of dead
game. Painting was his second interest, particularly the painting of
seascapes and dead animals. Of the collection of Franco's own
paintings which are included in his last doctor's memoirs, a
majority portray birds and animals which are either dead or
dying.[17]

Franco's enemies liked to depict him as a cruel and ruthless man,
but it is unlikely that the description bothered either him or his
followers. After all, such qualities were hardly alien to the military
traditions of his country while the falangists even welcomed them
as qualities likely to stiffen the nation. They would have been far
more insulted had he been regarded as feeble or incompetent.
Franco was certainly a harsh and cruel man without magnanimity,

but he was not a sadist, even though one sympathetic biographer records him 'chuckling with glee . . . as [he] drew up the daily execution lists' after the civil war.[18] Mussolini demanded the death penalty in order 'to make Italians more virile, to habituate them to the sight of blood and to the idea of death'.[19] But Franco, although he killed and executed far more people than Mussolini, thought of death in very different terms. One observer described Franco's attitude as 'the soldier's – especially the Spanish soldier's – indifference to life or death, the cruelty of the centurion'.[20] It was this indifference which enabled him to accept unnecessarily high casualty rates in the civil war,[21] and led him to order the execution of thousands of prisoners during and after it. Franco did not sanction the shooting of up to 200,000 people[22] after the war because he enjoyed the spectacle. He merely judged it to be necessary and, since he was impervious to suffering, he had no compunction about giving the orders. While lunching with a nazi businessman one day, he ordered the shooting of some republican militiawomen 'without changing the tone he would use for discussion of the weather'.[23]

Franco showed an astonishing cold-heartedness and lack of humanity towards almost everyone outside his immediate family and his circle of shooting companions. He rarely gave praise or even showed kindness to the most faithful of his supporters. Ministers who had served him loyally for years would learn of their dismissals from reading the newspaper at breakfast. One foreign minister, Colonel Beigbeder, enjoyed a confidential chat with Franco, in which he was encouraged to believe that his post was secure, only to open a newspaper 36 hours later to discover that he had been sacked.[24] Franco Salgado-Araujo, who served him in one capacity or another for over forty years, wrote of his egotism, coldness and indifference, and added that he had long given up expecting Franco ever to thank him for his loyalty and service.[25] If Franco had to make a political decision, no personal considerations were allowed to stand in his way. Every decision was the result of dispassionate calculation. Even so, the degree of his severity is often hard to understand. In 1937 he ordered the execution of one of Spain's most distinguished officers, General Batet, the man who had put down the Catalan rising of October 1934 intelligently and humanely, in notable contrast to the manner in which General Franco had suppressed the simultaneous revolt in Asturias. During the civil war Batet was taken from prison, where he had been for seven months, and shot on Franco's orders not because he had rallied to the defence of the republic but merely because he had refused to join the rebels.[26]

In old age Franco told his doctor that the secret of his success was that he was not a politician and did not understand politics.[27] It was a highly disingenuous remark. Whatever his shortcomings as a statesman, Franco was an immensely skilful politician. He was frequently lucky and he was sometimes naive, but the 'series of unexpected successes' which so puzzled Hoare in the forties continued almost without interruption for another thirty years. The secret of this success was not his ignorance of politics but his grasp of political reality, his understanding of the possibilities of a particular situation. According to one of his ministers, Franco's politics were 'more tactical than dogmatic [because] he was a *posibilista* who tackled problems with a sense of realism' rather than from any doctrinaire or ideological standpoint.[28] This is perhaps an understatement. As a politician Franco was a supreme pragmatist and his politics were innately empirical. His greatest achievement was to hold together the civil war coalition for nearly forty years by keeping a balance between its discordant factions. In contrast to some of his fellow dictators, Franco, although he enjoyed the exercise of power, was not mesmerized by its lure. Unlike Mussolini, he did not have to hold six or seven cabinet posts at the same time in order to demonstrate the extent of his authority. Franco directed from above, delegating to his ministers and arbitrating between them when necessary. His was a personal rule, but it was not megalomania. He created a system in which he possessed great power but seldom had to use it. He was often less the captain of his team than a referee controlling its behaviour.

Franco was a dictator through accident and not through ambition. He thus lacked many of the attributes of those who spend much of their lives plotting to become dictators. He was no demagogue in need of cheering crowds and public adulation but a weak public speaker with a thin, high-pitched voice. Nor was he a thinker or ideologue, ready with some half-baked theory on how to galvanize the Spanish people. Whatever else he was, Franco was not a fascist. He was a devout, conservative, military man with a small and basic stock of highly reactionary ideas. It was these ideas, the product of a simplistic, Catholic and extremely conservative interpretation of Spanish history, which became the guidelines for the organization of *franquista* Spain.

Franco expounded his version of Spanish history in a speech in April 1937.[29] For him there had been three stages in the life of the nation since the centuries of the 'Reconquest'. The first had been the Golden Age, the 'Christian Empire' of the Catholic Kings, Charles V and Philip II, a Spain based firmly in Castile and 'united to defend and extend throughout the world her universal and Catholic message'. This was the period of the true Spain, 'the most sublime and perfect moment of our history'. This magnificent era was followed by a calamitous period when the country degenerated into the 'bastardized, Frenchified and Europeanized Spain of "the liberals"'. During this time the true Spain had been represented by the carlist forces of Navarre and the north which tried to restore the glory of Catholic Spain in the civil wars of the nineteenth century. During the third and final period of the nation's history, the true Spain had been defended first by the regime of General Primo de Rivera (1922–29), then by a few small political parties of fascist inspiration, and finally by Franco himself and the men who supported him. On 18 July 1936 true Spain had risen to crush 'anti-Spain' by means of a revolt which was sometimes termed a crusade and sometimes a war of liberation but which was never referred to as a civil war. Franco always denied that it had been a war between Spaniards. 'Our victory has not been over our brothers,' he said in Burgos in February 1939, 'but over the world, over international forces, over Freemasonry.'[30] Spain, which Franco assured Winston Churchill was once again 'sound, virile and chivalrous',[31] had merely defeated her historic enemies. In God's name she 'had vanquished with heroism the enemy of truth in this century'.[32] Pragmatic and realistic though he was, even Franco was at times carried away by the rhetoric of the hour. He seems to have thought he could obliterate the memory of Spain's decadence and return to the glories of empire. In the summer of 1940 he visited Seville and signed his name in the golden book of the *Archivo General de Indias*. Beside his signature he wrote, 'before the relics of one empire, with the promise of another'.[33]

Franco's view of history was shared by his supporters and rapidly became the version taught to Spanish school-children. Millions of them were brought up to believe that the civil war had

been a 'war of independence . . . against foreign ideas,' fought by
'the Spanish army [which], once more carrying out its duty and
demonstrating its spirit of self-sacrifice, saved Spain from the red
revolution'.[34] From one publication put out by the vice-secretariat
of popular education in 1943, school-children could read 'the
wonderful legend of Spain' which pictured the country as a
princess in distress who is rescued by 'a rider on a white horse'
(Franco) and thereby 'freed from the poison distilled by envy'.[35]

The version presented to adults was hardly more sophisticated.
The forces of the republic were not composed of true Spaniards
but of people who had been so corrupted by foreign ideas that
they were no longer properly Spanish. In the gallery of anti-Spain
the chief villains were liberals, Jews, freemasons, socialists,
regionalists, anticlericals and communists. Attempts to weaken
Spain were blamed on their sinister machinations which were
given the generic and rather mysterious title, 'the Judeo-Masonic
conspiracy'. Although the communists were depicted by Franco
as being the most deadly of his opponents, this was done mainly
for political reasons. It was easier to unite the country, just as later,
in the 1950s, it was easier to portray himself as an indispensable
ally of the United States, if he said he was fighting the communists
instead of telling the truth, which is that he was fighting
liberalism. In 1936 the communists, with sixteen deputies in a
Cortes of 473, represented no conceivable threat to Spain, a fact of
which Franco was well aware: he did not bother even to mention
communism when he issued his manifesto at the beginning of the
rebellion.[36] Liberalism was the real adversary of the regime, the
historic enemy of true Spain since the time of the French
Revolution. When Franco proclaimed triumphantly that he had
'liquidated the nineteenth century which should never have
existed',[37] he meant that he had destroyed the legacy of successive
liberal governments. When he said that the nineteenth century was
'the negation of the Spanish Spirit,'[38] he meant that liberalism was
alien to Spain. Franco considered that liberalism was not only an
evil itself but, worse, it encouraged all the other vices peculiar to
anti-Spain. This view was well expressed by Rafael Calvo Serer,
who was originally an extreme conservative although he later
became an opponent of Franco: 'liberty of conscience leads to a
loss of faith, liberty of expression to demagoguery, ideological
confusion and pornography . . . Between fascists, catholics and

conservatives it has been possible to have a certain dialogue, which is impossible with radicalism and liberal democracy.'[39]

Had Franco accepted that he had been fighting a civil war in which the greater part of the Spanish people had remained loyal to the elected government, there might have been some chance of reconciliation afterwards. But his version of the conflict left no room for reconciliation. The enemies of Spain had been annihilated and must never be allowed to rise again. There could thus be no question of mutual forgiveness, no possibility of a genuinely national government to nurse the country after its terrible ordeal. Franco made no effort to unite post-civil war Spain but deliberately set out to divide it still further, to create a society split decisively between the conquered and their conquerors, between *los vencidos* and *los vencedores*. Spain was henceforth a country where the *vencedores* would have access to power, wealth and a certain degree of liberty, and the *vencidos* would not.[40] The demarcation was sharp and explicit. Perhaps it had to be. If Franco had conceded that his opponents had any rights at all, he would have been casting doubt implicitly on the legitimacy of his own rebellion. Therefore they had to be excluded. Raimundo Fernández Cuesta, secretary-general of the Falangist Party, made the position clear in 1951: 'Between their Spain and ours there lies an abyss which can be crossed only by repentance and submission to our doctrine. If they do not do this, it would be better for them to stay on the other side of the abyss and, if they try to cross it in secret, for them to perish.'[41]

Threatened by the ghosts of the nineteenth century and by their more radical descendants in the twentieth, Franco's Spain had to remain on a leash, denied freedoms of expression or information in case such concessions encouraged the return of the vanquished ideologies. Franco was quite clear about what he was not going to let the Spaniards have, and he was equally certain how they were not to be governed. A parliamentary democracy was out of the question. Such a system, which he regarded as 'inorganic', merely paved the way for communism.[42] Moreover, it was particularly inappropriate for Spain, at least according to his own reading of Spanish history. 'A century and a half of parliamentary democracy,' he once said, 'accompanied by the loss of immense territory, three civil wars, and the imminent danger of national disintegration, add up to a disastrous balance sheet, sufficient to discredit parliamentary systems in the eyes of the Spanish people'.[43] In its stead he proposed an entirely different system, which was known as 'organic democracy', in which the people would be represented not by political parties which 'sacrifice the interests of the nation to those of the party' but by 'natural' institutions, such as the municipalities, the syndicates and the corporations working harmoniously together for the good of the nation.[44]

Among the defenders of the true Spain which Franco had singled out in his speech of April 1937 were two small, quasi-fascist parties, the JONS (*Juntas de Ofensiva Nacional Sindicalista*) and the *Falange Española*, which amalgamated in 1934 to form the *Falange Española de las* JONS. Franco was neither intellectually nor temperamentally a fascist but he admired many things about this party and he shared its views on the decline of Spain. Both Franco and the falangists based their ideals on the belief that Spain was different from Europe and that solutions which were perhaps applicable to the problems of France or Britain were not applicable to Spain's. This was neither a new nor a radical idea. It had been put forward by several intellectuals of the so-called Generation of '98, by writers such as Unamuno and Americo Castro who sought among the ruins of their country's history the reasons for its present decadence. (In 1898 Spain had lost its last colonial possessions.) They were searching for the 'essence' of Spain and they found it in the harsh landscape and infinite horizons of Castile, 'the heart of Spain' and birthplace of the empire. Spain's essential character was Castilian, moulded during the *Reconquista* and epitomized by the *conquistadores* of the sixteenth century. The national character was thus formed long before the Enlightenment and owed nothing to the rest of Europe. Rationalism, liberalism and all the other ideas of eighteenth and nineteenth century Europe were at best irrelevant to Spain and at worst they polluted the character of the Spanish people. Castro concluded that the Spanish character was irreconcilable with the modern world.[45]

Although in other ways the *Falange* was as fascist as any other party being set up at that time in imitation of Mussolini, it did share this highly conservative view of Spanish history. It emphasized the importance of traditional values and it is significant that its support came mainly from the Castilian towns of Valladolid and Madrid. The *Falange* recommended 'a spirit of sacrifice and service, the ascetic and military sense of life'.[46] It pressed for national unity under the primacy of Castile and an aggressive foreign policy to acquire an empire that would include Morocco, other parts of Africa and, if possible, Portugal.[47] The party's two main sources of inspiration were Mussolini and Spain's Golden Age, but it is notable that its propagandists placed greater stress on Spanish history than on fascism.[48] One of them even tried to combine the two by claiming that the Spain of Ferdinand and Isabella was a fascist country and thus a precursor of Mussolini's Italy.[49]

The nature of Spanish fascism has been partially obscured by the charismatic figure of its chief, or *jefe*, José Antonio Primo de Rivera. A son of the dictator, General Miguel Primo de Rivera, José Antonio was very different from the fascist leaders of other countries. Although there were some ambiguous sides to his character, not least in his attitude towards violence, he was far from being a brutal and swaggering mimic of Mussolini. He was young, attractive and aristocratic, an educated man far too sceptical and honest to be a successful demagogue. An anglophile and an admirer of Kipling – unusual attributes in European fascists – he was a brilliant parliamentarian respected by politicians of the Left such as the socialist Indalecio Prieto and the republican Manuel Azaña. The attractiveness of José Antonio's character and the impressive manner of his death in the jail of Alicante in November 1936 have given Spanish fascism an idealized and romantic gloss which is wholly undeserved. In spite of its obsession with history and the glamour of its *jefe*, the *Falange* was a more or less orthodox fascist party which shared many of the characteristics of its Italian counterpart. It adopted the fascist salute, dressed its members in blue shirts (instead of black) and set up a paramilitary organization. Realizing that its aims could probably be achieved only by violence, it sought to abolish political parties and establish a totalitarian state. It often referred darkly to the plots of the 'Judeo-Masonic conspiracy' but since there were very few Jews in Spain and a great many freemasons, it concentrated its venom on the latter. As in Italy, it contained conservatives who supported it as the best means of preventing a socialist revolution and radicals who wanted to carry out a national-syndicalist revolution. Among the radical falangists were many, including José Antonio, who hated Spanish conservatives as much as they disliked the revolutionary Left. Ramiro Ledesma, one of the founders of the JONS, admired the anarchists[50] while José Antonio admitted that his economic views were similar to those of the *prietista* socialists.[51] Their principal criticism of liberalism and marxism was that the ideologies were anti-nationalist and un-Spanish. It was for this reason that the falangists became allies of the conservative Right.

In the general election of February 1936 the *Falange* had failed to win a single seat, yet by the end of that year it was the most important organization in nationalist Spain. It had been selected by General Franco as the political movement of his regime. Army officers automatically became members of the party and so did many government employees. All other political parties were banned. The *Falange* had become an instrument of state and in the process it lost its purity as well as its independence. In April 1937 Franco proclaimed the *Falange*'s amalgamation with the traditionalist carlists although fascism and carlism had little in common beyond authoritarian inclinations and a hatred of liberalism. The new formation, vast, amorphous and badly organized, was given the title *Falange Española Tradicionalista y de las Juntas de Ofensiva Nacional Sindicalista* (or FET *de las* JONS) and its new *jefe* was Francisco Franco.

As falangism became 'official', it soon lost its revolutionary spirit. Many of its original members, the old shirts or *camisas viejas*, had been killed in the early days of the rising and those who remained were quickly swamped by the crowds of new members who joined up not because they believed in falangist ideology but simply because they were pro-Franco and anti-republican. Franco, of course, would never have dreamt of joining the party in the ordinary course of events and only accepted it because he recognized the need for some form of political organization for his regime. He therefore took it over, adopted those parts of its programme which he found attractive and discarded the rest. The idea that the *Falange* was a revolutionary organization was naturally abandoned and those members who claimed its ideology was 'nothing less than the nationalization of the doctrine of Marx'[52] played little further part in political life. Falangist ideas on empire, totalitarianism and national-syndicalism were, however, retained, at least for a time. While Hitler and Mussolini were supplying Franco with military aid and later, when Germany seemed to be winning the Second World War, it was useful to keep up fascist appearances in Spain. After 1945, however, these were mostly dropped. Four months after the overthrow of Hitler, the law that had made the fascist salute compulsory was repealed by Franco.

Thus the *Falange* came to be just one of the components of the regime, an important one certainly, but not with any decisive power. In 1956 the secretary-general of the party produced statistics showing that the *camisas viejas* – that is, party veterans from before the rising – occupied less than five per cent of the posts in administration at municipal, provincial and national levels. [53] The *Falange* was useful to Franco because it was the only force which possessed a sort of ideology that might conceivably attract people to the regime. For this reason he encouraged the cult of José Antonio, who became the martyr-hero of the new state and whose name was emblazoned on the walls of Spanish cathedrals. After the war the dead *jefe*'s coffin was carried on the shoulders of falangists all the way from Alicante to the church in El Escorial where he was buried near the Spanish kings. José Antonio, generous, muddled and bold, a man of passion and self-doubt who possessed an heroic if misguided vision for his country, was thus used by a man who had none of these qualities and turned into the 'patron saint' of a regime he would have hated.

Franco manipulated the *Falange* unscrupulously whenever he needed to. In his hands it became what one observer described as 'a scarecrow that [he] picks up and shakes threateningly now and then'.[54] It was used as a counter balance to set against the other 'pillars' of the regime when Franco thought it necessary, but it was an organization whose power was almost continually in decline. It ceased to be a vital force in 1945 because it was no good trumpeting about empire and the 'virility' of fascism after Italy's embarrassing performance in the Second World War. Just as Franco hastily removed the signed photographs of Hitler and Mussolini from his desk and replaced them with those of the Pope and President Carmona of Portugal,[55] so he made a point of getting rid of some of the paraphernalia of falangism. But the party still had some jobs to do, organizing the syndicates and occupying at least two of the ministries at any one time. Not that this was particularly satisfactory because falangists were rarely given important cabinet posts and none of them ever occupied any of the crucial economic ministries. Nor was the syndical work much more rewarding: the *Falange*, in origin a national-syndicalist body, was given the task of running the state syndicates but was prevented from doing so effectively because it was not allowed to set up a genuine syndicalist system.

The *Falange* has seemed more important than it actually was because its presence was always visible and because its ideology became the staple rhetoric of the regime. Franco and his ministers were often saying the same things as José Antonio even if they had no intention of carrying them out. Consequently they gave the impression that falangism was a powerful and even a directing force when in fact it was not. Franco even admitted to one of his ambassadors that, as far as he was concerned, the purpose of the *Movimiento* (from 1958 the *Falange* was usually known as the *Movimiento Nacional*) was to act as a claque, or cheer leader, 'like a few people in a crowd who start clapping so that the others join in'.[56] Thus the *Falange* was used cynically by a man who adopted its language without adopting its programme. But probably it would have failed anyway. It had supported the losing side in the world war and, besides, it was disliked by most of the other elements of the regime, including the Church, many army generals, and the economists and businessmen associated with the mainly lay order Opus Dei. The Church may have had the same enemies as the falangists but that did not make them friends. Cardinal Segura, who considered the nazis were even worse than the communists, thought the falangists just as bad.[57]

In 1934 Ramiro Ledesma and José Antonio had drawn up the Twenty-Seven Points of the *Falange*, a document intended to contain the ideology and programme of the party. When Franco took control of the *Falange* and united it to the carlists, he adopted all these points except, for obvious reasons, the twenty-seventh which prohibited the party from allying itself to any other political organization. The Twenty-Six Points, as they were now known, became the official ideology of the regime and remained so until 1958 when they were effectively superseded by the Principles of the *Movimiento Nacional*.

Nothing illustrates better the decline of the *Falange* and the almost total irrelevance of its ideology to Spain in the late fifties than the text of these Principles. Gone are the old fascist dogmas of the Twenty-Six Points. There is no mention now of 'repudiating the capitalist system' (Point 10), 'nationalizing the banks' (Point 14) or 'expropriating land without compensation' (Point 21). There is no talk of totalitarianism or of setting up a national-syndicalist state. Instead of affirming that 'the historic destiny of Spain is imperial' or claiming for the nation 'a pre-eminent position in Europe' (Point 3), the new principles tamely 'aspire to the establishment of justice and peace between nations'. The ranting slogans of the thirties had been done away with because in the generation that followed the civil war, Spain had begun to change radically, and in the following generation it would change even more. Few Spaniards in 1958 were still dreaming the vision of José Antonio; the priority for most of them, and for the regime itself, was economic prosperity. On the twentieth anniversary of the *jefe*'s execution, the secretary-general of the *Falange*, José Luis de Arrese, summed up the feelings of the *camisas viejas* when he broadcast on national radio the following words:

> José Antonio . . . Are you satisfied with us?
> I do not think so.
> And I think not because you struggled against materialism and egotism, while today men have forgotten the grandeur of your words only to run like thirsty madmen down the path of materialism and egotism.
> Because you wanted a Fatherland of poets and of dreamers eager for a difficult glory, while men seek only a catering, round-bellied Fatherland, full of starch, though it possess neither beauty nor gallantry . . .
> . . . José Antonio, you are not satisfied with us. You who watch us from your place, from your twentieth of November, with a profound sense of melancholy and scorn.
> You cannot be satisfied with this mediocre, sensual life.[58]

The *franquista* state had begun by proclaiming itself 'a totalitarian instrument in the service of the national integrity' (Point 6 of the Twenty-Six Points) but it is debatable whether it was ever strictly totalitarian and it was certainly far from being so in its later years. The Spanish sociologist, Amando de Miguel, regarded the Twenty-Six Points as the ideology of a 'fascist totalitarian state' while the Principles of the *Movimiento Nacional* belonged to a state that was 'traditional authoritarian'.[59] But even while it retained its falangist ideology it was not truly totalitarian. Many years ago, Professor Juan Linz drew up his famous definitions of totalitarianism and authoritarianism and, if the *franquista* state is tested against his criteria, then it fits easily into the category of authoritarian regimes.[60] Franco's Spain was not subjected to one-party rule, it was not governed according to a particular ideology and its government made no attempt to mobilize the people in its support. Nor were Spaniards subjected to restrictions on travel, emigration, conversation or even censorship comparable to those imposed by totalitarian regimes elsewhere.

The ideology of falangism was not replaced by a different set of doctrines but by a sort of anti-ideology, a belief that Spain would get along much better without political ideas. The proponents of this idea were usually members or sympathizers of Opus Dei, some of whom took over the key economic ministries after 1957 and whose successors managed to dominate government until 1973. Henceforth Spain was to be administered not by idealists but by technocrats. Politics were to be abandoned and the country was to become 'depoliticized'. Spain would enter a new epoch, 'the twilight of ideologies',[61] in which the Opus Dei ministers would concentrate on the really important issue, the creation of a prosperous and efficient economy.[62] The technocratic ideal was disliked by many people of the regime – Manuel Fraga thought it complacent and politically dangerous[63] – but nevertheless it occupied the central position in government thinking throughout the sixties.

The lack of political ideology led to the depoliticization of the country. Spaniards, who had been exposed for so long to falangist demands for heroism and self-sacrifice, were now encouraged to take an interest in their material welfare. The regime wanted to channel people's enthusiasm into business, sport, economic development – anything, in fact, other than politics – and it succeeded. According to an opinion poll carried out in 1969, more than three-quarters of young Spaniards admitted to little or no interest in politics.[64] Football was the national passion and a Madrid sports paper became the newspaper with the highest circulation in the country. The men from the Opus and their supporters were delighted by this development. 'Political apathy,' claimed Gonzalo Fernández de la Mora, who was lauded as the chief ideologue of this anti-ideology and compared, oddly, by one admirer to Socrates,[65] 'is not a symptom of social disease but of health . . . The health of free states can be measured by the degree of political apathy. It is not a disturbing factor . . .'[66]

Franquista Spain was able to adopt in turn the ideologies of José Antonio and Fernández de la Mora simply because it was not a state which was governed according to ideologies. Instead of clear doctrines, it had a number of what Linz referred to as 'distinctive mentalities' which were not homogeneous and, indeed, were often contradictory. The government was usually able to adapt to changing circumstances and its survival owed much to the pragmatic skills of its dictator. Ultimately the most important feature of its existence was Franco's personal rule. He and his associates believed that they had created a system and planned to perpetuate it after his death through a *franquista* monarchy. But *franquismo*, or francoism, was not a system just as it was not even an 'ism'. It was more an attitude, or perhaps a collection of attitudes. Franco had nearly forty years of power in which he demonstrated great ability as a tactician and as a subtle politician. But he was not a statesman and he had no vision of the state which would succeed him. One of Franco's closest associates, Laureano López Rodó, said that Spain would be governed after his death 'according to the Fundamental Laws which he promulgated'.[67] This showed a surprising naïveté on the part of an intelligent man who had been responsible for much of Spain's economic development in the sixties. The Fundamental Laws were not a system of government but merely an aid to Franco's personal rule. They could not have survived without him.

For all its claims to permanence as the fulfilment of an historical destiny, *franquismo* was in the end little more than a personal rule sanctioned by victory in the civil war and extended by an unusually long life span. It had no consistent ideology but was guided by a number of simple, eclectic ideas which were easily discarded once their usefulness was over. Its institutions could never have been permanent and their dismantlement after Franco's death was inevitable. Ricardo de La Cierva, a supporter of the regime, prophesied before the end that there could not be *franquismo* without Franco as there was gaullism without De Gaulle, because gaullism was a political party while *franquismo* was merely an epoch.[68]

2
The Structure of the Dictatorship

In September 1936 the junta of nationalist generals in Burgos named Francisco Franco 'Head of Government'. Two days afterwards Franco gave himself the title of 'Head of State' and thus he remained. Although some of his fellow officers were irritated by the way he had so rapidly promoted himself, there was not much they could do about it. In a short time Franco had become Head of Government, Head of State, Generalissimo of the Armed Forces and *jefe* of the only political party. He retained all these posts for thirty-seven years until, at the age of eighty, he relinquished one of them, Head of Government, to Admiral Carrero Blanco.

Since it was the product of a military revolt, the regime obviously lacked any kind of legal basis. It was not accountable to anyone, nor was its leader. Franco believed that his victory had been ordained by God and by History and, in view of this, he felt there was no need to justify himself further. He had become *Caudillo* of Spain 'by the Grace of God', according to the inscription on the newly-minted coins, and he was 'responsible before God and History'.[1] The executive was Franco and it was not an executive which had to answer to any other body in the country. There was literally no formal limit to the powers held by Franco. He ruled conventionally through a cabinet with ministers who were named by him and who would resign if he told them to. But they were not responsible to the people, to a parliament or to anyone else. They were responsible only to Franco. As one commentator had observed, 'in Spain the principle of "one man, one vote" applied to only one man'.[2]

Franquista Spain had no formal constitution but was

administered according to a somewhat unco-ordinated series of
Fundamental Laws which were promulgated over a period of
thirty years. The first was the Labour Charter of 1938 and the
seventh and last, the Organic Law of the State (1967). The
ideological framework of the regime, which has already been
discussed, is encased in the Law on the Principles of the
Movimiento Nacional of May 1958. The emphasis throughout was
on the 'organic' nature of the state which was to have a political
system based on natural or 'organic' democracy, unlike Western,
liberal nations whose democracies were unnatural or 'inorganic'.
Organic democracy owed much to the theory of corporativism. In
such a system the people would be represented not by political
parties which are unnatural but by 'national interests' working
through 'natural organisms'.[3] The key natural organisms, such as
the municipalities, the syndicates and the various corporations
would send their representatives to the *Cortes* in Madrid. There, in
spite of the strong liberal traditions of the building, they would be
able, said Franco, 'to carry out the same functions as deputies
exercise in all other countries', with the crucial difference that they
would be 'dedicated exclusively to the service of the nation' and
would be able to perform their duties away from 'the passions of
party struggles'.[4]

'No one was ever born a member of a political party,' José
Antonio Primo de Rivera had said in a famous speech in the
Teatro Comedia of Madrid. 'On the other hand, we are all born
members of a family; we are all neighbours in a municipality; we
all labour in the exercise of a profession . . .'[5] To the falangist *jefe*,
the three main natural organisms of society were thus the family,
the municipality and the syndicate, in comparison with which the
political party was unnatural and artificial. It was one of the
falangist ideas which the regime adopted enthusiastically.
Although the *Cortes* was composed of deputies, or rather
procuradores, from a great many spheres (the Institute of Actuaries
and the College of Veterinary Surgeons both elected a *procurador*)
the most important categories were the national councillors of the
Movimiento and the three natural organisms of José Antonio.

The 'family' only received representation in 1967 after the
Organic Law decreed that two pi   adores familiares from each
province should be elected by heac   ⁻ families and by married
women. This group, which totalled   members of a *Cortes* of

562, was the only one to be directly elected; it could claim in fact to be the only important group to be elected in an even remotely democratic way in the entire history of *franquista* Spain.★ Nevertheless, it was a fairly modest concession since it applied to less than a fifth of the *Cortes*. Moreover, in practice candidates generally needed some form of government sponsorship in order to be successful. The measure was not a serious democratic reform and was not regarded as such by the Spanish people. More than forty per cent of them abstained in the 1967 elections and even more refused to go to the polls in 1971.

The *procuradores* for the *Movimiento Nacional* (112 members), the municipalities (111 members) and the syndicates (150 members) were either appointed or else elected by indirect and highly complicated methods which in effect ensured that only candidates acceptable to the government were chosen. In the syndical sector there were five separate electoral stages between the vote of the factory worker and the election of the *procurador*.[6] Most of those chosen by this method turned out to be officials of the regime already holding positions in the *Movimiento* or the syndical organization.

National-syndicalism, the key ingredient of the falangist ideology, was adopted as official policy of the *franquista* state. It was designed to solve the problem of class conflict by the creation of 'vertical' syndicates which all employees from the shop-floor upwards and all employers would be obliged to join. Neither group would need organizations of their own since their interests, being national, would be complementary rather than conflicting. Early in the civil war the anarchist and socialist trade unions were banned and in 1939 moves were made to set up a syndical system. In 1940 the Law of Syndical Unity was proclaimed and by the following year there were twenty-four syndicates (representing different sectors of industry, agriculture and the service industries), rising later to twenty-eight.

The regime had thus created a syndicalist structure and, had it

★The only other occasion when the Spanish people as a whole was consulted was at a referendum. This, however, was held only twice during the regime's lifetime, in 1947 to approve the Law of Succession, which officially made Spain a monarchy (though without, for the time being, a monarch), and in 1966 to ratify the Organic Law. As in most other undemocratic systems, the government obtained, on each occasion, well over ninety per cent of the votes cast.

wanted, it could have operated a genuine syndicalist system. But this was not in fact what it wanted. Whereas in Italy the corporative idea was championed, at least in theory, by Mussolini and the Fascist Party, in Spain it was only really supported by one faction of the victorious civil war coalition. Franco and most of his supporters were themselves lukewarm to the theory and regarded it as nothing much more than a means of controlling the working class. The representatives elected to the various committees inside the syndical structure were neither representative of the workers nor, since they were merely elected to consultative bodies, did they take part in making decisions. Labour questions were in practice settled not by them but by the minister of labour or, after 1968, by the minister of syndical relations.[7] The syndicalist idea (employers and employees working together instead of in conflict) was never given a proper chance in Spain. There was no balance between the two sectors. While the workers were on the whole controlled by the government, the large employers were usually able to by-pass the syndicates altogether and deal with the government departments directly.[8]

There was one attempt to establish genuine national-syndicalism in Spain and that was made by Gerardo Salvador Merino who was in charge of the syndicates from 1939 to 1941. His plans to set up a corporative system were so radical, however, that generals, industrialists and other conservatives clubbed together to get rid of him. While on his honeymoon he was accused of being a freemason (a serious charge in *franquista* Spain) and on his return he was sacked and banished to the Balearics.[9] Spain under Franco never became a corporative state. Neither the conservatives nor the *Caudillo* wanted it. But they did allow the *Falange* to set up the syndicalist machinery which, even if it did not function, was useful for controlling the workers and for the propaganda needs of organic democracy. The running of this 'system' and the administration of local government were the only really important duties performed by falangists during the last thirty years of the *franquista* regime.

The corporative idea was thus frustrated at the first stage since the corporations, or syndicates, were unrepresentative and power-less. It was finally sabotaged at the national level because the *Cortes*, apparently designed as a corporative chamber, ended up by being little more than a club for the regime's yes-men. In theory it was meant to be the legislature; in practice it did not legislate. It merely discussed those bills introduced by the government and, after occasionally making some minor amendments, it passed them. Of the several thousand laws enacted in the thirty years following its first session in 1943, only two were suggested by the *procuradores* themselves.[10] In spite of its solemnity, its complicated composition, and its pompous aura of legality, the *Cortes* was merely a rubber-stamp parliament. Although it had theoretic controls over the passing of new laws, in fact it seldom used them, while over the executive it had no control at all. The government's ministers were responsible to Franco not to the *Cortes*. They did not have to appear before the *procuradores* to defend themselves or to take part in debates. If they wished to, they could address the *Cortes* on some specific subject but they did not have to answer questions afterwards. The relationship between the *procuradores* and the government was entirely one-sided. The *Cortes* could be used or ignored as necessary.

In *franquista* Spain there was no separation of powers. The *Caudillo* was in virtually total control of the executive, the legislature and the judiciary. Although the creation of a number of high-sounding entities such as the Council of the Realm gave the appropriate impression of legality, these were usually ineffective consultative bodies that did nothing to restrict Franco's power. Franco used the institutions he had created to carry out his policy but he did not shrink from avoiding them if he found it easier. The government could by-pass the judiciary when it wanted and impose its own penalties just as it could ignore the *Cortes* altogether and legislate by decree. The power enjoyed by Franco was much greater than it seemed because he used it intelligently. He did not have to bluster to get his own way. He governed according to the principle of divide and rule but he divided his friends not his enemies. He ruled by keeping the components of his regime in a state of perpetual antagonism. Monarchists, falangists, technocrats and the rest plotted against each other and squabbled over policy. But Franco remained above the feuds, intervening only when they began to get out of hand. His arbitrations were always scrupulously even-handed because the balance had to be retained. If a falangist minister was to be sacked then one of his enemies – monarchist, carlist, technocrat or whatever – had to go too. If, during the Second World War, an anglophile was to be appointed to a high position, a supporter of Germany would get a similar job. In this way Franco remained unchallenged. During four decades of power, no one, not even the legitimate pretender to the throne, emerged as a threat to his rule.

Franco's regime provided the most stable government in Spain since the death of Charles III in the year before the French Revolution. It was also the only modern European dictatorship outside the communist countries which was not violently over-thrown. The longevity of a regime which was conservative and authoritarian and did little to rouse popular enthusiasm in its favour, requires a fuller explanation than a description of its dictator's skills. To put it simply, it survived because a determined minority wanted it to survive, because a larger group of people were not prepared to fight another civil war to overthrow it, and because the rest of the population was either coerced into accepting it or else prevented from doing anything that could conceivably be regarded as a threat to its existence.

Franquista Spain took a pessimistic view of the temperament and character of its subjects. It believed that Spaniards were not suited to liberty and claimed that in Spain too much freedom degener-ated into anarchy and convent-burning. 'We Spaniards restrict our liberties somewhat,' explained Alberto Martín Artajo, who was Franco's foreign minister between 1945 and 1957, 'precisely because of our love of liberty.'[11] In a speech delivered in 1951, Martín Artajo, a former pupil of the Jesuits and a leading member of *Acción Católica*, defined the *franquista* attitude to individual liberties. He explained that there were two types of rights: natural, fundamental rights, and less important, secondary ones. The primary rights, which the foreign minister believed were 'perhaps more secure in Spain than in any country in the world', included a man's right to 'worship his God, found a home, educate his children, work and go about with dignity and independence'. Compared with these, political liberties such as the right to strike, the right to form trade unions or political parties, and the right to a free press, were not important. These were 'secondary, accessory liberties of an inferior order' which were 'from one point of view a luxury' that Spain did not need. In what might be described as a somewhat Jesuitical argument, Martín Artajo concluded: 'General Franco loves liberty, loves his freedom as much and perhaps more than many others; but precisely because of this love of these holy liberties that were inherited from his ancestors, he takes care to protect them against the abuse of the enemies of liberty.'[12]

The *franquistas* were convinced that the curtailment of individual liberties was an essential condition for the preservation of order in Spain. Notwithstanding this precept, which was truly one of the elemental dogmas of *franquista* Spain, they produced in 1945 the *Fuero de los Españoles*, or Charter of the Spanish People, which guaranteed all those rights which Martín Artajo and his colleagues considered to be 'accessory liberties of an inferior order'. The date of this document, which was published shortly after Germany's defeat in the Second World War, indicates that the Charter of the Spanish People was in fact of minor relevance to the Spaniards themselves and was produced for the benefit of the victorious democratic powers which were unlikely to be impressed by a regime which allowed its subjects to do little more than 'go about with dignity and independence'. Certainly, the Spaniards were systematically barred from enjoying those controversial political liberties listed in the Charter. The great Spanish liberal, Salvador de Madariaga, claimed that the Charter was 'the most mendacious document ever penned. It guarantees every right which the government tramples upon daily: freedom, where any man is at the mercy of any official and never knows whether his day will not end in jail . . . justice, when none is admitted unless it suits the regime; opinions when none are allowed but those that please the dictator.'[13]

The Charter contains thirty-six articles which set out the rights and duties of the Spanish people. Most of these do not need to be discussed and it can be conceded that those regarded as 'primary rights' by Martín Artajo were indeed respected, with the exception of the first, a man's right to 'worship his God'. Protestants and other non-Catholics were not free to worship in public in *franquista* Spain and thus the state did not guarantee religious freedom but merely recognized a person's right to freedom of conscience. But it is those three political rights, which taken with the right to vote in elections are the vital prerequisites of democratic government, that need to be examined: freedom of expression, freedom of association and freedom of assembly. All three were guaranteed in articles 12 and 16 of the Charter but only with conditions. For example, the free expression of ideas was permitted so long as it did not 'endanger the fundamental principles of the state'. Similarly, Spaniards were allowed 'to assemble and associate freely for lawful purposes and in accordance with the Law'. Obviously it was up to the government to define 'lawful purposes' and to decide what did or did not 'endanger the fundamental principles'. There was a further restriction in the Charter which said that the exercise of these rights must not 'go against the spiritual, national and social unity of Spain' (Article 33). The adjectives were carefully chosen. They were directed against anticlericals, separatists and marxists who were deemed to be the respective enemies of the nation's 'spiritual, national and social unity'. In other words, the regime's principal opponents were prevented from exercising the rights set out in the Charter.

Throughout the life of the regime Spaniards were simply denied these three basic rights. Censorship and other controls were applied to ensure that there was no freedom of expression anywhere except in private conversation. Books were banned, newspapers censored and theatres closed. Although the situation improved after Manuel Fraga's Press Law of 1966, nothing approaching a free press existed until after Franco's death.

The Spaniards' right 'to assemble and associate freely' was no more respected than their right to say and publish what they liked in public. Freedom of association did not mean that Spaniards were free to join political parties or free trade unions but merely that they were allowed to join *the* political party or *the* state trade union, although this was not much of a privilege since all workers were forced to join the syndicates and many officials had to be members of the *Movimiento*. If a citizen wanted to form another association he could do so only if he could prove to the civil governor of his province or to the ministry of the interior that the aims of his association coincided with the Principles of the *Movimiento Nacional*. A Law of Associations was passed in 1964 which proclaimed in the preamble that the right of association was 'one of the natural rights of man' but then went on to state that associations would not be permitted if they had 'aims contrary to the fundamental principles of the *Movimiento* or to the other fundamental laws' or if they could be considered 'a grave danger to the political and social unity of Spain' (Articles 1 and 2). Apart from commercial associations and various other non-political institutions, the only associations outside the *Movimiento* which were permitted in *franquista* Spain were Catholic ones. Even these were accepted only on condition that they had 'exclusively religious aims', although some of them did in fact become increasingly political in the sixties.

The right to free assembly was, if anything, even more restricted than the others. It was regulated by two ordinances issued in 1939 and 1940 which were never amended. These required that any meeting or conference of more than twenty people which was not held under the auspices of the Church or the *Movimiento* needed the approval of the ministry of the interior. If a meeting was held without such authorization, then the police would break it up and its organizers would be fined and in some cases imprisoned. In 1967 the Duchess of Medina Sidonia received a 5,000 peseta fine and a one year prison sentence for having organized a public meeting to protest about an incident in which American aircraft collided and deposited unexploded atomic bombs near the village of Palomares.[14]

One of the few basic human rights which the regime did not accept in theory and then contradict in practice was the right to strike. It would have been illogical had it done so since the whole beauty of the syndical idea was that it would make labour conflicts redundant. The 1938 Labour Charter, the first of the Fundamental Laws, started that any 'illegal act . . . which seriously disturbs or endangers production, shall be punishable by law'. The Penal Code of 1944 followed this up by declaring that strikers would be punished for sedition. The position of labour improved marginally during the fifties. In 1957 the elections for the syndicates' shop stewards became less cumbersome and more open, while the following year a sort of collective bargaining was introduced. In 1965 the *Cortes* revised the Penal Code so as to differentiate between types of strikes. Henceforth workers would no longer be prosecuted if they took part in strikes that were not politically motivated. Stoppages, however, that were considered to have a political nature or else affected essential national services, were still regarded as seditious. Nevertheless, the revision of the Penal Code did give formal recognition to a fact which had been obvious for years – that even with the (admittedly fraudulent) syndical system labour conflicts had not disappeared.

The Spain of 1969 was undeniably a less oppressive and illiberal state than the Spain of 1939. In 1969 a newspaper editor could publish articles that would have been struck out by the censor ten years earlier. A worker could strike over bad working conditions without being packed off to prison. Yet on the whole the improvements were not substantial ones and the political nature of the regime changed little during its long existence. Spaniards were still kept on a leash, even if the leash was now rather longer. Repression and not reconciliation had been used to consolidate the regime in the 1940s and it was repression, though of a less brutal and arbitrary kind, which kept it in place thirty years later.

A full discussion of the post-civil war repression is outside the scope of this book. Even the less partisan historians give wildly different estimates of the numbers of people executed by the new regime.[15] The repression was undoubtedly on a very large scale. Anyone who had been a member of a trade union, a masonic lodge or a republican or left-wing political party, anyone who was a supporter of Basque or Catalan nationalism, anyone who since 1 October 1934 had 'helped to undermine public order, or after 18 July 1936 [had] impeded the *Movimiento Nacional* . . . by definite acts or by being grievously passive'[16] was liable to imprisonment or execution. Even if they survived, the *vencidos* were to play no part in the new Spain of the *Caudillo*. Repression still made sure of that, long after the end of the civil war. Communist miners accused of fomenting strikes in Asturias, were tortured and imprisoned. So were Basque nationalists or suspected members of the anarchist trade unions. The *Guardia Civil* demonstrated its traditional brutality in the methods used to smash illegal strikes, break up unauthorized meetings and interrogate prisoners. The regime was unrelenting in its persecution of the defeated. Although during the sixties it began to allow liberals and christian democrats to publish mild criticisms of the regime, its repression of the hardline opposition, particularly communists and Basque separatists, continued.

In the face of this repression, the Spanish citizen had little opportunity for legal redress. The Organic Law stated that 'the Judiciary shall enjoy complete independence' but in practice it enjoyed no such thing because the *franquista* Judiciary, like the Legislature, was almost entirely dependent on the Executive. The government could usually count on a verdict favourable to itself but, when it wanted to make sure, it often resorted to special courts such as military tribunals, which were frequently used in trials of a purely political nature, and the Public Order Court set up in 1963 to deal with people suspected of 'undermining the foundations of the State, altering public order, or creating anxiety for the national conscience'.[17] In neither of these types of courts did an opponent of the regime have much chance of an acquittal. Nor were the constitutional guarantees listed in the Charter of the Spanish People of much help to a citizen since these were rarely respected when the regime was dealing with its enemies. Article 18 of the charter, which declared that 'any arrested person shall be set free or turned over to the judical authorities' within seventy-two hours, was frequently suspended when the government wished to deal with Basque separatists or Asturian miners.

In any case the administration could suspend the constitutional guarantees for a whole area or even the entire nation if it saw fit, and its only obligation was to inform the tame *procuradores* in the *Cortes* beforehand. From 1956 onwards a regime whose principal boast was the preservation of peace and order found itself repeatedly declaring a state of emergency and suspending articles of the charter. A state of emergency was declared eleven times in the following years, usually in the Basque provinces of Vizcaya and Guipúzcoa, but on four occasions in the whole of Spain. The articles most frequently suspended were Article 18 (habeas corpus) and those guaranteeing inviolability of the home (Articles 14 and 15). Ironically, in 1969 the government decided to suspend those rights which it had never respected in the first place: the rights of expression, assembly and association.

The denial of human rights and the repression needed to enforce it were the central means used by the regime to ensure its survival. But they did not by themselves maintain the *franquistas* in power. Without the active support of a number of Spaniards and the passive acceptance of many more, the regime would not have survived. An American embassy official who claimed in the 1940s that Spain was ruled by 'a government without the people, above the people, and against the people,'[18] exaggerated even at the time. Applied to the sixties, the remark would have been even less accurate. After the rising Franco had the support of perhaps a third of the nation. Almost half the electorate had voted for the centre or right-wing parties in 1936, and it can be assumed that more than half of those who voted against the Popular Front's candidates in February would have supported a revolt against its government in July. In the 1940s, after the worst civil war Europe has ever seen, many people who had supported the republic were grateful to the regime for the restoration of order. During the fifties and sixties, antagonism towards Franco and his government was diluted by the country's growing economic success. The workers may not have had rights, but many of them had jobs and job security, and their standard of living was improving.

The army created the regime in 1936 and remained its bulwark and guarantor thereafter. Although its influence over government policy declined, particularly when the technocrats took charge of the economy, it remained the first and most vital 'pillar' of the dictatorship. The armed forces always had at least three officers in the cabinet (in charge of the ministries of the army, navy and airforce) and usually several others as well. Of the 114 ministers who served in Franco's cabinets, forty of them were military men.[19] The other 'pillars' were the *Falange*, whose decline has already been discussed, and the Church.* None of the components of the regime changed as radically as the Church in the years between 1936 and 1975. In March 1939 Pope Pius XII sent Franco a telegram in which he thanked God for 'Spain's Catholic victory'[20] and at the time the Spanish Church stood almost unanimously behind the *Caudillo*. Thirty years later it was deeply divided and in 1971 a majority of the delegates at the first joint assembly of bishops and priests voted for a resolution which in effect asked forgiveness for having supported Franco so strongly.[21]

Other, less important groups that rallied to Franco in 1936 were landowners, monarchists and the leading men in the financial and industrial worlds. In many cases these categories overlapped, as businessmen had been buying agricultural property since the selling-off of Church lands in the nineteenth century. Considering themselves threatened by the republic's agrarian reform programme, the great aristocratic landowners instinctively supported the rising. But their political influence in Spain had long since been in decline and they never became a vital component of the regime. Bankers, however, came to play an increasingly important role in

---

*There are fuller descriptions of the role of the Church in *franquista* Spain in chapter 4, of the monarchists in chapters 4 and 5, and of the armed forces in chapter 12.

franquista Spain and became one of the most powerful economic forces. It was the bankers and businessmen of the Basque country, not those from Catalonia, who were fervent supporters of the regime. The financial and industrial oligarchy of Bilbao was almost the only sector of the Basque population to support Franco during the civil war and to continue to do so afterwards. It provided Franco with so many of his ministers that, second only to Madrid, the Basque country was the region most represented in the cabinet.[22]

Although Franco made little effort to court monarchist sentiment during the rising and did not even declare Spain to be a monarchy in principle until eleven years afterwards, the supporters of the Borbón family (known as the Alfonsine monarchists after Alfonso XIII, the last King of Spain) enthusiastically welcomed his attempt to overthrow the republic. After the civil war some of them, such as the Duke of Alba, who was then ambassador in London, tried to persuade Franco to step down in front of the legitimate heir, Don Juan de Borbón. Franco, however, ignored them, partly because he was determined to remain in power himself and partly because he did not consider Don Juan, who was liberal and anglophile, to be an appropriate representative of the new state. Apart from declaring Spain a monarchy in 1947, he made no further moves towards restoring a monarch until 1969 when he designated Prince Juan Carlos, the son of Don Juan, as his successor. In spite of this, most of the Alfonsine monarchists remained loyal to the regime. When they had to choose between their allegiance to Franco and their loyalty to Don Juan, living in self-imposed exile in Portugal, few of them seem to have had much difficulty in making their decision.

There was another group of monarchists who were even more ardent in their support for the rising than the Alfonsine legitimists. These were the carlists who in the nineteenth century had fought two bitter civil wars in attempts to impose an absolute monarchy under Don Carlos, the brother of King Ferdinand VII, and later under his grandson. Although originally based in northern Spain along the entire length of the Pyrenees, by the end of the century carlism had lost many of its adherents to the nationalist movements of Catalonia and the Basque country. Popular support for the movement was thereafter found only in Navarre. In 1936 the carlists rose for Franco, and Navarre became the only province in

Spain where there was a *popular* rising against the republic. The carlist *requetés* were important troops in the battles in the north and proved to be a more effective military force than the falangist militia. Even in *franquista* Spain, however, the carlist movement was an anachronism and it had little influence after the civil war. Their cause was not helped by the death of the carlist pretender in 1936 which robbed the movement of such legitimacy as it had previously been able to claim. The following year, the carlists, or traditionalists as they came to be known, were amalgamated against their will with the *Falange* and their most prominent political leader, Manuel Fal Conde, was sent into exile. Their independence was over. A small number of so-called carlists joined Franco's cabinets, usually as ministers of justice, but they were in reality merely Basque conservatives with reactionary views on religion and society rather than proponents of a carlist restoration. A carlist pretender, Don Javier de Borbón-Parma continued to claim the throne, but as he was French and Franco refused to give him Spanish nationality, he was not a serious claimant. Over the years he did little more than irritate the regime with his preposterous ambitions, and in 1968 he was expelled with all his family. Towards the end of the dictatorship the official carlist position became nonsensical when Don Javier's son Hugo (who called himself Carlos Hugo to sound more carlist) tried to turn the movement (until then the most reactionary, Catholic component of a reactionary, Catholic regime) into a socialist party.

All these groups had some stake, however limited, in the regime. None of them received all of what they wanted but most of them got enough to keep them loyal. Even those, such as falangists and traditionalists, whose influence was always in decline, remained tied to Franco simply because they had nowhere else to go. The only conceivable alternative to the regime was a liberal and possibly left-wing democracy which, from their point of view, was bound to be worse than Franco. So the components stuck together, even though some of them were plainly incompatible. As rewards, they each received control of some part of Spanish life. The Church regulated the moral life of the nation while members of *Acción Católica* were for many years in charge of the ministries of education and foreign affairs. Opus Dei members were given the key economic ministries in 1957 and, in conjunction with the bankers, directed the country's economic advance. The armed forces provided the personnel for all their own ministries – no civilian was ever in charge of a defence ministry in *franquista* Spain – and for several others as well including the minister of the interior in the 1960s and the vice-president of the government from 1962 to 1973. The other components were accorded much less. The falangists controlled the syndicates and the ministry of labour, the traditionalists had the ministry of justice, while supporters of Don Juan occupied briefly the ministry of education and for a longer period the ministry of public works.

Franquista Spain was thus governed by a limited pluralism. Although ultimate power remained in the hands of one man, the country was administered not by a single party but by a reluctant coalition of diverse groups. This coalition stuck together for nearly forty years and did so principally because of the skills of Franco and the weakness of his opponents. It represented a regime which relied for its survival mainly on the repression of the Spanish people. Yet its survival depended on other factors as well. It needed to acquire supporters who, if not devoted to *franquismo*, at least had an interest in keeping it in power. That it was able to do this was largely a matter of luck. American aid and the state of the world economy provided the right conditions for the social and economic transformation of Spain in the 1960s. It was this transformation which helped to make the regime more attractive to Spaniards. Ironically, however, it eventually helped to destroy it. The economic and social changes were so far-reaching that they undermined the political foundations of a regime whose nature had scarcely evolved since 1936. Had Franco's successors tried to perpetuate *franquismo*, they would have found the political position untenable.

3
Non-Political Revolutions (1959–75)

There were nearly forty years between the day General Franco became Head of State and the day of his death at the end of 1975, and during that time Spain underwent a more radical transformation of its society and its economy than at any other period since the thirteenth century. José Solís, one of the longest-serving falangist ministers, claimed that Franco had 'transformed a sandal-wearing Spain into one of the dozen most prosperous nations in the world'.[1] How far the *Caudillo* or his regime was responsible for the economic success is a point which will be discussed later. What is indisputable is that a society which had been backward and predominantly rural in 1936, had become, within forty years, industrialized and largely urban-based.

During the decade which followed the civil war the Spanish economy showed few signs of recovery and it was not until 1952 that income per capita reached its 1935 level. In 1959 agriculture was still contributing a higher percentage of the country's gross national product than manufacturing industry.[2] Over two-fifths of the labour force, or about 4.9 million people, were employed in agriculture and, according to one historian, there were more people working on the land in 1960 than in 1900.[3] In the last fifteen years of the *franquista* regime more than forty per cent of the country's farm workers left the land. Followed by their families and other people whose livelihood depended on the rural population, they made the one-way journey to the nearest town. If they failed to get jobs there, they would go on to the provincial capital, to the great cities, or even abroad. Perhaps five million

Spaniards, from a population that in 1960 numbered just over thirty million, abandoned the land. Most of them came from the poor agricultural regions of Castile, Extremadura and Andalusia – fourteen provinces lost nearly a quarter of their populations in a single decade[4] – and most of them ended up in Madrid, Barcelona or Bilbao. During the fifties and sixties more than a million people migrated to the capital and only slightly fewer arrived in Barcelona. It has been estimated that by 1970 1.6 million people had left Andalusia and that nearly half of them were living in Barcelona.[5]

The rural exodus was caused largely by the new opportunities in Spanish industry after 1959 and by the prospect of well-paid jobs abroad. Between 1960 and 1975 nearly a million and a half new jobs were created in industry and construction and more than two million in the service sector.[6] However, since the country's population grew by nearly five million over the same period,* these were not enough to absorb the migrants from the countryside. The regime, which in its early years had tried to dissuade Spaniards from working abroad, now encouraged the emigration of the surplus work force. Between 1961 and 1972 a million and a half Spaniards emigrated abroad, nearly all of them to Europe where they found work in the factories of Germany, Switzerland and France.[8]

If new opportunities in the cities provided one incentive for the farm worker to pack his suitcase and leave home, living conditions in the countryside and the depressed state of agriculture provided others. The historic problems of Spanish farming still showed few signs of solution in 1960. The *minifundios*, tiny, uneconomic parcels of land, were still the predominant feature of rural life in Galicia and the northern provinces; the *latifundios* still dominated the agricultural world of Andalusia and Extremadura. There were still three-quarters of a million *jornaleros*, or day labourers, in southern Spain, men who stood about in the plazas of Andalusian pueblos waiting to be hired by farm managers from the *latifundios*. Their employment was, at best, seasonal. Southern agriculture has always concentrated on a few large crops and seldom provides employment all the year round. In the province of Jaén, the largest

*The population of Spain was 28.4m in 1950, 30.9m in 1960, 34.0m in 1970, 35.6m in 1975 and 37.7m in 1981.[7]

olive-growing district in the world, labourers had work in January, when the olives are collected, and in the spring when the trees are pruned. For the rest of the year about 100,000 *jornaleros* were without work.

The uprooting of hundreds of thousands of under-employed people from Extremadura and Andalusia was unavoidable, given the growing population and the government's failure to establish sufficient industries in these regions. But elsewhere the migration was unnecessarily heavy. In 1950 the agricultural population of Castile was too high but by 1975 it was definitely too low. Anyone who travelled through the Castilian *meseta* during the seventies would have been struck by the sense of desolation and decay: the crumbling villages with their dwindling populations, the old stone houses with caved-in roofs and broken window panes, the decadence and ruined splendour of the palaces of the hidalgos. On many of the buildings would be scrawled slogans like the old anarchist demand, *la tierra para el que la trabaja* – 'the land for he who works it' – but the cry is irrelevant now for there are not enough people in Castile to farm the land. In many parts of the *meseta*, fields and orchards are left uncultivated and stifled by weeds.

It was not only the peasants and farm workers who left. Shopkeepers, blacksmiths, carpenters – people who depended for their living on a thriving rural community – followed close behind. In many cases this meant the virtual destruction of village life. Around the fine medieval town of Sos del Rey Católico, on the border of Aragon and Navarre, there are skeleton villages with no inhabitants at all. In most of Castile it is mainly the old who are left: by 1973 a considerable majority of the nation's agricultural workers were over fifty-five years old.[9] In one of his most recent novels,[10] the Castilian writer Miguel Delibes describes how a political candidate and two of his supporters arrive at a village where they hope to hold a meeting. They ask an old man where they might find the other villagers and he tells them they will have to go to Bilbao. Elsewhere Delibes has written evocatively of this uprooting – of abandoned fields and broken families, of the destruction of an age-old culture, of the dehumanization of the young who desert family, land and nature for the bright lights of the city, and of the old who refuse to leave their land and sacrifice their lives to it, last witnesses to a culture and final practitioners of a way of life that will die irrevocably with them.[11] In strict economic terms the uprooting was a success because the prosperity of the nation was fuelled by the new industries and by the money which the emigrant workers sent home. But in human terms its consequences were terrible because it was too extensive, because it was unplanned and because it happened too quickly.

Once industrialization had got under way, the regime, reversing its earlier policy, encouraged the rural exodus. At the beginning the government had tried to persuade the peasantry to stay on the land. After all, such support as Franco's uprising had enjoyed among the working classes came from the rural areas of Castile and Navarre, while before 1936 the appeal of the Falangist Party had been limited to the provinces of Madrid and Valladolid. Spanish writers from Unamuno to Delibes have praised the qualities of the Castilian peasant and it has long been an article of faith among right-wing intellectuals that the essence of Spain, its true spirit and eternal values, reside in the towns and villages of the Castilian *meseta*. It would indeed have been ironic if a regime, which claimed spiritual descent from the Castile of Isabella la Católica, had immediately acquiesced in the destruction of traditional life in Castile and Andalusia.

Any serious attempt to keep the small farmers and labourers on the land would have required strong government action in the shape of agrarian reform. During the Second Republic (1931–6) most political parties had agreed that agrarian reform was necessary although they disagreed strongly over what kind of reform should be introduced. While the parties of the Left disputed the merits of collectivization and the setting-up of individual peasant holdings, the Right was divided between those who actively favoured serious reform and those who were interested only in making cosmetic changes for the purposes of propaganda. José Antonio Primo de Rivera had argued for radical agrarian reform – for which he was denounced as a bolshevik by the conservative newspaper *ABC*[12] – and Manuel Giménez Fernández, the minister of agriculture during the conservative government of 1934–5, proposed a series of reforms which would have turned insecure tenant farmers into independent smallholders. But agrarian reform from the Right was always obstructed by the conservative landed interests which refused to allow the *latifundios* to be broken up. It was they who sabotaged the plans of

Giménez Fernández and they who ensured that during the *franquista* dictatorship there were no radical changes in the pattern of land ownership. Agrarian reform under Franco was thus limited from the beginning by the regime's refusal to deal with the *latifundios*. Although legislation in 1953 provided for expropriation of under-exploited land which would then be made available for settlement, this was apparently never used.[13]

Nevertheless, for ideological and propaganda reasons, the regime made much of its desire to settle tenant farmers on individual plots of land, and it was for this reason that the *Instituto Nacional de Colonización* (INC) was set up in 1939. According to Franco, 'internal colonization' would be carried out according to three principles: 'the economic one of the nation, which is to increase production; the social one, which is to satisfy the needs and longings of the peasant classes . . . and that of justice, respecting the legitimate rights of property.'[14] As these principles tended to contradict each other, and as 'respecting the legitimate rights of property' received priority over 'satisfying the needs . . . of the peasant classes', the effectiveness of the INC was limited. According to one estimate, 23,000 family plots were established between 1939 and 1951, 19,800 during the fifties, and only 9,900 in the sixties.[15] The colonies, or settlements, built by the INC among newly-irrigated land, were undoubtedly attractive places in which to live. But, as they benefited only about 50,000 families, they went little way towards solving the problem of land hunger. Ultimately the problem was resolved not by agrarian reform but by migration. During the fifties and sixties barely 2,000 families were settled by the INC in the province of Jaén. In the same period nearly 350,000 people left the province to look for work outside.[16]

A more effective body than the INC was the *Servicio Nacional de Concentración Parcelaria* (SNCP), which was set up in 1952 to deal with the problem of the *minifundios*. If the *latifundios* were the historic scourge of southern agriculture, the *minifundios* were the chief obstacle to agricultural productivity in the north. In Galicia, the Basque provinces, parts of northern Castile and the Cantabrian coast, the land was divided into millions of small-holdings, most of them smaller than an acre. In Galicia alone there were fourteen and a half million small-holdings in 1959, with an average size of about a third of an acre.[17] The average farmworker was having to look after twenty-six tiny pieces of land often dispersed over a considerable area. Obviously the situation had to be altered if northern agriculture was ever going to provide more than a subsistence livelihood for those who worked in it. Thus a number of laws were passed during the fifties and sixties with the aim of reorganizing the *minifundios* into more manageable holdings. In spite of the peasant's attachment to his land and resistance to change, much was achieved by the SNCP and between 1954 and 1975 nearly eleven million acres had been reorganized throughout the country.[18] Nevertheless the agriculture of northern Spain remained among the most backward of Europe. The traveller to Navarre during the later seventies still came across large numbers of old men ploughing minute, barely accessible fields with a couple of mules, while in Galicia the commonest sight in the countryside remained the old woman in black, grazing her solitary cow by the wayside.

If the Castilian peasant seemed, to many Spanish conservatives, to be the embodiment of national virtues, his counterpart in Andalusia, the underpaid, underemployed, often anarchist, *jornalero*, represented what they most feared and detested. Yet there was little cultural or racial difference between the two, since Castile had conquered western Andalusia in the thirteenth century, colonized it and expelled its Moorish inhabitants. The chief differences between them were their working and living conditions, and it is astonishing that so few conservatives, with the exception of a small group of people such as Giménez Fernández, should have realised this. As late as 1956 most of the agricultural workforce in western Andalusia were still *jornaleros*, labourers hired by the day and often unemployed for months at a time. In Castile three-quarters of the agricultural population either owned or rented their own farms. It is hardly surprising, therefore, that Castile should have been politically and socially conservative while Andalusia was the historic centre of rural anarchism. But it was not a connection that the Spanish Right was able to make. In 1959 the *latifundios* still covered seventy per cent of Extremadura and western Andalusia,[19] and at the time of Franco's death Spain had perhaps the most unequal land distribution in Europe.[20]

Anarchist anger had been directed not so much at the extent of the *latifundios* as at the way they were exploited. It often used to be said that owners devoted large areas of their estates to shooting and the breeding of fighting bulls, but this appears to have been no longer true after 1930. What is certain, however, is that the *latifundios* were often badly run and under-exploited. Until recently there was little capital investment in either machinery or fertilizers, and agricultural productivity in Andalusia was as a result much lower than the national average. The chief cause of this neglect has been the owners' lack of interest in their estates. In Spain it is still considered eccentric to live in the country unless one is obliged to, and the most that can be expected of a great landlord is that he should occasionally visit his property. One historian has calculated that '. . . among the 262 grandees who collectively owned 355,000 hectares of arable land in southern Spain in 1933, only 14 had been born there and all of these came from large cities, not from the countryside'.[21] During the *franquista* dictatorship this pattern continued and spread even to the smaller landlords. When a British anthropologist went to live in an Andalusian hill village in the 1950s, he found that nearly all the local landlords had gone to live in Jerez or Málaga.[22]

Nevertheless, if the degree of landlord absenteeism did not diminish, there was, in the last years of Franco's rule, a considerable improvement in the productivity of the *latifundios*. The Guadalquivir valley, which crosses Andalusia in a diagonal from the south-west to the north-east, is one of the most fertile areas in Spain and well suited to mechanization and intensive cultivation. Between 1960 and 1975 the number of tractors in the country increased more than six-fold and many of them were used to plough up the former pastures and scrubland of Andalusia. Banks and companies began investing in the southern arable lands and by the seventies the agriculture of the Guadalquivir had become capitalist. The south, which had been under-exploited ever since the defeat of the Moors, was now in danger of becoming over-cultivated. The hillsides of the Guadalquivir Depression around Carmona or Osuna are now so extensively ploughed that there is no room for hedges, woods or anything else. Only a few trees and the occasional white farm house punctuate the monotony of this vast brown landscape.

The mechanization of agriculture has naturally led to even fewer jobs in the countryside and the balance has not been redressed by the large irrigation works which have been taking place in areas such as the Guadalquivir itself and the plain of Granada. The *jornaleros* can still be found in the plaza of Carmona or other pueblos of Andalusia, standing patiently in their scores with arms folded, waiting for the farm managers to arrive, while a few tractors do their work for them in the plains outside the town. It is ironic that the neglect of the *latifundios*, which contributed for so long to the lack of employment in the south, should give way to such labour-saving efficiency, and without any intervening period when Andalusia's agricultural population might at last have enjoyed some prospect of stable employment. By the time of Franco's death, things were getting even worse for many of those still trying to make a living from the land. The world economic recession was well under way and tens of thousands of southern emigrants were returning from a Europe in which they could no longer find work. If they went home to Andalusia, they were likely only to swell the numbers of *jornaleros*, and even if they did find an agricultural job, it would probably be insecure and badly paid. In 1973 the regime was paying much less attention to its agricultural population than it had done a generation earlier, and a farmworker earned barely half the wages of a construction worker and about two-fifths of what an employee in the service sector was taking home.[23]

Autarky, the economic system based on self-sufficiency which was adopted by the regime after the civil war, was a very Spanish solution to the nation's problems. It was a kind of economic Pyrenees, a barrier set up to protect Spain from the competition of the rest of the world. Dependent on protection and a high degree of government involvement in the running of the economy, it was not a new theory. Free trade had only briefly flourished in Spain in the nineteenth century and elements of autarky had been important features of the economic policies of Spanish governments since the 1890s.[24] The continuation of the system after 1945 was to some extent forced on Spain by its exclusion, on account of the nature of its regime, from Marshall Aid. But autarky was, in any case, a natural policy for a regime that prided itself on its nationalism and spirit of self-sacrifice. It might not make a nation wealthy but at least it would make it self-sufficient, independent of the influences of other countries. Spain, declared the Industrial Law of October 1939, must be 'redeemed from the importation of exotic products'.[25]

Whatever other advantages autarky may have had, economic

success was not one of them. During the forties, industrial production grew at the rate of about one per cent a year and agricultural production increased even more slowly. Autarky created large, inefficient industries incapable of exporting and suitable only for the domestic market; a huge, incompetent bureaucracy endlessly dealing with permits, licences and quotas for the importation of vital raw materials, and a thriving black market in foodstuffs. By the early fifties, as the economies of France and Italy started to expand rapidly, it began to dawn on some Spanish economists that they would have to abandon autarky altogether or else accept that Spain would fall further and further behind the rest of Europe.

Spain had not been allowed to join the United Nations in 1946 but its ostracism by the West came to an end with a change in American policy after 1950. With the outbreak of the Korean war in 1951 and the relations between the United States and the Soviet Union at their coldest, American defence chiefs began to look for new allies. Spain was an obvious choice, partly for strategic reasons and partly because it was a widely-held belief in the United States that Franco had been the only man ever to inflict a military defeat on communism. President Truman is reported to have told the US generals: 'I don't like Franco and I never will, but I won't let my personal feelings override the convictions of you military men.'[26] Negotiations between the two countries began immediately and by 1953 agreements on defence and economic assistance had been signed. The scale of American aid to Spain was smaller than it had been to the democratic countries of Europe and it came with more conditions. Economic aid tended to arrive in the form of surplus raw materials from America, such as cotton and soya bean oil; military aid was usually spent on the purchase of American weapons and the construction of bases to be used by US forces. Nevertheless, the assistance from Washington, which in the decade following the agreements totalled over a billion dollars,[27] did contribute to the stimulation of an economy which from 1951 was at last beginning to show perceptible growth.

Autarky, however, did its best to hamper the industrial revival. Growth depended on the importation of raw materials and equipment, but the tariff barriers on these were so high, and the productivity of Spain's insulated industry so low, that it was practically impossible for a business to manufacture anything competitive for export. Industry was therefore forced to produce for a home market which was clearly not large enough to support further industrial growth. Efforts by the government to stimulate domestic demand with high wage rises led to an inflation rate in 1957 of over sixteen per cent. Combined with a huge public sector deficit, this led to a balance of payments crisis that nearly bankrupted the country. Plainly it was time for some drastic change.

Liberalization of the economy was not an attractive proposition for many Spaniards, particularly those connected with the *Falange* who regarded the abandonment of autarky as a betrayal. It meant not only admitting that the country had been following the wrong path for twenty years; it entailed adopting the economic system of countries such as Britain and France which falangists had long regarded as decadent and unheroic. Moreover, there was also the danger that liberalization of the economy would lead to political liberalization as well. Political authoritarianism and economic autarky were natural allies, and were regarded by many people as inseparable. On the eve of the crisis, the powerful, state-owned *Instituto Nacional de Industria* (INI), emphatically rejected economic liberalism as a solution to Spain's problems. In a report on its activities written in 1957, INI declared that 'the old doctrines of economic liberalism have finally been left behind . . . the ideals of personal profit, economic supremacy and technological progress at any price, have been superseded by new, more generous ideas.'[28] But in the crisis years between 1957 and 1959 neither INI nor the *Falange* had anything positive to suggest. The situation was so bad that the economy either had to be opened up, or else closed completely to foreign influences – a policy which would inevitably have led to a severe reduction in the standard of living.

The proponents of liberalization consisted of a few business-men, a handful of economists, one enterprising bank (the Banco Urquijo) and two men who became ministers in 1957, Alberto Ullastres, the minister of commerce, and Mariano Navarro Rubio, the minister of finance. The political importance of Ullastres and Navarro Rubio, and their membership of the Opus Dei organization, will be discussed in the next chapter. In the dramatic change in economic policy that took place in 1959 they were the crucial figures. Discarding the customary rhetoric of the regime, they set out to convince people that the economy must be stabilized and opened up. Yet it is very unlikely that they would have managed to persuade Franco to allow them to carry out their policies had it not been for outside pressure as well. The *Caudillo* knew little about economics but all his instincts would have made him hostile to economic liberalism. It was the offers of help from the United States and organizations such as the International Monetary Fund (IMF) and the Organization for European Economic Co-operation (OEEC) which made the difference. They were prepared to support Spain with $544 million in credits and drawing rights on condition that the government introduced a number of liberalizing measures.[29]

The outline of the so-called Stabilization Plan (no formal plan ever existed) was contained in a memorandum sent to the IMF and the OEEC in June 1959 in which the government declared that 'the moment has arrived to change [its] economic policy so as to place the Spanish economy in line with the countries of the West, and to free it from the policy of interventionism which, inherited from the past, is not appropriate to the needs of the present situation'.[30] The measures proposed and carried out by the government included the abolition of import licensing on 180 commodities, the devaluation of the peseta, a freeze on wages, higher interest rates, a reduction in public expenditure and the encouragement of foreign investment. These severe deflationary measures drove the country immediately into recession, causing an increase in unemployment, a fall in consumer demand and a sharp drop in investment. Nevertheless, inflation had been conquered and the balance of payments restored. From 1961, when the recession was over, the economy began to grow rapidly and for more than a decade Spain enjoyed the fastest growth rate in Europe.

Most of this growth was concentrated in industry and construction, and by 1975 industry had increased its share of exports from 21 per cent of the total in 1961 to 78 per cent.[31] Among the most successful new industrial products were chemicals and machinery but the fastest growing area of all was ship-building. By 1975 Spain had become one of the world's most important producers and was exporting $125 million worth of ships.[32] During the fifteen years after the Stabilization Plan, Spanish industry was expanding at an average rate of 8.6 per cent a year while the economy overall was growing at an annual rate of 6.9 per cent.

This level of growth naturally brought about radical change in the country's living standards, particularly among the urban population. For every person who owned a telephone, a car or a television set in 1961, in 1975 three had telephones, nine had cars and twenty-nine owned televisions.[33]

By carrying out the measures proposed in the Stabilization Plan, the government established a climate in which economic growth could take place. A few years later it decided to promote economic development directly and in 1964 it launched the First Development Plan, based very closely on the successful French model of the 1950s. This was the first serious piece of regional planning undertaken by the dictatorship and its essential ingredient was the establishment of special areas where industrialists would be encouraged to build new factories. The objective was to create industries in areas other than Madrid, Barcelona and Bilbao, and so do something to stem the rush of people leaving the poorer provinces for the capital and the industrial cities of the north. However, in spite of the government's use of credits and tax concessions to encourage businessmen to move to the new areas, they were not a great success. Investment in the special areas was much lower than had been expected, except in Vigo, and the number of jobs created was also far less than the government had hoped. Accepting the relative failure of the experiment, the government decided not to create any new special areas in its Third Development Plan (1972–5).

Franco's supporters have attributed Spain's economic success to the policies of his government just as his detractors assert that the boom was merely a consequence of American aid, emigrant remittances and the introduction of package holidays. Both claims are only partly true. Italy also benefited from tourism, the money sent back by Italians working abroad and the financial assistance provided by the US after the Second World War, but the Italian christian democratic governments are usually given credit for their country's economic 'miracle'. Plainly the liberalizing policies of Ullastres and Navarro were crucial for the success of the 1960s because they established a framework in which businessmen could operate successfully. But the actual development of the economy was not achieved by the government, which enjoyed indifferent success in its regional planning, but by a dynamic private sector taking advantage of government incentives and the new economic climate. Having said that, one has to admit that the high growth rate was only partly sustained by the industrial achievement. The neo-liberals had been determined to solve the balance of payments problem and they managed to do so, but not, as they intended, through exports alone. Without the $700 million being sent home (1970) by emigrant workers, or the $3,404 million being brought in by more than thirty million foreign tourists (1975),[34] the country would have been faced by a balance of payments crisis that would have ended the economic miracle.

Spanish society during the dictatorship was a strange mixture of radical change and unbending conservatism. The most reactionary government the country had suffered for centuries had presided over the most far-reaching social and economic changes since the greater part of Moorish Spain had been conquered in the thirteenth century. Millions of people had abandoned the countryside, a modern industry had been created and a prosperous middle class had come into existence. Yet amid all the upheavals and innovations, traditional attitudes and behaviour often survived. There were still many people, among the underground Left as well as the *Falange*, whose outlook and ideology remained firmly rooted in the 1930s. The attitudes of the landed aristocracy belonged to a still earlier epoch.

The political power of the old aristocracy had long disappeared and much of its economic strength had gone too. But it still enjoyed enormous social prestige, as Franco realized when he created a number of new titles. The aristocracy, however, no longer dominated the *latifundios* as it had done under the old monarchy. The dukes of Medina Sidonia had long since been forced to sell their estates, while the Medinaceli family went into industry in an effort to restore its fortunes after the duke's second marriage in the 1920s had led to the dispersal of most of its land.

The Spanish aristocracy, which Gerald Brenan refused to term feudal on the grounds that 'feudalism implies a sense of mutual obligations that has long been entirely lacking in Spain',[35] had a well-deserved reputation for frivolity. Anyone who reads the memoirs of the Marqués de Villavieja,[36] which were published during the civil war, is likely to conclude that few classes in history have done more to provoke a violent revolution. With the money that came in from their estates, where they never lived and which they seldom visited, the noblemen were able to roam around Europe, renting grouse moors in Perthshire, playing polo at Hurlingham, or simply 'relaxing' in Biarritz. There was and is a curious admiration for Britain among Spanish aristocrats and few of them, in spite of their respect for Franco, wanted Germany to win the Second World War. Their anglophilia was not typical of the pro-British feelings of other foreigners and did not extend to an admiration for representative government, or for the principle of equality before the law or, indeed, for the respect of individual liberties. What they most esteemed about Britain were its field sports and the discipline of its public schools. The Chilean poet, Pablo Neruda, visited the Alba family's abandoned palace in Madrid during the civil war and discovered a copy of Kipling's poem 'If' – that famous hymn to self-discipline – in a gold frame by the duke's bedside.[37] Alba himself was a great admirer of the British public schools and extolled 'that wonderful training of character that is given in England and that all of us who have received it appreciate so much'.[38] During Franco's rule the Spanish upper classes often sent their children to British schools, the girls to convents and the boys usually to Jesuit schools such as Beaumont College or Stonyhurst. A glance at the Old Boys list at Stonyhurst reveals the names of an assortment of counts, dukes and marquesses.[39]

The elite of *franquista* society, however, was formed less by the aristocracy than by the new brand of bankers and businessmen. The aristocracy supported the 1936 rebellion and appreciated Franco for destroying the republic, but it was not really *franquista*. It was conservative but usually monarchist, and it had little taste for Franco himself and even less for the *Falange*. Franco's Spain was dominated by its chief product, the middle classes. After 1959 the regime attempted to *embourgeoiser* Spain and its minister of education even declared that 'our national preoccupation is to create middle classes'.[40] The Twenty-Six Points, the repository of falangist ideals, were abandoned in 1958, and autarky went the year after. The regime no longer wished to make the Spaniards heroic, but simply to make them prosperous. The *camisas viejas*, the falangist old guard, moved off into the wings, and the bankers and technocrats took over. Spain became a country of financial scandals, property speculation and materialist values. Church attendance declined while bars and night clubs sprung up in the cities and even small towns acquired their *discotecas*. Garish chalets

began to sprout on the slopes of the Guadarrama foothills at El
Escorial, though a more inappropriate place would be hard to
imagine. In former working-class areas such as Cuatro Caminos
in Madrid, the small brick houses with their tiled roofs and
wrought-iron balconies were torn down and replaced by standard
blocks of eight or nine storeys, with similar green blinds and
strands of ivy dangling from their concrete terraces. In the districts
of Madrid the degree of middle-class penetration could usually be
deduced by the profusion of ivy and dwarf conifers.

One of the most curious things about *franquista* Spain was its
indifference towards the fate of its historic buildings. It is hard to
understand how a regime which justified itself through constant
evocation of the country's past, should not only have acquiesced
in the destruction of much of Spain's architectural heritage, but
should have actively encouraged and even taken part in it. José
Antonio Girón, a civil war veteran and one of Franco's ministers,
was endlessly appealing to the morality of the past and preaching
the need for sacrifice, but his main occupation during the sixties
was the accumulation of a large personal fortune by developing
the Costa del Sol.[41] Only Toledo and Santiago de Compostela
were preserved from the speculators; in Salamanca, Seville,
Granada and elsewhere they were given a free hand. But while
knocking down old palaces and putting up apartment blocks in
their places was one of the quickest ways of making money in the
sixties, this despoliation was not all carried out in the name of
greed. 'Progress', or rather the idea some officials had of progress,
was another culprit. The impression was often given that it was
enough to preserve a city's cathedral and town hall, and that
anything else could be sacrificed on the altar of 'progress'. The
biggest vandal in Seville was José Hernández Díaz, Rector of
Seville University and later mayor of the city. Author of a book
on Goya and of a four volume study of the archaelogical and
artistic wealth of Seville, Hernández Díaz was a professor of fine
art and President of the *Comisión de Monumentos Históricos y
Artísticos de la Provincia de Sevilla*. Such a man might have been
expected to revere his city's architecture. Yet during his term as
mayor he presided over acts of official barbarism such as the
demolition of the beautiful palace of the Medina Sidonia family
and its replacement by one of the ugliest department stores it is
possible to conceive. Once Hernández Díaz had set such an

example, Seville naturally acted as a magnet for anyone who felt like picking up some easy money by obliterating a piece of its history. Old Seville might have disappeared altogether had not a young aristocrat, the Duke of Segorbe, formed a pressure group called *Pro Sevilla* which effectively put an end to speculation in the city.*

The dictatorship was determined to make Spain a prosperous country but it made little effort to ensure that the new wealth was shared either by different classes or by different regions. In each of the Basque provinces income per capita in 1973 was more than twice that of Andalusia or Extremadura.[42] In 1973 a report revealed that Andalusia had the lowest living standards in western Europe.[43] Social inequality was not reduced by either the tax system or by welfare. The Spaniard was expected to fend for himself. If he was unable to earn a living in the countryside, he had to go to the city. But even if he found a job in the city he was unlikely to find somewhere to live because the government's housing programme, although more impressive than some of its critics have alleged, could not keep up with the pace of the rural exodus. Many of the migrants went to the *chabolas*, or shanty-towns, that fringed Madrid and Barcelona, and built themselves shacks with whatever materials they could find. There they remained until they could afford to rent a flat in one of the blocks being constructed by private developers (sometimes with government subsidies), or until they were forced out when the *chabolas* themselves were bulldozed in the early seventies.

Spain thus acquired many of the features of western industrial society – pollution, traffic jams and so on – without some of its redeeming aspects. At a time when European governments were extending their social services, Spain was in real terms reducing its expenditure on welfare.[45] In the late sixties, when the rest of Europe was putting more than five per cent of its Gross National Product into education, Spain was spending only two per cent.[46] At the same time Spaniards were paying less tax than any other

*One of the most bewildering acts of the 1950s was the destruction of Cervantes's birthplace in Alcalá de Henares and its replacement by a much larger building called the Casa de Cervantes. This was done not for reasons of progress or profit but presumably because it was felt that Cervantes's memory was better served by a big, grand building which was not his house than by a small, cramped one which was.[44]

people in Europe and the differences in income between rich and poor were extremely high. The ratio between the income of the richest tenth of the population and that of the poorest tenth was double that of Britain and three times that of Holland.[47] As Cardinal Herrera lamented in 1968, 'the only thing that has not developed is social justice'.[48]

4
Inside the Regime: the Struggles for Reform

All through the years of the dictatorship, the forces defeated by Franco in the civil war continued to oppose his regime either from exile or from underground movements inside Spain. Simultaneously, from within the regime, groups of people were pressing for reforms in the political, economic and social structures of the country. From the early forties monarchists were trying to replace Franco by a king; during the fifties and sixties Catholic groups were trying to liberalize certain aspects of Spanish life while members of Opus Dei attempted to transform the economy; and in the sixties and early seventies a group of liberal conservatives tried to bring about an *apertura*, or 'opening up' of the regime. All these efforts were opposed unconditionally by the *Falange*, and most of them were rejected by Franco. Only the economic reforms, proposed by the Opus Dei ministers, were fully carried out. A number of political changes were made but they did little to alter the political character of the regime. As a disillusioned former supporter complained in 1968, 'everything is the same and will stay the same. The regime will reach its last day with the same inflexibility it had on its first.'[1]

The first group of Franco's supporters to demand a change were the monarchists, supporters of Alfonso XIII, who had gone into exile in 1931 and abdicated in 1941, and then of his son, Don Juan de Borbón. The monarchists had supported Franco's uprising against the republic and many had fought in the civil war. Among them were some of the most prominent nationalist generals, such as Kindelán, Aranda, Varela and Orgaz. These men, who had

been colleagues of Franco and knew his weaknesses, argued that
he was not the right man to rule Spain in peacetime and should
retire once the war was over. He had carried out the duties of a
Spanish patriot and should now hand over to the legitimate
monarch. The monarchists argued that there could be no
permanence in a regime based on the personal rule of one man and
in 1943 a number of them, who were also *procuradores* in the
newly-inaugurated *Cortes*, wrote to Franco asking him to withdraw in favour of a 'Catholic, traditional monarchy'.[2]

The monarchists did not form a homogeneous group but were
divided between a majority that wished to placate Franco and a
minority that wished to oppose him. To most of them there was
no real contradiction between monarchism and francoism: they
wanted both, a traditional monarchy carrying out *franquista*
policies. If, they argued, Don Juan was to identify himself fully
with the regime, then there would be no problem and Franco
would no doubt hand over to him at a later date. Unfortunately
for them, the pretender refused to support the dictatorship and
towards the end of the world war he was becoming publicly
critical of Franco's policies. This placed those monarchists with
dual loyalties in a difficult position. Many of them did not care
greatly for Franco himself but recognized the importance of his
achievement. The future monarchy, they believed, had to be tied
closely to *franquista* principles or it would not survive. A liberal
monarchy, to which Don Juan aspired, would be dangerous and
might return Spain to the anarchy from which Franco had only
recently rescued it. In the years after 1943, as the breach between
the pretender and the dictator widened, these people had to take
sides and most of them, often with regret, turned their backs on
the heir to the throne. Only a few, such as Pedro Sainz Rodríguez,
Franco's first minister of education, stayed with Don Juan, who
lived on in frustrated exile in Portugal. A few more remained
ambivalent. The Luca de Tena family tried to uphold the
monarchist cause through its newspaper *ABC* but it was forced to
make concessions to the regime to avoid the closure of its paper.
José María de Areilza managed to combine an ardent monarchism
with a highly successful public career. An associate of Ledesma
and Primo de Rivera in the early thirties, and later a member of the
Falange's *Junta Política*, he became, after the civil war, mayor of
Bilbao, director general of industry, and ambassador to Buenos

Aires, Washington and Paris. During the sixties he began to distance himself from the regime and, on renewing his links with Don Juan, he became secretary of the pretender's privy council in 1965. Within a short time he had established a reputation as a reformer and a leader of Spain's liberal conservatives. Few people were surprised when, after Franco's death, he was chosen as foreign minister in the first government of the monarchy.

Most of the monarchists initially supported, then timidly opposed and finally acquiesced in Franco's rule. The attitude of the Church was very different. From a position of outright, obsessive support, it moved slowly into a position of guarded criticism and finally into opposition and rejection of the regime. Considering that several thousand priests had been killed in the republican zone during the civil war, the Church's enthusiasm for the nationalists was understandable. But the degree of fanaticism and intolerance it displayed after the war was, for a European Church in the twentieth century, truly astonishing. For the Church, as for Franco, the war had been a crusade and there was no room for mercy or reconciliation at the end of it. Those who resisted the crusade deserved punishment, and a number of Basque priests who remained loyal to the republic were shot afterwards without an audible protest from the Church.*[3] 'On the soil of Spain,' proclaimed the Bishop of Salamanca early in the war, 'a bloody conflict is being waged between two conceptions of life, two forces preparing for universal conflict in every country of the earth . . . Communists and Anarchists are sons of Cain, fratricides, assassins of those who cultivate virtue . . . [The war] takes the external form of a civil war, but in reality it is a Crusade,'[5] Shortly after the 'crusaders' had won, they were publicly congratulated by the Pope[6] and the Spanish Church settled down to enjoy the fruits of its victory. For a long time Franco was preserved from criticism. To the Bishop of Orense, his regime remained 'a bulwark of the Catholic faith . . . the only country which has resisted and defeated the hordes of the Godless'. Franco's Spain, he declared in a pastoral letter, 'will be the star to which all European

---

*Cardinal Gomá later said in a letter to the Basque leader, José Antonio Aguirre, that the Church had not remained silent over the executions. It had not protested in public, however, because, in the Cardinal's view, this would have been less effective than doing so in private.[4]

nations will again turn their eyes.'[7]

Franco rewarded the Church for its support by granting it a list of privileges so long that it found itself in a position of power it had not known since the days of the Hapsburgs. A century and a half of efforts to separate church and state were nullified: bishops sat in the *Cortes* and in the Council of the Realm, huge subsidies were paid out of the state budget, moral and educational issues became the preserve of the Church. Spain officially became a 'Catholic state', considering as 'a seal of honour its obedience to the Law of God, according to the doctrine of the Holy, Catholic and Apostolic Church, the one, true and inseparable faith of the national spirit *which will inspire the country's legislation*'[8] (my italics). The nation's moral life was organized by the ecclesiastical authorities. Religious teaching became compulsory in all schools and control of text books was largely in the hands of the Church. Divorce became illegal, adultery a crime, contraception was prohibited, and civil marriage was forbidden if either partner was a Catholic. The Church's duties extended over vast areas of Spanish life: it could decide how people should not dress, what they should not do, and what they should not read – in 1957 they even managed to ban the works of Miguel de Unamuno. One example of the Church's attitudes in 1959 is provided by the words of the then Cardinal Primate of Spain: 'Public bathing on beaches, in swimming pools or from river banks constitutes a special danger for morality. Mixed bathing must be avoided because it almost always gives rise to sin and scandal. As for engaged couples, they must shun solitude and obscurity. Walking arm in arm is unacceptable. It is scandalous and indecent to walk about linked in any way whatsoever.'[9]

The Vatican had been delighted by Franco's victory in the civil war and Pius XII had declared: 'the nation chosen by God as his principal instrument for the evangelization of the New World and as the impregnable bastion of the Catholic faith, has just given the proselytes of materialist atheism in our century the most shining proof of the supremacy of the eternal values of religion and the spirit over all things'.[10] The Papacy's admiration for Franco continued into the fifties and in 1953 a Concordat was signed between Spain and the Vatican. This document, which ratified the gains made by the Church during the war, also resolved the one outstanding problem between Franco and the Vatican: the presentation of bishops. The dictator insisted that he had the right to nominate bishops and archbishops, and on this issue the Vatican had to concede, although it did reserve the right to appoint apostolic administrators for sees that had fallen vacant as well as titular bishops to act as auxiliaries where necessary.[11]

The Vatican's enthusiasm for Franco diminished, however, a few years later, after the election of Pope John XXIII. Spain may have been 'the impregnable bastion of the Catholic faith' but its political system was repugnant to the new Pope. In two great encyclicals (*Mater et Magistra* 1961 and *Pacem in Terris* 1963), and in the Second Vatican Council (1962–5), the Catholic Church proclaimed its new stand on human rights. To the dismay of the *franquistas*, the Vatican endorsed all those rights – freedom of expression, freedom of association, freedom to elect one's rulers – which the regime, with the help of the Spanish Church, had been denying for a generation. The political effects of the Second Vatican Council were far-reaching. Catholics throughout Spain began to re-examine their government in the light of the new papal doctrines and many soon adopted christian democrat positions. Two of the advantages enjoyed by the Spanish Church under Franco – freedom from state censorship for Church publications and freedom of association for Catholic organizations so long as they did not interfere in politics – were now put to use. *Ecclesia*, the weekly publication of *Acción Católica*, began to disseminate the ideas contained in the encyclicals, while Joaquín Ruiz Giménez, a friend of the Vatican and a former ambassador to Rome, set up a monthly review called *Cuadernos para el Diálogo* in which mild criticisms of the regime were tolerated. Simultaneously, two branches of *Acción Católica*, the *Hermandades Obreras de Acción Católica* (HOAC) and the *Juventud Obrera Católica* (JOC), adopted increasingly political roles and became involved on the side of the workers in the great labour disputes of the sixties.

The Church itself reacted cautiously to the encyclicals and it was not until after the appointment of Mgr Vicente Enrique y Tarancón as Cardinal Primate in 1969 that a majority of the bishops wholeheartedly accepted the Vatican line. Before then a number of bishops had spoken out against social injustice and in 1967 the archbishops of Murcia and Madrid had infuriated the *Falange* by refusing to allow memorial services for Hitler to be held in their dioceses.[12] But most bishops were reluctant to abandon the regime, in contrast to the lower clergy which became increasingly radical during the sixties. More than half the priests who replied to an opinion poll conducted by the Church in 1970 defined themselves as politically of the Left.[13] Many of them shared the views of Dom Aureli Escarré who, as Abbot of Montserrat, had denounced the regime and the Church in an interview .with Le Monde in 1963: 'We do not have behind us twenty-five years of peace but only twenty-five years of victory. The victors, including the Church which was obliged to fight on their side, have done nothing to abolish this division between victors and vanquished: this represents one of the most lamentable failures of a regime which calls itself Christian, but whose state does not follow the basic principles of Christianity . . . The future depends upon the manner in which today's problems are solved – the social problem, the problems of democracy, liberty and also of justice . . . Ultimately it is a problem of Christianity: to be or not to be authentic Christians, both in the individual sense and in the collective, that is to say, political, sense. As a body, our politicians today are not Christians.'[14]

The Church finally withdrew its support for the regime in the early seventies and, by doing so, managed to avoid an anticlerical reaction after Franco's death. In September 1971 the first joint assembly of bishops and priests voted on a resolution which apologized for the Church's role in civil war. The resolution – 'we humbly recognize and regret the fact that we did not play our true role as ministers of reconciliation among our people when they were divided by a fratricidal civil war' – did not gain the two-thirds majority required for its adoption, but a clear majority voted in its favour.[15] Shortly afterwards, in January 1973, the bishop's conference voted by nearly three to one in support of a resolution calling, among other things, for the removal of bishops from the Cortes, the separation of Church and State, and an end to Franco's right to nominate bishops.[16] To supporters of the regime the attitude of the Church was treasonable and franquista loyalists inveighed against 'red bishops' and 'communist priests'. One fanatical group, which called itself the Guerrilleros de Cristo Rey, went about assaulting the 'apostates'. To Franco himself, the 'desertion' and 'ingratitude' of the Church was one of the saddest events of his life.[17]

After the Second Vatican Council, the regime's 'Catholic'

supporters – that is, members of lay organizations like *Acción Católica* – were confronted by a similar problem to that faced by the monarchists twenty years earlier: the objects of their dual loyalty were moving into opposing camps. But in the decade before the election of Pope John, they had become one of the most important components of the regime. During the civil war and the global conflict which followed, the army and the *Falange* had been the most prominent of the regime's supports. But after the defeats of Italy and Germany, the *Falange* was hastily relegated and confined to running the ministry of labour and the *Movimiento*. Franco foresaw the international problems he would face after the Second World War and thus he searched around for presentable, non-fascist representatives to negotiate with the outside world. Fortunately, there were a number of skilled men connected to *Acción Católica* and the related *Asociación Católica Nacional de Propagandistas* (ACNP) who were prepared to do this. Two of the most important of these figures were Alberto Martín Artajo and Fernando María Castiella who between them held the ministry of foreign affairs from 1945 to 1969. Martín Artajo, who was president of *Acción Católica*, was chosen as foreign minister in 1945, but before accepting the post he asked the Cardinal Primate to advise him whether he should take it. The Cardinal told him to accept the appointment because it would 'result in the common good of the Fatherland and of the Church'.[18] As foreign minister Martín Artajo was extremely useful to both his allegiances. A man who would have been regarded as a right-wing christian democrat in Italian politics was obviously a more suitable representative in post-war Europe than any of his military or falangist colleagues. The negotiations over the Concordat were successful largely because they were carried out by Martín Artajo with the help of another ACNP member, Joaquín Ruiz Giménez, who had been appointed ambassador to Rome in 1948.

Not everyone, however, who was connected to *Acción Católica*, remained an upholder of the regime. The lay working-class associations, HOAC and JOC, moved into almost overt opposition in the early 1960s when, among other things, they backed the strike of the Asturian miners. Later a number of ACNP members formed the *Tácito* group to campaign for an *apertura* in the early seventies, while one of the most influential reformers inside the regime was Federico Silva Muñoz, a man tied closely to the

ACNP and minister of public works between 1965 and 1970. But the first and most prominent ACNP member to break ranks was Martín Artajo's protégé, Joaquín Ruiz Giménez. A tall, impressive man, transparently honest and almost obsessively self-critical, Ruiz Giménez became ambassador to the Vatican at the age of thirty-five. Less than three years later, before the negotiations over the Concordat were completed, he was summoned home and appointed minister of education. His principal aim as minister was to broaden the range of university teaching in the country. During the immediate post-civil war years, republican sympathizers in the universities were sacked and replaced by men ideologically committed to the regime. Since only a limited number of falangists had sufficient academic qualifications to deserve professorships, the standard of teaching dropped dramatically. Ruiz Giménez tried to improve matters by opening up intellectual debate and appointing those who, while not actively opposed to the regime, were at least critical of some of its features. He encouraged debate inside the universities between liberal Catholics and radical falangists. Two of the men he promoted were Pedro Laín Entralgo, who became Rector of Madrid University, and Antonio Tovar, whom he appointed Rector of the University of Salamanca. Both men had been falangist intellectuals whose ideas were changing and both ended up eventually in the opposition.

Ruiz Giménez's policies were detested by most *franquistas* and in 1956, after riots in Madrid University and clashes between students, they were able to obtain his dismissal. He was not wholly dismayed because he was already finding his position difficult to justify. As ambassador in Rome, Ruiz Giménez had met and been impressed by reformist leaders in the new Christian Democrat Party. In the early fifties he went through a 'crisis of conscience' and felt more and more alienated from Franco's Spain. As minister of education he believed in the peaceful evolution of the regime but the strength of resistance from the Right made him doubtful that liberal reforms could come from within the system. After leaving office he combined his work as an academic, first at Salamanca and then at Madrid University, with a legal practice in which he spent much of his time defending trade unionists and leaders of the underground opposition. He was greatly influenced by the Second Vatican Council, which he attended, and by the papal encyclical, *Pacem in Terris*. He promised John XXIII that he would try to spread the new Vatican ideals inside Spain and in 1963 he established *Cuadernos para el Diálogo* which, presumably because of the Vatican links of its founder, did not suffer the degree of persecution and censorship experienced by other publications. Convinced finally of the futility of trying to reform *franquismo* from within, Ruiz Giménez resigned from the *Cortes* in 1964 and passed into opposition.[19]

The men of *Acción Católica* and ACNP represented a reasonably wide section of Spanish opinion, ranging from rigid conservatism to left-wing christian democracy. Their chief rivals, members of the largely lay order Opus Dei, presented a more homogeneous group: with one or two well-publicized exceptions, the most prominent men of the Opus were politically on the Right and interested chiefly in economic issues. This secret and mysterious organization, which one critic termed 'the Holy Mafia',[20] dominated Spanish political life from the Stabilization Plan until 1973. Founded in 1928 by an Aragonese priest, José María Escrivá de Balaguer, Opus Dei expected its members to occupy important positions in the state. The order's conquest of power after the civil war was a remarkable achievement. During the 1940s a number of its members became university professors and in 1957 three of them joined the government. Ullastres as minister of commerce, Faustino García-Moncó as his under-secretary, and Navarro Rubio in the ministry of finance were responsible for the Stabilization Plan of 1959. During the 1960s, with the help of other members of the Opus such as Gregorio López Bravo, who became minister of industry, and Laureano López Rodó, who was in charge of the development plans, they carried out the transformation of the Spanish economy. The other components of the regime were forced to retreat before the rapid advance of the Opus and the ubiquitous presence of its members in the apparatus of state. By 1970 eight of the nineteen cabinet ministers belonged to Opus Dei and at least four others were closely linked to it. The order controlled the seven economic ministries (finance, commerce, industry, development, agriculture, housing and public works) as well as the vice-presidency and the ministry of foreign affairs.

The aims of the Opus men in government were economic prosperity and political tranquillity. They liberalized the economy and encouraged people to make money because they believed that this would lead to a depoliticization of the country. Political ideologies, they argued, were a thing of the past, the phenomenon of an under-developed society. Ninety per cent of contemporary politics, argued Gonzalo Fernández de la Mora, the ideologue of 'technocracy' and a sympathizer of Opus Dei, consisted of technology and economics.[21] These were in the process of making the old ideologies redundant. Politics should be concerned only with 'the maintenance of order, the increase of national income and the fair distribution of wealth'.[22]

For the technocrats of Opus Dei, economic reforms and the development of the country would make political reforms unnecessary. But to many other people it was absurd that an anachronistic political structure should survive during a time of modernization and economic progress. Businessmen who had supported or acquiesced in Franco's dictatorship during the early years felt that by the sixties a change was needed. To them, an autocratic regime which may or may not have been appropriate to the problems of the 1930s, and which had barely evolved since, was plainly unsuited to an industrialized Spain hoping to join the European Economic Community. Those who pressed for political reforms from economic motives often supported an *apertura* for other, more pragmatic reasons as well. In 1962 Franco entered his seventies but until 1969 he made no move to designate a successor. Even then there was much uncertainty as to the nature of the state that would follow him. Franco could claim that everything was 'well tied up' and López Rodó could assure people that the country would continue to be governed according to the Fundamental Laws,[23] but most people were apprehensive about the future. It was largely in order to remove the possibility of civil conflict after Franco's death that reformers inside the regime began campaigning for an *apertura*. As Joaquín Garrigues, a prominent liberal conservative later to become a minister in the governments of Adolfo Suárez, warned during the last year of the dictatorship: 'It is only by taking the risk of possible change . . . that one can control the change. Otherwise, the social forces which are bringing pressure to bear on the institutions of state will end by triumphing as did Ho Chi Minh in Saigon. By rubbing out everything and starting again.'[24]

The man who best represented the spirit of *aperturismo* during the 1960s was Manuel Fraga Iribarne, a young Galician professor with a brilliant academic record. Fraga, who became minister of information and tourism in 1962 at the age of thirty-nine, had little respect for the ideas of the Opus technocrats. Fernández de la Mora's 'theory of the end of ideologies in an ideology composed of empiricism, complacency and justification of the status quo. It proclaims what the Right have always proclaimed: "We are the ones who know and the others have to obey."'[25] Politics, in Fraga's view, could never be abolished and a technocrat who evaded moral and political responsibilities would become 'something humanly despicable and politically very dangerous'.[26] Fraga's idea of an *apertura* was to introduce political reforms from inside the system, reforms that at the same time would 'preserve the positive elements of the regime – the defence of law and order, authority, efficient administration . . . the creation of millions of jobs, the construction of great public works, the improvement in Spain's prestige.'[27] Fraga valued the *franquista* achievement – 'thirty years of tranquillity after a century of anxiety' – and he was not, at any rate at this stage, a democrat. He called himself a 'man of the centre' trying to find 'a balance between tradition and development . . . between immobilism and irresponsible radicalism'.[28] In fact he was a conservative of authoritarian temperament, trying to modernize the country because reforms were necessary if chaos and violence were to be avoided after Franco's death.*

The ministry of information in 1962 was an ideal job for an *aperturista* to tackle. The previous incumbent, Gabriel Arias Salgado, who had been in charge of censorship for almost a generation, had turned Spain into a cultural wasteland. As under-secretary for education in the forties, and from 1951 minister of information, Arias Salgado had created an appalling press, which few people bothered to read, and an atmosphere of intolerance and narrow-mindedness which no great artist could

*All the same, his views had evolved since the late forties when he had written a deplorable work of propaganda for the Diplomatic Information Office. In this book Fraga made the preposterous claim that 'the glorious rising of July 18, 1936, was one of the most popular politico-social movements recorded in history. Impartial observers and objective historians are bound to recognize that it was the greater and the better part of the country that rose on July 18 against an illegal, corrupt Government, which was preparing the most sinister of red revolutions from within the Cabinet.'[29]

live in. The list of forbidden authors was enormous and included
Joyce, Hemingway, Camus, Malraux and Voltaire; even novels
such as *Madame Bovary* and *The Charterhouse of Parma* were banned
because they were regarded in some way as subversive. The
cinema and theatre were ruthlessly censored and the works of
García Lorca, the great poet and playwright murdered by Franco's
supporters at the outbreak of the civil war, were prohibited. When
a theatre club tried to produce Graham Greene's play *The Living
Room* in Barcelona in 1952, the ministry of information insisted on
a number of grotesque changes. Among other proposals it was
suggested that one character should be praying while committing
suicide so as to leave open the possibility that she might go to
heaven.[30]

Some writers such as Miguel Delibes or Camilo José Cela
remained in Spain in spite of the censorship, but usually only if
they were apolitical authors: Delibes, as we have seen, wrote
about rural life in Castile, while Cela was at his best describing
encounters with local eccentrics in the Alcarria. Writers with a
broader scope, such as Madariaga, Alberti or Ortega y Gasset,
went abroad, as did most of Spain's other great artists such as
Picasso and the cellist Pablo Casals. Ortega, one of the major
Spanish thinkers of the Generation of '98 and not in any sense a
man of the Left, eventually returned to Spain. When he died in
1955, Arias Salgado sent the following orders to editors of the
press: 'Each newspaper may publish up to three articles on the
death of Ortega y Gasset: one biographical piece and two
commentaries. All articles on the writer's philosophy must
emphasize his errors in religious matters. On the front page
photographs of the funeral parlour, the death mask or the corpse
may be published, but not photographs of Ortega during his
lifetime.'[31]

The first article of the 1938 Press Law declared that 'the
organization, supervision and control of the national (sic) institution of the press belongs to the state.' The press was indeed
virtually 'nationalized', much of it published directly by the
government through the *Falange*, the rest of it controlled by
means of censorship and the appointment of falangist editors.
Most of the pre-civil war publications were immediately banned
and those that survived were deeply conservative newspapers such
as *Ya*, which was published by *Editorial Católica* (the publishing

house of *Acción Católica*), and the monarchist *ABC*. Even these could not be trusted to toe the line with sufficient accuracy. During the Second World War the government foisted boorish falangists with nazi sympathies upon both papers in order to stifle the pro-allied sentiments of some of the editorial staff.[32] Sometimes it would send an article to a newspaper and insist on its publication. In May 1944 the Marqués de Luca de Tena, *ABC*'s proprietor, opened his own newspaper to discover a scurrilous and hysterical attack on José María Gil Robles, a politician and fellow-monarchist whom he had no wish to insult. The author of the piece, which had been imposed by the *Delegación de Prensa*, turned out to be Arias Salgado himself.[33]

After the Second World War the *ABC*'s monarchist loyalties, although not often apparent in its articles, made the paper particularly vulnerable to the censor's whims. Presumably in revenge for its proprietor's known allegiance to Don Juan, *ABC* often found itself unable to report on any monarchist activities taking place anywhere in the world. Among other items removed by the censor were a portrait of the King of Norway, the news of the death of Prince Eugen of Sweden, and a description of the wedding dress worn by Britain's Princess Elizabeth. In 1962 the government even tried to extend its censorship to Greece when a Spanish monarchist decided to publish a newspaper, *Diario Español de Atenas*, for a few days during the celebrations of the wedding between Prince Juan Carlos, Don Juan's son and heir, and Princess Sofia, the daughter of the king of Greece. Franco himself ordered the Spanish foreign ministry to demand the prohibition of this temporary paper, but the Greek prime minister replied that it was impossible: 'In Greece,' he said, 'there is a parliament and the government cannot take this kind of arbitrary action.'[34]

Shortly after his appointment as minister in 1962, Manuel Fraga announced that there would be a new law on information. In the event Spaniards had to wait until 1966 for the law and even then it was a law that dealt only with the liberalization of the press (*Ley de Prensa*) and not with other parts of the media. Fraga claimed that his new law would mean 'a real liberty, without armed gangs, without duels or challenges, without cartels or monopolies, without licentiousness or abuses. It will be a liberty to keep Spain pure, not to smear it or to destroy it.'[35] The chief feature of the

Ley de Prensa was the removal of prior censorship by the state and its substitution by voluntary or self-censorship on the part of the editors. The first article of the law stated that Spaniards should enjoy the right 'to freedom of the expression of ideas . . . by means of printed material' but the second article set limits to this freedom in much the same way as the Charter of the Spanish People had dealt with this and similar 'rights' in 1945. The press could publish what it liked provided it showed 'respect for truth and morality; obedience to the principles of the *Movimiento Nacional* and other fundamental laws; the needs of national defence, state security, the maintenance of law and order, and external peace; the respect due to institutions and persons in expressing criticism of public and administrative action; the independence of the courts, the safe-guarding of the privacy and honour of individuals and families.'[36]

Although the *Ley de Prensa* managed to dispel some of the repressive atmosphere, with the result that the Spanish press improved considerably, it was a far from liberal law either in principle or in application. In fact, as a consequence, newspapers were fined and particular issues confiscated with much more frequency than before. Fraga thought that Spaniards should be grateful to him for his new law and he was particularly harsh with those who infringed it. In 1968 he twice suspended publication of the daily *Madrid*, which, he claimed, had systematically abused the liberty of the press.[37] *Madrid* was run by two 'dissident' members of Opus Dei, Antonio Fontán and Rafael Calvo Serer, and its columns became increasingly critical of the regime after 1966. (Five years later, when Fraga was no longer minister of education, the paper was closed down altogether.) Among others who suffered was the christian democrat, Joaquín Ruiz Giménez. After publicly calling for a revision of the Concordat in the autumn of 1966, Ruiz Giménez was removed by the government from the editorship of *Cuadernos para el Diálogo*, allegedly because he was not a professional journalist and did not have the necessary qualifications to be editor of a magazine.[38] For a regime which had imposed wholly unqualified falangists as editors of *Ya*, *ABC* and many other papers, for a government whose minister in charge of the press (until 1962) had no journalistic experience whatever, it was ironic that a man who had been ambassador to the Vatican and minister of education could have been considered unsuitable to edit a monthly magazine.

Nevertheless, in spite of its limitations, the *Ley de Prensa* was a reforming measure. Access to information became much easier than before and books on most subjects, even marxism, could be found without much difficulty. In 1970 George Orwell's *Homage to Catalonia* was published in Catalan with only one passage deleted by the censor.[39] Three years later an economist with strong communist sympathies was able to publish an extremely critical history of the dictatorship which remained on the best-seller list for several months.[40] The *aperturistas* had won a victory, however imperfect, in the struggle to achieve information. It was natural that they should now turn their attention to broadening the regime's definition of freedom of association. From 1968 until the end of the dictatorship, the principal struggle within the regime was between the *aperturistas* and their 'immobilist' opponents, or *inmovilistas*, over the issue of 'political associations'.

Since the civil war there had been no political parties in Spain – except, of course, for the *Falange* or *Movimiento* – and Franco had often repeated that there never would be. Yet even the *Caudillo* thought the Spaniards should be allowed to participate a little more in political life, and in the late sixties there was much discussion about setting up political associations within the *Movimiento*. These were intended to reflect not the range of ideas in the country as a whole but only the range of ideas among the regime's supporters. The Statutes of the *Movimiento*, which were issued at the end of 1968, contained an article dealing with the future establishment of such associations, and some *aperturistas* optimistically believed that Spain would soon possess a limited political pluralism. However, a plan introduced shortly afterwards by the minister of the *Movimiento*, José Solís, showed how limited the government's scheme was. The Solís Statute, as it came to be known, foresaw 'associations of public opinion' rather than political associations, and even these would be set up under so constrictive a framework that no serious *aperturista* could contemplate taking part. Three months after the statute had been approved by the National Council of the *Movimiento*, Solís was replaced as minister by Torcuato Fernández Miranda who quickly buried the scheme which had, in any case, never received Franco's signature. A few months later, Fernández Miranda produced his own plan for political associations to be made legal so long as they accepted the ideology of the *Movimiento*. However, although he remained minister for another four years, he made no effort to put his plan into practice. Over the central issue of political reform, the *aperturistas* had been defeated.

A further setback for the reformers occurred in October 1969 when Fraga was sacked in the same reshuffle which removed Solís. Two months earlier the government had been severely embarrassed by the worst of a number of financial scandals which broke during the last years of the dictatorship. On the strength of fraudulent returns on export sales, a textile firm called Matesa had been receiving huge credits from the Banco de Crédito Industrial. The money gained from the company's declarations totalled more than ten billion pesetas (about £75 million), much of which was subsequently invested privately abroad. Three economic ministers, all of them members of Opus Dei, were involved, and Fraga and Solís, well-known opponents of the Opus, hoped to make political capital from the scandal. They should have studied Franco's methods more clearly. On several occasions, notably in 1941 and 1956, Franco had shown that he liked to balance his dismissals. When, during the Second World War, he sacked the pro-British army minister, General Varela, he also got rid of the pro-German foreign minister, Serrano Suñer, who was his own brother-in-law. In 1956, when he decided that the liberal, anti-falangist Ruiz Giménez had to leave the ministry of education, the secretary-general of the *Falange*, Fernández Cuesta, went as well. So it was in 1969. The Opus Dei ministers had to go (although they were replaced by other members of the order) but Fraga (who as minister of information had allowed the press to report the scandal in detail) and Solís accompanied them.

Franco later relented over Solís, who had served him loyally for many years, and brought him back into the government six years later. But Fraga was not forgiven. Not only had he helped to embarrass the regime – or at least he had done nothing to limit its embarrassment – he had also, in the eyes of the most fervent *franquistas*, done more than anyone to undermine Spanish morals. To them the *Ley de Prensa* had not only opened the regime to criticism; worse, it had also been responsible for bringing pornography to Spain. In fact, pornography was, by the standards of other western countries, still extremely limited, but it was sufficient to dismay both Franco and his vice-president, Admiral Carrero Blanco. Between them they decided that there would be no more reforms. *Aperturismo* and its champion would be discarded and a policy of 'continuation', or *continuismo*, would be followed instead. Reforms, as they thought the last few years had well demonstrated, were disastrous for Spain. Carrero, who liked to write under the pseudonym Ginés de Buitrago, put forward his views on *aperturismo* in the *Movimiento*'s paper *Arriba*.[41] Before 1936, he argued, Spain had been like a drunkard who had nearly died from his excesses. Just in time he had been saved by a doctor and had then recovered and become a new man – until wicked friends tempted him back to drink. In contemporary Spain, Carrero alleged, the *aperturistas* played the part of wicked friends. If political parties and the 'demo-liberal system of inorganic democracy' returned to Spain, the drunken excesses of the past would return with them.

After Franco himself, the key figure of the regime was Luis Carrero Blanco. In 1941 he was appointed under-secretary to the presidency and for the next thirty-two years he was Franco's right-hand man, becoming minister in 1951, vice-president in 1967 and president (that is, prime minister) in 1973.* Carrero's influence in the formation of governments was immense and he frequently addressed memoranda to the *Caudillo* with suggestions for the appointment and dismissal of ministers.[42] According to Laureano López Rodó, a protégé of Carrero and the dominant minister in the cabinet between 1965 and 1973, he was a man without ambition who accepted his appointments only because of a strong sense of duty.[43] Although, apparently, he would have liked to retire from politics, he did not do so because it would have been a desertion of Franco. Carrero was a natural 'number two' who defined himself as 'a man totally identified with the political work of the *Caudillo* . . . My loyalty to his person and his work is total, transparent and pure, without any shadow of private reservation or blemish of mental reserve.'[44] His loyalty was indeed remarkable, extending to the suggestion that Franco should make himself king.[45]

In spite of his strong sense of duty, his deference to Franco and

*The prime minister in Spain is called *presidente del gobierno*. Franco remained prime minister (as well as Head of State) until 1973 when he handed over to Carrero.

his lack of flamboyance, Carrero Blanco was a fanatic. Hater of communism, freemasonry and liberalism, his most intense hatred was directed against Judaism, which he called 'the true enemy' of Spain. Judaism was worse than all the other 'isms' because it was the original, the ancestor of all subsequent evils. In an absurd book published in 1941 he claimed that Spain's enemies of Jewish descent included the Reformation, the Enlightenment, liberalism, masonry, atheism and communism. In the contemporary struggle which Spain, 'the paladin of the Christian faith', was waging, Judaism's weapons included 'separatisms', 'internationalisms', atheism, Marxism and 'capitalist imperialisms'.[46] As an older man, he became a prominent exponent of the 'better dead than red' school of thought. 'The avoidance of war is of little value . . .' he told a sympathetic journalist in 1968, 'if political subversion is not contained, because it is better to be blown up by a nuclear explosion than to go on living as part of a Godless mass of slaves.'[47]

The government formed after the Matesa affair – nicknamed *monocolor* because of the predominance of the Opus men – remained in office for nearly four years until Carrero, who was a strong sympathizer but not a member of Opus Dei, became prime minister in June 1973. Franco was by then eighty and was at last feeling his age. The previous year he had been obliged to preside over the victory parade sitting down, and López Rodó noticed that he had started to doze off during cabinet meetings.[48] Carrero had been offered the job before but had turned it down with the remark that Franco was the best prime minister the Spaniards could wish for.[49] But by 1973 it was plainly time for Franco to hand over the running of the government, and Carrero formed a new cabinet without most of the Opus Dei ministers. It did not last long. On 20 December of the same year, Carrero Blanco was assassinated by members of the Basque separatist group ETA. It was the greatest blow the dictatorship had received in its entire history, and López Rodó, then foreign minister, realised that it meant the end of the Franco regime.[50] From then until the death of Franco himself two years later, the government was in permanent crisis as it tried to deal with a wave of strikes, increasing terrorism, and the activities of an opposition which knew that the regime was dying.

The new prime minister was Carlos Arias Navarro, a dry,

unimaginative man whose ambition had been to become a Madrid notary rather than a politician.[51] His only experience of government was as minister of the interior during the six months of Carrero's government, but before that he had been director-general of security and mayor of Madrid. During the civil war he had been state prosecutor in Málaga (after its 'liberation' by Franco's forces in February 1937), where he had acquired an apparently well-deserved reputation as 'the butcher of Málaga',★ and it was evidently his hard, repressive past which persuaded Franco to choose him to counter subversion and impose order after Carrero's assassination. According to his own account, Arias told Franco that 'the job [was] too important for my humble merits and meagre strengths' but the *Caudillo* interrupted with the words, 'your loyalty is enough'.[53]

The *aperturistas* saw some hopeful signs in the formation of Arias's cabinet. It was not, by any standards, a reforming government but it was the first since before 1957 to contain no trace of Opus Dei influence. Furthermore, the appointment of Pio Cabanillas, an associate of Fraga, to the ministry of information, seemed likely to herald a further liberalization of the press. But the most encouraging event for the *aperturistas* was a speech made by Arias on 12 February 1974 in which he called for a number of political reforms. Of these, the most important was yet another

---

★Arias was state prosecutor in Málaga from 1937 to 1939. While it is impossible to ascertain the exact extent of his personal responsibility for the executions that took place, the repression in Málaga was extremely savage both during the civil war and afterwards. The following is an extract from a letter sent by the British consul in the city to the ambassador in Madrid on 31 August 1944:[52]

'I have for a long time been endeavouring to ascertain the total number of executions carried out since Málaga was "liberated" on 8th February, 1937. I have now obtained the following statistics which, I have every reason to believe, are quite reliable as they were secured from official records:-
a) The "Reds" were in control of Málaga from July 18th, 1936, until February 7th, 1937, and during that time they executed or murdered 1,005 persons.
b) During the first week of "liberation", that is from February 8th to 14th, when no courts were functioning, 3,500 persons were executed by the Nationalists.
c) During the period from February 15th, 1937, to August 25th, 1944, a further 16,952 persons have been "legally" sentenced to death and shot in Málaga.'

project to set up political associations. The others were plans to reform the *Cortes*, to make local government more democratic and to revise trade union law. The prime minister constructed his speech carefully, using words and phrases designed to placate both the *aperturistas* and the *inmovilistas*.[54] Certainly the vocabulary of *aperturismo* was all there – the references to 'open doors', 'bold innovation', 'the demands of a changing society' and so on – but so were the heavy phrases of *franquismo* – the insistence on a rigorous maintenance of law and order, 'the applicability of permanent, fundamental principles', the importance of continuity, authority, duty and obligation. 'The new government,' Arias assured the Right, 'adopts with honour the entire history of the Regime.'

Although Arias tried hard not to upset the *inmovilistas*, the extreme Right almost immediately launched an offensive against 'the spirit of 12 February'. This group regarded itself as a 'last ditch' bastion of 1930s *franquismo* and came to be known as 'the Bunker'. Its most articulate leaders were Blas Piñar, founder of the neo-fascist paper, *Fuerza Nueva* ('New Force'), and José Antonio Girón, a former minister of labour who in 1974 became president of an association of civil war veterans, the *Confederación de Ex-Combatientes*. These two could count on the support of a number of newspapers such as *El Alcázar* and the *Movimiento*'s chief organ, *Arriba*, various *camisas viejas* such as Raimundo Fernández Cuesta, and a variety of shadowy groups such as the *Hermandad de Defensores del Alcázar de Toledo*. Their most extreme supporters were a group of fanatics calling themselves the *Guerrilleros de Cristo Rey* ('Warriors of Christ the King') led by Mariano Sánchez-Covisa. Typical of their activities were beating up 'red priests' and slashing Picasso canvasses. But the Bunker's most important supporters were those holding official positions in the army or the institutions of state. Many *procuradores* in the *Cortes* and members of the *Movimiento*'s National Council were followers of Girón. So were generals such as García Rebull, a former captain-general of Madrid, and Iniesta Cano, the commander of the para-military *Guardia Civil*. So indeed were some of the ministers themselves. Although officially in favour of the 12 February programme, both the minister of the *Movimiento*, José Utrera Molina, and the minister of justice, Francisco Ruiz Jarabo, were natural allies of the Bunker. So was Luis Peralta España, under-secretary at the ministry of the interior, who later became national secretary of Girón's *Confederación de Ex-Combatientes*.

Girón began the offensive against Arias in April, two months after the prime minister had set out his programme. His savage attack in *Arriba*[55] on Arias's reformism was complemented by Blas Piñar who warned Spaniards during the following month that the civil war was not yet over.[56] In September Blas Piñar came out in open opposition to Arias. In an unsigned article in *Fuerza Nueva*,[57] he told the prime minister that he could not collaborate with him in any way and warned that the democratization he was urging would be achieved over a legion of corpses. While the spokesmen of the Bunker assailed the government through the press, their followers took to the streets. At the smallest opportunity groups of them would rush around Madrid giving the fascist salute and chanting the falangist anthem *Cara al Sol*. In December, on the first anniversary of Carrero's assassination, about 200 of them charged about the city shouting 'Long Live the 18 July! Down with 12 February!' After a short demonstration in the street where Carrero had been killed, they were led by General García Rebull to the church of the Jerónimos where an official commemoration service was to take place. 'We will invade the church,' he shouted, 'although we have not been invited. Let us sing, but we must also shout "Down with the traitors!".' They started off, reciting martial songs on the way, but were diverted by the sight of the French embassy. There they forced their way into the courtyard and began insulting the French by calling them assassins and democrats. After yelling *Cara al Sol*, they rushed off again and eventually reached the church. Crowding around the entrance, they bombarded the invited guests with insults or, in the case of prominent members of the Bunker, with acclamation. When Mgr Vicente Enrique y Tarancón, the Cardinal Archbishop of Madrid, appeared, he was greeted with shouts of 'Tarancón to the firing squad'. Arias arrived shortly afterwards to loud cries of '*mantequilla! mantequilla!*' ('butter! butter!') by which the demonstrators declared their opinion of the prime minister as a man of butter.[58]

Arias, whose entire life since 1937 had been dedicated to the maintenance of law and order, resented this criticism of his supposed weakness. As a man of the Right, he regarded left-wing criticism as natural and unavoidable, and he cared nothing about it. But these rebukes from his erstwhile comrades were different.

He brooded over them and subsequently began to harden his policy. Within weeks of his 12 February speech, it had become clear that Arias was withdrawing from his commitment to *aperturismo*.

The idea that there was anything liberal (as opposed to reformist) about the new government had already been dispelled by Arias's approval of the garrotting of a Catalan anarchist in March and a crackdown on the Left which by June had resulted in the arrests of more than 500 alleged communists and trotskyists. Simultaneously, he provoked a confrontation with the Church by ordering a 'red bishop', Mgr Añoveros, out of the country. Añoveros, who as Bishop of Cádiz-Ceuta in 1960s had attacked the *latifundistas* of Andalusia, was now Bishop of Bilbao and a supporter of the moderate aspirations of Basque nationalism. In February 1974 he preached a sermon proclaiming the Basques' right to preserve their own identity and was promptly placed under house arrest. On 3 March Añoveros was told to leave the country; he refused. During the following week he began to receive strong support from other Spanish bishops and, once the Vatican had come out strongly on his side, the government was forced to climb down.

Neither Arias's crackdown on the Left nor his treatment of Añoveros had mollified the Bunker. Nor did his actions during the summer, even though these were often specifically designed to placate the hardline Right. One of the Bunker's chief targets was General Manuel Díez-Alegría, the chief of the army general staff. Díez-Alegría was well known to be an open-minded and rather liberal officer, quite unlike the majority of his colleagues. Some of these believed, or at least affected to believe, that he might play in Spain the role that General Spinola had played in Portugal – the Portuguese revolution was then a terrifying spectacle for the Spanish Right – and consequently they clamoured for his dismissal. In the middle of June, without explanation, Arias agreed to their demands and a government decree announced that Díez-Alegría had been replaced by General Fernández Vallespin.

Even more surprising was Arias's treatment of one of his ministers, Pio Cabanillas, an *aperturista* and a friend of Fraga, and thus another object of right-wing hatred. Although during his ministry issues of magazines were still being confiscated at a steady rate, there was a new atmosphere of liberalization in the press. Newspapers were discussing and sometimes even criticizing actions of the government. They were commenting, often favourably, on events abroad such as the Portuguese revolution. Some were also, so the Bunker claimed, spreading pornography. Certainly there had been a change in the attitudes of the press towards sexuality. Towards the end of Franco's life even the conservative and 'respectable' magazine *Blanco y Negro* was publishing lengthy reports on nude bathing, teenage sexual habits and 'gay power español'. Predictably, the Bunker was horrified and the removal of Cabanillas became one of its immediate objectives. This was achieved in October 1974 with the help of Franco who, on recovering from a nearly fatal illness at the end of the summer, was shown a sample of the press's 'pornographic' output during Cabanillas's ministry. The dismissal was the worst setback the reformers had received from Arias's government and lost the prime minister his remaining supporters among them. From that time many prominent *aperturistas* came to the conclusion that reform from inside the regime was now impossible and would have to wait until after Franco's death. Thus Cabanillas's departure from the government was followed by the resignations of a number of people in government positions. The minister of finance, Antonio Barrera de Irimo, resigned from the cabinet in sympathy, while Cabanillas's deputy, Marcelino Oreja, also resigned as under-secretary at the ministry of information. Barrera's example was followed by Fernández Ordóñez, the president of INI, and with him went the director of studies, Miguel Boyer, and two of his deputies. In all, eleven senior officials connected with the ministry of information, including Ricardo de La Cierva and Juan José Rosón, resigned their posts. Few careers were damaged by these resignations. In the years following Franco's death, Oreja, Rosón, La Cierva and Fernández Ordóñez – as well as Cabanillas – all became cabinet ministers; in 1982 Boyer and his deputy, Carlos Solchaga, became the leading economic ministers in the first socialist government since the civil war.

Arias was prepared to do many things to appease the Bunker but he was not prepared to abandon the principal reform suggested in his 12 February speech. In another speech, in Barcelona in June 1974, he assured his audience that political associations would be admitted and in the following September he promised that an appropriate law would be in force before the end of the year. At the beginning of December he went on television to announce a proposed statute that recognized the right of all Spaniards 'to associate freely for political action . . . and to exercise that right . . . within the orbit of the *Movimiento*' (Article 1). Arias himself seemed somewhat apologetic about the limitations of the statute and, but for the hostility of Franco and the Bunker, he would probably have been more generous. The Statute of Political Associations was extremely restrictive and the rights which the Spaniards were supposed to enjoy under it were, in fact, more limited than those which technically they had been enjoying ever since 1945 when the Charter of the Spanish People recognized their right 'to assemble and associate freely for lawful purposes and in accordance with the Law'. The statute laid down that any association set up under its auspices must have at least 25,000 members spread over not less than fifteen provinces, a provision designed to prevent the Basques and Catalans, who were each concentrated in only four provinces, from forming their own associations. In addition, any association would have to accept the Fundamental Laws and could, if it misbehaved, be dissolved by the National Council of the *Movimiento*.

Arias had been in a difficult position because he realized that, if the idea of *asociacionismo* was going to work at all, then the *aperturistas* must be encouraged to set up their associations. Without them the whole project would become a farce and the associations would merely act like clubs for the regime's most stalwart supporters. Yet the prime minister knew he could not persuade the reformers to join in without offering them a broader statute which would further antagonize the Bunker. In the end he opted for a narrow statute and tried to persuade the reformers to accept it by claiming that it was in fact broad enough for all to take advantage of, except for separatists and communists.[59] But neither the Bunker not the *aperturistas* were fooled. The *inmovilistas* realized that the statute was not an opening to democracy and, in spite of their opposition to the whole project of associations, most of them accepted it. The National Council of the *Movimiento* approved the statute by 95 votes to none with only three abstentions (from reformist councillors) and even García Rebull, who during the debate proclaimed his 'fanatical *antiasociacionismo*', voted in favour.[60]

In March Arias reshuffled his government and dismissed José Utrera Molina, the minister of the *Movimiento* and the most pro-Bunker member of the cabinet. Utrera was replaced by the more moderate Fernando Herrero Tejedor who, after his death three months later in a car accident, was followed by Solís. Before returning to the post he had held from 1957 to 1969, Solís had been actively involved in plans to set up a vast association initially known as the *Alianza del Pueblo* and later as the *Unión del Pueblo Español* (UDPE). In July the UDPE, which had quickly collected its 25,000 members, became the first association to receive the approval of the National Council of the *Movimiento*. Under the presidency of a young protégé of Herrero Tejedor called Adolfo Súarez, the UDPE was planned as the great association of *continuismo*, an organization that would carry on the work of Franco without sinking into the Bunker or making concessions to the *aperturistas*. A number of other putative associations also applied for permission from the National Council but all of them were connected in some way with the regime. Manuel Cantarero del Castillo, a radical falangist who believed that the *Falange*'s ideals had been perverted, submitted a proposal to set up *Reforma Social Española*, through which he hoped to bring about a social democratic transformation of the regime from within. Among the *aperturistas* only Federico Silva Muñoz, a successful former minister of public works and now a somewhat timid advocate of reform, responded to the statute. He announced the formation of the *Unión Democrática Española* with the aim of establishing an association designed to attract the regime's christian democratic supporters.

But most of those who considered themselves christian democrats refused to go with Silva. José María Gil Robles, the old CEDA* leader now in his late seventies, condemned Silva as a collaborator and refused to consider him as a christian democrat.[61] Proclaiming his total opposition to the statute and his refusal to participate in Arias's project, Gil Robles nevertheless announced that he would be forming the *Federación Popular Democrática* in order to seek 'democratic solutions inspired by the principles of

*The CEDA (*Confederación Española de Derechas Autonómas*) was a coalition of Catholic parties formed to contest the elections of 1933. Until the next elections in February 1936 it was the largest force in the republican parliament.

Christian humanism'. Joaquín Ruiz Giménez, regarded by many as the country's leading christian democrat, also refused to co-operate with Arias. 'I am not a marxist,' he declared, 'but the marxists will have to participate in the future. The contrary would be an injustice and an enormous political error.'[62] Even *Tácito*, a group of young christian democrats on the fringe of the regime, would not form an association. Many of them had held official posts up until the dismissal of Cabanillas – some of them continued to do so afterwards – but even for them the statute was too narrow. Marcelino Oreja, a *Tácito* member who had resigned from the ministry of information in solidarity with Cabanillas, was one of the three people who had abstained in the vote on associations in the National Council. 'Unless we open a political road now which the people will use,' he had argued during the debate, 'we will be only history tomorrow.'[63] The rest of the group were in agreement with him: they could not support the 'statute of the *antiasociacionistas*'. In a statement *Tácito* claimed 'that the statute has had to make such concessions to [the Bunker] that the spirit of 12 February cannot be recognized in it'.[64]

The future of Arias's experiment, however, depended on the participation of Manuel Fraga. The former minister of information, now ambassador in London, was the earliest, loudest and most energetic advocate of *aperturismo*. He had been talking for some time about setting up 'a great association of the centre' and at the end of January 1975 he flew into Madrid to discuss the proposal. Swarms of journalists followed him as he hurried around Madrid, meeting ministers, talking to Arias, sounding out possible supporters. Another leading *aperturista*, the monarchist and former ambassador, José María de Areilza, pledged his support, declaring that his identification with Fraga was such that he would go anywhere with him in the service of Spain.[65] It was predicted that an association based on an alliance between Fraga and Areilza, and possibly with Silva as well, would become a crucial factor in the politics of post-*franquista* Spain. But Fraga asked for more than Arias was prepared to concede. He insisted that the objectives of any association he might establish would include free trade unions and a legislative chamber elected directly by universal suffrage. Once again Arias was torn and once again he remained true to his old loyalties. It was better to see the collapse of his project altogether than consent to the establishment of an association which seemed to be a poorly-disguised political party aiming for full, or 'inorganic', democracy. It was not, of course, Arias who could decide whether or not Fraga's association would be legalized: that was the prerogative of the National Council of the *Movimiento*. But the attitudes of the prime minister and his government were sufficiently discouraging for Fraga to realize that his chances of persuading that incurably conservative body to agree to his plan were not high. Disheartened further by the appearance of the UDPE, and the government's evident support for it, Fraga withdrew. In July he, Areilza and Cabanillas set up not the much-heralded association of the centre but a 'business association' to promote political studies.

With the failure of Fraga's scheme, the efforts of the *aperturistas* to reform the regime came to an end. There was nothing they could now do except to wait until Franco's death and press hard for reforms in the early months of the monarchy. Francisco Cambó, the Catalan businessman and politician, had declared during the crisis of 1917, 'the most conservative thing is to be a revolutionary; if we do not act, the revolution will come from below.'[66] It was a sentiment which many *aperturistas* were echoing during the last months of Franco's life. As Fernández Ordóñez warned shortly after his resignation as president of INI, change was 'the only ultimate guarantee of civil peace'.[67] Another reformer, Joaquín Garrigues, argued that the time had come to compromise with the opposition: 'We winners of the civil war must concede something if we want democracy in Spain. We must reach agreement with the "other side" over sharing the national cake . . . Spain's leading economic interests will have to concede democratic trade unions, high wages and shorter factory hours, and profit margins more like those elsewhere in western Europe.'[68] This was a blatantly pragmatic attitude from a man who identified with Franco's victory – although he had been a small boy at the time – but realized that the preservation of those gains achieved by Franco required radical change. His ideas were typical of many ambitious young men with *franquista* backgrounds who were determined to play a political role in Spain after Franco's death. A number of them, like Garrigues, became ministers in the centrist governments of the late seventies, and in the meantime they were laying plans for the formation of putative political parties. Garrigues himself, who was described in one magazine as a potential John F. Kennedy, gave up a number of business posts in 1973 and devoted himself to politics. Two years later he decided to set up a society with the aim, among other things, of promoting Spain's political, cultural and economic integration into Western Europe. During this activity, which eventually led to the formation of the *Federación de Partidos Demócratas y Liberales*, Garrigues tried hard to dissociate himself from the line of the older generation of *aperturistas* represented by Manuel Fraga. In Garrigues's view, Fraga was a reformist *franquista* and not the man of the centre he was claiming to be. He declared that he felt 'neither ideologically nor historically close to Señor Fraga. We are different. While he may have changed in recent times, his politics are well to the right of mine.'[69]

Once the associations issue had been settled, Arias made it clear that his government was not going to promote further reform. Of the three other bills which he had envisaged in his 12 February speech, one of them, the revision of trade union law, never reached the statute book, while the other two, originally designed to reform the *Cortes* and local government, ended up by virtually preserving the status quo. On the broader issue of general constitutional reform, Arias was adamant: he believed it to be 'not necessary, nor useful, nor opportune. Before thinking of constitutional reform, one should exhaust the possibility of extracting from the prevailing legality all the wealthy contents [of our own constitution]'.[70] Three months later, in June 1975, Arias made a tough, highly conservative speech to the *Cortes* in which he once again rejected constitutional reform. This speech, which marked the beginning of a new period of repressive government, also included attacks on the Left and the regional movements.

Arias's new hard line was at least partly caused by an increase in terrorist activity. In the twenty months following the assassination of Carrero, ETA killed a further 40 people (more than half of them policemen or members of the *Guardia Civil*) while other extremist groups such as FRAP (*Frente Revolucionario Anti-Fascista Patriótico*) also claimed victims. In April 1975 the prime minister reacted by declaring a state of emergency in the provinces of Vizcaya and Guipúzcoa and suspending five articles of the Charter. In August he issued a strong anti-terrorist decree making the death penalty mandatory for anyone convicted of a 'political' killing. Suspected terrorists would be tried in military courts and police were given unrestricted powers to search homes and hold people for five days without charging them with an offence. Under this decree eleven members of ETA and FRAP were condemned to death three weeks later. Six of these were subsequently reprieved but on 27 September, in spite of the Pope's appeals for clemency, the remaining five were executed. The incident caused consternation in the country and provoked widespread criticism abroad; it also led to the reprisal killing of six policemen within the next week. But Franco reacted in his usual manner. Making his final speech to crowds of cheering supporters in the Plaza de Oriente in Madrid, he declared: 'All is part of a masonic leftist conspiracy of the political class in collusion with communist-terrorist subversion in the social sphere.'[71]

The repressive policy of the Arias government was not directed only against terrorists. In the summer of 1975 it seemed prepared to lash out at any opposition. Intellectuals, trade unionists and 'communist priests' were rounded up, army officers suspected of being democrats* were arrested, and a number of well-known magazines were fined and suspended for long periods. The situation was so bad that Ruiz Giménez believed that the country was experiencing the 'psychological preparation for another civil war'.[72] It was at this moment that Spaniards were diverted from politics by the long death-bed struggle of Francisco Franco.

During the first half of 1974, Franco, at the age of eighty-one, had been in good health. One minister, who joined Arias's government in January of that year, was struck by the *Caudillo's* mental clarity and his sharpness of memory.[73] But in July of the same year Franco became seriously ill with phlebitis and handed over his powers as Head of State to his designated successor, Prince Juan Carlos, the son of Don Juan and grandson of the last king of Spain. Contrary to expectations, however, Franco recovered and six weeks later he resumed power. During the autumn he regained his strength with the help of physical exercises and a new doctor, and by the end of November he was fit enough to go shooting again. Although he sometimes expressed a desire to retire to a Carthusian monastery – an idea that he had been considering for the previous ten years – he was soon hard at

*They were accused of being members of the *Unión Militar Democrática*. See below p. 234.

work.[74] By the end of the year he had fully recovered and was keeping a stern eye on his prime minister's plans for political associations.

In the autumn of the following year Franco fell ill again and this time he understood that there would be no recovery. He wrote his political testament but otherwise tried to carry on as normal. On 30 October he suffered a heart attack and six days later he was rushed to the Ciudad Sanitaria La Paz, where surgeons carried out the first of a series of operations. On 20 November, in the early morning, he finally died. He had been kept alive pointlessly for several weeks after it became clear that he was on his death bed. Throughout that time, during which he lay in great agony, Franco had behaved with the dignity and bravery that were characteristic of him. On the day of his death it is said that the shops of Barcelona ran out of champagne,[75] but in most of Spain he was mourned as a great leader. He had ruled Spain for nearly four decades and during that time his reign had never been seriously threatened. No foreign head of state went to his funeral but scores of thousands of Spaniards stood around in the cold Madrid streets, wating for a chance to file past the *Caudillo*'s coffin as it lay in state in the Palacio de Oriente. Millions of Spanish people who had disliked the regime and opposed its policies, felt reverence and admiration for Franco. To them he was Spain's leader; the majority had lived under no other.

5
The Opposition

Writing in 1946, shortly after he had ceased to be British ambassador in Madrid, Sir Samuel Hoare commented: 'If the strength of a government is the weakness of the opposition, the Franco regime was less precarious than many of its foreign critics and émigré opponents imagined.'[1] The weakness to which he referred was born of the disunity that had plagued the republic from the beginning of the civil war. In the years after 1939 the republican losers continued to quarrel among themselves and thus contributed to the consolidation of the *franquista* regime. The extent of their failure can be measured by the fact that Franco's chief opponents refused to co-operate with each other until after his death.

Many of the republican leaders had fled to France in January 1939 after the fall of Barcelona. Some, such as the socialist prime minister Juan Negrín and his communist allies, returned to Spain for the last few weeks of the war. Manuel Azaña, the greatest of the republican leaders, remained in France and on 28 February, the day after Britain and France recognized Franco's government, he resigned as president. Powerless and dispirited, unable to prevent the violent rivalries within the government, he had spent the last months of the war writing a profound and moving play about the divisions which had destroyed the republic.[2] When resistance on the Madrid front ended in March, the remaining leaders followed him to France. The communists, who had dominated the last government, went from there to Moscow. Most of the rest stayed in Paris until the German invasion of 1940, when the Gestapo handed over the unlucky ones to Franco, who shot them.* Others

*Two ministers, Julián Zugazagoitia and Joan Peiró, were shot, as well as the Catalan leader, Lluis Companys, president of the *Generalitat*.

escaped to Mexico, the only country, apart from the Soviet Union, which had positively supported the republic. Over the following decades the exiled leaders, and the men who came after them, plotted the overthrow of Francisco Franco.

Although Franco proclaimed the end of the war on 1st April 1939, guerrilla warfare continued for some time afterwards. It was widely believed that the collapse of Germany in the Second World War would lead to a new onslaught against the *franquista* regime, and Spanish exiles, many of whom had been fighting in the French *maquis*, crossed the Pyrenees to take part in the expected insurrection. In October 1944 a communist force of about 2,000 guerrillas invaded Spain but was easily defeated in the Valle de Aran by the troops of General Yagüe. The communists were slightly more successful when they operated in small bands in the mountains and for the next four years they carried out a number of violent raids throughout Spain. In spite of their efforts, however, they received little support from the local populations and by 1947 the *Guardia Civil* had destroyed many of their groups. The following year the communists received orders from Moscow to change tactics and the guerrilla campaign was soon discontinued. Almost simultaneously, however, the anarcho-syndicalist CNT* decided to step up its terrorist activity inside Spain. Small groups of guerrillas living in France crossed the Pyrenees and, linking up with former CNT militants still living in Catalonia, they carried out bank robberies, shot policemen and distributed anarchist propaganda. In 1949 they placed bombs in the Barcelona consulates of those Latin American countries considered to be friendly to Franco. The years 1949 and 1950 were the principal ones for anarchist terrorism but by the end of the second year most of the groups had been caught by the police and those taken alive had been shot. In 1955 a splinter group from the CNT began a new series of raids but this had been virtually wiped out by the winter of the following year. The most famous of the *guerrilleros*, Francisco Sabate, known as *El Quico*, continued his spectacular exploits until 1960 when he was killed near Barcelona.[3]

The activities of anarchist *desesperados* were of little concern to the republican leaders in Mexico, Paris and Moscow. These spent

*The CNT (*Confederación Nacional de Trabajo*) had been, at the outbreak of the civil war, the largest trade union in Spain. Its strength was concentrated in Andalusia and Catalonia.

their time forming committees, passing resolutions and trying to prevent the rest of the world from accepting Franco's regime. Their behaviour suggested that they were more concerned with conserving their own legitimacy than with doing anything to damage Franco. The regime set up in 1931 was regarded as sacred, and the preservation of its institutions seemed for them to be the highest goal imaginable; thus they were led to reject co-operation with other opposition forces such as the monarchists. Different governments-in-exile followed each other with mounting irrelevance, clinging to the diplomatic support of Mexico and half a dozen countries in Eastern Europe. In January 1945, 72 deputies of the *Cortes* reassembled in Mexico, a pathetic reunion of a body which had lost 127 of its members during the civil war. The meeting was symbolic and nostalgic but nothing more. The republican institutions were like plays without an audience, of interest to no one but the actors. As one former socialist deputy remarked, 'the only thing we are doing is to die gradually'.[4] The republicans enjoyed one victory when, in 1946, the United Nations General Assembly referred to Spain as 'a Fascist regime patterned on . . . Hitler's Nazi Germany and Mussolini's Fascist Italy' and recommended the breaking of diplomatic relations. But in 1950 the resolution was revoked and an American ambassador was soon installed in Madrid. Further defeats for the republicans took place in 1952, when Spain joined UNESCO, in 1953 when it signed agreements with both the United States and the Vatican, and in 1955 when it became a member of the UN.

The largest of the political parties which had supported the republic had been the socialists (*Partido Socialista Obrero Español* – PSOE). The divisions which had bedevilled the party since 1933 – Madariaga claimed that they had made the civil war inevitable[5] – continued into exile. At the end of the war the socialists had been divided into three factions: a reformist, social democratic group led by Indalecio Prieto; a radical but anti-communist faction grouped around the former prime minister, Francisco Largo Caballero; and the followers of his successor, Juan Negrín, who worked closely with the leaders of the Communist Party (*Partido Comunista Español* – PCE). Prieto, the most forceful and, with Julián Besteiro, the most talented socialist leader of the period, had struggled for years to prevent Largo Caballero from turning the PSOE from a party of reform to a party of revolution. He had failed and in the critical years after 1933 the socialists had abandoned social democracy and embraced the idea of marxist revolution. But after the disaster the *prietista* wing recovered and by 1947 it was able to dominate the party conference in Toulouse. The PSOE would not collaborate again with the PCE which according to Prieto, was not 'a fraternal party' but 'a rival, adversary and enemy'.[6] The socialists still in Spain, declared one prominent member of the party, shared a hatred of falangism and a distrust of communism.[7]

The position of the party inside Spain in the years after the civil war was catastrophic. A number of socialist militants fought alongside communist guerrillas during the forties, particularly in the Asturian mountains, but party members were usually more concerned with trying to retain some semblance of organization. This was, indeed, almost impossible in the circumstances, since the most dedicated militants were either dead, or in prison or in exile. Those who were still at liberty in Spain were watched by the police and attempts to commit the crime of 'reconstituting the Socialist Party' usually ended in arrests and long prison sentences. Successive national executive committees, painfully organized by survivors, were discovered by the police and their members arrested. By 1950 more than 1,200 PSOE members were imprisoned in Burgos; by 1953 members of six different executive committees were under arrest.[8]

The state of the party in exile was, though very different, not much healthier. Following the defeat of Germany, most of its 8,000 members based themselves in France, where they remained, waiting for something to happen. The PSOE and the socialist trade union, the *Unión General de Trabajadores* (UGT), held conferences on the northern side of the Pyrenees at Toulouse, but they were able to offer few ideas on how to overturn Franco. Like the republican government-in-exile, which Prieto despised for its uselessness and self-importance, the socialists were waiting for others to liberate Spain for them. Many believed that the defeats of Italy and Germany in the Second World War would be followed by the downfall of the *franquista* regime. It was logical, they argued, that the child of Hitler and Mussolini should disappear with its parents. But Franco had not joined the Axis, he had not allowed German troops to enter Spain and his support for Hitler had been largely verbal. In Allied eyes, Franco had not been sufficiently quisling to deserve to be overthrown by Allied troops. Britain, France and the United States declared in a joint note in March 1946 that they would like to see the 'peaceful departure of Franco, the abolition of the *Falange* and the establishment of a provisional government' which would bring about an amnesty, the return of the exiles and free elections.[9] But they themselves were not prepared to help. It was up to the Spaniards to get rid of Franco.

The Allies' refusal to treat Spain as one of the defeated powers was, for the republicans, the second betrayal. In 1936 Britain and France had proclaimed their support for the legal government but had refused to sell it the weapons needed to defeat the military uprising. Ten years later they once again declared their opposition to Franco and once again did nothing positive against him. The result was that Franco won the war and then the peace through the refusal of the Western democracies to do anything more than oppose him vocally from the sidelines. The discovery that their reliance on the West had been misplaced was depressing for the republicans, but it did introduce at least a degree of realism into the conferences of the exiles. The most realistic and far-sighted of the socialist politicians, Indalecio Prieto, understood that the one chance the Spaniards had of overthrowing Franco by themselves was in the creation of a broad alliance of opposition forces. Only the communists, who had alienated so many groups through their arrogance during the civil war, would be left out. Anybody else who could be considered democratic and *antifranquista* would be included. Prieto realized that, once the military option had been closed, the only possible alternative to Franco was a constitutional monarchy under Don Juan de Borbón. Heedless of the protests of the government-in-exile, which refused to entertain the idea that Franco might be succeeded by anything other than a republican government, the old socialist leader thus devoted his energies to negotiating an agreement with the monarchists. 'Not to reach an agreement would be lamentable,' he declared, 'not to attempt it would be criminal.'[10]

Hitherto, there had been little common ground between the socialists and the supporters of the monarchy. When Largo Caballero was preaching revolution in 1936, the exiled monarch, Alfonso XIII, was telephoning Mussolini and begging him to send aeroplanes to help the uprising.[11] Don Juan himself had arrived in

Spain a fortnight after the beginning of the rebellion and offered to fight for the nationalists – an offer which Franco tactfully turned down. At the end of the war he congratulated Franco effusively on the 'liberation' of Madrid[12] and, even when he was at his most critical of the dictator, he did not deny the legitimacy of the uprising, claiming that it had been necessary to save Spain from anarchy[13] But it did not take Don Juan long to understand that the reconciliation which Spain needed after the civil war could not be achieved under Franco. Ironically, this was something that Franco himself realized because, when he refused Don Juan's request to serve in the nationalist forces, he told him that a future king would have to come as a conciliator and not from the ranks of the victors.[14] It was a strange remark for the dictator to make. Once the war was over he rejected Don Juan's offer to 'reconcile' the Spaniards and even denied that there was any need for reconciliation.

Early suggestions for a monarchical restoration came, as we have seen, from people who had supported and often fought for Franco in the civil war. Some of his most senior generals wrote to him in 1943 suggesting that the time had come for him to give way to a monarchy. They and other monarchists argued that it would be a disaster for Spain if Franco was still in power after the Allies had won the war. If Don Juan, who had once served in the British navy, was on the throne, they believed Spain would be safe from the threat of Allied retribution. But if Franco was still there, argued one of them, Spain would be treated as one of the defeated powers and the dictator's refusal to step down would lead to anarchy.[15] It was an argument that Don Juan himself was to use in his manifesto from Lausanne of March 1945 in which he declared that Franco's regime, 'inspired from the beginning by the totalitarian systems of the Axis powers, so contrary to the character and traditions of our people, is fundamentally incompatible with the situation which [the Second World] war is creating in the world.' Spain, he argued, was running 'the risk of seeing itself dragged into a new fratricidal conflict and of finding itself totally isolated from the world.' He was thus asking Franco to recognize 'the failure of his totalitarian concept of the state and to abandon power' so as to permit the restoration of the monarchy. 'Only the traditional monarchy,' he declared, 'can be the instrument of peace and concord to reconcile the Spanish people. Only it can achieve respect abroad . . . and bring about a harmonious synthesis of order and liberty . . .'[16] However, although he strongly disapproved of Franco's policies, Don Juan refused actively to oppose the regime or to countenance any kind of revolt: 'I am not raising the banner of rebellion,' he proclaimed at the end of his manifesto, 'nor inciting anyone to revolt. But I wish to remind those who support the present regime of their irresponsibility in helping to prolong a situation which will bring disaster to the country.'[17]

This honourable but passive position made matters difficult for his followers. A majority, as we have seen, believed that Franco would eventually step down, and therefore they urged Don Juan to adopt a more conciliatory attitude towards him. When the pretender refused to ingratiate himself with Franco, most of these men stood by the dictator and did little more for the monarchical cause. Others, of whom the most prominent was José María Gil Robles, urged Don Juan to take a more active position and put himself at the head of the *antifranquista* forces.

Like Prieto, Gil Robles had been one of the great political figures of the republic. Pugnacious and self-confident, he had become leader of the powerful, right-wing CEDA party in his mid-thirties. In 1935 he was appointed minister of war and the following year he was the Right's chief representative in its attempt to hold off the Popular Front's challenge in the February elections. It was the high tide of European fascism and many people were looking for a Spanish '*Duce*' to rid the country of Largo Caballero and his friends. Gil Robles, with his robust, demagogic speeches, looked and sounded the part. He had established the right credentials by his strutting, arrogant behaviour in the *Cortes* and his demands for still greater repression after the Asturian uprising. He had allowed the governments of 1934–5 to overturn the achievements of earlier republican administrations. He had failed, when it was in his power, to prevent the Right from sabotaging the agrarian reforms proposed by Giménez Fernández. Gil Robles perhaps did more than anyone to destroy popular faith in the republic, but he was not the man to destroy the republic itself. When he failed narrowly to win the 1936 elections, the Right deserted him to look for new, more extreme heroes such as José Calvo Sotelo and José Antonio Primo de Rivera. Contrary to appearances, Gil Robles could never have been the saviour the Right was looking for. He was not a fascist, nor even a potential one. In the words of Salvador de Madariaga, he 'was a convinced parliamentarian too deeply committed to a Republican-Parliamentarian mode of life to be in any way acceptable to Fascism or susceptible to it.'[18] When he died in 1980, Don Juan remarked that Spain had lost a fine democrat.[19]

In spite of his past and his responsibility for events which ultimately led to the military uprising, Gil Robles became the pre-eminent figure of the conservative opposition to Franco. He had assisted the Right in its work of dismantling Azaña's reforms at least partly because the CEDA depended on financial contributions from the Right. But he had never really been a man of the Right himself and when he saw it in power in the early forties he was horrified. 'The Spanish Right', he declared, 'is not prepared to forget that it was the victor of a civil war. It has always been narrow-minded and lacking in generosity, but now it is more so than ever.'[20] Other people with Gil Robles's background and dislike of the Left would, perhaps, have compromised with the new regime, or at least criticized it discreetly from within. But Gil Robles went into full opposition and determined to work for Franco's downfall. In 1942 he went to see Don Juan to discuss strategy.

In contrast to the majority of the monarchists, Gil Robles realized from the beginning that Franco would never allow Don Juan to become king. 'Franco has no other ideal than to keep himself in power,' he declared in 1944.[21] Consequently there was no point in trying to promote good relations between the pretender and the dictator. He told Don Juan that he should stop vacillating and giving the impression that a monarchical restoration depended on the good will of a dictator. Don Juan should make an emphatic statement declaring his hostility to the regime and aim to become the leader of the democratic opposition to Franco. At the same time he should set up an efficient organization abroad and his supporters should resign from their posts in Spain. But Gil Robles understood the problems that Don Juan had to face. In a letter to Madariaga in the summer of 1946, he pointed out that 'the King has to pursue with great skill a dual policy of immense difficulties. On the one hand he has to split the *franquista* bloc, gaining the support of the forces which support the regime. On the other, he has to secure the collaboration of the non-revolutionary Left.'[22] The task was perhaps impossible in the circumstances, but it was one worth trying. And it was appropriate that the work of reconciliation should be attempted by two great adversaries of the 1930s, Prieto on behalf of the Socialist Party, and Gil Robles for the newly-established *Confederación de Fuerzas Monárquicas*.

Prieto and Gil Robles began negotiations in London in October 1947 and a year later a joint socialist-monarchist document – known as the Pact of St Jean de Luz – was handed into the embassies of the western democracies in Paris and Madrid. It was accompanied by a note from Don Juan in which he declared that, while he had taken no part in the negotiations, he approved of and encouraged the actions of the *Confederación de Fuerzas Monárquicas*. The agreement was imprecisely worded and included no reference to the monarchy or to socialism. A provisional government – no mention was made of its nature but by implication it would have been a constitutional monarchy – would consult the nation, through elections or a referendum, over the future character of the regime. It would also, among other things, grant a political amnesty, prevent reprisals, eliminate totalitarian influences and guarantee freedom of worship.[23]

The importance of the pact lay not in its contents, which were somewhat banal and did not amount to much of a political programme, but in the fact that it had been agreed by two groups of people who in the past had never agreed on anything. Unfortunately, the pact achieved nothing and it soon broke up with loud recriminations. But it was not entirely useless because it did provide an important precedent. More than twenty-five years later, socialists and monarchists (with Gil Robles still among them) again came together to form the core of an opposition whose moderation was crucial to the success of the later transition to constitutional monarchy.

The Pact of St Jean de Luz failed for a number of reasons. To begin with, neither Prieto nor Gil Robles, both of them talented, abrasive characters with a tendency to despise their colleagues, was representative of their parties. Prieto was a social democrat disliked by republicans and radical socialists, while Gil Robles was an opposition monarchist loathed by those monarchists who were quite comfortable inside the regime. The notion that Franco's monarchist generals should collaborate with PSOE militants was, of course, anathema to both sides. But blame for the failure must lie primarily with Don Juan. The pretender admired Gil Robles and encouraged the negotiations with Prieto, but he was not prepared to go all the way with him. He had stated repeatedly that he would not become a conspirator or the leader of a revolt. He was not willing to cut all links with the regime and he even jeopardized the pact itself by meeting Franco on the dictator's boat shortly before it was due to be signed. In Don Juan's defence it should be said that his view of Spain could never be merely that of an opposition leader. He was the representative of a dynasty which had ruled Spain for two hundred and fifty years and he was not prepared to endanger the future of his family by going into full opposition. Over the last thirty years most of the royal families of Europe had been unseated and in the previous decade the crowned heads of Italy, Romania, Bulgaria, Albania and Yugoslavia had gone into exile. The Bourbons were a much older dynasty than the Balkan royal families, but Don Juan knew that Franco was capable of preventing a restoration of his line. Although Spain technically became a monarchy in 1947, this by no means ensured that he or his heirs would eventually occupy the throne. When, in 1965, one of his ministers tried to persuade Franco to designate the future king, the dictator replied that the problem was that there were four pretenders.[24] The fear that Franco might exclude his family and even choose a carlist claimant was undoubtedly one of the causes of Don Juan's reluctance to make many concessions to Gil Robles and the socialists. He felt that his family must remain tied to Spain, however much he might dislike the regime, and it was for this reason he decided that his heir, Prince Juan Carlos, should be educated there.

After the break with the monarchists, which came in 1951, the fortunes of the Socialist Party reached their lowest point. Relations between the party in exile and members in Spain were distant and poorly co-ordinated. In 1953, when many of its internal leaders were in prison, the party contained only 3,000 members. There appeared little that they could usefully do and much time was spent complaining about those who had 'betrayed' them: the West, particularly the United States, which Prieto accused of having allowed Franco to consolidate himself, and Don Juan, who also became one of the old socialist's favourite targets of abuse. Like the other great political forces of republican Spain –

the anarchists and the republican parties – the PSOE had become almost irrelevant in the struggle against the dictator. After 1956 the main opposition came not from the exiles but from forces inside Spain, from workers, students and intellectuals who were often united by little but a common desire to challenge the oppressiveness of the *franquista* state.

The first open display of opposition came from students in 1956. Since the appointment of Ruiz Giménez as minister of education in 1951, there had been a more liberal atmosphere inside the universities, and this had been encouraged by men such as Pedro Laín Entralgo, the new rector of Madrid University. Students became increasingly critical of the low standards of teaching and the restricted nature of the courses they could follow. They also found the activities of the *Sindicato Español Universitario* (SEU), the falangist-run union to which they were forced to belong, more and more irksome. In February 1956, after the government had annulled student elections at Madrid University, students occupied a number of faculties and the SEU offices. Armed falangists attacked them inside the university and later during a demonstration outside the ministry of education. In response to the disturbances, a number of liberal students and intellectuals – described by *Arriba* as 'assassins against Spain'[25] – were arrested. Astonishingly, the government suspended articles 14 and 18 (which stated that a person could not be held for more than 72 hours without charge) of the Charter of the Spanish People and stopped classes at the university. Three weeks later, when the classes began again, a pamphlet was circulated which, after calling for the release of those arrested, ended with the words 'Down with the SEU!' and 'Down with Blas Himmler!' (the name of the minister of the interior was Blas Pérez). The authors of the pamphlet were arrested and at the subsequent trial the prosecutor asked for a five-year prison sentence. But as Gil Robles, who was the defending lawyer, pertinently asked, how could it be regarded as an insult to give the interior minister the name of a man who, only a few years earlier, had been so highly regarded by the Spanish authorities?[26]

The unrest at Madrid university led to the formation of the *Agrupación Socialista Universitaria*, a student group which included a number of the PSOE's future leaders. In the early sixties it was followed by other opposition unions such as the *Federación*

Universitaria Democrática Española, which in 1962 organized demonstrations in support of striking workers in northern Spain. By the mid-1960s few students were paying any attention to the official union, a fact which the government recognized by abolishing the SEU in 1965 and replacing it by student associations. These, however, were no more popular, and in the university elections of 1965–6, 80 per cent of students either abstained or returned blank ballot papers.[27]

While opposition to the regime became increasingly vocal in the universities, a similar though far more important movement was taking place among the industrial working class. Before 1962 labour conflicts in Spain were rare. The country's 'historic' trade unions, such as the socialist UGT and the anarcho-syndicalist CNT had been declared illegal by Franco during the civil war, and many of their members had been shot or imprisoned. Under the dictatorship the workers were organized in 'vertical' syndicates which in origin were designed to represent both workers and management but in practice represented neither. During the late 1950s, workers who realized that their interests were not being properly represented in the official syndicates, began to set up their own committees to act on their behalf. In the industrial regions of Asturias and the Basque provinces, *comisiones obreras* (workers' commissions) were formed to deal with a particular situation. They organized strikes to demand better pay or working conditions and then, when the dispute was over, they dissolved themselves. The *comisiones* remained spontaneous and temporary until the 1960s. In 1962 they organized the first major strikes of the dictatorship, closing the Asturian coalfields, and later, strikes in Catalonia and the Basque country. From then on they were an important and permanent institution and in 1967 they held their first national assembly in Madrid.[28]

By the mid-1960s the *comisiones obreras* (CCOO) had established a parallel organization to the official syndicates. Since they were palpably more representative of the workers than the syndicates, businessmen and, indeed, government had to take notice of them. It was tacitly understood that labour disputes would often be settled only through negotiations with the *comisiones*. During this period the CCOO enjoyed a semi-legal existence and some of their officials even took part, successfully, in the state's syndical elections. Various *franquista* officials, aware of the inadequacy of their syndicates, hoped to incorporate the *comisiones* into the syndical structure. But this indicated a disastrous misreading of their real nature. The remnants of the 'historic' unions in exile claimed that the CCOO were collaborators and, in the most literal sense, they were. But it was collaboration of a double-edged kind. The *comisiones* might help the government to solve industrial problems but these were often problems which they had caused intentionally in the first place. They were essentially an opposition force, and a far more effective one than the UGT or the CNT.

The government's unofficial toleration of the *comisiones* came to an end after they had organized a huge demonstration in Madrid in 1967. Although the government had warned that all demonstrators would be arrested, more than 100,000 workers marched through the streets of the capital shouting 'free trade unions', 'Franco no, democracy yes,' 'unity between workers and students'. This was too much for the regime and the CCOO leaders were arrested. From now until Franco's death the *comisiones* were savagely repressed. In June 1972 nine men were arrested and charged with being leaders of the *comisiones obreras*. A Madrid public order court found them guilty and sentenced them to an average of eighteen years' imprisonment – Marcelino Camacho, the best-known of the CCOO leaders, was given twenty-eight years – although the sentences were later reduced.

The government's new attitude was prompted by the tardy realization that the *comisiones*, far from being potential collaborators, were a well-organized, increasingly political, opposition force dominated by members of the Communist Party. The PCE and the CCOO both denied that there was a link between them, and in the early days the *comisiones* had contained many Catholic militants and socialists as well. But during the sixties the well-organized communists had extended their influence in the CCOO to the detriment of other groups and by the middle of the decade they were in control of the *comisiones* in Asturias and in the powerful metal-workers *comisión* in Madrid. Camacho himself was a member of the PCE executive committee, although this was not known at the time; Sartorius, another CCOO leader, later became vice-secretary-general of the party.

The infiltration of the *comisiones* had been a natural objective for the PCE. In 1948 the party had ordered its guerrillas to give up the armed struggle and three years later it was encouraging workers to infiltrate the syndicates so that they could press for better conditions from within the system. When workers began to choose their own delegates to represent them through the *comisiones*, a large number of communists were usually selected. They possessed a dedication and a discipline which were remarkable. Of all the enemies of the dictatorship, the communists were the ones who struggled hardest and suffered the most. A Catalan opponent of Franco, who was not a communist, has recorded the courage and cheerfulness of a PCE militant who, having served nineteen years in prison for being a member of the party, was condemned shortly after his release to another sixteen years.[29] Another Catalan, who was strongly opposed to the PCE on ideological grounds, refused to criticize the communists in any way, simply because they were so much the bravest of the opposition. 'We others have done some things, been arrested and jailed a few days – but they have suffered everything, beatings and years in jail, and are absolutely dedicated.'[30]

During the sixties the Communist Party acquired considerable prestige among Spaniards. Apart, of course, from the *Movimiento*, it was the one real party inside Spain and the only opposition force which most people knew anything about. The PCE was in many ways the natural home for those who wanted to do something about opposing the regime: one young aristocrat joined it after an exhilarating gondola ride with La Pasionaria* in Venice. A large number of intellectuals, who would not have been communists had they been living in a democracy, joined the party in the sixties. Most of them resigned after the struggle against Franco had ended.

The PCE gained strength from the repeated and intemperate attacks which Franco and the Church had been making against it since 1936. In 1958 Madariaga, whose anti-communism and anti-francoism were about equal, complained that 'the regime unwittingly acts as the best recruiting agent for Communism by dubbing as Communist every adversary it wishes to deprive of his liberty'.[31] But Franco knew what he was doing. He realized that a strong Communist Party meant, paradoxically, a weak opposition. He and his advisers strove to keep the memory of the civil

*Dolores Ibarruri, known as La Pasionaria, was born in 1895. She was a prominent figure during the civil war, secretary-general of the party from 1942 to 1960, and afterwards president.

war alive by harping on about the threat from communism. They knew they would always defeat the communists; they were less certain they could contain the democrats. Thus they sought to present the future in terms of 'them or us', communism or Franco, in the hope, at least partly justified, that by this method they would keep the middle classes loyal to the regime.

The history of the Communist Party was, as Franco well knew, its greatest weakness, and the regime's supporters enjoyed publicizing the communist role in the civil war. The party had been a minor component of the Popular Front, winning only 16 of the Front's 267 seats in the elections of February 1936. Yet during the course of the civil war, communist influence had grown spectacularly so that within two years the party had come to dominate the republican government. As nearly all the weapons which the republic received came from the Soviet Union, and as the International Brigades were run largely by their French and Italian comrades, the communists had found themselves in a position of great strength. They had then used that position to take control of the police and much of the army and from there they had bullied and often persecuted any of their supposed allies – anarchists, socialists, republicans and other left-wing groups – who refused to follow the party line. The communists had ended the war disliked and distrusted by people on all sides. The memories of their behaviour during the war years led to their exclusion from those opposition fronts organized during subsequent decades by socialists and other opponents of Franco. A further disadvantage, one which haunted them up to the 1980s, was the fact that the party's most senior leaders had played prominent, often notorious, roles in the civil war. Apart from La Pasionaria, there was Santiago Carrillo (secretary-general from 1960 to 1982), the man widely held responsible for the massacre at Paracuellos in November 1936,* and Enrique Líster, a leading republican general who left the party in 1970 to form his own, pro-Soviet group.

---

*Several thousand captives were taken from republican prisons in Madrid and executed at Paracuellos del Jarama; modern estimates range from 2,400 to 8,000. It seems certain that the massacres were carried out by members of the Communist Party, but it is still not clear who gave the orders. Two recent books on Paracuellos differ on many aspects of the massacre, not least on the personal responsibility of Carrillo.[32]

The PCE shared many of the problems of the other parties in exile. Its membership inside Spain was decimated during the forties, there were problems of comunication between communists in exile and those in the interior, and quarrelling groups of leaders in Moscow and Mexico spent much time denouncing each other. But the party also had a problem peculiar to itself: a tendency to split repeatedly so that by the 1970s there were a large number of rival organizations with similar names, divided by nuances that were difficult to discern by outsiders. Self-proclaimed maoists, trotskyists and marxist-leninists broke away to form new groups, to break up shortly afterwards and then to re-group under a slightly different name. These schisms took place side by side with a number of expulsions. From 1948–9, when 'Titoite bandits' were expelled from the party, to 1969, when the 'Sovietophiles' were ordered out, the leadership was ruthless in stamping out dissent. Carrillo's policy of removing anyone who disagreed with him continued into the post-*franquista* period and was partly responsible for the party's electoral collapse in 1982.

Nevertheless, in spite of its past and the dramas of its internal squabbles, the PCE did manage to become the most serious opposition force to Franco. The crucial factors in its success were the strength of its organization and the dedication of its militants, particularly those inside the *comisiones obreras*. A further reason was the change of policy which occurred during the leadership of Carrillo, who took the party from neo-Stalinism to a point where it became the most radically 'eurocommunist' party in Western Europe. On a number of issues, such as his acceptance of the mixed economy and his rejection of the doctrine of the dictatorship of the proletariat, Carrillo's thinking was ahead even of his Italian counterpart, Enrico Berlinguer. He was also advocating future co-operation with socialist and Catholic groups – what the Italians later called the 'historic compromise' – long before the Chilean coup of 1973 had revealed the dangers of attempting a marxist revolution in democratic countries far from Russian influence. During his time as secretary-general, Carrillo also transformed the party's attitude towards the Soviet Union. In 1956 the PCE had made no criticism of the Russian invasion of Hungary; in 1968 the plenary union of the party's executive voted by 66 votes to 5 to criticize the invasion of Czechoslovakia.[33] The party declared its 'profound sympathy' for the policy of the Czech communists and even La Pasionaria, who had followed the Moscow line obediently for four decades, protested to the Kremlin.[34]

The polarization of Spain during the civil war – a polarization that was subsequently exploited with great skill by the regime – made it difficult for Franco's moderate opponents to secure much of a following. But neither this disadvantage, nor the impossibility of reaching a wide audience, deterred a number of individuals from setting up small, clandestine organizations in opposition to Franco. One of these was formed by a group of repentant falangists headed by Dionisio Ridruejo. In Italy and Germany socialists and social democrats had turned to fascism and nazism. In Spain the process was reversed and a number of fascist intellectuals, who had become disenchanted with the *Falange*, adopted social democracy. A few, such as Manuel Cantarero del Castillo, remained inside the party and hoped to restore some of its former idealism. Others deserted it altogether and renounced their falangist past.

After José Antonio Primo de Rivera, Dionisio Ridruejo was the most charismatic figure in the *Falange*. Poet, idealist and a fine orator, Ridruejo was only twenty-three when the civil war began. Within two years he had become one of the *Falange*'s most senior figures and director-general of nationalist propaganda. By the end of the war, however, he was already feeling guilty about his role as a falangist and disenchanted by the nature of the new regime. He resented the fact that the *Falange* had lost its radical idealism and become a bourgeois and reactionary movement. In 1940 he resigned as director-general of propaganda and the following year he enlisted in the 'Blue Division' to fight alongside the Germans in Russia. On his return in 1942 his disenchantment with all kinds of fascism was complete. He refused all positions offered him and resigned from his remaining posts inside the party, an action which led to his banishment to the town of Ronda. For the next thirty years Ridruejo was to be one of the most courageous and persistent of Franco's critics. In 1956 he backed the student rebellion in Madrid and spent six weeks in prison as a result. A few months later he founded a social democratic group called the *Partido Social de Acción Democrática* (PSAD). In 1957 he made some disparaging remarks about the regime in a Cuban magazine and was promptly arrested again. When a judge granted him bail, he was re-arrested and accused of illegal association.[35] For this he was sentenced to twenty months in jail, although he was pardoned before he had served his full sentence. During the sixties his life followed the same pattern: outspoken criticism of the state coupled with attempts to set up an opposition front, followed by further spells in prison.

Other intellectuals pursued the same course as Ridruejo. The philosopher Aranguren, in early life a *Caudillo*-worshipper who once claimed that no man was less free than a democrat,[36] acquired a reputation as a progressive Catholic who recognized the value of marxism. Tovar and Laín Entralgo were others who had eulogized Franco and nazi Germany in the past,[37] only to end up among the regime's democratic opposition. These, and others like them who were associated with the PSAD, realized that they had been wrong, but none of them seemed as repentant of their past as Ridruejo. They were prepared to make excuses for themselves, but Ridruejo was not. His life after 1942 often seemed to be lived in atonement for his youthful years in the *Falange*.

A more considerable opposition group than the reformed falangists around Ridruejo was the christian democrats. As we have seen, a number of those who considered themselves as christian democrats were among the regime's most stalwart supporters in the early years, and a few remained so until the death of Franco. But for anyone whose politics resembled those of De Gasperi and the Italian christian democratic Left, or whose ideas were in any way similar to those of John XXIII, full-hearted collaboration with the regime was obviously difficult. Two christian democrat groups, which were closer in thought and sentiment to the Italians than to *Acción Católica* or the ACNP, were formed during the fifties. One was an organization, later to be headed by Gil Robles, called *Democracia Social Cristiana*. The other was *Unión Demócrata Cristiana* (at one time known as *Izquierda Demócrata Cristiana*), which was founded after the Madrid University riots of 1956. Its leader was the old CEDA deputy, Manuel Giménez Fernández, minister of agriculture during the republic and then professor of canon law at the university of Seville. Giménez Fernández was a liberal conservative, a rare breed in Spain and an object of particular dislike for the Right. He was repeatedly offered official posts by the regime but refused to collaborate in any sense until political parties were permitted. He remained an enthusiastic advocate of agrarian reform and recommended the nationalization of the banks. Although he regarded Franco as 'the most intelligent and least bad of the *franquistas*',[38] he was a persistent critic of the regime's corruption and incompetence. Admitting that repression in Eastern Europe was worse than in Spain, his group nevertheless described the regime as 'the dirtiest, emptiest and most useless of [those dictatorships] which Europe has known in recent centuries.'[39]

When Giménez Fernández died in 1968, the most prominent christian democrat in Spain was Joaquín Ruiz Giménez. He was also one of the most radical. At a time when European christian democracy was generally becoming more conservative, Ruiz Giménez was advocating the extension of public ownership to many areas of the economy. Admitting in 1969 that he was more and more attracted by nationalization, he declared that public services, urban property, large tracts of the countryside and unspecified 'means of production' should be transferred to state control.[40] He called his group merely *Izquierda Democrática* (Democratic Left) because, although his own ideas were inspired by christian principles, he did not want to see the emergence of confessional parties in Spain.[41]

Another opposition group set up in the late fifties was *Unión Española*, whose principal founders were two conservative monarchists, Joaquín Satrústegui and Jaime Miralles. Both of them had fought for the nationalists in the early days of the rising and believed that the civil war had been necessary to put an end to the chaos caused by the republic. But as Satrústegui said, in a speech at a dinner in Madrid's Hotel Memfis in 1959, the civil war was also a tragedy and the country's future must be founded not on tragedy but on reconciliation. For this reason he proposed a monarchical restoration. Another speaker at the dinner – the three main speakers were all heavily fined afterwards – was a socialist academic, Enrique Tierno Galván. A somewhat incongruous figure inside *Unión Española*, Tierno supported the restoration of a liberal monarchy under Don Juan because he saw it as the only means of achieving a peaceful transformation of the regime. He regarded himself, however, as a marxist socialist, and a few years later he joined the Socialist Party. But he was too independent, too ambitious and too disrespectful of the party's exiled leadership for him to be comfortable in the PSOE, and he was soon expelled. In 1968, claiming that the new generations of socialists did not want to be led by an exiled leadership which had lost touch with the country,[42] he formed the *Partido Socialista del Interior* (PSI).

During the late fifties and early sixties people from these groups would meet each other and representatives of the exiled parties in attempts to put together a united opposition front. These were never entirely successful. The Pact of Paris of 1957 was signed by all the major organizations in exile, except the communists who were automatically excluded, but had no support from the interior. In 1961 the *Unión de Fuerzas Democráticas* was created, consisting of *Izquierda Demócrata Cristiana* as well as the exiles, but the anarchist CNT refused to take part. Even at the most famous *antifranquista* meeting of all, the Congress of Munich in 1962, the opposition forces were divided. The congress was criticized not only by the communists and anarchists, but also by some republican leaders and by the Catalan government in exile.

The Congress of Munich was inspired by Salvador de Madariaga, then president of the Liberal International, who conceived the idea of organizing a large conference where Spaniards from outside and inside the country would meet to promote a democratic alternative to Franco. The principal object of the exercise was to show the Spanish people, as well as the rest of the world, that Spain did not have to choose between Franco and communism.[43] There was a middle way. Accordingly, in June 1962, 118 Spaniards, of whom two-thirds were then living in Spain, congregated in Munich. The representatives from the interior included Ridruejo, Gil Robles, Satrústegui and Miralles. Among the delegates from abroad were the exiled leaders of the Socialist Party, Basque nationalists and various republicans. After two days of discussions, the delegates agreed to work for 'the establishment of institutions authentically representative and democratic which will guarantee that the government is based upon the consent of the people'.[44]

The Spanish people learnt about the congress from a scandalously inaccurate article which appeared in *France Soir*, extracts of which were reprinted in the Spanish press.[45] This gave the impression that all Spain's enemies had declared war on Franco and were feverishly plotting the downfall of the regime. The account of the meeting between Gil Robles and the socialist leader Llopis gave Franco a propaganda opportunity and the state press had a field-day denouncing the 'traitors'. Communism, capitalism, masonry and other familiar demons were once again trying to undermine the nation. According to *Arriba*,[46] Gil Robles was a 'coward and reactionary, a persistent traitor to the fatherland' while a different falangist publication described him as a 'repulsive jellyfish'.[47] The conference undoubtedly damaged Franco's international standing but it did nothing to weaken his image inside Spain. Indeed, he profited from it because he was able to persuade people that it was not the regime which was being attacked, but Spain itself.

After the conference, some of those who had been living in Spain, such as Ridruejo, stayed in exile. Others, like Satrústegui, Miralles and the christian democrat Álvarez de Miranda, were given the choice of exile or confinement on the island of Fuerteventura. They went to Fuerteventura. On returning to Madrid's Barajas airport, Gil Robles was told to get on the first flight out of Spain but, as this was going to Dakar, he was allowed to remain, under guard, until the next aeroplane left for Paris.[48] In exile he discovered that the Munich conference, and his actions in particular, had been disowned by Don Juan, and he promptly resigned, with much bitterness, from the pretender's privy council.

Munich was the high point in the history of the *antifranquista* opposition. Never again did it achieve such publicity either inside or outside the country. In 1967 another pact was signed in Paris – among the signatories were Gil Robles, Ridruejo and Giménez Fernández – but it led to nothing. The next event of significance did not take place until 1974 when the Communist Party tried to end its isolation by forming a coalition called the *Junta Democrática*. Even then mistrust of the communists was so high that important sections of the opposition – notably the Socialist Party and the *Izquierda Democrática* of Ruiz Giménez – refused to join in. The junta thus consisted of the PCE, the *comisiones* and a number of mavericks such as Rafael Calvo Serer, a former right-wing conservative and a supporter of Don Juan, and Carlos Hugo, the carlist pretender who was trying to convert his reactionary followers to socialism. It also included an Andalusian group claiming to be both socialists and regional nationalists, and, more importantly, Tierno Galván's band of socialists, which now changed its name to the *Partido Socialista Popular*. The junta, which was formed in Paris in the summer of 1974, put forward a programme of impeccably democratic aims, but insisted that there could be no compromise with the existing regime. There had to be a break, or *ruptura*, with *franquismo*. Calvo Serer argued that it was impossible to reform the regime and he attacked *aperturistas* such as Fraga and Areilza, as well as Juan Carlos himself, for being prisoners of the *franquista* institutions.[49]

Demands for a *ruptura* were also made by the junta's rivals, the *Plataforma de Convergencia Democrática*, which was set up a year later and consisted of most of the rest of the opposition. Like the communists and their allies, the leaders of the *plataforma* had little faith in the future monarchy of Juan Carlos. As one socialist leader remarked, 'we intend to oppose from the very start the kind of compromise with the past that he represents'.[50] The *plataforma* included Ridruejo's social democrats, *Izquierda Democrática*, the socialist trade union (UGT) and a number of other groups, including the carlists who had just abandoned the *Junta Democrática*. But the crucial component of the coalition was the Socialist Party.

The PSOE had spent more than two decades during which it had seldom been heard of. Rodolfo Llopis, its secretary-general until 1972, was an elderly man obsessed by the threat of communism. He was largely ignorant of modern Spain and he made little effort to resurrect the party in the country. With the support of a handful of other exiled leaders in Mexico and France, he had retained control of the PSOE and refused to share power with its members in the interior. At the conferences which the party held regularly in Toulouse, delegates from across the Pyrenees had been refused the right to vote on the grounds that it was impossible to discover the number of members living in Spain.

From the early 1960s, socialists inside Spain had complained of their subordination to a leadership which seemed interested in little more than its own perpetuation. But it was not until the end of the decade that they made any progress towards reducing the power of Llopis. In 1970, at the eleventh conference in exile, a young Sevillian labour lawyer called Felipe González argued for a radical change in the party's balance of power. Despite the opposition of Llopis, more than three-quarters of the delegates supported González, and a decision was taken to elect a new executive committee consisting of seven members in exile and nine from the interior. From then on the position of Llopis declined. In 1972, faced by growing criticism both in Spain and abroad, he decided to postpone the twelfth conference, but a majority of the leadership opposed him and the conference went ahead in August. A few months later, he summoned a rival conference where his principal success was in attracting the support of Tierno Galván, the man whom he had expelled from the PSOE some years earlier. But he needed a lot more than the enigmatic Tierno to arrest his decline. The party membership was rallying to the dynamic leadership of González, the new secretary-general, and his colleagues. In January 1974 the 'renovated' PSOE received the support of the Socialist International.

The socialists in Spain were still much weaker than their communist rivals. After so many years of inertia, their bases were reduced to Andalusia, Asturias and the Basque country. In the early seventies members of the new executive committee travelled across Spain, visiting old militants, building up contacts, reviving the almost defunct trade union.[51] Although by 1974 the party had only 4,000 members, about half of whom were in exile, it was at last setting up an organization capable of sustaining a political party. Its rejuvenation was well-timed. When it re-emerged on the eve of Franco's death, it presented a modern, energetic and attractive image. Moreover, in contrast to the grizzled civil war veterans at the head of the Communist Party, it was led by a man who had been born three years after the war had ended.

The attitude of the government towards the activities of the opposition during Franco's last year was curious. Arias, the prime minister, alternated between bouts of repression and periods of hesitancy. Probably he simply did not know what he ought to do. The party leaders, apart from the communists, were living openly in Spain and were known to be meeting other opposition leaders. Sometimes they were left alone and sometimes they were arrested. In November 1974 a number of them, including Ridruejo, González and the son of Gil Robles, were arrested at dinner in a private house in Madrid and taken to the *Dirección General de Seguridad*. Ruiz Giménez, who by chance had left the house before the arrests were made, learnt of the incident and hurried to join them. Finding the senior police officer, he insisted that, as he also had been at the dinner, he ought to be arrested as well. But the officer refused.[52] There was, as Ruiz Giménez recognized, a 'league table of toleration'.[53] He and the other christian democrats were more or less tolerated by the regime and so was Tierno. Although they could not hold meetings, they were able, for example, to make statements to newspapers without being sent to prison. Such leniency was rarely accorded to other members of the opposition, and never to the communists.

In October 1975 Tierno declared that the opposition groups were in the process of forming a united democratic front, but they were too late. Within a month Franco was dead and the opposition was still disunited, as indeed it had been ever since the uprising nearly forty years earlier. Its components had been kept apart by suspicion of the communists, the weakness of the socialists, the short-sightedness of the republicans and the ambiguity of the monarchist position. Their leaders had been often dogmatic and doctrinaire, and at the same time ineffective. The failure of Franco's opponents, however, was not entirely their own fault. The regime had used repression and other, more subtle tactics to keep its critics at bay. Censorship had prevented the opposition from being heard and a technocratic society had been promoted in order to encourage a climate of political apathy. Spain had become what Ridruejo called a 'political desert'[54] which ensured that the Spaniards either did not receive or else were not receptive to the appeals sent them by the opposition. For most of those who had heard of Ridruejo, he was a falangist poet who had gone off the rails rather than the leader of a social democratic group. Of the small, embryo parties set up by him and so many others, a large majority of Spaniards had not the slightest knowledge. Only after Franco had died could they come out into the open and make themselves known.

6

The Resurgence of Local Nationalism

Spain, wrote José Antonio Primo de Rivera, 'is a unity of destiny in the universal. Any conspiracy against that unity is loathsome. Any kind of separatism is a crime which we will not forgive.'[1] Like many of José Antonio's sayings, this one was 'adopted' by the *franquista* state. Article 1 of the Principles of the *Movimiento Nacional* proclaimed Spain 'a unity of destiny in the universal' and declared that the 'sacred duty and collective task of all Spaniards' was to work for 'the unity, greatness and freedom of the fatherland'.

The question of unity was, and is, a *franquista* obsession. No right-wing orator can hope to be taken seriously unless his speeches contain regular references to 'the sacred and indissoluble unity of the fatherland'. In a famous phrase, the right-wing monarchist leader, José Calvo Sotelo, once said that he would prefer *una España roja a una España rota*, a red Spain to a broken Spain.[2] It was a sentiment shared by many *franquistas*. Communism, they declared, was their principal enemy, and they rallied supporters to their cause by claiming to wage a crusade against 'atheistic marxism'. But separatism was for them a more insidious and also a more dangerous foe. For purposes of propaganda, they could claim that communism was an imported ideology which stalinist Russia was trying to impose upon catholic Spain. But they could not convincingly blame foreign powers for the rise of local nationalism in the Basque country or Catalonia. Since the beginning of the last century, right-wing Spaniards have developed a hatred of many 'foreign' things – liberalism, marxism, freemasonry and so on – but their most violent loathing has been directed against the regional movements inside Spain. 'We prefer a communist Asturian miner,' declared a falangist newspaper in Valladolid, 'to a separatist Basque priest.'[3] In the short testament which was read out after his death, Franco referred four times to the unity of the fatherland, and besought his countrymen to maintain it in defiance of 'the enemies of Spain and of christian civilization'.[4]

The *franquistas*' passion for unity was based on the supposed connection between 'unity' and 'greatness' in sixteenth-century Spain. They argued that the country had once been great and united, but for generations it had been weak and disunited. If Spain was to become great again, they believed, they should return first to the old formula and unite the country around Castile. These people suffered from an overwhelming nostalgia for that century when Castile was the greatest power in Europe, the nation which conquered the Moorish kingdom of Granada, defeated the French in Italy, repelled the Turkish menace at Lepanto, and then conquered, colonized and 'christianized' the New World.

Many of their ideas derived from the work of a writer who was neither a *franquista* nor a falangist. José Ortega y Gasset believed that Castile had been responsible both for Spain's greatness and for its decadence. He declared that Spain had been made by Castile and suggested that 'only Castilian heads had adequate organs' for understanding the great problem of Spanish unity.[5] For a century, Castilian strength, energy and enterprise had made Spain great, until 1580 when the process of disintegration began. Castile turned inwards, becoming 'suspicious, narrow, mean, resentful'.[6] In the words of the poet Machado, 'wretched Castile, once supreme, now wrapped in tatters, despises what she does not know.'[7] The transformation of Castile, according to Ortega, led inevitably to the decomposition, first of the empire, and then of Spain itself. He argued that Basque and Catalan nationalism were the logical results of Castilian weakness and incompetence. Once the empire had been reduced to a few islands, it was only natural that the people of the peninsula should ask whether there was any point in remaining tied to Castile. They could not be expected to live simply for 'the resonance of the past', and so, understandably, they had turned to regionalism. By 1920 Spain had become less of a nation than 'a series of water-tight compartments'.[8]

The version of history propounded by *franquistas* and falangists was based at least partly on a simplistic interpretation of Ortega's simplistic thesis. They concluded that Spain's recovery depended on the regeneration of Castile – which José Antonio called 'the depository of eternal values'[9] – and the suppression of regional movements. The lesson they drew from history was that Spain could only be great if it was united, and they pointed to the Spain of the Catholic Kings as the ideal to which they should return. There, they claimed, was the first real nation of Europe, united more than two centuries before the union of England and Scotland, and nearly four centuries before the unification of Italy or Germany. Spain, wrote the falangist author Pemartín, 'was already a nation under Ferdinand and Isabel, at a time when the other nations of Europe were nothing more than feudal conglomerations'.[10]

This view was based on a disastrous misreading of Spanish history. The marriage in 1469 between Ferdinand, heir to the throne of Aragon,* and Isabel, heiress to the Castilian crown, led to a dynastic, not a political, union. When James VI of Scotland ascended the English throne in 1603, the kingdoms were separate states, and remained as such until the union a century later. The situation in Spain after 1469 was similar. Political unity did not come to the country for two and a half centuries after the marriage of Ferdinand and Isabel, and then it was imposed, after the Catalans had been defeated in two wars, by a different dynasty. During the period of its greatness, Spain was never a unitary state. Aragon retained its constitutional system – so different from that of authoritarian Castile – its coinage, laws and system of land tenure.[11] Its king needed the approval of the local *cortes* before he could raise money or send Castilian troops through Aragonese territory.[12]

The union of crowns came at a bad moment for Aragon. Whereas Castile was richer, more powerful and more populated than in any previous period, the eastern regions of the peninsula were in economic and political decline. One hundred and fifty

---

*The kingdom of Aragon included the autonomous 'nations' – each with their own *cortes* – of Valencia, Aragon and Catalonia, and the island of Majorca. In the 12th century the Count of Barcelona married the daughter and only child of Ramiro II of Aragon, and their successors were known as the kings of Aragon.

years earlier, Aragon had been a major power, with a Mediterranean empire that included Sardinia, Sicily and even Athens. Barcelona, with its banking and its textile industry, had been the first city of Spain. But economic recession, recurrent plagues (the population at the end of the fifteenth century had dropped to less than two–thirds of the 1365 figure), and civil wars had destroyed much of that prosperity. For several generations after the union of the crowns, Aragon remained a poor relation of Castile. The Castilians largely excluded Catalonia from taking part in their economic boom by preferring Genoese bankers to those from Barcelona, and they prevented the Aragonese from joining them in the exploitation of America.[13]

The fundamental problem with the dynastic union was that it took place at a time when Castile was unnaturally strong and overpopulated, and Aragon was unnaturally weak and underpopulated. A century later, when Castile's dynamic period came to an end, the Catalans began their economic recovery, and the balance between them gradually changed. From then on, the Catalans grew steadily more resentful at the subordinate role they were being required to play as a consequence of the marriage of 1469.

At the height of its power, Castile doubtless could have forced political unity on the rest of Spain, as Richelieu was to do in France a century later. But the Spain of Philip II, so intolerant of religious and racial diversity, was curiously indifferent towards the question of political disunity. It was only when Castile's economy was in ruins, its lands drained of men and resources for wars in the Netherlands and elsewhere, that a bankrupt government in Madrid tried to reduce the autonomy of Catalonia. The effort was made too late, and ended disastrously. By 1640 Castile was too poor and too weak to impose itself on the rest of the peninsula. The attempt to persuade Catalonia to pay its fair share of taxes caused a revolt in which the Catalans proclaimed their allegiance to the French king. The rebellion was followed by a long war – Barcelona did not surrender until 1652 – and by a revolt in Portugal (which had been annexed by Philip II in 1580). By the end of the war, most of Catalonia had been recovered (the northern districts were ceded to France), but Portugal was irretrievably lost.

Spain did not finally become a unitary state until the War of the

Spanish Succession ended in 1714, leaving a French prince, Philip V, on the throne.* Earlier Philip had offered to respect the *fueros*, or liberties, of Catalonia, but the Catalans rejected him and his offer, and rose in support of the Austrian claimant. When Barcelona was captured in 1714, after another lengthy war, the Bourbons were in no mood to preserve Catalonia's institutions: the *fueros* or 'foral system' (a combination of medieval laws and customs) were abolished, the universities and the Barcelona city council swiftly dismantled. Catalonia's remaining privileges, such as its coinage, special tribunals and commercial laws, disappeared in the early part of the nineteenth century.

The reduction of Catalonia's political autonomy coincided with an increase in population and the beginnings of an industrial revolution. Brandy and textiles were its chief products, and by the 1790s it had, after Lancashire, the highest concentration of dyers and weavers in Europe.[14] Light industry flourished during the nineteenth century, and Barcelona's population increased from 88,000 in 1818 to more than half a million by 1897.[15] This new manufacturing industry may not have been particularly efficient – it needed heavy protection against English products – but it made Catalonia a region that was very different from and much more advanced than Castile. It also led to the creation of a different kind of society. By the middle of the nineteenth century, Catalonia was the only area of Spain which possessed an industrial working class and a significant middle class.

As the economic and social discrepancies between Castile and Catalonia grew, Madrid's political domination over Barcelona seemed more and more ridiculous. Gradually, Catalans became more confident of their strength, and more conscious of their history and traditions. Catalan, which had not existed as a literary language since the early sixteenth century, enjoyed a revival. To begin with, this was largely folkloric and romantic, but later it became serious, leading to the foundation of newspapers and other publications in Catalan. Poets began to write about Catalan history, eulogizing past achievements and thus encouraging the emergence of a sense of Catalan national identity.

Catalan nationalism did not appear as a political movement until

*It is ironic that Spanish unity in a centralized state, which Franco and his supporters so revered, should have been achieved not by the Catholic Kings but by a French monarch during the 'decadent' and despised eighteenth century.

the last moments of the nineteenth century. The problem with Catalonia, one of its intellectuals has lamented, is that its nationalism arrived too late.[16] Catalonia was still fighting the carlist wars when the rest of Europe was producing new nations. Yet there are few similarities between nineteenth-century Spain and Italy or Germany during the era of their unification. As Ortega pointed out, Spain's regionalist movements were largely reactions against the backwardness and indolence of its political capital. In Italy the unifying impulse came from Piedmont, economically and politically the healthiest region in the country. Had it come from Naples, and *against* the wishes of Piedmont and the north, unification would not have taken place.

Eighteen ninety-eight, when Spain lost Cuba and the remaining imperial possessions, was a crucial year in the development of Catalan nationalism. The scale of the disaster, the waste of men and money, highlighted the folly and incompetence of the Madrid government. The Catalan middle classes saw the need to turn Spain into a modern, industrial state, but realized they could not do so through the existing liberal and conservative parties in Madrid. Political power still lay largely with the landowners of Castile and Andalusia. As the Catalan leader Cambó later remarked, individual Catalans had held important positions in the state, but the 'Catalan spirit' had never been present in Spanish governments.[17] Their failure to persuade Madrid to reform the state convinced many Catalans that they should look for a Catalan solution to their problems. In 1901 they founded their own political party, the *Lliga Regionalista*, an organization which eschewed separatism in favour of autonomy, and was determined to transform Spain from an 'oligarchic and semi-feudal' country into a 'modern bourgeois state'.[18]

The year 1898 also had an effect on Spain's other industrial region, Vizcaya, the north-western province of the Basque country. Vizcaya already had a regional movement, rural in its outlook and radical in its aims, that was entirely different from Catalan nationalism. The two regions had indeed little in common. The Basque country had no advanced Mediterranean culture, and lacked a glorious medieval past. It was a backward region recently enriched (or in Basque rural eyes, recently ruined) by the exploitation of its minerals. The only similarities between the Basque country and Catalonia were that they both experienced industrial revolutions (though Vizcaya's had been much quicker) and that they both had a tradition of autonomy. As we have seen, Catalonia lost its *fueros* in 1714, but the Basques, who had supported Philip V, were allowed to keep theirs.

The three Basque provinces* had been united to the kingdom of Castile since the thirteenth and fourteenth centuries. But the retention of their *fueros* gave them a very real measure of independence. The Basques enjoyed a number of economic and commercial rights, they were exempted from military service, and their foral councils could decide what taxes should be paid to Castile. On occasion the northern provinces could even sign international treaties.[19]

Until the wave of industrialization in the last quarter of the nineteenth century, Basque society was conservative, intensely catholic, and based largely in the countryside. In 1833 the Basque provinces (except for the few large towns) rose in support of the carlist cause, not because they believed strongly in its dynastic claim, but because they shared its outlook and its hatred of the centralizing policies of Madrid. Reverence for tradition, defence of the *fueros*, hatred of anticlericalism and distrust of the cities were all tenets shared by the Basques and the carlist rebels.

In 1837 the government dissolved the foral councils of Alava, Guipúzcoa and Vizcaya, but two years later a compromise peace was made at Vergara. Most Basques were more interested in the preservation of their *fueros* than in the monarchical ambitions of Don Carlos, and were prepared to accept a peace that guaranteed these. Although the Basques had to make a number of concessions, the foral system was restored at Vergara, article one of the treaty confirming the *fueros* of Navarre and the Basque provinces 'without prejudice to the constitutional unity of the monarchy'. This phrase, which was greeted with protests at the time, was later turned into a symbol of the Basques' loss of independence. The provinces' allegiance to Spain, Basque nationalists subsequently claimed, had been for five centuries *voluntary*. They had voluntarily accepted the Castilian king as their king, and in the process had retained their sovereignty. Vergara, regarded by radical carlists as 'the great betrayal', was later denounced by radical Basques as the abduction of their sovereignty.

*Vizcaya, Guipúzcoa and Alava. Basques consider that Navarre is also Basque territory, as well, of course, as the Pays Basque in south-western France.

The grandson of Don Carlos ordered his followers to rise again in 1872, and once more they were supported by the Basque provinces. Four years later, after the inevitable defeat,* the prime minister, Cánovas del Castillo, introduced a new law for the Basque country. Rejecting the suggestion that the time had come to abolish the *fueros* altogether, Cánovas decided that the Basques could keep their juntas and foral councils but must surrender their fiscal independence and their right to exemption from military service. When the juntas and the councils refused to accept these conditions, the government dissolved them, and thus effectively destroyed the foral system. In 1878, however, it established the system of the *concierto económico* which restored the Basques' financial independence from Madrid.

Modern Basque nationalism has several ancestors, but by far the most important of them is the carlist movement. The fact that nationalists today do not share its religious fanaticism or its dynastic intransigence, does not invalidate the vital role which carlism played in the development of Basque nationalism. Telesforo Monzón, the most prominent radical nationalist in the Basque country after Franco's death, accepted the carlist heritage without hesitation. The Basques, he declared in 1979, had been fighting the same war for 150 years. The first carlist war, the second carlist war, the civil war, and the contemporary campaign of ETA were all part of the struggle for the restoration of Basque sovereignty.[21]

After its defeat, carlism lost most of its popular support, except in Navarre. In the Basque country, and to a lesser extent in Catalonia, its adherents were attracted to the nascent nationalist movements. The apostle of Basque nationalism, Sabino Arana-Goïri, was the son of a prominent carlist, and in early youth he also considered himself a carlist. He accepted carlism's reactionary ideas, its religious intolerance, its hatred of liberalism and freemasonry. When he renounced carlism, he did so, not because he disagreed with its views on politics or religion, but simply

---

*Gerald Brenan has compared the carlists after 1840 with the Jacobites in Britain after 1715.[20] There were also similarities between the Jacobite rebellion of 1745–6 and the second carlist war. Like the highland Scots, the carlists were difficult to beat on their own ground, in the hills and mountains of the Pyrenees; similarly, they lacked the resources to capture a defended city or to come close to threatening the capital.

because he had come to believe that neither the carlists nor the Madrid liberals had the right to rule Vizcaya.* In that year, 1882, Arana was convinced by his brother Luis that the Basque country did not belong to Spain.† From that moment he decided to devote the rest of his life to the development of an ideology which would lead to Basque independence. 'If I knew that my death would revive my fatherland,' he announced in the famous speech at Larrazábal, 'I would give my neck to the axe not once but a hundred times.'[23]

In the Larrazábal speech, which he made to a small group of Basques in 1893, Arana proclaimed his motto, *Jaungoikoa eta Lagizarra*, 'God and the Old Law'. By the 'Old Law', he meant the Basques' laws, their customs, their race and their language. These were the four indispensable ingredients of his nationalist teaching, and he used them to demonstrate the essential differences between Spain and the Basque country.

Sabino Arana claimed that the Basque people had the longest tradition of independence in the world.[24] They had been con-quered neither by the Romans nor by the Arabs, and their union with Castile had not infringed this independence. Over the centuries they had constructed an egalitarian society,‡ based on the notion that all Basques were 'noble', without constraint or interference from Spain. In 1379 the same person had become Señor de Vizcaya and King of Castile, but this had not entailed any loss of sovereignty. The *fueros* were not privileges granted by an outside power but the laws of a people who had been completely independent until 1839. Vergara and the law of 1876 were thus illegal because Spain had no right to tamper with the laws of a different people. The abolition of the *fueros* was the action of a foreign government which had conquered and was now enslaving

*He also came to the conclusion that neither had the right to rule Guipúzcoa, Alava or Navarre, and that France similarly had no right to the Pays Basque.

†This is one of the sacred events in Basque nationalist lore. Fifty years later, when the Basques celebrated their first *Aberri Eguna*, day of the (Basque) fatherland, it was held to commemorate the 'revelation' of Sabino Arana.[22]

‡Basque society was very different from Castilian or Andalusian society, and certainly much fairer. But, as with the question of historical independence, too many claims have been made for it by nationalist propagandists. Modern Basque historians have shown that Basque egalitarianism was in fact little more than a myth.[25]

the Basque people. The present task for the Basques, he asserted, was to unite so as to regain their rights. Basque nationalism, he said, was 'not a revolutionary policy which demands anything new, but a restorationist policy which aims to return the ancient and legitimate state of liberty to a people which has lost it against its will.'[26]

Arana saw Vizcaya in sentimental terms, as a rural paradise which was being ruined by the arrival of thousands of 'Spanish' immigrants needed to work the mines and iron foundries around Bilbao. He believed that the immigrants – whom he disparagingly referred to as *maketos* – were corrupting the Basque race, and declared that it was necessary to refrain from having social or sexual relations with them. For Arana, the principal aim was to preserve the purity of the Basque race. Between the Spaniards and the Basques, he believed, there was no racial connection. The Spaniards were a mixture of all the peoples that had settled in Spain: Celtic, Phoenician, Greek, Roman, Germanic and Arab. The Basques, by contrast, were a pure race speaking a pure language.* Their distinguishing characteristics, claimed Arana, were intelligence, nobility, capacity for hard work, devoutness, dignity and cleanliness. This made them very unlike the Spaniard who was lazy, stupid, idle, servile, dirty, greedy, adulterous, criminal, and 'in need of a foreign invasion from time to time to civilize him'. The Spanish race was 'the most abject in Europe', 'the most vile and contemptible', 'effeminate and depraved at one and the same time'.[29]

·   After the preservation of the Basque race, Arana's next priority was the preservation of *euskera*, the Basque language, which had been contracting its frontiers ever since the eleventh century.[30] Arana himself could not speak Basque until after his 'revelation', when he went off to study it.† Having done so, he claimed that the Basque language was as original as the Basque race,‡ and that all Basques should be encouraged to speak it. The Castilian

*Although this is nonsense, the origin of the Basques remains a mystery. There has long been a theory that they were the inhabitants of Iberia in pre-Roman times, and survived because they were not conquered by the legions. Various people have found similarities between Basque and such diverse languages as Finnish, Turkish, Hungarian, Aztec, Hebrew and Dakota.[27] A contemporary researcher has discovered close similarities between carnival rites in a Basque village and those in a district of Bulgaria.[28]

language, like the Castilian himself, had a corrupting influence on the Basque country. 'All the world knows,' declared Arana, 'that immorality increases in those areas where *euskera* is no longer spoken; and that the blasphemousness, the profanity and the immoral and criminal customs of the *maketo* invader gain ground in Vizcaya in direct proportion to the conquests made by the Castilian language.'[33]

Arana's nationalist ideas were thus a reaction to the abolition of the *fueros* and to the subsequent industrialization of Vizcaya. The imposition of massive heavy industry on a mainly rural society and the arrival of a large immigrant population were perhaps the principal factors behind the emergence of Basque nationalism. Under the foral system, the iron mines had been owned by the municipalities, and it was forbidden to extract ore for the benefit of 'foreign kingdoms'.[34] Once this ban had been relaxed, as a consequence of the law of 1876, the exploitation of the iron mines increased enormously. Vizcayan iron was much prized in the rest of Europe because its low phosphorous content made it suitable for Henry Bessemer's revolutionary method of making steel. After the carlist war, iron production leapt from an annual pre-war figure of about 250,000 tons, to a million tons in 1877 and six million in 1899.[35] The industrial revolution, which was fuelled by the exploitation of the iron mines, was centred around the Vizcayan capital, and in the last twenty years of the century this area was radically transformed. During the short lifetime of Sabino Arana (1865–1903), the population of Bilbao increased by nearly five times. By 1900 nearly half the city's inhabitants were '*maketo* invaders'.[36]

When Arana founded the *Partido Nacionalista Vasco* (Basque Nationalist Party – PNV) in 1895, he represented a small,

---

†Later nationalist leaders, such as Aguirre and Monzón, also went to the countryside to study Basque. The Basques' ignorance of their own language is an indication of the weakness of Basque culture compared to Catalan. The idea that a Catalan nationalist leader might not speak Catalan is absurd.

‡*Euskera* was doubtless at one stage an original language. But it was no longer so in the nineteenth century, as Arana well knew. He himself invented Basque-sounding words to replace those which appeared to him to have Latin roots.[31] According to one source, nearly three-quarters of the words in the Basque vocabulary came from Latin or Romance languages.[32]

reactionary movement without visible political prospects. Its supporters were confined to those areas of Vizcaya affected by industrialization (nationalism had little following in Guipúzcoa until the First World War, and was irrelevant to Alava until the Second Republic). It had no support from the urban working class, or from Basque intellectuals,* or from a large majority of the middle classes. It seemed, indeed, little more than an invention of its founder, who had concocted an ideology from a blend of carlism, Basque mythology and pseudo-history.†

Basque nationalism might have remained fanatical and unimportant had it not been joined, in the final years of the nineteenth century, by a group of men who had formed the *Sociedad Evskalerria* (the Basque Society). They had little in common with Sabino Arana. Liberal, anti-carlist, participants themselves in the industrialization of Vizcaya, they nevertheless possessed a strong feeling of Basque identity, and were passionately in favour of the restoration of the foral system. The society was shunned by the rich new bourgeoisie, which after all owed its wealth to the government's decision to abolish the *fueros* and sell off the mines; the shipping magnate, Ramón de la Sota (afterwards knighted by George V for lending his fleet to Britain during the First World War), was the only great industrialist to support Basque nationalism. But many lesser members of the Bilbao middle classes joined the society. Their approach to the question of nationalism was quite distinct from Arana's. They did not have his fanaticism, they cared little about his mythology, and they were not opposed to industrialization. As in Catalonia, the failings of the Madrid government persuaded many of them to embrace local nationalism.

---

*The opposition of Basque writers was notorious. Baroja thought the nationalists stood for little more than religious intolerance, and were trying to turn the Basque country into a 'Paraguay in the time of the Jesuits'.[37] Unamuno detested the movement and once made a speech in Bilbao in which he welcomed the future disappearance of the Basque language, and of the Basques themselves.[38] This astonishing performance gave the opponents of Basque nationalism a 'great name' to use in their attacks on the movement.

†Among his other lasting inventions are the Basque flag, the *ikurriña*, whose design is based on the Union Jack, and the name which the Basques usually call their country, Euskadi.

With the incorporation of the *Sociedad Euskalerria* into the PNV, Basque nationalism became a political force, and it was soon winning municipal elections in Bilbao. Arana remained its leader, and the carlist influence was still dominant, but in 1900 the PNV was a less intransigent party than it had been a few years earlier. In the last years of his life, even Arana became more realistic and pragmatic, abandoning his more primitive ideas and advocating some degree of co-operation with Spain. What lay behind his 'Spanish evolution', however, and what he was really suggesting, remain unclear, because he died soon afterwards, leaving his followers mystified. They have been arguing ever since whether his 'conversion' was tactical or real.

After Arana's death in 1903, the PNV split into two factions, a division which has lasted, with some vagaries, for the whole of the twentieth century. Perhaps it was inherent in the circumstances of its formation, because the space between Ramón de la Sota and Arana in his pre-'Spanish' days was too wide to fit comfortably within a single political party. Under the leadership of Arana's brother Luis, the radical nationalists, the pure *sabinianos*, became increasingly critical of Sota and his brand of liberal regionalism. In 1921 the PNV formally divided, and its reunification in 1930 was an uneasy, half-hearted affair. The regionalists, who were in a majority, wished to collaborate with the republic and hoped to obtain from the government a statute of autonomy. But the *sabinianos*, the faction grouped around the *Jagi-Jagi* paper, disdained all dealings with Madrid, and continued to demand independence.

By 1931, after several decades of existence, the Basque and Catalan nationalist movements had had little success. The sole achievement of the *Lliga* had been to obtain the *mancomunidad* in 1913, which granted the Catalans a measure of control over their schools, social services and communications. For the first quarter of the twentieth century, Barcelona was plagued by labour disputes. The demands of the powerful anarchist movement, and the obtuse and repressive reactions of the Madrid government, turned the Catalan capital into a battleground where between 1919 and 1923 several hundred people were killed. Street terrorism, perpetrated partly by the anarchists and partly by government agents, so alarmed the businessmen of the *Lliga* that they were prepared to sacrifice their political ideals in return for the restoration of order. In 1923 they welcomed the coup d'état of General Primo de Rivera, the father of the future leader of the *Falange*.

Until 1923 Catalan nationalism had been a largely conservative movement, backed by the local clergy and by members of the middle classes. Primo de Rivera, who was highly unsympathetic to regionalist movements,★ helped to make it more radical. He abolished the *mancomunidad*, forbade Catalan to be taught in schools, and suppressed even minor manifestations of Catalan feeling such as performances of the *sardana*, the famous national dance. His repressive policies merely strengthened the Catalans' nationalist sentiments – as Franco's were to do a generation later – and undermined the *Lliga*, which had welcomed him. Within a short period the Catalans were fed up with Primo de Rivera and with the king who had acquiesced in his dictatorship. In 1931 Barcelona voted by a large majority for the establishment of a republic.

The Catalan nationalists finally accomplished their main objective – an autonomy statute – during Azaña's government in 1932. The statute, which José Antonio and many future *franquistas* regarded as 'a crime against Spain',[40] went much further than the *mancomunidad*. It gave the Catalans their own government, the *Generalitat*, with control over most local issues, and proclaimed Catalan as an official language of the region. The measure, which was received enthusiastically in Barcelona, cemented Catalonia to the republic and ensured its loyalty to the government during the civil war.

The advent of the republic was not welcomed in the Basque country as it had been in Catalonia. The conservative, catholic leaders of the PNV were suspicious of the republicans' intentions respecting the Church. In 1931 they successfully contested the elections in alliance with the carlists, although carlism and Basque nationalism were by now only distantly related. They held similar views on the religious question – the PNV deputies walked out of the *Cortes* following the approval of an article in the constitution which disestablished the Church and paved the way for the expulsion of the Jesuits – but on little else besides. The carlists

★'Regions?' he is reported to have said once. 'Out of the question. A quarter of a century's silence about regions, usually the mask of separatism . . . and Spain will have been freed from one of her gravest perils.'[39]

detested the republic and everything it offered; the Basques were prepared to accept it if, like the Catalans, they received a statute of autonomy. In the 1933 elections the Basque nationalists still regarded the left-wing parties as their main enemies, and only when it became clear that no conservative party would give them a statute, were they prepared to collaborate with the Left.

The PNV's decision to remain loyal to the republic after Franco's uprising outraged many right-wing Basques as well as their former carlist allies in Navarre, who were among the rebellion's most enthusiastic supporters. To them it seemed inconceivable that the Basques should fight with the Popular Front – whose radical policies they disliked – against a movement with which, on all essential questions save the issue of autonomy, they were in agreement. The PNV was not in fact enthusiastic about the Popular Front government, and it did not allow the type of revolutionary experiments taking place in Catalonia and 'the red zone' to be performed in the Basque country. But the party leadership believed the government would reward the PNV for its loyalty with a statute, and for that reason it opposed Franco.

After heavy lobbying by the socialist leader Prieto, and oblique warnings from the PNV that its allegiance was not unconditional, the *Cortes* did finally approve a statute of autonomy in the autumn of 1936. The statute was broad enough to be acceptable to the regionalist wing of the Basque Nationalist Party, but it was rejected by the *Jagi-Jagi* faction. When José Antonio Aguirre, the PNV leader, was elected president of the provisional Basque government in Guernica, a group of hardliners chanted 'Statute no! Independence yes!' On the same day, 7 October, Arana's brother Luis left the PNV in protest against its 'adulteration of the nationalist creed'.[41]

The new Basque government, consisting of members of the Popular Front parties as well as the PNV, was in a difficult position from the beginning. Whereas Catalonia was far away from the front line and in no immediate danger of attack, the Basques had already lost large chunks of their territory. Alava, the southern and least 'Basque' of the three provinces, had been captured at the start of the uprising, while San Sebastian and most of Guipúzcoa had fallen in September. Cut off from France and from the rest of republican Spain (except for the narrow coastal strip which stretched to Asturias), the Basques were reduced to a single province. Vizcaya, moreover, was not a difficult target for Franco's armies, and it was 'softened up' beforehand by the bombing of Durango, Bilbao and Guernica. After a spring offensive, Bilbao fell in June 1937 – the secrets of its defences betrayed by a Basque engineer – and Aguirre's government went into exile.

Since the end of the sixteenth century, Spanish rulers have had the choice of two policies to pursue with regard to the non-Castilian regions of Spain. The alternatives were discussed during Philip II's reign when the council of state was making up its mind how to deal with certain difficulties in Aragon. The Duke of Alba declared that, 'given three or four thousand men, he would wipe out Aragon's liberties; to which the Marqués de los Vélez . . . replied that this was not the advice to give the king if he wished to see him retain his territories, but that the way to preserve them was to respect their *fueros* and observe the conditions under which they had been inherited.'[42] Few of Spain's leaders have followed the wise counsel of Vélez. Franco, like Primo de Rivera before him, decided to take the Duke of Alba's advice.

The two sides of Franco's policy were the establishment of a highly-centralized system of government and the use of large-scale repression in the defeated areas. The autonomy statutes were suppressed, the recently re-established foral councils abolished, and administration was carried out by civil governors responsible to Madrid. In a decree-law of June 1937, Vizcaya and Guipúzcoa were termed the 'traitor provinces', and punished by the annulment of the *concierto económico*. A large number of people on the defeated side were shot after the fall of Bilbao; the town's new mayor, Areilza, rejoiced that his city was being 'redeemed for ever from the red scum in the service of Moscow, and the Vizcayan nationalist scum in the service of separatism'.[43] Repression in the Basque country remained at a high level throughout the dictatorship. Of the eleven states of emergency declared between 1956 and 1975, all but one were applied to Vizcaya, Guipúzcoa or both.

The one class in the Basque country to welcome Franco's victory was the industrial and financial oligarchy of Bilbao, which returned in style to its huge villas in Neguri.* With the exception of the Sota family, which had most of its property confiscated, the higher ranks of the Bilbao bourgeoisie loathed Basque nationalism, sharing Areilza's opinion of Euskadi as a 'horrible, evil and inhuman nightmare', the product of socialism and the 'imbecility' of Vizcayan nationalism.[44] This class was among the most enthusiastic supporters of the new regime, providing numerous ambassadors, cabinet ministers and other senior officials. During the fifties and sixties it presided over a second industrial revolution in the Basque country, financed largely by two of the country's great banks, the Banco de Bilbao and the Banco de Vizcaya.

The Catalan middle classes, more liberal-minded and civilized, had not supported General Franco's uprising. In January 1939 some of them welcomed his army's entry into Barcelona because they wished to see an end to the war and to the violent quarrels between the communists and their anarchist rivals. They were the spectators, and sometimes the victims, of a long round of intolerance and violence: they had not liked the rising or the attempted revolution, and they did not now like the repression. Few Catalans participated in the government of the new regime. When Cambó, the old leader of the *Lliga*, returned to Catalonia after the war, he was horrified by the sight of people giving the fascist salute. Declaring that he would not return until he could greet people with his hat, he left the country and died abroad.[45]

The repression in Catalonia was similar to what it had been in the Basque country, except on a larger scale. Many thousands of prisoners were executed between 1939 and 1943, including Leuis Companys, the president of the *Generalitat*, who, as he faced the firing squad, took off his shoes and socks so that he could die touching the soil of Catalonia.[46] One of the regime's chief targets, in both regions, was the local language. In 1939 Ridruejo went to Barcelona with a load of falangist propaganda, but was forbidden to distribute it because it was written in Catalan. Afterwards he recalled 'the closed-down institutes, the translated commercial signs, the proscription of language-teaching, and the cities and towns full of impertinent exhortations: "talk in Spanish!" "speak the language of the empire!" etc'. Many years later, long after he had

---

*Neguri is a monument to the vulgarity of nouveau riche life in the early part of this century. It is also a dramatic illustration of class divisions. Built on the right bank of the River Nervión, it preserved the oligarchy from the pollution of its own factories, and – as there is no bridge connecting it to the left bank – from contact with the proletariat it had imported to work them.

left the *Falange*, he protested to Franco that the regime was treating Catalonia like a foreign country under occupation.[47]

The dictatorship prevented Basque and Catalan from being taught in schools and forbade the publication of newspapers or magazines in either language. Mass could not be celebrated in Basque unless it was before 8 o'clock in the morning,[48] and all kinds of cultural groups – dance companies, choral societies and so on – were banned. At Barcelona University the chairs of history, literature and Catalan were all suppressed. When, in 1952, a chair of Catalan and Catalan literature was finally permitted, it was located at the University of Madrid; in the same year, as a concession, the Basques were given a chair for their language – in the University of Salamanca!

The regime's actions in the conquered regions were designed to stamp out Basque and Catalan nationalism once and for all. But they were often so petty and vindictive that they merely irritated the population and made it more determined to resist. To change the name of Barcelona's concert hall or to make its main street the *Avenida José Antonio*, had no practical value whatever. In the Basque country the policy was even more senseless. To name the streets of a district of Bilbao after all the generals who had fought against and finally conquered the Basques only helped to instil in the defeated a desire for revenge.[49]

Catalonia also suffered from economic discrimination. The government understandably decided to help the development of backward areas in preference to those already industrialized. But its policy in Catalonia was evidently to hinder, rather than simply ignore, the economy. Once other areas had caught up with Catalonia, so ran the curious argument, the Catalan problem would disappear.[50] The government took measures to ensure that the Barcelona stock exchange did not function properly,[51] and it refused to provide sufficient electricity supplies, with the result that Catalan industry was often paralysed by power cuts.[52] According to Ridruejo, Catalans who wished to set up or invest in new industries were frequently told that they could only do so outside Catalonia.[53]

Regionalist sentiment survived in both Catalonia and the Basque country because the people wanted it to. As children could not learn Catalan at school, their parents brought them up to speak it at home. The aggression displayed by the dictatorship had the opposite effect of what was intended. It served to stimulate feelings of Catalanism in many people who had not previously cared about it. By the 1960s, when Catalonia was enjoying a cultural revival, nationalist sentiment was stronger and more widely-spread than before the civil war.

In both the Basque provinces and Catalonia, the recovery and resurgence owed much to the help of the local clergy. After Navarre, the Basque country is one of the most devout regions in Spain. Anticlericalism has had little appeal there, because the priests have remained much closer to the population than in other parts of the country. The Bishop of Vitoria refused to sign the collective letter of the Spanish bishops supporting the 1936 uprising, and he was soon expelled from the country. The 'crusade' also failed to attract the local priests, some of whom were shot and many others arrested and deported. A generation later, the Basque clergy was in the vanguard of the *antifranquista* opposition. In 1960, 339 priests signed a letter denouncing the barbarism of police practices, and others followed this during subsequent years with a number of open letters, protests and other demonstrations of hostility. Several priests became supporters and collaborators of ETA.

In Catalonia, by contrast, anticlericalism had a long history, and church attendance in Barcelona was the lowest in the country. Nevertheless, the clergy was traditionally a supporter of Catalan nationalism, and the Archbishop of Tarragona was not allowed to take up residence after the civil war because he too, like his colleague in Vitoria, had refused to sign the collective letter. During the dictatorship, a leading centre for the *antifranquista* opposition was Montserrat, the Benedictine monastery near Barcelona. There the monks worked hard to keep the native culture alive, continuing to sing in Catalan and to celebrate the masses of Catalonia's most distinguished musician, Pablo Casals.[54] Montserrat also played an important political role through its abbot, Dom Aureli Escarré, the most tenacious and courageous of Franco's ecclesiastical critics. After several years of opposition, Escarré made his most famous attack on the regime in an interview in *Le Monde* in 1963 (see above p. 56). The following year 400 Catalan priests signed a letter supporting Escarré and criticizing the regime, but the Vatican considered it prudent to relieve him of his duties, and he retired to Milan. He was succeeded, however, by an abbot who promised to continue his policy.[55] Several years later, 300 of Catalonia's most distinguished painters, musicians and intellectuals barricaded themselves in the monastery in protest against the government's conduct in the trial of Basque guerrillas at Burgos.

Two events about mid-way through the dictatorship demonstrate the strength of the Catalanist revival. The first was the campaign against the Barcelona daily newspaper *La Vanguardia*, whose editor, Luis de Galinsoga, was a protégé of Franco. Galinsoga, whom the government imposed upon the unfortunate paper after the fall of Barcelona, despised Catalonia: during the civil war he had even suggested in a *franquista* paper that it should suffer the fate of Carthage, '*Delenda est Catalonia*'.[56] More than twenty years later he had an argument in a Barcelona church with a priest who was preaching in Catalan (which he was allowed to do on one Sunday a month). After an abusive exchange, Galinsoga left the church shouting that all Catalans were excrement. The remark echoed across Barcelona, and a boycott of *La Vanguardia* was organized: orders were quickly cancelled and advertising withdrawn. As the campaign continued and grew in strength, the Madrid government met to discuss the matter, and concluded reluctantly that Galinsoga would have to resign.

A few months later, in May 1960, there was an incident at a Barcelona concert during a visit that Franco was paying to the city. As it was the hundreth anniversary of the birth of the Catalan poet Maragall, there was a rumour that Franco had permitted – for the first time since the civil war – a performance of the poet's 'Hymn to the Catalan flag'. In the event it was disallowed, and a part of the angry audience stood up and sang the hymn itself. The police then charged in and dragged away some of those singing. Over the next few days, others allegedly connected with the affair were also arrested and tortured.* On learning of the police brutality, crowds gathered outside the archbishop's palace in Barcelona, beseeching him to intercede with Franco. In spite of their pressure, which lasted several days, the archbishop chose to

---

*One of those tortured by the police was Jordi Pujol, a young aspiring banker, who had had little connection with the incident, although he had been one of the organizers of the anti-Galinsoga campaign. Pujol, a future leader of Catalan nationalism, was sentenced to seven years' imprisonment, of which he served thirty months.[57]

remain silent. From Montserrat, however, Escarré sent a strong protest.[58]

Catalonia's cultural 'renaissance' of the sixties – exemplified by singers such as Raimon and Serrat, and by the large increase in the number of books published in the vernacular – coincided with Manuel Fraga's period at the ministry of information. As in the rest of the country, his appointment brought with it a relaxation of censorship and a less oppressive atmosphere in cultural matters. In 1964 he made the almost heretical claim that the use of Catalan did not 'threaten the unity of the fatherland',[59] and two years later he permitted the publication of *Tele-Estel*, the first periodical in Catalan to be published since the civil war. Repression and censorship, however, still continued, and people who attended illegal gatherings were arrested and fined. In the late sixties an American anthropologist came across the mayor of a Catalan town who insisted on hearing the lyrics of any folk-song before it was sung.[60] In 1968 Fraga prevented Joan Manuel Serrat from taking part in the Eurovision song contest because he intended to sing in Catalan.

Towards the end of Franco's life, a prominent nationalist could claim that Catalonia had ended the phase of linguistic and cultural recovery, and all it now needed was the restoration of its political rights. The sixties and early seventies witnessed a growing feeling of self-confidence, a new optimism about the region's future. Among the large majority of Catalans there was broad agreement on the essential political changes that must be made after the dictatorship had gone. The 'Assembly of Catalonia', set up in 1971 by almost all the *antifranquista* forces in the region, had three specific aims: an amnesty for exiles and political prisoners, the restoration of democratic rights, and the re-establishment of the institutions and principles of the autonomy statute. This political consensus among Catalans, combined with their cultural revival and the strength of their traditions, gave them the confidence that after Franco's death they would be able to recover their rights without resorting to violence.

There was no such feeling of confidence in the Basque country, where nationalism aroused more controversy and where the local culture was still on the defensive. The Basques also had enjoyed a linguistic revival, and by the late sixties they were building their own schools to propagate their language. But political divisions in the Basque provinces were wider and deeper than in Catalonia. Among the Catalans, there were the normal political differences between Left and Right (although the latter were usually liberal conservatives rather than *franquistas*), but nearly all of them shared a feeling of Catalanism and a desire for political autonomy that fell short of independence. Socialists and communists were usually sympathetic to nationalism in Catalonia, whereas they had always been unsympathetic towards it in the Basque country.* Among Basques there was not only a Left/Right divide, but an even wider gulf between nationalists and anti-nationalists, which was made worse by the very intransigence of both sides. Nationalism had many more enemies in the Basque country – inside as well as outside its borders – than it had in Catalonia.

In exile, Basque nationalism remained, as always, divided into factions. Aguirre, president of the short-lived Basque government, continued to collaborate with politicians of the republic, and his government-in-exile included representatives of the Popular Front. His objective, shared by most of the PNV, was to overthrow Franco, bring back the republic, and develop Basque autonomy in accordance with the 1936 statute. But the 'pure' nationalists, heirs of Arana and the *Jagi-Jagi* faction, rejected this line. For the radicals, the statute was not enough. What mattered was the actual experience of government, those months of quasi-independence before the fall of Bilbao. The statute, the radicals claimed, had been superseded by events and was now redundant. 'I have known a sovereign government in a sovereign state,' Telesforo Monzón declared many years later. 'I have belonged to a government which had its own army, its own navy, its own passports and its own coinage. None of these were included in the supposed statute of 1936.' The Basques, he claimed, had fought Franco for their independence, not in defence of the Statute.†[63]

The PNV became an ineffective body in exile, its members

---

*'We socialists,' wrote a Bilbao socialist leader in 1902, 'have always fought against the nationalism of Arana because it is uncivilized and reactionary, and because we consider it inhuman . . . and based upon an unjust hatred of other Spaniards.'[61]

†Monzón, who broke with Aguirre on this issue, claimed that he had not bothered to read it, even though he was minister of the interior in a government which, but for the statute, would not have existed.[62]

dispersed and dispirited. It began to lose touch with its supporters in the Basque country, and with the ideas of the post-war generation of nationalists. In, the early fifties, a group of young Basque intellectuals, still attached to the PNV, set up a radical organization to promote a revival of Basque nationalist sentiment. Disenchanted with the caution and lethargy displayed by the ageing leaders of the PNV, they broke with the party in 1958, and the following year set up *Euskadi ta Askatasuna* (ETA – Basque Homeland and Liberty).

ETA's ideology was a direct descendant of the *sabinianos* and the *Jagi-Jagi* group. The early leaders based their ideas firmly on the teaching of Sabino Arana. They endorsed the historic myths propounded by him and other propagandists: the nobility and egalitarianism of Basque society, the complete independence it had enjoyed until the nineteenth century, the conquest and occupation of a foreign power. Everything that was wrong with the Basque country was the fault of Spain (except in the northern provinces where it could be attributed to France).

ETA began as a simple nationalist movement, with the independence of the Basque country as its sole objective. Like Arana, it was anti-marxist and had little interest in social change. Its roots were deep in the countryside of Vizcaya and Guipúzcoa, and it reacted to the second industrial revolution much as Arana had done to the first, complaining vigorously about the 'massive invasion' of Spanish immigrants.[64] But ETA soon abandoned Arana's racism, partly because some of its leaders were not of Basque origin, and partly because racist doctrines were no longer fashionable outside southern Africa. The claim of racial superiority was substituted by an assertion of cultural-linguistic superiority. ETA did not relinquish the idea that Basques were superior to Spaniards, but merely altered the basis of the claim. While the preservation of the race was for Arana the first priority, ETA concentrated on the preservation and diffusion of the language.

The movement's first ideologue was Federico Krutwig Sagredo, whose book *Vasconia* (published under the pseudonym Fernando Sarrailh de Ihartza) appeared in 1963. Krutwig accepted the bulk of Arana's ideas, except for his views on religion and race – he later said the PNV founder was more racist than Hitler[65] – and advocated a state with borders that included not only the Basque provinces but the ancient territories of the duchy of

Vasconia and the kingdom of Navarre.[66] He brought marxism and the theory of class struggle into Basque nationalism, and later claimed that the Basque country was a victim of colonialism and imperialism, exploited for the benefit of Madrid.★[67]

At the time of its establishment, ETA did not advocate armed struggle, and the question was not debated by its leaders until after 1962. Some suggested that Gandhi's policy of non-violence should be adopted, but they were over-ruled by others who argued that non-violence could only be successfully employed against 'civilized regimes'. It could not be used against a regime which gave a man a seven year sentence for burning a Spanish flag.[68] As it was not possible to negotiate with the dictatorship, remarked Krutwig, the Basques must accept a revolutionary war. In a phrase reminiscent of Mussolini, he declared that it was 'better to die like men than live like beasts deprived of their nationhood.'[69]

By the middle sixties there were three distinct currents inside ETA. One pressed for a guerrilla war, another promoted the idea of proletarian revolution, and a third stuck to the original line of anti-marxism and cultural resurgence. The 'proletarian' wing briefly achieved dominance, but the other two distrusted it and regarded its doctrines – which included the notion of working-class solidarity throughout Spain – as insufficiently Basque. At the organization's fifth assembly (held in two parts in December 1966 and March 1967) they clubbed together and threw the 'proletarians' out. Shortly afterwards, the 'cultural' wing withdrew from ETA, because it understood the folly of starting a guerrilla war in the Basque country.

The fifth assembly was the most crucial in ETA's history because it committed the organization to violence. Its leaders began a frenetic study of liberation movements in other parts of the world, receiving inspiration from contemporary struggles in Cuba, Algeria, Vietnam and Palestine.† Eventually they opted for

---

★This claim cannot be taken seriously. Anyone who travels around Spain and sees the quantity of Basque banks up and down the country will have a clear idea of which regions are economically exploited and which are not.

†ETA was very impressed by the zionist movement, and particularly by Menachem Begin, the terrorist leader who later became prime minister of Israel. The blowing-up of the King David Hotel in Jerusalem, in which 91 British and Arab lives were lost, was an exploit ETA was determined to emulate.[70]

a maoist strategy without seeming to notice that there might be a difference between a guerrilla war in a small, heavily-industrialized region, and one in a vast rural landscape about a thousand times larger.[71]

The armed struggle began in 1967, and the first deaths occurred in June of the following year: a *guardia civil* and an ETA leader. Two months later, ETA killed Melitón Manzanas, a police officer in Guipúzcoa well known for his brutal interrogation methods, and the government declared a state of exception. Over the next couple of years hundreds of Basques were rounded up and imprisoned. Between April and July 1969, 85 Basques were given prison terms for political offences. Five priests, who had gone on hunger strike to protest against police methods, were each given sentences of ten or twelve years. By the end of 1969, 21 priests were in the special prison block at Zamora, a figure that was later increased to 30.[72] In December 1970, after a farcical trial, a military court in Burgos sentenced six Basques to death (for their alleged participation in the murder of Manzanas) and nine others to gaol sentences averaging 35 years. (Two days later, the condemned men were reprieved by Franco and given prison terms of 30 years.)

Those *franquistas* who maintained that the Basque problem was merely a problem of order, should have been disabused by the events leading to the Burgos trial. These had demonstrated that heavy-handed repression simply stimulated ETA. The organization lost nearly all its leaders – many to Franco's prisons, others to exile abroad – but it found replacements. Far from dissuading Basques to join ETA, Burgos encouraged recruitment. It also won ETA the support of thousands of Basques, who identified with its struggle and regarded the convicted as national heroes.

The well-known cycle – violence, repression, more violence, more repression – carried on into the seventies. ETA continued its inner feuding, factions being repeatedly expelled for not following the ideological line of the moment. The victors of the fifth assembly, thrown out at the sixth in 1970, had regained control of ETA by 1972. In 1974 the most extreme among them split from the main organization and reconstituted themselves as ETA-militar. In response to the ruthless policy of the regime, this body became increasingly violent itself, concentrating almost all its energy on terrorism. In December 1973 it carried out its most celebrated operation, the assassination of Carrero Blanco in Madrid. The following September it committed its worst atrocity: in imitation of the blowing-up of the King David Hotel,[73] it destroyed the Cafe Rolando in central Madrid, killing 13 people and causing 84 further casualties.

PART TWO

The Transition 1975–79

7
The Return of the Monarchy

In 1947 General Franco proclaimed Spain a kingdom. This proclamation, which was made in the first article of the Law of Succession, was presumably intended to emphasize the difference between *franquista* Spain and the Spain of the Second Republic. It was not an announcement heralding the return of the monarchy. The second article of the law confirmed Franco as Head of State, and the sixth gave him the power to designate a successor either as king or regent. Spain thus became a kingdom without a king, or even an heir-apparent, since Franco did not choose his successor until 1969.

The *Caudillo* held strong views on the type of monarchy that would succeed him. As he told Don Juan in a letter written in 1942, it should be modelled on the 'revolutionary, totalitarian' monarchy of the Catholic Kings and their immediate successors, Charles V and Philip II.[1] Many years later he stressed that the new monarchy would be 'traditional, Catholic, social and representative', a 'monarchy of the *Movimiento Nacional*', inspired by the rising of 1936.[2] There could be no question of a liberal monarchy because, according to Carrero Blanco, it would make Spain a vassal of England and lead to communism.[3] Thus the *franquistas* took pains to point out that, although the royal family itself might be restored to the throne, they were not restoring the old, decadent monarchy of Isabella II or Alfonso XIII. When Franco talked of bringing back the monarchy, he was careful not to use the verb *restaurar*, which means to restore, but *instaurar*, which means to set up or establish.

The Lausanne Manifesto of 1945 had shown Franco that the heir to the throne envisaged the type of monarchy that was anathema to the spirit of 18 July. In the *Caudillo*'s eyes, Don Juan was a liberal anglophile, badly advised and under the influence of freemasons.* Franco decided, perhaps as early as 1943, that he would not be succeeded by such a man. He did not tell Don Juan of his intentions, however, and continued to send advice to the exiled pretender, asking 'God to enlighten your understanding, forgive your errors and curse those who direct you from the straight path'.[5] The behaviour and attitudes of Don Juan were no doubt partly responsible for Franco's decision to delay the choice of a successor. But the delay did not matter to Franco because he had clearly decided to remain Head of State until his death. The return of the monarchy was going to be a slow process, accomplished in stages, and it was not going to interfere with his rebuilding of the true Spain.

Franco brought back the red and yellow flag in 1936, and the following year he re-established the Royal March as the country's national anthem. But although he professed to be a monarchist,[6] he made little effort to satisfy monarchical sentiment until his proclamation of 1947. Even the Law of Succession irritated the monarchists, and Don Juan angrily denounced it, refusing to accept that his right to the throne was in any way dependent on a decision of Franco. Since Alfonso XIII's abdication in his favour, Don Juan's right to the Spanish throne was indeed unquestionable, and was regarded as such by the overwhelming majority of monarchists. He could not accept that Franco should remain Head of State, or that the dictator should have the right to choose his successor.

In 1948, a year after the Law of Succession, Don Juan had an interview with Franco on the *Caudillo*'s boat. Although Franco tried to turn the conversation towards uncontroversial subjects such as fishing and shooting, Don Juan insisted that they talked about politics. Franco remarked that, although Spain was now a kingdom, the monarchy was not strong enough to govern. Don Juan declared that it was absurd for Spain to be a kingdom while any type of monarchist activity was illegal. 'How am I going to

*Freemasonry was one of Franco's obsessions, and much of the world's evil he ascribed to it. He believed that, among others, Mendès-France, Perón, the Italian Communist Party and the Gibraltarian government were controlled by masonic lodges. He thought that freemasonry was very close to communism and maintained that 'the bastion of international masonry' was the *New York Times*.[4]

send my son to Spain' he asked, 'when it is considered a crime to shout "Long Live the King!", when all kinds of monarchical propaganda are forbidden, and when my supporters are fined and persecuted?'[7] The previous year Don Juan had held the first meeting of his privy council in Estoril, but the Duke of Alba was not present, because the government had refused to give him a passport. 'It is the first time in the history of Spain', complained the nobleman, 'that a duke of Alba has not been permitted to go to the summons of his king.'[8]

Franco and Don Juan held two further interviews, in 1954 and 1960, in a private house in Extremadura. Although the two men disliked and distrusted each other, they needed to remain in touch. On both occasions Franco told shooting stories and treated the pretender to lectures on Spanish history. But the principal subject of conversation was the education of Prince Juan Carlos. Franco wanted the prince to be educated in Spain, and the two men agreed that he should attend the Zaragoza military academy as well as receive naval and air force training before studying at Madrid University.

By the early 1960s a number of prominent *franquistas*, including Carrero Blanco and López Rodó, had come to the conclusion that Franco's successor should be Juan Carlos. There was an array of possible candidates, including the carlist family of Borbón-Parma, and the Borbón-Dampierre nephews of Don Juan. But strong arguments could be made against all of them: the Borbón-Parma family was French, while Don Jaime, the elder brother of Don Juan and father of Alfonso and Gonzalo de Borbón-Dampierre, had long since renounced his rights. López Rodó and his associates knew that monarchist support in Spain was not strong, and that it would be even weaker if the main Borbón line was discarded in favour of some lesser branch. Thus, if Franco had excluded Don Juan, his son became the only plausible candidate. During the middle sixties, when Franco was already in his seventies, López Rodó persistently tried to persuade the dictator to choose Juan Carlos. The *franquistas* knew that the prince was a risk, but they hoped and believed that, after his Spanish education and a long spell in the armed forces, he would free himself of his father's influence and embrace the idea of a *franquista* monarchy.

While Juan Carlos remained the most likely choice, other ideas were being canvassed in *franquista* circles. A number of traditionalists had gone over to Don Juan in 1957, but other carlists remained faithful to Don Hugo, in spite of his failure to attain Spanish nationality. They were delighted by Hugo's marriage to Princess Irene of Holland in 1964, but their hopes collapsed when he and his family were expelled from Spain in 1968. Another idea, promoted by anti-monarchists inside the *Falange*, was to set up a regency under one of the generals, possibly General Muñoz Grandes. Two of the proponents of this plan, Admiral Nieto Antúnez and the falangist minister Solís, later espoused the cause of Alfonso de Borbón-Dampierre.[9] One pretender who does not appear to have received support from anyone was the Archduke Francesco-José Carlos Habsburgo-Lorena y de Borbón, who put himself forward as the true carlist heir in January 1969.

After sustained pressure from Carrero and López Rodó, Franco finally agreed to name Juan Carlos as his successor in July 1969. Against the wishes of Don Juan, the prince accepted the designation, explaining to his father that although he did not wish to usurp his position he believed he had no choice in the matter. On 16 July Don Juan received a letter from Franco asking him to sacrifice personal ambitions for the good of the country. Two days later, while the *franquista* establishment was celebrating the anniversary of the 1936 uprising in the gardens of La Granja, Don Juan's reply was transmitted to Fraga, the then minister of information. Fraga's response to a statement which was predictably critical of both the decision and the regime which made it, was typically *franquista*. He claimed that it constituted an attack on the Fundamental Laws and therefore could not be published. When part of it did finally appear in a newspaper, Don Juan's words were distorted to ensure that they contained no suggestion of criticism.[10]

The *Cortes* voted in favour of Franco's choice by 419 votes to 19 with 9 abstentions. Juan Carlos thus became the designated successor and spent much of the next six years at the dictator's side at official functions. His position was not entirely secure, however, because Franco had the right, which he had granted himself in the Law of Succession, to change his mind.

The *juanistas* refused to accept that Franco's decision meant the end of Don Juan's hopes of succeeding to the throne. They opposed Juan Carlos not simply out of loyalty to his father but because they, like the *franquistas*, believed that the prince would be only a monarchical facade, and that behind him the regime would continue as before. 'The real choice,' wrote Calvo Serer in *Le Monde*, 'is between a monarchy camouflaging a dictatorship . . . and a legitimate monarchy which would establish modern democracy in Spain.'[11] He argued that, as it would be impossible for Juan Carlos to open up the regime without breaking his oath of loyalty to Franco, it would be better for him to abdicate in favour of his father as soon as he became king.

Neither the partisans of Don Juan nor the supporters of other candidates were strong enough to influence Franco. In July 1974, when the *Caudillo* appeared to be on his death bed, he handed over his powers as head of state to Juan Carlos. Forty-five days later he took them back again, and Juan Carlos returned to the shadows until finally he became king in November 1975. On his accession he encountered a certain amount of goodwill but little admiration or enthusiasm. Few people expected him to be anything more than what the *franquistas* had intended – a *franquista* with baubles. It was well known that he was no intellectual, that his reading tastes were simple, and that his abilities seemed confined chiefly to yachting and other sports. Moreover, he had not created much of an impression during his short period as head of state in the previous year. He had made no major pronouncements, and had spent much of the time in his holiday home. His critics seemed to think he should have been making promises of liberalization at a time when Franco was still alive and *franquistas* were in full control of the state.

The new king was an unknown quantity and few people knew whether his ideas had been influenced more by Franco or by his father. On Don Juan's side were liberal public opinion, the European leaders (some of whom came to the coronation) and most of the Church: at a service to celebrate his accession, the Archbishop of Madrid declared that liberty should be neither a concession nor a subject for negotiation because it was a basic right to be enjoyed by everyone. Ranged against the liberals were the memory of the dead *Caudillo*, the formidable group of *franquista* politicians who had been giving advice to the prince since the sixties, and the armed forces in which he had served for so many years. But the *franquistas* lacked a single, dominant figure to guide the king. There had been such a man, Admiral Carrero

Blanco, but he had been assassinated by ETA two years earlier. Had he still been prime minister, in place of the hesitant Arias, Juan Carlos would have found it impossible to make a democratic opening without a fierce confrontation with the *franquistas*. Moral considerations aside, the murder of Carrero was probably the only thing the Basque guerrillas ever did which furthered the cause of Spanish democracy.

Later it became clear that the king had been all along on the side of Don Juan. He realized that it was neither possible nor desirable to carry on with the dictatorship after the dictator had died. Like his father, he wanted to be a constitutional monarch and Spain to be a modern democracy. But he could not tell this to the country without jeopardizing his whole strategy. Spanish democrats did not understand his predicament and were thus disappointed when he made an ambiguous speech at his investiture which contained only a few hints of change. They were also annoyed by his refusal to grant an immediate and far reaching amnesty for political prisoners.

Juan Carlos was right to go slowly. He knew that kings were not popular in Spain, chiefly because the country had been ruled by so many bad ones over the previous two centuries. Franco once said that, if the Spaniards were asked to choose between a monarchy and a republic, the monarchists would not get ten per cent of the vote.[12] Even the monarchists themselves admitted that they were few in number, and the reason that people were prepared to tolerate a king was because they believed he might be a force for stability at a critical period. Among the political opposition Juan Carlos had little support, the Left being divided between republicans and those prepared to accept a monarchy under Don Juan. Among the *franquistas*, he received support only because he had sworn to observe the Principles of the *Movimiento Nacional*. Half a century earlier, his grandfather, Alfonso XIII, had betrayed the constitution by appointing a dictator, and several years later he was rejected by the Spanish people and sent into exile. If Juan Carlos had broken his oath and ignored the Principles, he might well have been faced by a *franquista* revolt backed by the army. As he had little active support among the rest of the population, he would probably have fulfilled the prophecy of the communist leader Carrillo, and gone down in history as Juan the Brief.

Among the advice which the king was receiving from Spain's impatient democrats, was the suggestion that he should govern by decree rather than through the existing institutions.[13] Juan Carlos did in fact threaten to call a referendum or use exceptional measures if the institutions were consistently obstructive. But he knew that it would be dangerous to do so, as such a course would incur the profound resentment of the *franquistas*. He therefore decided that the only prudent policy was to persuade the *franquistas* themselves, or at any rate the more moderate of them, to reform their own institutions. This was bound to be a difficult and lengthy business, involving threats and cajolery, but at least it would make it difficult to claim that Juan Carlos had broken his promise to Franco.

The key figure in the king's strategy was Torcuato Fernández Miranda, whom he made president of both the *Cortes* and the Council of the Realm. These appointments dismayed the democrats because Fernández Miranda was a man with an irreproachable *franquista* past. As minister of the *Movimiento*, he had ensured that there would be no law on political associations while Carrero was alive. But he had also been tutor to the king, and Juan Carlos knew him to be both faithful and flexible. Fernández Miranda was a 'behind-the-scenes' figure with a fine legal mind and a somewhat machiavellian reputation. He understood the institutions as well as anyone, and he was the ideal person to plan their dismantlement. Within a short time of his appointments, it had become known that he was the man selected by the king for the task of persuading the *franquistas* to reform.

Juan Carlos needed a prime minister who would co-operate with Fernández Miranda, and he knew that Carlos Arias, who had headed the government for the past two years, was not the right man. But he did not dare to make too many changes at the same time, so he asked Arias to remain and bring some reformers into his cabinet. The confirmation of Arias as prime minister was a depressing piece of news for the country's democrats, because they knew from past experience that it was impossible to convert him to democracy. Nevertheless, during the formation of his government, he told his future ministers that his programme was to go steadily and irreversibly towards the complete democratization of the political system.[14] He even told the press that all parties, with the exception of the communists, should be recognized.[15]

The new cabinet was largely a mixture of reformers, men of the *Movimiento*, and military conservatives. Two of the leading *aperturistas* joined the government, José María de Areilza as minister of foreign affairs and Manuel Fraga as minister of the interior. Antonio Garrigues, an elderly liberal who, like Areilza, had once been ambassador to Washington, became minister of justice. From the far right of the political map, Admiral Pita de Veiga was confirmed as naval minister, while General Fernando de Santiago was appointed vice-president for defence matters. Arias had intended to keep the long-serving Solís as minister of the *Movimiento*, but Fernández Miranda went to see him with another suggestion. He proposed that the new minister should be Adolfo Suárez, a young and ambitious politician from Avila who had once been the vice-secretary general of the *Movimiento*. Arias argued that Franco would have wished him to keep Solís in his position, and only agreed to appoint Suárez when Fernández Miranda suggested moving Solís to the ministry of labour.[16]

The government was thus disunited from the beginning. As Areilza noted in his diary, it contained some people who wanted to reform the system radically, and others who wished to change it as little as possible.[17] Although he himself had a *franquista* past that went back to the thirties, Areilza was the leading advocate of reform. For some years he had believed that his mission in life was to civilize the Spanish Right, and then to persuade it to carry out political reform. In spite of his close association with fascism during his youth – a link which in later life he went to great lengths to gloss over – Areilza was an urbane, intelligent man, and a good choice as foreign minister. His favourite tactic in his new job was to fly around Europe announcing the imminence of democracy, and hope that the ponderous and reluctant government would back him up. His chief role, or so he saw it, was to gain European support for his policy. Within a week of his appointment, he was in Paris prophesying that there would be general elections before the end of the following year. He also told a press conference that Santiago Carrillo should be given a Spanish passport.

Like his former friends in the Bunker, Arias was horrified by the behaviour of his foreign minister. But he did not dare to reprimand him because Areilza had only joined the government on condition that its chief objective was the establishment of democracy.[18] It is difficult to understand what was going on in the prime minister's head when he formed his government, because plainly he was not prepared to set up a democracy similar to those in western Europe. Perhaps he thought he could merely fudge the issue, enact a few reforms, call the result democracy, and hope for the best. Arias was a timid and anxious man, and in the photographs of that period his expression resembles that of a puzzled monkey. In his office he kept a huge portrait of Franco – there was only a small photograph of the king in the room – and he seems to have spent much of his time wondering what Franco would have done in his position. When one of his ministers suggested he should meet the veteran christian democrat, Gil Robles, Arias replied, 'Would Franco have received [him]? No, right? Well then, neither will I.'[19] His reactions were always those of a loyal *franquista*. When another minister mentioned that a small, unknown Parisian theatre was producing a play that was apparently disrespectful of Franco, Arias's reaction was to suggest that a play disrespectful of De Gaulle or Giscard should be performed in Madrid.[20]

If Arias was worried by the shadow of General Franco, he was equally perturbed by the criticism of his *franquista* friends. One day he was out shooting with some of them when he received a telephone call informing him of some strikes in Madrid. Upon telling this news to his fellow hunters, they unanimously advised him to be tough and uncompromising in his reaction. Arias, apparently, was deeply impressed by their attitude.[21] Strikers, like separatists and communists, could not be tolerated by a true *franquista*. Nor could pornographers. On one occasion, the prime minister was handed a document detailing the quantity and variety of sexual acts that were being shown in Madrid cinemas. He was very upset and proposed taking immediate measures to deal with this wave of eroticism.[22] With all this, it was perhaps not surprising that, only two months after the formation of a government which was supposed to bring in democracy, Arias should have announced to a mixed committee of the government and the National Council: 'What I want is to continue *franquismo*. And while I am here or elsewhere in public life, I will be nothing but a strict follower of *franquismo* in all its aspects . . .'[23]

Predictably, the Arias government was not a success. It was

muddled, divided, and unsure of what it was meant to be doing. The cabinet meetings did not consist of discussions about policy but of long statements from the ministers about the affairs of their particular departments. They were also extremely lengthy. In his diary Areilza recorded how the meetings habitually lasted ten or twelve hours without settling anything. He became so obsessed about such time-wasting that he took to asking the ministers of other countries how long their cabinet meetings lasted. He discovered that in Spain they took three times longer than anywhere else.[24]

At no time did the first government of the monarchy have a coherent policy on political reform. The leading ministers all made contradictory statements about their real aims. Only Areilza called unequivocally for the establishment of full democracy. Fraga, who had been regarded as the regime's leading reformist for the past ten years, also called for democracy, but of a more limited kind. It was to be democracy as defined by Fraga, one that excluded communists, separatists, and anarchists.[25] As for Arias, his statements were usually so obscure that they were open to a variety of interpretations. Observers only agreed on the fact that they were highly conservative. In his major speech to the *Cortes* on 28 January 1976, Arias talked about 'Spanish democracy', with the inference that this was something quite different from the democracies of other countries. He talked vaguely about reforms and political parties, but he said nothing about free trade unions, he merely hinted at general elections, and he announced that there would not be a wide-ranging political amnesty. When he referred to Franco, which he did repeatedly, or when he talked about public order or other subjects close to their hearts, he was cheered by the *procuradores*. At the end of his speech he was given an ovation because they knew he had spoken not as a democrat but as a sympathizer of the Bunker.[26]

So it went on: much confusing and contradictory talk of political reform, and little action. A joint committee of the government and members of the National Council was set up to discuss proposals for reform. But the Bunker was sufficiently entrenched in the National Council to make the committee useless. The Council was prepared to make some concessions over the suffrage, but only on condition that there was no danger of the Right losing power. If one chamber was to be elected by universal suffrage, it argued, the other, possessing equal powers, would have to be appointed.

Nevertheless, in spite of so much muddle and hesitancy, the government did finally put forward a number of reforms. These were chiefly the work of Garrigues, the justice minister, and Fraga, the minister of the interior. In February the government agreed to modify the law on the prevention of terrorism and to introduce a bill on the right to hold political meetings and demonstrations. The Law of Assembly was debated in the *Cortes* in May and passed almost unanimously. It was not, however, a very liberal law. Anyone who wished to demonstrate had to ask for the government's approval at least ten days before the event was due to take place. Even then the government reserved the right to name the place where the demonstration might be held, or even to ban it altogether.

The two crucial reform measures were a law on associations and the reform of the Penal Code, which were debated by the *Cortes* at the beginning of June. By then, however, the Bunker had decided that the reforms were going too far. Some of the Right had, of course, been upset by even the mildest changes suggested by Arias, and in March Blas Piñar had told a rally in Madrid: 'If the government does not enforce the basic laws of General Franco, we, the men of *Fuerza Nueva*, will take to the streets and do it ourselves.'[27] But the Bunker did not organize itself properly until the middle of May, when 126 *procuradores* signed a statement opposing the government's reformist policies. Shortly afterwards, it mobilized its supporters to attack a bill which proposed to legalize political parties so long as they were not excluded by the reformed Penal Code, and on condition that they respected the Fundamental Laws.

The Bunker's assault was led in the *Cortes* by the old falangist leader, Raimundo Fernández Cuesta, who claimed that political parties were less democratic than the system of organic democracy based on Primo de Rivera's three representative elements: the family, the municipality and the syndicate. He was followed by other speakers who condemned the attempt to dismantle a system which had brought peace and unprecedented prosperity. As the principal author of the bill, Fraga should have been the minister to defend it before the *Cortes*. But Arias was irritated at being constantly upstaged by Fraga and Areilza, so he gave the task to the almost unknown minister of the *Movimiento*, Adolfo Suárez. In an impressive speech, Suárez disarmed the *Cortes* by praising the dictatorship, its attainment of peace and social justice, its achievements of cultural and material well-being. He described the reform not as the demolition of what had already been achieved, but as the completion of Franco's work. Spain was now a pluralist society, and the new law would simply recognize and legalize those forces which already existed.[28]

The minister's speech impressed people on all sides. Areilza noted that Suárez had said what Arias should have been saying six months earlier.[29] On the morning of 9 June, at the end of the debate, the Bunker could drum up only 91 *procuradores*, or one fifth of the *Cortes*, to vote against the bill. A majority among almost all types of *franquistas* was prepared to trust the government, except for the armed forces. Of the fifteen generals in the *Cortes*, only one, the vice-president of the government, voted in favour of the bill.[30]

The Bunker reacted badly to its defeat, and in the afternoon of the same day, when the debate on the reform of the Penal Code began, the atmosphere in the *Cortes* was tense. This reform was crucial for the government because it complemented the earlier bill. According to the existing law, it was an offence to set up or even belong to a political party, and therefore the Penal Code had to be changed if the new Law of Associations was to be effective. Considering the ease with which the first bill had been passed, there should have been no problem with the second. But the mood in the *Cortes* had changed, and the tension increased when it was learnt that a local *jefe* of the *Movimiento* had been assassinated in the Basque country. As *procuradores* of the Bunker launched an impassioned attack on the bill, government ministers discussed what should be done next. Areilza and Fraga urged Arias to carry on and submit the bill to a vote. But others, including Suárez, advised him not to risk a defeat. Arias hesitated, as usual, but in the end he decided to withdraw the bill and send it back to be re-drafted by the Justice Committee. It was a disastrous decision, wiping out the success that had been achieved only that morning. Moreover, the government now looked ridiculous: Spain was left with a law which permitted political parties, while it retained a Penal Code which prohibited them.

The government's credibility, dented by its dithering attitude to political reform, was further damaged by its handling of day-to-day affairs. The problems which confronted it were admittedly considerable. The government had to deal simultaneously with political terrorism, the activities of the opposition, a huge increase in labour disputes and a disastrous economic situation. In the first year of the monarchy, there were more than ten times as many strikes as there had been in the last year of the dictatorship.[31] These had political causes – the labour force putting pressure on the government to bring in democratic reforms – as well as economic roots. Arias had first come to power in January 1974, and his period in office coincided with the beginning of the world economic recession. The prime minister had little enough experience of politics, but he knew nothing at all about economics. In any case, it seemed to him more urgent to solve the political problems than to attempt to deal with the economic difficulties. Until 1973, Spain had enjoyed a high growth rate, low unemployment and large currency reserves, and the economic ministers did not seem to realize that these would be affected by the recession and the rise in oil prices. Very little, therefore, was done to adjust the economy to the new circumstances, and the result was catastrophic. Inflation reached 20 per cent by the middle of 1976, bankruptcies and unemployment soared, and the balance of payments showed a sharp deficit. Industrial investment and productivity both dropped together. When the minister of finance proposed taking drastic action, he was opposed by most of the other ministers. The political situation was considered far too delicate for the cabinet to demand austerity. Until the question of political reform was settled one way or the other, the economic problems would have to wait.[32]

The government's neglect of the economy, coupled with its hesitations and failures over political reform, did much to weaken its popularity. So did its attitude to the problems of order. Fraga had joined the government with a liberal reputation, which he had cultivated during his previous two years as ambassador to London. But it was the kind of liberalism which shone brightly when compared to someone like Carrero Blanco, yet looked very dim when compared to the real thing. Moreover, even if Fraga was a liberal in his ideas, he was not so in his behaviour. He was perhaps the right man to liberalize the press laws in 1966, but he was certainly not the man to keep order during a period of political ferment ten years later. Fraga was a natural 'law and order' politician, and his behaviour as the nation's policeman during the first half of 1976 lost him his liberal reputation.

For the first month or so, there were few problems, and Fraga instructed the police to behave with restraint. But he over-reacted as soon as he was seriously challenged, by ETA, by the Communist Party, or by strikers in Vitoria. He became increasingly arrogant and assertive, insisting on tough responses to situations which required sensitive handling. The man who saw himself as a centrist politician, a practitioner of 'the art of the possible',[33] turned out to be a typical *franquista* in government. His ally Areilza wondered what had happened to him, since his manner at cabinet meetings was almost always aggressive, violent and threatening.[34] His outbursts against ETA and the Communist Party were frequent and even hysterical, and his policy towards both was that of a hardline authoritarian. While he arrested those communist leaders he could lay hands upon, he demanded emergency powers against the Basques. 'With military courts and the death penalty', he claimed, against all available evidence, 'I will get rid of the Basque problem within a year, cost what it may.'[35]

Fraga's attitude towards the opposition was particularly strange for someone professing to be a democrat. At the end of March the *antifranquista* opposition at last united, the *Junta Democrática* (led by the communists) and the *Plataforma de Convergencia Democrática* (led by socialists) coming together to form *Coordinación Democrática*. The new body promptly issued a manifesto in which it affirmed its opposition to the regime and the policy of the government. Fraga's reaction was to invite half a dozen of his fellow ministers to the best restaurant in Madrid, and inform them that he was going to arrest the leaders of *Coordinación Democrática*.[36] When each of his guests advised him to be cautious, Fraga replied that the group contained communists who could not be tolerated. The opposition reacted to the subsequent arrests by calling for a demonstration on 3 April. Although this was quickly banned by Fraga, several thousand people defied him and took to the streets of Madrid. Predictably, the event led to a confrontation with the police, and to the arrest of another hundred people.

Fraga was in effect treating the opposition as Franco had done, not as his political opponents but as the enemies of the country.

Yet Franco was running a dictatorship where opposition was not tolerated, while Fraga was supposedly trying to lead the country to democracy. If he wanted his opponents to co-operate in the new democratic system he was proposing, surely it was foolish to persecute them in the meantime? But the point was lost on Fraga. Referring to *Coordinación Democrática* in an interview, he said: 'I do not recognize their position and I despise them – not all of them. Mainly I think it is a group of fellow travellers of the Communist Party, so I do not take it seriously.'[37] Given this type of response to a body which contained most of the *antifranquista* opposition, it was only logical that the leaders of *Coordinación Democrática* should have been unimpressed by the democratic claims of the Arias ministry.

The king's first government lasted barely six months, and for most of its short existence there was constant speculation about its successor. It was widely recognized that the vacillations and mistakes of the Arias cabinet – what the foreign minister termed 'the comedy of errors'[38] – could not be allowed to continue. In March the magazine *Cambio 16* called for the government's resignation on the grounds that it neither would not could govern.[39] Around the king and his advisers there was a mood of exasperation. Don Juan warned his son to get rid of Arias or the monarchical experiment would collapse.[40] As for the king himself, he could not understand what had happened to his prime minister: Arias was suspicious of everybody, he could not make a decision, his government was incoherent.[41] Juan Carlos was an indiscreet man who found it difficult to keep his opinions to himself. During the spring he was interviewed by Arnaud de Borchgrave, and on 26 April *Newsweek* published an article in which it was claimed that the king considered Arias to be an unmitigated disaster. Although the article was not repudiated by Juan Carlos, Arias continued in office for another two months, resigning only when asked to do so on 1 July. He was rewarded for his services by being made a marquis and a grandee of Spain.

Arias had been a bad prime minister from the beginning, ever since he succeeded Carrero Blanco in January 1974. Franco had chosen him because he was a conservative with a reverence for 'order', but he was not really a politician, certainly not a statesman. In government he revealed himself as a man of small imagination, with little idea of what he ought to be doing.

Cabanillas, whom he sacked as minister of information, called him 'the sphinx without a secret', and it was a good description.[42] After the king's accession, Arias presided hesitantly over a government which was supposed to bring about a change he did not believe in. He had always been a loyal servant of Franco and of the regime of 18 July, and that was what he remained after their demise.

8
Suárez and the Defeat of the Right

The logical successor to Arias was Areilza; six months earlier it would have been Fraga. The two reformers had been by far the most conspicuous members of the Arias government. While it was generally agreed, however, that Areilza had been a successful foreign minister, few people thought that Fraga had distinguished himself as minister of the interior. Besides, Fraga's temperament was against him, and it was felt that the king would not appreciate his hectoring and authoritarian manner. Areilza, therefore, was the favourite, and it was outside his house that journalists congregated on 3 July, the day that the Council of the Realm met to choose the *terna* – a list of three candidates from which Juan Carlos would select the prime minister.

Areilza realized, however, that there was no chance of his name appearing in the *terna* unless the councillors knew that he was the king's choice. The Council of the Realm was a highly conservative body which included among its sixteen members such luminaries of the Bunker as Girón and Antonio María de Oriol. Areilza, like Fraga, was too liberal for them. They would only have voted for him after massive pressure from the king and the president of the council, Torcuato Fernández Miranda. But Juan Carlos was not prepared to interfere. His policy was still to persuade the *franquistas* to reform their own institutions, not to bring in a distrusted liberal to do it for them.

Thirty-two candidates were discussed by the council, thirteen of whom were eliminated without a ballot. Seven more were quickly voted out, including Fraga and Areilza, who each received only five positive votes. Various lengthy and complicated electoral procedures were then used by Fernández Miranda to reduce the remaining twelve to nine, then to six, and eventually to three. The final list consisted of two former ministers, Silva Muñoz and López Bravo, who received fifteen and thirteen votes respectively, and the current minister of the *Movimiento*, Adolfo Suárez, who came third with twelve votes. Fernández Miranda told waiting journalists that he was now 'in a position to give the king what he has asked me for', and went off to see Juan Carlos. Whether he was merely referring to the list of candidates, or whether he was alluding to the fact that the king had asked him to ensure that a certain name was in the *terna*, was not clear. There is no doubt, however, that Fernández Miranda employed his elaborate and confusing voting systems simply to get the almost unknown Suárez onto the list. Once that had been achieved, the rest was a formality. Suárez was summoned to the Zarzuela Palace that evening, and asked to form a government.[1]

The new prime minister was forty-three years old. He had good looks, great charm, and immense ambition. He came from a lower middle-class family in a small town near Avila, and was consequently regarded by some of Madrid's 'sophisticated' political class as a provincial upstart. It was said that he was slightly too well-dressed, the parting of his hair never deviated, the right smile was invariably assumed for the photographers. He was an astute man, with a natural understanding of politics, but he was ill at ease with intellectuals. A man such as Areilza, who could speak five languages and discuss a large number of subjects, made him feel inferior.[2] Suárez himself appears not to have had any cultural interests, and a hostile biographer has even claimed that he never managed to read a whole book from beginning to end.[3] He followed football closely, he enjoyed swimming and playing tennis, but he allowed himself few other distractions. According to one of his associates, he was 'a man programmed purely and simply for politics'.[4]

From his student days, Suárez's ambition had been to become a senior official of the *franquista* regime. But a young man from an unknown provincial family needed patronage if he was to be successful in the nepotistic world of *franquista* officialdom. So in 1956 he joined the office of Fernando Herrero Tejedor, the civil governor of Avila. Although Herrero remained his principal patron until he was killed in a car accident in 1975, there were several others. Suárez was a natural ADC, deferential and eager to be helpful, and he attached himself to a number of senior *franquistas*: Alonso Vega, Carrero and, most important of all, Fernández Miranda. This assiduity bordered on sycophancy. He was prepared to go a long way to please his superiors, even, it is said, to the extent of holidaying in the flat next door to the interior minister if it might help his career. In the last years of the Franco regime he rented a house near La Granja apparently so that he could invite distinguished people to swim, dress and dine with him on the day of the 18 July celebrations.[5]

In 1967 Suárez was elected to the *Cortes* as a *procurador* from Avila, and the following year he became civil governor of Segovia. In 1969 he moved to Madrid to take up the post of director-general of the national radio and television company. After these early successes, his career went into eclipse until March 1975, when Herrero Tejedor, recently appointed as minister of the *Movimiento* came to the rescue of his protégé and made him his deputy. Within a few months both Franco and Herrero were dead, and Suárez was a minister in the king's first government. His old patrons were either dead or out of power, but he no longer needed them: he had had the good fortune to attract the country's two most powerful men, the king and Fernández Miranda. During the Arias government he saw both of them regularly. He went to football matches with Juan Carlos, and he went to Fernández Miranda when he needed political advice. Months before his appointment, the two men had marked out Suárez as a possible prime minister. In June, when Suárez delivered his successful speech to the *Cortes* on political reform, he confirmed their hopes. Three weeks later, Arias was dismissed.

Adolfo Suárez was a clever choice as the man to carry out the strategy devised by the king and Fernández Miranda. To begin with, he was a card-carrying *franquista*, not one who had ever been involved in repression or corruption, but a *franquista* nevertheless, and one who was trusted by other *franquistas*. In May 1976, when the National Council of the *Movimiento* had to elect a new member, the *franquista* councillors had preferred Suárez to Franco's son-in-law (who had asked for their vote 'in the name of the *Caudillo* Franco') by 66 votes to 25.[6] Secondly, he understood the regime – he had been in the *Cortes* and had occupied posts in the *Movimiento* – and he knew where the power lay. And thirdly, he had few political principles and fewer political ideas. In 1975 he was happy to wear the blue shirt of the *Falange* and make pro-Franco speeches. A year later he was sounding as if he had been a democrat all his life. The hatred which many on the Spanish Right have felt for Suárez stems from the time of his apostasy.[7] He considered himself to be a loyal *franquista* in 1975, a christian democrat in 1976, and a social democrat in 1977.[8] In fact he was none of these things. To him they were merely labels which could be altered or discarded whenever it was convenient to do so. Politics was the art of getting on with the job, compromising where necessary and refusing to allow ideological considerations to interfere with the running of government.

Following the news of Suárez's appointment, shares fell drastically on all three of Spain's stock exchanges. Throughout the country the announcement was greeted with dismay, astonishment and indignation. The disappointed candidates were furious. Fraga fired off letters to the king and to Suárez saying that he did not wish to continue as a minister. His private opinion was that the prime minister designate was a nonentity, and that his government would collapse before long. Four other ministers also announced their unwillingness to continue, including the other well-known reformers, Areilza and Antonio Garrigues. Both men were amazed by the choice and believed that it represented a step backwards. They thought Suárez had been appointed to slow down the reform programme and to set up a 'facade democracy'.[9] A few days later, when it was known that Suárez's plan was in fact to accelerate the pace of reform, they appear to have regretted their decision. Garrigues spoke to Alfonso Osorio, the minister closest to Suárez, and suggested that Areilza would, after all, accept his old post.[10] But it was too late; the government was almost complete. Besides, Suárez was relieved that he would not have to deal with Fraga and Areilza in cabinet. The two older *aperturistas* had dominated the previous government, and Suárez, inhibited, inexperienced and over-shadowed, had seldom spoken. The last thing he now wanted was to be overawed by his own ministers.

Thus the second government of the monarchy was weaker than its predecessor. This was partly the fault of those ministers who refused to co-operate out of pique, partly the fault of Suárez who made no attempt to persuade them to change their minds, and partly the fault of Juan Carlos himself. The king liked and respected Areilza, and much of the success he had enjoyed abroad, on his visits to Washington and elsewhere, he owed to the preparations and advice of his foreign minister. In July 1976 he chose not to make Areilza prime minister, a decision which in the circumstances may well have been correct, but he should have informed him of his plans. Had Areilza been summoned and told that the appointment of Suárez was designed to speed up the reform programme, he would have remained as foreign minister and the government would have benefited from the experience of one of the country's wisest politicians.

Experience was the quality which the new government most obviously lacked. Excluding the four military ministers who remained unchanged from the previous cabinet, most of its remaining members were in their early forties. Since the government was not expected to survive for long, no well-known politicians were prepared to risk their careers by joining it. In the end Suárez had to rely on a number of young, right-wing christian democrats whom few people had heard of. The most influential was Osorio, the second vice-president and the prime minister's right-hand man. Three ministers came from the *Tácito* group, and four, including Osorio, were members of the *Unión Democrática Española*, the association set up the previous year by Silva Muñoz.

The dismay caused by the designation of Suárez was aroused once more by the announcement of his government. There was some relief that its composition was not as *franquista* as Suárez's past had led people to fear, but there was general agreement that its talents were second-rate. Ricardo de La Cierva, a conservative historian who later became one of Suárez's ministers, recalled the judgement of the Conde de Mayalde on the politicians of a previous regime: 'they have all our defects and none of our virtues'. In a celebrated article in *El País*, which he entitled 'What an error! What an immense error!' La Cierva described the cabinet as 'the first *franquista* government of the post-Franco era', and predicted its imminent collapse.[11] Three other aspiring politicians, all of them future collaborators of Suárez, described his cabinet variously as trivial, third-rate and a 'fourth division team'.[12]

Within a fortnight of its formation, however, the government was already looking more effective and united than its predecessor. In its first declaration it announced that sovereignty resided in the people, and proclaimed its intention of working for 'the establishment of a democratic political system based on rights and civil liberties, on equality of political opportunity for all democratic groups and the acceptance of genuine pluralism'.[13] The programme of political reforms was certainly more coherent than anything Arias had suggested. The plan was to prepare a new bill of political reform, to be debated by the *Cortes* in the autumn, and then submitted to the country in a referendum. Once this had been achieved, the government would open negotiations with the *antifranquista* opposition and ask for its co-operation in the holding of free general elections before 30 June 1977. The resulting parliament would assemble to pass a law of constitutional reform, which the Spaniards would have the opportunity to approve in a further referendum.

The declaration came as a surprise to many who, accustomed to the vacillations of the Arias governments, no longer believed that political reform would come from an unelected government. The derision provoked by the appearance of the Suárez cabinet subsided and even opposition leaders expressed the hope that the country might finally be on the road to democracy. Apart from its commitment to political reform, the government had also announced its recognition of regional diversity and its acceptance of the principle of free trade unions. Furthermore, it agreed to ask the king to grant an amnesty to all political prisoners innocent of violent crimes. A fortnight later Juan Carlos granted an amnesty which led to the release of about half of the country's 600 political prisoners.

The first piece of important legislation which the government presented to the *Cortes* was the reform of the Penal Code, the measure that Arias had hastily withdrawn in the fiasco in June. The bill, which contained modifications to the code's articles on freedom of expression and on the rights of assembly and association, was duly passed, but only by a small majority. Its most controversial feature was the article permitting the legalization of political parties. Although Suárez was at the time opposed to the legalization of the Communist Party, he wanted the text to be kept as vague as possible to give himself room to manoeuvre. The Bunker, however, wanted to ensure that the party could never be legalized and so it introduced an amendment outlawing 'national and international communist groups, associations, and parties'. This proposal was defeated, but so was the government's alternative, and in the end the *Cortes* settled for a formula which outlawed those parties 'that, subject to international discipline, want to set up a totalitarian regime'.

Before going ahead with the reform programme, Suárez made the wise decision to discuss his plans with senior officers in the armed forces. He knew that the Bunker would oppose him but, although this was a nuisance, it was not really important. The army, on the other hand, was powerful enough to wreck the entire constitutional experiment, and thus its support from the beginning was crucial. On 8 September, therefore, Suárez invited the leading generals, admirals and air force officers to a meeting where he told them of the reforms he intended to make. He was at his most charming, chatting confidentially to the officers, reminding them of his attachment to the old regime, assuring them that the changes in the Penal Code did not mean that the Communist Party would be legalized.[14] The generals, evidently, were full of praise for him.[15] Two days later the cabinet discussed the proposed Law for Political Reform, and none of the four military ministers objected to it. As the minister of the navy later remarked, his conscience could approve of the reforms because they were being carried out legally using the machinery of the *franquista* state.[16] Suárez was delighted with himself, convinced that he had converted Franco's generals to democracy.

A fortnight later, however, General Fernando de Santiago, the first vice-president of the government, resigned. He had been out of sympathy with the reform programme since the declaration in July, when he had left a cabinet meeting in disgust because of the government's announcement that sovereignty resided with the people. Since power came from God, he told Osorio, it was impossible for him to admit the principle of popular sovereignty.[17] In September he had accepted the programme of political reform, but he could not swallow the plan to dismantle the syndicates and permit free trade unions. To General De Santiago, the legalization of the *comisiones obreras*, dominated as they were by members of the Communist Party,* would be as inadmissible as the legalization on the PCE itself.

De Santiago was replaced by Manuel Gutiérrez Mellado, a

---

*By 1976 four-fifths of the members of the CCOO secretariat were also members of the Central Committee or Executive Committee of the PCE.[18]

liberal general and a friend of Díez-Alegría, the chief of staff sacked in 1974 for being too liberal. The crisis might have ended there had not De Santiago decided to inform his colleagues of the reasons for his resignation. In a private letter which was, however, widely circulated, he explained that the government was proposing to legalize 'the trade unions responsible for the outrages committed in the red zone [area held by the republicans in the civil war], and the CCOO, the trade union organization of the Communist Party.'[19] This letter, and another applauding De Santiago which General Iniesta, a stalwart of the Bunker, published in *El Alcázar* a few days later,[20] presented Suárez with a problem. The prime minister understood that the army had to be appeased, but he could hardly tolerate insubordination. And under the existing law, officers were allowed to express themselves in public only if they submitted their texts to the military authority of their region. As obviously neither of the generals had done this, Suárez decided to discipline them. Iniesta and De Santiago were thus removed from active service and placed in the reserve.

The proposed Law for Political Reform was sent to the *Cortes* on 16 November, and debated for two and a half days. In the build-up to the debate, the government employed the tactic used by Suárez when he had defended the Arias reforms in June. It tried to persuade the *franquistas* that the bill did not constitute a break with the previous regime; it should be seen instead as the logical conclusion of the *Caudillo*'s work. As Osorio argued, Franco had 'made democracy possible by carrying out the social and economic transformation of the country'.[21] It was now up to the *Cortes* to carry out the political transformation.

While this argument carried some weight with moderate *franquistas*, it did not impress the Bunker. The men of the hard Right knew that they were being asked to commit political suicide, and they reacted accordingly. While Girón fulminated against 'the traitors', Blas Piñar's *Fuerza Nueva* declared: 'We are the opposition, and by this we mean all those who continue to be faithful to the ideals of 18 July, those who are still loyal to the *Caudillo*, and above all, those who love Spain more than anything else after God.'[22] In the *Cortes* Piñar rejected the claim that the bill was in any way a continuation of *franquismo*. It contradicted the Principles of the *Movimiento*, and it conflicted with 'the political philosophy of the Spain which arose from the Crusade'.[23]

Piñar was followed by other representatives of the far Right. One speaker got up to say that he was a member of the Bunker and proud of the fact. He had been physically at the side of General Franco on the morning of 18 July, and spiritually there ever since.[24] Another *procurador*, José María Fernández de la Vega, opposed the bill because it meant transferring the basis of Spanish 'democracy' from the organic representativeness of the family, the municipality and the syndicate, to a system of 'inorganic suffrage'. In his eyes the Spanish system of representation was far superior to those existing in western Europe,[25] and he condemned the bill as 'obsolete, antisocial, reactionary, divisive, anti-historical and anti-national'.

The government knew that if the opposition consisted only of the Bunker, there was no danger of losing the vote. The important thing, therefore, was to concentrate on trying to convert that large array of ex-ministers and ex-officials who were thoroughly *franquista* in sentiment but regarded themselves as less obstructive and more civilized than the bunker. The government thus used converted *franquistas*, such as Fernando Suárez, a former minister, and Miguel Primo de Rivera, the nephew of José Antonio, to preach to the unconverted. The tactic was even more successful than expected. The government had to make a number of minor concessions, principally on the nature of the proposed electoral system, in order to gain the support of a large number of *procuradores*. But the size of its victory was still spectacular. Perhaps the *Cortes* was so accustomed to supporting governments that it could not bring itself to vote against the government which proposed its abolition. Only 59 hard-core members of the Bunker opposed the bill, and 13 others abstained. Among the 425 who voted in favour were many of Franco's ministers, including Arias, Fernández de la Mora, Licinio de la Fuente, López Bravo, López Rodó, Martín Artajo, and Solís. None of them can have liked the bill, but they voted for it, partly because they considered it inevitable, and partly because they needed at least one democratic credential if they themselves were going to compete in the new democratic system.

The Law for Political Reform, passed almost exactly a year after the death of General Franco, was the first major constitutional achievement of the monarchy. Nearly three years after Arias had first aired the possibility of reform in February 1974, the government had passed a measure intended to bring democracy to Spain. The law accepted the principle of popular sovereignty, brought in universal suffrage, and recognized the need for political pluralism. It implied the abolition of the chief *franquista* institutions, the 'organic' *Cortes*, the *Movimiento* and the National Council (the Council of the Realm was retained), and opened the way for elections to a bicameral legislature. The new *Cortes* would consist of a *Congreso de los Diputados*, with 350 members, and a *Senado*, with 207 elected senators. As for the electoral system, the government had originally favoured proportional representation for both chambers. But a large number of *procuradores*, particularly those attached to the conservative coalition *Alianza Popular*, which Manuel Fraga was then organizing, preferred the British majority system. As Suárez knew that the left-wing opposition would only accept proportional representation, he could not allow the *Congreso* to be elected by any other method. But he did concede that the senators would be elected by a simple majority, and he also agreed to the demands of *Alianza Popular* that there would be a minimum number of deputies for each province, a measure that was bound to lead to the over-representation of the more rural areas. He also agreed to take steps to avoid the 'inconvenient fragmentation' of the *Congreso* by fixing a minimum percentage of votes which parties would have to obtain before they could be represented.

The law also referred to the powers of the king, who at the time was still enjoying those granted to the Head of State by the Organic Law of 1967. Under the new law the king could submit any political question, constitutional or otherwise, to a referendum. He could dissolve the *Cortes* and call for new elections, and by implication he could appoint the prime minister. He could also designate senators to a number not greater than one fifth of those elected (in practice this meant 41).

Four weeks after the law had been passed by the *Cortes*, it was submitted to the Spanish people in a referendum. The government campaigned hard and unscrupulously for a positive response from the electorate, but the country's other political forces were divided. The extreme Right naturally opposed the government, Girón, Piñar and Fernández Cuesta stalking the country with the slogan 'Franco would have voted no'. The *franquistas* in *Alianza Popular* called for a 'yes' vote, as did a number of small centre-right parties which were being set up in preparation for the elections. Various liberal and christian democratic groups decided not to advise their followers on how to vote, but most of the left-wing opposition, including the communists and the socialists, tried to persuade voters to abstain. The *antifranquista* opposition was in a quandary. It certainly wished for political reform, but felt that the government should have consulted it beforehand. It had long argued that reforms should not be imposed by Franco's heirs, but should be agreed upon by a provisional government which would include the main parties of the opposition. The Left's attitude towards the Law for Political Reform was thus conditioned not so much by the contents, though it disliked some of these, but by the manner in which the law had been enacted. Angered by the way in which Suárez had ignored it, the Left reacted by trying to sabotage the reform. It was a short-sighted and self-defeating tactic which merely led to the strengthening of the prime minister's position.

The referendum, which was meant to bring the country nearer democracy, was carried out in a highly undemocratic manner. In some ways it resembled the referenda of the previous regime more closely than those called by other countries of the West. The government threw its whole weight behind the 'yes' campaign and denied its opponents a chance to put their case to the public. The leaders of those political parties which had already been legalized were given some television coverage, but since all the left-wing parties were still illegal, this was not much of a concession. It was not unlawful to campaign for an abstention, but in practice left-wing meetings were often broken up, and people found handing out pamphlets opposing the government were arrested. Furthermore, the manner in which the country was being asked to reply was bound to encourage an affirmative vote. People who voted 'yes' knew why they were voting: either they were supporters of Suárez or they were opponents who nevertheless believed that he would set up a genuine democratic system. A 'no' vote could mean that a person thought the reforms were either too much or too little, while an abstention could mean all sorts of things. In any case, it was difficult for left-wing voters to decide to abstain when they were not given the means to find out why their leaders were advocating abstention.

The result of the referendum was another triumph for Suárez, and once again he won more easily than he had anticipated. 77.7 per cent of the electorate voted, and of these 94.2 per cent voted 'yes'. 2.6 per cent voted 'no', a figure which accurately reflected the Bunker's strength in the country, and the remaining votes were blank or null. The left-wing opposition did almost as badly as the Right. 22.3 per cent is not a high rate of abstention in an election, and the chances are that a good many of those who abstained did so for reasons of health or lack of interest, rather than because they agreed with the leaders of the Left.

In spite of its humiliation in the referendum, the extreme Right refused to accept that it had been beaten. 'We do not feel we have been defeated in the referendum,' declared *El Alcázar*. 'We did our duty and now we shall go onto the offensive'.[26] It was as good as its word. Over the following weeks the Right launched a campaign of violence intended to produce an atmosphere of such tension that the army would be forced to intervene and set up a military government. Right-wing mobs destroyed bookshops and libraries. One group broke in to a Madrid restaurant and forced everybody present to sing *Cara al Sol* and shout *Arriba España!* At a service commemorating the assassination of Carrero Blanco three years earlier, Fernández Miranda, whom the Right correctly identified as its wiliest enemy, was assaulted. The worst outrage took place at the end of January when gunmen burst into a building near Madrid's Atocha station and murdered five labour lawyers attached to the *comisiones obreras*.

Most of this violence was blatant and undisguised. But a mysterious group called GRAPO (*Grupo Revolucionario Antifascista Primero de Octubre*) was more subtle in its terrorism. GRAPO either was or pretended to be an extreme left-wing movement, the product of a schism in the Communist Party in the later sixties. Its programme was certainly left-wing, and so were its gunmen who were caught or shot by the police. But other left-wing groups claimed that GRAPO was in fact controlled by the extreme Right, and used as a weapon to 'destabilize' the country at psychologically difficult moments. This was also the view of General Gutiérrez Mellado, the vice-president, and probably of Suárez as well.[27] GRAPO's operations appeared too obviously timed to benefit the Right for it to be credible as a left-wing organization. The kidnapping of such a pillar of the establishment as Antonio María de Oriol, for example, only four days before the referendum, seemed clearly intended to frighten people into voting 'no'.

Apart from its worries over Oriol (who was rescued by the police in February) and the violence of the extremist Right, the government ended 1976 on a good note. It had been in power for only six months and it had achieved a lot. It had, admittedly, failed to deal with the country's pressing economic problems, and there had been little progress in the struggle against political terrorism either in Madrid or in the Basque country. But Spaniards wanted Suárez to concentrate on political reform, and he had responded. Within a few months, he had done what was necessary to give them a real prospect of democratic government. Throughout the country there was a mood of euphoria. The man who had been scorned by the political class in July had become a national hero by December.

The successful policy had been planned by the king and Fernández Miranda. But Suárez had shown considerable tactical ability in carrying it out. He had governed by that mixture of intuition, compromise and improvisation that characterized his later governments. And he had succeeded. By intelligent man-oeuvring, he had regained the initiative for the monarchy and for the government. Unlike Arias, he had known what to do, and in what order he had to do it. Thus he began by tackling the Right, trying to persuade the army and the moderate *franquistas* to support him. Only when he had achieved this, could he go on to the next step. The hard-core Right had to be reduced to the irreducible – the Bunker and the terrorists – before he was strong enough to tackle the Left. His success in the *Cortes* followed by his triumph in the referendum placed him in a position of strength which the opposition could not ignore. Burying its demands for a break with the regime, the Left was forced to accept that it had no option but to negotiate with the prime minister on his terms.

9

1977: the General Elections

The *antifranquista* opposition had watched the progress of the Suárez government with a mixture of frustration and reluctant admiration. It maintained that Spain's democratic forces should have some role in the building of a democratic system; and it resented the way in which a former official of the *Movimiento*, who had never previously shown any inclination towards democracy, was imposing political reforms on the country. Nevertheless, it realized that it could not continue to condemn those reforms, which were approved by a majority of the Spanish people, without losing credibility. In December 1976, therefore, it appointed a commission to negotiate with the government.

Over the previous nine months, the attitude of the left-wing opposition had altered considerably. On 29 March the leaders of the newly-formed *Coordinación Democrática* had held a press conference in which they denounced the Arias government, criticized the reform programme, and insisted on a *ruptura* with the *franquista* regime. They also demanded an amnesty, the release of political prisoners, the recognition of political and trade union liberty, the observance of human rights, and the acceptance of the rights of the different 'nationalities' and regions of Spain.[1] As we have seen, the Arias government was not prepared to tolerate this sort of thing, and many of the opposition's leaders were arrested on the orders of Fraga. Although some of them were almost immediately set free, those connected with the Communist Party, whom Fraga referred to as 'my prisoners',[2] remained in prison.

During the first half of 1976 there was very little communication between the government and the opposition. Only Areilza, who called for a 'national pact' between the two sides, made an effort to talk to opposition leaders. Fraga held one meeting with González, but his arrogance merely antagonized the young socialist leader.[3] Arias met no-one. In view of the government's attitude – which was either to ignore the Left or to put its leaders in prison – the hostility of the opposition was understandable. In mid-summer almost the entire *antifranquista* opposition, ranging from communists to christian democrats, signed a declaration attacking the government and calling for its replacement.

Within weeks of the formation of the Suárez government, the opposition had begun to modify its criticism. It recognized that the political climate had altered, and that Suárez, in spite of his political origins, was very different from Arias. The declarations of the new government surprised opposition leaders by their unambiguous references to political reform. Less than a month after their denunciation of Arias, they composed another, more conciliatory declaration in which they called for a dialogue with the government.[4]

Suárez realized that he had to carry out his reforms without the help of the opposition if he was to receive the support of the *franquistas*. But he also knew that he would have to deal with the opposition more tactfully than Fraga had done if he wanted its co-operation at a later date. Within weeks of becoming prime minister, he thus embarked upon a series of meetings with opposition leaders. On 10 August he talked to González, who found him a much easier person to deal with than Fraga. The socialist leader left the meeting impressed by Suárez's political realism and announced that he was optimistic about the future.[5] Suárez considered González to be intelligent and patriotic, and believed that he would not ultimately insist on a *ruptura*.[6]

By the autumn of 1976 the chief issue for the opposition was whether or not it should continue to call for a *ruptura*. The hardline elements of *Coordinación Democrática* still demanded a break with the regime, but others were wavering. In October the opposition issued another series of demands including the immediate forma-tion of a government of 'broad democratic consensus', but social democrats and christian democrats refused to sign it. Like the liberals, they realized that a *ruptura* was neither practicable nor desirable.[7] The establishment of a provisional government to preside over a period leading to a general election was in principle a fine idea. But it had no chance of success, because the government understood that such a move could destroy the whole reform programme. The peaceful transition from dictatorship to democracy in Spain was only possible if it was done *legally*, that is, if it was carried out by the institutions of the previous regime. If the democratic reforms were approved by the *Cortes*, then it would be difficult for the Right to repudiate them later on. But if the government ignored the institutions, as the opposition suggested, and introduced democracy by decree, it would almost certainly provoke a civil conflict or a military coup.

The argument between reform and *ruptura* became increasingly unrealistic as the government simply went ahead with its reform programme. For a while González and other leaders limited their demands to a *ruptura pactada*, a negotiated break, and finally dropped the subject altogether. Once Suárez had converted the *Cortes* and the Spanish people to his point of view, there was little alternative but to concede. Nonetheless, it was a considerable concession to make. The battle over reform or *ruptura* was in effect a struggle for control of the democratic process. By abandoning its demands and accepting the rules laid down by Suárez, the opposition was accepting that the new, democratic regime would be run, at least initially, not by democrats but by men of the old regime.

Franco had always identified the Communist Party as his chief opponent. In numbers, organization, and the dedication of its militants, it exceeded the rest of the opposition put together. Many observers predicted a brilliant future for the party in the post-Franco years, comparable perhaps to its sister parties in Italy or France. On Franco's death the socialists in Spain were weak, divided, and few in number. There was thus a strong possibility, as in Italy, that the Communist Party would become the predominant force of the Left. But the Spanish communists, unlike their Italian comrades after the Second World War, had a controversial and discreditable past. Their energy and determination might attract the most politically active section of the population, but by the end of the *franquista* period a large majority of Spaniards had little interest in politics.[8] Moreover, while fascism had ended disastrously in Italy, *franquismo* could claim a number of successes. In consequence, there was not the desire for radical change in Spain in 1975 that there had been in Italy thirty years earlier. The Spanish people wanted change, but they had become sufficiently prosperous under the dictatorship to wish for reform rather than revolution.

Opinion polls taken in the first months of the monarchy suggested that the main political forces of democratic Spain would be christian democracy and a socialist-social democratic alliance.[9] These findings were an indication of Spaniards' attitudes rather than a reflection of support for a particular party. Those who said they favoured christian democracy were expressing vague support for a conservative, catholic party similar to those which existed in Germany or Italy. They were not announcing their intention to vote for the left-wing followers of Ruiz Giménez or the right-wing followers of Silva Muñoz, because they probably knew little of the numerous and quarrelling groups which all claimed to be christian democrats. It was much the same with those who declared support for socialists or social democrats. There were at least twenty parties to choose from, although many of these were little more than sets of initials devised by different groups of friends. The social democrats had produced one impressive figure, Ridruejo, but he had died in the summer of 1975. His successors formed a number of 'parties' which then pursued a course of merging with, and seceding from, other, practically identical 'parties'.

The socialists did at least have one set of initials inherited from the past. But this was claimed by both the 'renovated' PSOE of Felipe González and the 'historic' PSOE of Rodolfo Llopis. There were also a large number of regional parties, as well as the PSP of Tierno Galván. On Franco's death, the best-known of these groups was the PSP. Tierno was a long-standing member of the *antifranquista* opposition inside Spain, and he had done more for the socialist cause than Llopis and his friends had achieved in Toulouse. His party had little popular support but it had attracted a number of intellectuals, and it received financial support from Mexico and Venezuela. The PSP might well have become the main socialist group if González had not received the support of the Socialist International.

The 'renovated' PSOE had the advantage of its name, as well as the fresh and attractive leadership of González and his colleagues. But the decisive factor in the defeat of its rivals was the support it received from socialists abroad. In December 1976 the Suárez government allowed the PSOE – although the party was still illegal – to celebrate its first conference in Spain for forty-four years. Among the 38 'fraternal' delegations sat the leaders of European socialism: Mitterrand, Brandt, Palme, Foot and Nenni. The moral and financial backing which the Europeans provided for the PSOE helped to establish it as the leading socialist party in Spain. During the six months between the conference and the general election, the PSOE swallowed up most of the regional socialist groups, and accepted a number of 'refugees' from the rival party of Llopis. The enthusiasm which González attracted around the country was remarkable: even he was surprised by the thousands who flocked to a party that a few months earlier had barely existed.[10] The transformation of the PSOE into a major political organization was largely the work of Alfonso Guerra, the deputy leader of the party. Guerra had been a close friend of González since the early sixties, and together they had rebuilt the Andalusian section of the PSOE. In character he was almost the reverse of González: ruthless, controversial and demagogic. But he was an excellent administrator and a crucial figure in the party's successful development. Guerra took on the unpopular work of building the party structure and uniting the components of Spanish socialism. He attracted criticism and made a large number of enemies inside and outside the party. By doing so, he allowed González to cultivate the image of an innocent and attractive politician who refused to take part in mud-slinging or machiavellian manoeuvres.

Guerra enjoyed making inflammatory speeches full of sarcastic references to other politicians, but this was done partly to satisfy the party's revolutionary wing. The PSOE leadership, dominated by Basques and Andalusians, was politically moderate. González and most of his colleagues were social democrats by conviction, and were 'encouraged' to take a moderate line by the German Social Democratic Party (SPD). The PSOE adopted the rose-in-fist symbol from the radical French socialists, but took little else from Mitterrand's party. It turned to Germany for financial support and political backing. In 1975–6 González visited Germany several times and became a protégé of Brandt, the former chancellor. The SPD provided the PSOE with substantial funds* and thus had considerable influence on its behaviour. During the first half of 1976, when Arias was refusing to talk to the opposition, the principal means of communication between the

Spanish government and the main Spanish socialist party appears to have been through the German embassy. When Areilza had a complaint about the PSOE's political stance in March 1976, he telephoned the ambassador to ask him to deal with it. The following month the ambassador visited Areilza to explain that, although the Germans were able to influence the PSOE, they could not prevent it from becoming more radical if the government refused to introduce democratic reforms.[11]

In the exhilarating atmosphere prevailing at the conference in December 1976, González put the need for party unity above other considerations. He was not prepared to have a repeat of the 'reform versus revolution' controversy that had plagued the party in the 1930s. The executive committee thus found itself saddled with a 'political resolution' and a 'programme of transition' which were far more radical than it would have liked. The PSOE defined itself as a 'class party and therefore a party of the masses, marxist and democratic', before giving a confusing and largely meaningless explanation of what it meant by marxism.[12] It also called for the suppression of capitalism and the socialization of the means of production, a process that would be begun by nationalizing the leading banks and companies. González, however, was less interested in the ideology of a hypothetical socialist government than in the negotiations he was about to begin with Suárez. From his point of view, the important thing was to persuade the party to drop the demand for a *ruptura* and to accept that the transition to democracy would have to be negotiated with the government. And he wanted to do this without antagonizing his supporters by challenging their favourite dogmas. González, like Suárez, was a

---

*The SPD was not the only German political party to give financial backing to Spanish groups. The christian democrats provided funds from the Konrad Adenauer Foundation, and the free democrats supported Spanish liberals through the Friedrich Naumann Foundation. All three had offices in Madrid to administer the funds. As the Socialist International had already recognized the PSOE, the SDP's task was straightforward, but the other foundations had difficulty in deciding which liberal or christian democratic groups to support. While the free democrats and the christian democrats were opposing each other in Germany, their foundations ended up backing the same party, the *Unión de Centro Democrático*, in Spain. Both of them, however, were also giving money simultaneously to other groups. To some Spaniards it was ironic that the country which had done so much to destroy their democratic government in 1936 should have been teaching them about democracy forty years later.

good judge of priorities. He persuaded his party to back him on the question of negotiations and did not worry too much about the rhetoric of the conference resolutions. Later, when it came to drawing up the manifesto for the elections, González simply dropped all references to marxism, the class struggle and revolution.

Through international recognition, historic legitimacy and astute leadership, the PSOE was able to unite the great mass of Spanish socialists. The only groups outside the PSOE which seemed capable of attracting any support were Tierno's PSP, the *Federación de Partidos Socialistas*, the remnant of Llopis's following, and a small group of Andalusian socialists. The christian democrats, potential adversaries of the PSOE, hoped to embark on a similar process of unification. But the obstacles were even greater. Gil Robles and Ruiz Giménez, the historic leaders of Spanish christian democracy, received the support of their counterparts in Italy and the rest of Europe. But both men were in the opposition and christian democracy could not flourish in Spain without *franquista* support. Ruiz Giménez was close to the socialists on many issues, while Gil Robles refused to co-operate with anyone who had collaborated with Franco.* Between the two of them, they managed to alienate most of christian democracy's natural constituents.

Alfonso Osorio, the vice-president and leading christian democratic figure in the government, tried unsuccessfully to put all the factions together in one party. Christian democrats were split not only between those, such as the *Tácito* group and the UDE, who had supported Franco, and those who had opposed him. They were also divided on current issues such as the question of legalizing the Communist Party. In addition, there was the opposition of the Church, which did not want to support either the factions of Gil Robles and Ruiz Giménez or the creation of a new christian democratic party. The Cardinal Archbishop of Madrid told Osorio firmly that he did not wish to see any party use the name 'christian democrat'.[13] Confronted by the opposition of the Church and the intransigence of Gil Robles, Osorio

---

*Ruiz Giménez, of course, had collaborated with Franco when he was minister of education in the early fifties. Gil Robles considered, however, that his colleague had repented sufficiently of his past (as indeed he had) to be acceptable.

abandoned his project of building a united party and concentrated on bringing some of the smaller groups into a coalition with other centre-right formations. Gil Robles and Ruiz Giménez formed an alliance to contest the elections by themselves, while a group of right-wing christian democrats, headed by the former minister Silva Muñoz, broke away from the UDE to join Fraga.

The designation of Suárez as prime minister had been a great blow to Manuel Fraga. He had arrogated to himself the dual role of architect of reform and guarantor of order, but the king had suddenly taken it away and given it to someone else. Fraga was very hurt: he was described by one associate as behaving like a wounded bear.[14] He felt he had sacrificed years preparing the way for reform, and he bitterly resented the fact that the project had been handed over to someone who had never before shown it the slightest interest.[15]

For a few weeks after his disappointment, Fraga refused to make plans or to talk of the future. Then, with characteristic energy and determination, he threw himself into the task of building a political party. Two of his closest allies were Areilza and Cabanillas, and it was expected that he would try to form a liberal-conservative party with them. In mid-September the three lunched together and Fraga told the others about his plans. Far from setting up the much-vaunted liberal-conservative party – the 'civilized Right' which Areilza proposed – he intended to fashion a great alliance of the *franquista* Right. When Areilza asked him how far right he was prepared to go, Fraga listed the names of a number of Franco's ministers who had already agreed to join him.[16] Areilza and Cabanillas were appalled. With the exception of the highly conservative Silva Muñoz, not one of Fraga's new allies had been an advocate of political reform. Indeed, they had been among the most vigorous opponents of democracy all their lives: Fernández de la Mora had even written books on the subject, which Fraga at the time had thought absurd.[17] Perhaps the most surprising name in the list was López Rodó, the former economics minister and leader of the Opus Dei 'team', who had been Fraga's principal adversary in the cabinet during the 1960s.

Fraga's politics had been moving to the right since leaving the Spanish embassy in London. On returning to Spain he was greatly impressed by the crowds which filed past Franco's coffin in Madrid.[18] Perhaps the scene convinced him that the country was more conservative than in fact it was. When he decided to create a party of the *franquista* Right, he believed he could capture the support of 'sociological *franquismo*' – that is, the new middle classes which had gained most from the economic boom of the 1960s. So he went ahead and put together *Alianza Popular* (AP), a coalition supported by eight former ministers and 180 *procuradores* of the *Cortes*. It was a tremendous misjudgement. There were many people who were grateful for the economic benefits of the sixties who nevertheless wished for political reform. Like Fernández de la Mora, Fraga seems to have believed that prosperity deadened, rather than stimulated, political interest. He did not understand the temper of the country and its desire for change. The prime minister's talents may have been lesser than Fraga's, but Suárez was the man the country then wanted – and probably needed.* Suárez incarnated the aspirations of the new Spain in a way which Fraga was unable to understand. While Suárez responded to the national mood, Fraga sent himself off into political exile. In six months he destroyed his reformist reputation, firstly as an intolerant and imperceptive minister, and then as the founder of a *franquista* party. In the words of one commentator, he had ended up a few millimetres from the Bunker against which he had struggled for so long.[20]

Areilza and Cabanillas were invited to join Fraga's party, but they hastily refused. Areilza believed that political reform had to come from the Right not the Left, but he did not see how it could be done by a party which included people such as Fernández de la Mora. It had to be done by liberal conservatives, by people who did at least genuinely believe in political reform. Cabanillas wanted to set up a centre party, backed if possible by the government, which would prevent the polarization of the country between *Alianza Popular* and the Left. He argued that this party should not be christian democrat in complexion because it would need to attract liberals and social democrats as well. For some months a number of people, including members of the *Tácito* group, had been laying the foundations for such a party, the *Partido Popular* (PP), and in the autumn they were joined by

*The abilities of the two men reminded one politician, a supporter of Suárez, of Clemenceau's remark: 'Poincaré (or Fraga) knows everything and understands nothing; Briand (or Suárez) knows nothing and understands everything.'[19]

Areilza and Cabanillas. At the beginning of December, six weeks after the establishment of *Alianza Popular*, the party was launched in Madrid.

Many people besides Areilza and Cabanillas were trying to fill the wide political space between Fraga and González. They formed a large number of 'parties', some of them so small that it was joked that their membership would fit in a single taxi. Once these largely imaginary parties had been set up, their leaders began to negotiate coalitions with similar groups. When they saw that Areilza was having considerable success in attracting people to his public meetings, a number of them decided to ally themselves to the *Partido Popular*. Two liberal leaders offered to join their groups to Areilza on condition that they received third and fourth places on the electoral lists in Madrid.[21] They were followed shortly afterwards by a group of social democrats. But the most important party which joined – the only one, apart from the PP, which had any national support – was the *Partido Demócrata Cristiano*. This party consisted of a number of people who had left Ruiz Giménez because he was too left-wing, and a number of others who had broken with Silva Muñoz because he was too right-wing. It thus represented an alliance of lukewarm *franquistas* and moderate opponents. Unfortunately it was the closest the christian democrats would get to unity. Strenuous efforts were made to persuade Ruiz Giménez to join them, but he deferred to Gil Robles. As the elections approached, he seemed to realize that the intransigence of Gil Robles was leading him to political oblivion, but he stayed with him until the end.

While about 200 political parties made preparations for elections to be held on 15 June, the government had to define the electoral rules. This was done by two decree laws in February and March 1977. The first modified the Law of Political Associations passed by the Arias government the previous June by removing the obligation for a party to adhere to the Fundamental Laws of the old regime. Under the decree law, all that a party had to do was to hand in its credentials to the ministry of the interior, which would decide within ten days whether to legalize it. If the case was a dubious one – that is, if there was some doubt whether the party in question came into the 'totalitarian' category defined by the Penal Code – it would be referred to the Supreme Court.

The second decree-law established the electoral system and

various regulations governing the conduct of the elections. Most of these had already been discussed in the Law for Political Reform, but their details had been left for the government to work out. It had been agreed that each province would form a constituency and that the system of election would be a type of proportional representation. It had also been decided that each province would elect a minimum number of deputies, which in practice meant that all of them would choose at least three representatives. (Ceuta and Melilla, the enclaves in Morocco, would each elect one deputy and two senators.) If strict proportional representation had been followed, Barcelona would have had forty-one deputies, Zamora two and Soria one. The system adopted, which gave Barcelona thirty-three, Zamora four and Soria three, thus favoured the most rural areas at the expense of the cities. In each province a party would present a list of candidates for as many seats as the constituency possessed. The lists were 'closed' so that the elector could only choose a party and not a particular candidate. The seats would be subsequently allocated according to the D'Hondt system, a complicated method which prevents too much fragmentation in parliament and leads to the over-representation of large parties.* For the upper chamber an entirely different system was introduced. All provinces would elect four senators only, irrespective of the population, except for the Balearic and Canary Island provinces which would each choose five. The senators would be elected on a 'first past the post' system although, as each elector could vote for only three

---

*The decree-law gives the following example of a hypothetical province whose eight seats are contested by six parties. The 480,000 votes are shared between list A (168,000), B (104,000), C (72,000), D (64,000), E (40,000) and F (32,000). These are then divided consecutively by numbers from 1 to 8, which gives the following table:

	1	2	3	4	5	6	7	8
A	168,000	84,000	56,000	42,000	33,600	28,000	24,000	21,000
B	104,000	52,000	34,666	26,000	20,800	17,333	14,857	13,000
C	72,000	36,000	24,000	18,000	14,400	12,000	10,285	9,000
D	64,000	32,000	21,333	16,000	12,800	10,666	9,142	8,000
E	40,000	20,000	13,333	10,000	8,000	6,666	5,714	5,000
F	32,000	16,000	10,666	8,000	6,400	5,333	4,571	4,000

From this table, the highest eight figures are taken, giving four seats to A, two to B, and one each to C and D.

communist, because it implied that being a member of the party was no longer a crime. The PCE was euphoric, believing that the episode made its legalization inevitable.[26]

On 24 January right-wing terrorists carried out the 'Atocha massacre', and two days later the PCE and the *comisiones obreras* organized a massive demonstration around the funerals of the murdered labour lawyers. Scores of thousands of mourners marched through the centre of Madrid. There were no incidents, no indiscipline. The Communist Party was displaying its strength and its restraint before the nation. According to Alfonso Osorio, his closest associate in the government, one of the people most impressed by the demonstration was Adolfo Suárez. Until then he had believed that it was not possible to legalize the PCE; after that exhibition he concluded that it was impossible not to legalize it.[27] The entire project of reform would collapse, he believed, if the communists were barred from taking part.

The communist strategy was to stay prominently in the public eye without doing anything provocative which might lead to accusations of subversiveness or irresponsibility. In early February senior representatives of the French and Italian communist parties went to Madrid and announced that Georges Marchais and Enrico Berlinguer had accepted Carrillo's invitation to take part in a 'eurocommunist' summit in Madrid. A few days later, the government asked the Supreme Court to make a judgement on the PCE's application for registration. Suddenly, while the matter was still *sub judice*, Suárez decided to hold a secret meeting with Carrillo. It was a bold move which contained many risks, but it worked. Suárez set out to persuade Carrillo to accept the national flag (i.e. to abandon the republican standard), the monarchy of Juan Carlos, and the unity of the nation. The communist leader agreed, subject to various conditions, including of course the legalization of his party. Like many others, Carrillo was captivated by the prime minister's charm, and he later described the meeting as one of the 'crucial' events of the transition.[28] The two men understood each other and established a relationship which contributed significantly, over the following few years, to social, as well as political, stability in Spain.

At the end of March, the Supreme Court met and decided that the question of legalizing the Communist Party was outside its competence. The government was divided in its reactions to the news, but Suárez believed that he had no alternative but to go ahead and legalize. Public opinion now favoured legalization, and even the conservative catholic newspaper *Ya* declared that it would be disastrous to keep the PCE banned.[29] Martín Villa, the interior minister, and General Gutiérrez Mellado, the vice-president in charge of defence matters, supported Suárez. Only Osorio, from among the small group of ministers who were consulted, disagreed. He argued that the army had been promised that the reforms would be carried out within the framework of the law; a hasty decision by the prime minister would mean breaking that promise. Suárez and Gutiérrez Mellado claimed that there was no problem with the army: the senior officers and the military ministers had been consulted, and, although they did not like the decision, they would accept it without creating difficulties. The prime minister thus went ahead with his plan, and on 9 April, in the middle of the Easter weekend, the Spanish people learned from radio and television that the Communist Party was now legal.[30]

Unfortunately, it was not only the people who heard the news in this way. A number of senior ministers on holiday in various parts of the country were astonished to learn that the government had taken such an important decision without consulting them. Some of them threatened to resign, but were dissuaded by Osorio, who pointed out that resignations at such a critical moment would leave the king in a perilous position.[31] The civilian ministers thus remained in the cabinet, although several accused Suárez of opportunism and believed that he had overridden the law for the sake of short-term political advantage.

In the armed forces the news was received with even greater consternation. On Easter Monday the minister for the navy, Admiral Pita da Veiga, resigned in disgust. The following day the Supreme Army Council met and condemned the government's decision. Every general present was opposed to both the legalization of the PCE and the manner in which the law had been ignored. Many, apparently, wished to ask Juan Carlos to dismiss Suárez and Gutiérrez Mellado from their posts.[32] In the end they agreed on a document which denounced the legalization of the Communist Party, and announced that the army was accepting the decision only from a sense of duty and patriotism.

Suárez and Gutiérrez Mellado had indeed handled the affair

badly. The PCE plainly had to be made legal if democracy was going to work, but the legalization should have been done properly. Improvisation was the hallmark of Suárez's government, and frequently it paid off. But on this occasion his casual treatment of the law, and his blithe disregard for the sensibilities of the armed forces, nearly led to disaster. In September 1976 Suárez had promised senior officers that he would not legalize the Communist Party; the following April he should at least have informed them that he had changed his mind. But in spite of the assurances to their cabinet colleagues, neither Suárez nor his military vice-president discussed the matter with the armed forces. According to his own version, Gutiérrez Mellado merely told the other military ministers that there was a possibility of legalizing the PCE if the Supreme Court's judgement proved positive.[33] But taking a decision on the advice of the country's highest legal authority was very different from taking it on the advice of two or three ministers. The legalization of the PCE, which was a crucial step in Spain's progress towards democratic government, was also a seminal event in the army's disillusionment with the new regime.

Apart from fixing the rules and deciding who could participate in the elections, Suárez had to decide what part he personally would play in the forthcoming contest. Many people argued that he should remain neutral during the elections and not stand as a candidate himself. But he was too ambitious a politician to stand aside, and by the end of 1976 he was discussing the possibility of forming a centrist coalition. Fraga had occupied the space on the Right, while the Left was dominated by the PSOE and the PCE. But in the centre and centre-right of the political spectrum, there was still a great deal of confusion. Some of the small parties joined together to form the *Centro Democrático* at the beginning of 1977, but judged from almost every standpoint – members, organization, and the stature of its leaders – it was weaker than its prospective rivals. To Suárez it seemed an obvious vehicle for him to take charge of and transform into an election-winning machine.

Most of the centre's leaders were unknown outside political circles in Madrid, and none of them had the style or the appeal of Suárez. The only one with the prestige necessary for a party leader was Areilza, who enjoyed considerable popularity in the country. Suárez could deal with the other leaders of the centre, who were of his generation and without much political experience. But he could not deal with Areilza who, apart from being older and more sophisticated, gave him an inferiority complex.[34] He wanted to be the undisputed leader of the centre coalition and he knew that Areilza would be a rival. Therefore he had to go. In March 1977 Suárez asked Osorio to tell the leaders of the *Centro Democrático* that if they wanted the government's support in the elections, they would have to jettison Areilza.[35] Osorio introduced the subject bluntly at a dinner to which the leaders of the *Partido Popular* (except for Areilza) and the *Partido Demócrata Cristiano* – the chief components of the *Centro Democrático* – had been invited. His audience did not like Osorio's suggestion, but at the same time they realized they would have to go along with it. With Areilza they might win a few seats, but opinion polls indicated that they would be heavily defeated by *Alianza Popular*; with Suárez and the support of the government, they might win the election outright. A couple of days later, Cabanillas told Areilza of the dilemma which he and his colleagues had been presented with, and the old statesman gracefully surrendered.[36]

As soon as he had heard that the *Centro Democrático* had abandoned Areilza, Suárez entered into negotiations with its various factions. He even summoned Areilza and Cabanillas to a meeting in which, after apologizing for Osorio's behaviour and telling them untruthfully that the minister had not in any way been speaking on his behalf,[37] he outlined his plans for the new party. Areilza left the prime minister's office, captivated by his charm and impressed by his intelligence and tactical ability. He disagreed with the project of creating a political party from government rather than first building a popular base in the country, but he did not wish to be an obstacle to Suárez's plans, and he quickly resigned as vice-president of the *Partido Popular*.* It was not the end of the old man's career, although Suárez tried to make it so. Whatever other qualities he had, Suárez showed little generosity towards his rivals. The previous year he had offered Fraga a humiliating position;† now he tried to exclude Areilza

---

*Apparently as a result of government pressure, Cabanillas rather than Areilza had been elected president of the party at its conference in February 1977.[39]
†In September 1976 Fraga was offered the presidency of the *Tribunal de la Competencia*, a minor law court dealing with commercial matters.[40]

from public life. Not only was the former foreign minister forced out of the party he had helped to found: at least two people were later removed from the electoral lists because of their close relationship with him. During the following two years Areilza disappeared from public view, denied even the opportunity of appearing on the state-owned television. When he asked Suárez for a place in the lists for the second elections in 1979, his request was curtly turned down.[38]

The decree-law of March 1977, which contained the electoral rules, included an article which banned certain people from standing as candidates in the elections. Among those declared ineligible were all government ministers, with the curious exception of the prime minister. The publication of the decree-law immediately produced speculation about the intentions of Suárez. The political world was divided over whether he should participate in the elections or stand aloof. Carrillo hoped that Suárez would stand in order to prevent Fraga from dominating the *Cortes*. The socialists, however, declared that it would be unfair for the government to take part. One commentator argued perceptively that the candidature of Suárez would simply turn the elections into a second referendum on the prime minister's reform programme.[41] Suárez paid little attention to the debate because he had long since decided that he would stand. However, it was not until the end of April that he announced his decision, and not for a further week that he confirmed that he would be the first candidate for the centre coalition in Madrid. He was standing, he claimed, in order to avoid the polarization of the country between Right and Left.

In many ways Suárez was a very modern politician. He understood the importance of television and image building. He did not believe in stumping the country, holding great rallies for his supporters. Nor did he think it worthwhile to create a party with popular, 'grass-roots' participation. A modern political party, he believed, should be controlled not by its members but by 'six or eight' people.[42] The centrist coalition, which received the title of *Unión de Centro Democrático* (UCD), was not, therefore, a 'popular' party. As one of its leading christian democrats complained, it was 'not born by natural means, it was born with forceps, from power'.[43]

All through the early months of 1977, the 'taxi parties' had been flocking to join the centre coalition. Apart from the *Partido Popular* and the *Partido Demócrata Cristiano*, the UCD contained four social democratic parties, four liberal parties (two of which left the coalition before the elections) and regional parties from Galicia, Murcia, Andalusia, Extremadura and the Canary Islands. Besides these, the coalition included a large number of *franquista* bureaucrats – *azules* or 'blues' as they were called – who were personal followers of Suárez or the interior minister, Martín Villa. It was a pretty motley collection of groups – the philosopher Aranguren described it as a 'bazaar where one can find anything one wants'[44] – led by a pretty motley collection of people. Enrique Larroque, who left the UCD because he was not given a place on the lists, described it as 'an *Alianza Popular* of the second division: AP has ex-ministers and the UCD ex-under-secretaries.'[45]

The most immediate task facing the UCD was the construction of electoral lists in the fifty different provinces. Leopoldo Calvo-Sotelo, the minister for public works, resigned from the government in order to organize lists that would satisfy the party's diverse components. It was a difficult job because each group considered itself to be more important than it really was, and therefore entitled to a large number of winnable positions. The best Calvo-Sotelo could do was to try to limit the jealousy and the latent antagonism between different factions.[46] He did not always succeed. Several groups threatened to walk out of the coalition if they did not get what they wanted. Fernández Ordóñez, one of the social democratic leaders, announced his departure on learning that an associate, Rafael Arias Salgado, had been given the fifteenth place in the Madrid list.[47] He only relented when Arias Salgado was found a suitable position in Toledo. Oscar Alzaga, a leading christian democrat, discovered that Calvo-Sotelo had demoted him from eleventh to twelfth place in the Madrid list, and therefore decided that, although he would stand in the election, he would make no contribution to the campaign.[48] The behaviour of aspiring deputies was often frivolous and irresponsible. At times personal ambition seemed the only motive keeping them all together: one group of social democrats, led by José Ramón Lasuén, first attempted to form a coalition with the PSOE *históricos*, then tried to negotiate a pact with *Alianza Popular*, and only joined the UCD at the last moment because it seemed the most likely means of gaining seats.★[49]

Eventually, just before the deadline, the lists were completed. Apart from Larroque, there were no significant casualties, but the process had caused a good deal of bad feeling. The main cause of annoyance was the introduction of so many *azules* – 57 of them became deputies – at the top of the lists. The 'democrats' in the UCD, many of whom had been in the opposition, were indignant at being displaced by men who had made their careers in the *Movimiento*, the official trade union, or as mayors and councillors of the old regime. But they had to accept it because Suárez insisted on bringing in men he knew and trusted; and without Suárez the coalition was nothing. Of the various parties in the UCD, the social democrats of Fernández Ordóñez and the liberals of Garrigues Walker received more than their fair share of places. The christian democrats received less. Although they had only one party in the coalition, it was larger than the eight liberal and social democratic parties put together. They also formed the largest group inside the *Partido Popular*. Furthermore, the UCD's potential voters on the centre-right were more likely to be christian democrats than liberals, of whom there were very few in Spain, or social democrats, many of whom would vote for one of the socialist parties. The sacrifices which the christian democrats had to make in the formation of the UCD led to a disaffection among them which grew in subsequent years and eventually led to the destruction of the party.

When the election campaign began in May, there were 163 parties listed on the Register of Associations.[50] Between them they put up more than 6,000 candidates; in Madrid nearly 600 people contested the city's 32 seats in the *Congreso*. At the beginning of the campaign, the electorate was understandably confused by the proliferation of parties with similar names and similar programmes: according to one opinion poll, 60 per cent of the electorate had not made up its mind how to vote.[51] There were far too many parties to choose from. A socialist voter, even if he eliminated the small left-wing parties and those with a regional base, still had a choice of three: González's PSOE, Tierno's PSP (which had allied itself to the *Federación de Partidos Socialistas* and was fighting the election under the surprising name of *Unidad Socialista*), or the

---

*Lasuén was elected to the *Congreso* in 1977 but was later expelled from the UCD. Eventually, at the third attempt, he joined up with Fraga, and was elected as a deputy for *Alianza Popular* in 1982.

rather pathetic coalition formed by the remnants of Ridruejo's social democrats and the surviving members of the Llopis group. A christian democrat had to choose between the UCD, *Alianza Popular* – which also contained christian democrats – and the coalition set up by Gil Robles and Ruiz Giménez.

The campaign itself was confusing. 'The important thing to bear in mind,' said one Catalan politician, 'is that the Right is pretending to be the Left, and the Left is pretending to be the Right.'[52] Allowing for the exaggeration, the remark contained a strong element of truth. There were a lot of *franquistas* masquerading as democrats. Almost half of AP's successful candidates had been ministers in Franco's governments; twenty-four of the deputies elected for the UCD had been *procuradores* of the *Cortes*.[53] On the Left both the socialists and the communists emphasized their moderation. No correlation existed between the resolutions passed at the PSOE's conference in December 1976 and the electoral propaganda issued five months later. There was a lot of talk of liberty during the campaign, but none about marxism, republicanism or the class struggle, all of which the party officially supported.[54] As for the communists, they tried to be more moderate still, stressing the fact that there were many believers and even priests inside the party.[55] Carrillo went around looking as respectable as possible, in a suit and tie, and was careful to attack nobody to the left of Fraga. He even praised Suárez, referring to him as his 'most trustworthy adversary' in the elections.[56]

Apart from the various groups of the extreme Right, which regarded ballot boxes as waste-paper baskets, perhaps the only party which went into the elections flying its true colours was *Alianza Popular*. Fraga had constructed a party that was unashamedly *franquista* and appealed – at a time of international recession – to the nostalgia of the economic success of the sixties. He had even recruited Carlos Arias to his side. Announcing that he would be a candidate for the *Senado*, the former prime minister proclaimed that he was still totally loyal to Franco and not ashamed of the fact.[57] AP's campaign was dominated by Fraga, who barnstormed the country trumpetting the need for law and order. The crowds at his rallies chanted 'Fraga! Fraga!' interspersed with cries of 'Franco! Franco!'.

Fraga, González, Tierno and Carrillo fought hard and energetic campaigns, filling the country's bullrings and stadiums with thousands of their supporters. Suárez, who insisted that the election would be won on television,★ did not campaign at all, except shortly before polling day when he visited his home province Avila. The rest of the UCD held occasional meetings but, as its leaders were almost entirely unknown, few people bothered to turn up. As the campaign progressed, opinion polls indicated growing support for the PSOE, but Suárez remained confident that his party would still win. On 13 June, however, the president of Icsa Gallup informed Osorio that his latest poll put the socialists more than three percentage points ahead of the UCD. Suárez tried to prevent the publication of the poll, but Osorio countermanded him, and it appeared in *Ya* on the following day, the eve of the elections. Osorio hoped that the likelihood of a socialist victory would attract the undecided to the UCD.[58]

On 15 June 1977 nearly eighteen million Spaniards voted in the first democratic elections since 1936. The abstention rate was just over 20 per cent; nowhere, except in Galicia and Tenerife, did it reach 30 per cent. As the results began to come through during the evening, it seemed at first as if González's socialists would triumph. They easily defeated the UCD in Barcelona, Valencia and Bilbao, they won narrowly in Asturias and Andalusia, and they were only a few thousand votes behind in Madrid. The news was greeted with delight by many PSOE supporters – a large crowd of them began chanting victory slogans in the streets of the capital – but there was consternation at the party's headquarters. Its leaders had neither wished nor expected to win: they were terrified by the prospect of coming to power at such an early stage in the transition. They knew that they were not ready for the country, and that the country was not ready for them.

At the prime ministers's offices in the Moncloa Palace, the optimism suddenly evaporated. Suárez, who had remained confident that his personal magnetism would secure victory,

---

★The decree-law of March 1977 stated that all parties would have the right to free television and radio space during the campaign. It also provided for the formation of a committee, with representatives of the major parties, to oversee the coverage of the elections by the media. In spite of this, the network remained fully in the hands of the government, and the opposition received very little coverage. Constant television appearances by Suárez contributed to the result.

retired to his study where he chain-smoked and talked about organizing the UCD properly in opposition.[59] But during the early hours of the morning, as the results from the rural provinces became known, the UCD's position improved. It gained half of the votes and two-thirds of the seats in Extremadura and Old Castile; in Galicia it captured 20 out of 27 seats, and 10 out of 13 in the Canaries. In two of the smallest provinces, Soria and Avila, it won all three seats.

The UCD's success in the rural provinces had disastrous consequences for *Alianza Popular*. Fraga won four seats in Galicia (his home region), three in Madrid, but only one each in Catalonia, Valencia and the Basque country. López Rodó just managed to win in Barcelona, but Martínez-Esteruelas, another of the *franquista* former ministers, was a casualty in Teruel. In the capital, Carlos Arias failed to be elected senator.

In spite of errors in adding up the votes – the final figures were not announced until long after the election – it had become clear by dawn on 16 June that the UCD would be the largest party in the new parliament, and that the PSOE would be the principal party of opposition. With 34.7 per cent of the vote, the UCD had gained 165 of the *Congreso*'s 350 seats; the PSOE had won 29.2 per cent of the vote and 118 seats. All the other national parties were losers. So far from emulating their Italian comrades, who had gained more than 34 per cent of the vote in their national elections the previous year, the PCE won less than 10 per cent of the votes and only 20 seats. Fraga, with 8.2 per cent of the votes and 16 seats, did even worse, achieving the kind of result usually obtained by the Italian neo-fascists. Tierno Galván's PSP, which lacked the funds and glamour of the PSOE, elected six deputies, three of them for Madrid. Of the remaining seats, 23 were won by nationalist parties in Catalonia and the Basque country, and two by independents. The christian democrats of Gil Robles and Ruiz Giménez (1.1 per cent of the vote) won no seats at all; nor did the PSOE *históricos* (0.6 per cent) or the *Falange* (0.26 per cent).

The electoral law had been widely criticized beforehand as likely to benefit the parties of the Right, but, in application, its most obvious feature was the way it favoured the larger parties of both Left and Right. The UCD received just over a third of the votes but obtained nearly half the seats; the PSOE also received a higher percentage of seats (33.7) than of votes. All the other national parties, however, did proportionately worse in seats than in votes. *Alianza Popular* polled nearly a quarter as many votes as the UCD, but elected less than a tenth as many deputies. The only small parties that had a chance of gaining representation were regional ones with concentrated support in a small area. A Catalan nationalist coalition and the Basque Nationalist Party were able to win eleven and eight seats respectively, and thus become the fifth and sixth largest parties in the new *Congreso*. Nevertheless, a considerable majority of the electorate in both Catalonia and the Basque country voted for parties that were 'national' rather than 'nationalist'.

The elections for the upper chamber, carried out under a different system, gave the UCD a small overall majority. Of the 207 seats, the government coalition won 106 and the PSOE 47. *Alianza Popular* and the PSP gained only two each, and the communists none at all. The remaining seats were won mainly by regional parties and by independents.

In the end, and after a scare on election night, the prime minister's intuition had paid off. Suárez won the election practically by himself. His well-groomed appearances on television, coupled with his record over the previous year, carried the day. It did not matter that he headed an 'entirely phantom party . . . without history . . . without programme . . . [and] without ideology'.[60] The television image could defeat real parties, both on the Right and on the Left. Felipe González was also, in many ways, a creation of the media. His party gained six times as many seats as the communists and twenty times as many as the PSP. Yet only twelve months earlier, González, like Suárez, was almost unheard of, whereas Carrillo and Tierno were well-known figures.

The result was also a victory for the young over the old. Neither of the winning parties contained a prominent figure either of the old regime or of the opposition. The *franquistas* and the *antifranquistas* had both been defeated. Perhaps they had simply been around for too long: Carrillo and Gil Robles had been bogeymen since the thirties. All of the older politicians who, one year earlier, might have been expected to play an important role in the transition had been left either without seats or in charge of minor parties without much influence: Fraga, Areilza, Arias, Ruiz Giménez, Gil Robles, Tierno, Carrillo. The Communist Party, the protagonist of the *antifranquista* struggle for so many years, had been rejected almost everywhere except in Barcelona. The PSP, the one socialist group to have acted against Franco, had been defeated by a party only recently returned from exile.

The most humiliating electoral performance was that of the christian democrats of Gil Robles and Ruiz Giménez. They polled barely 200,000 votes, and did not come near to winning a seat. The conditions that had favoured the creation of christian democratic parties elsewhere in Europe after the Second World War did not exist in Spain thirty years later. Anticlericalism, which had been such a potent force during the Second Republic, hardly existed, and the Church did not want to see the rise of a new confessional party. But the annihilation suffered by the coalition at the election owed more to the failings of its leaders. Gil Robles was too old and too stubborn; Ruiz Giménez, the most honourable of men, proved to be neither a politician nor a leader. It was folly to stay out of the government coalition, just as it was folly for a christian democrat party to compete for left-wing, *antifranquista* votes.

Considering that the country had not enjoyed a democratic election for forty years, the electorate showed surprising sophistication. In 1936 Spaniards had abandoned the centre; in 1977 they converged upon it. The result was not a victory for the Right over the Left, but for the moderate Right over the *franquista* Right, and the moderate Left over the radical Left. The UCD's real adversary was *Alianza Popular*, just as the PSOE's main rivals were the PCE and the PSP.[61] The voters had picked their side of the spectrum, and then chosen the moderate option. Many people, who were tempted to vote AP or PCE, decided to vote UCD or PSOE both because they did not want to waste their votes, and because they saw the need for moderation at a critical moment in the nation's history.

In the end most Spaniards gor the result they wanted. Only those who voted for *Alianza Popular*, the christian democrats, or the fringe parties on either side, were really dissatisfied. Many people who voted socialist or communist knew that it would be dangerous for their parties to win. They were happy for Suárez to continue in government, at least for a while. He had successfully carried out the first half of the transition; it was best to allow him to complete it.

10
Consensus and the Constitution

The two newly-elected chambers of the *Cortes* found themselves in a strange position. Although they had been elected by a democratic system, they still had to operate within the framework laid down by the previous regime. Franco's governments had not been responsible to the *franquista Cortes*, and Suárez's government was not legally responsible to the democratic *Cortes*. Suárez, whom the king confirmed as prime minister two days after the elections, had clear ideas about the situation: the government's job was to govern, while the task of the *Cortes* was to devise a new constitution.* Once the constitution had been accepted, and the new rules set out, the role of the *Cortes* would be expanded.

Neither Suárez nor the *Cortes* made an impressive start to their terms. In spite of the country's political and economic problems, the *Congreso* devoted its first real debate to an absurdly trivial affair. At the end of August a socialist deputy was roughed up by police during a demonstration in Santander, and the PSOE decided that there would have to be a debate on the matter. In the *Congreso* the socialists called for the resignation of the interior minister but, as no other party supported them, they were easily defeated by the votes of the government party.

Suárez also seemed unaware of the pressing nature of the country's problems. He showed such indolence during his first three months in office that people began to wonder whether the man who had dismantled the *franquista* structure was the right

*The parties of the Centre and Left were in agreement that the new *Cortes* should prepare a constitution. *Alianza Popular* had argued that it was unnecessary to do more than reform Franco's Fundamental Laws.

person to construct the new democracy. His behaviour resembled that of an official of the previous regime: he refused to explain his policies on television, and he refused, except on one occasion, to talk to journalists. His treatment of the *Congreso* was particularly disdainful: he neither made a statement nor answered a question.

Immediately after the elections, Suárez decided that his new government would adopt a social democratic stance. Spaniards had voted for the Left, he reasoned, and therefore it was necessary to govern from the centre-left. Besides, he had come to the conclusion that he himself was a social democrat, and so in the future he would contest the centre-left ground with Felipe González.[1] His intention was perhaps to emulate De Gasperi: to use a centre party, backed by right-wing votes, to pursue left-of-centre policies.

The government which emerged at the beginning of July, however, could only be described as centre-right. Alfonso Osorio, who had become disenchanted with Suárez's style of leadership and believed that his new direction was 'a crass mistake',[2] decided not to remain in the government. But five ministers from the previous cabinet were retained, including Oreja, Martín Villa and Gutiérrez Mellado. Among the new ministers were the leaders of most of the small parties which had formed the UCD, including Cabanillas and the chiefs of three separate liberal groups. There were also a number of christian democrats and a couple of social democrats. Perhaps the only suggestion of a left-wing shift was the appointment of Fernández Ordóñez, the UCD's leading social democrat, as minister of finance. Yet he had been a *franquista* official until 1974, when he resigned as president of INI, and he could not really be considered a man of the Left. The most original feature of the new cabinet was the reorganization of the defence ministries: Suárez broke with *franquista* practice by refusing to give the three branches of the armed forces their own separate ministries, and appointed Gutiérrez Mellado as overall minister of defence.

Two major problems, which had been largely ignored by previous governments, faced Suárez after the 1977 elections. The first, which will be discussed in the next chapter, was the regional question and the related problem of political terrorism. The second was the disastrous state of the Spanish economy.

Suárez, like Arias and indeed Franco, knew little about

economics. Since the assassination of Carrero Blanco, governments had concentrated on trying to prevent political upheaval,
and the economy had been allowed to deteriorate. Arias had been
in power as the world recession began to hit Spain, but he had
neither the knowledge nor the will to make an effort to adjust the
economy to the new situation. As inflation steadily rose, he tried
to buy social peace by agreeing to huge wage increases. Suárez
similarly refused to grapple with the economic problems, arguing,
probably rightly, that his first government did not have the
authority to impose the necessary austerity measures. He thus
continued his predecessor's policy of running down the country's
reserves in an attempt to appease labour demands. Neither of
them were successful because the workers were striking for
political reasons more than for wage rises: they were demanding
amnesties, free trade unions and democratic government. In spite
of salary increases that outstripped inflation – real wages in
industry rose by 47 per cent from 1973 to 1978, four times the
average of the OECD countries[3] – the number of strikes increased
more than tenfold. In 1976 Spain lost 156 million working hours
through strikes, compared to less than 15 million the year before.
It had become the country with the highest strike record in the
world, outdistancing Canada and Italy.[4]

After experiencing a growth rate which had averaged 6.5 per
cent a year over the previous decade, the economy grew by a bare
one per cent in 1975. The rise in oil prices, particularly damaging
for Spain with its lack of energy resources and other raw
materials, aggravated a number of problems which had been
disguised by the expansion of previous years. The country's heavy
industries – iron and steel, mining, ship-building and motor cars –
were inefficient and in need of restructuring. With the recession,
many firms faced the prospect of bankruptcy. In addition, the
crisis led to declining investment, high unemployment, rapid
inflation, and a large balance of payments· deficit.

Unemployment increased by more than two and a half times
between 1973 and 1977. The jobless figure in 1977 stood at
832,000, or 6.3 per cent of the work force.[5] Unemployment was
particularly bad among the young and in Andalusia, where it was
exacerbated by the return of many emigrants no longer able to
find work in the factories of Europe. The inflation rate increased
in similar proportion to the rise in unemployment, growing from

11.4 per cent in 1973 to 24.5 per cent in 1977.[6] Meanwhile the balance of payments, which had been positive in the years up to 1974, showed a deficit of $4.3 billion in 1976 and $2.2 billion a year later.[7]

Enrique Fuentes Quintana, the new vice-president for economic affairs, was perhaps the most distinguished member of the new cabinet. An independent-minded academic economist, he decided to tackle the problems with a series of measures that contained both keynesian and monetarist ideas. He proposed to devalue the peseta, create new jobs, reform the tax system, end bank secrecy, impose a credit squeeze, and limit wages to a level several points below the anticipated rate of inflation.

Neither the business community nor the trade unions reacted favourably to these proposals, and the government itself was sluggish in putting most of them into practice. By the autumn the situation was getting steadily worse, and the inflation rate in October was running at 27.4 per cent. Many people began to wonder whether Spanish democracy, which had been born in spite of terrorism and the *franquistas*, might be strangled by economic failure. It was feared that, unless things improved quickly, the country would succumb to a Videla or a Pinochet.[8] At a time when the government was being criticized from all sides, the UCD's leading christian democrat, Fernando Alvarez de Miranda, made the embarrassing suggestion that it should give way to a government of national unity.

At the beginning of October, Suárez finally did act. It was one of the prime minister's eccentricities that he allowed a problem to accumulate for months without attending to it, and then suddenly produced a flurry of activity and solved it in a few days. On 5 October he invited the country's political leaders to discuss the economic problems, and within days they had agreed upon an emergency plan.

The Moncloa Pacts, as the plan based on the proposals of Fuentes was known, were essentially an agreement between Suárez and the Left. The prime minister was offering the opposition a programme of social reforms, and in return he was asking for the co-operation of the unions and the left-wing parties in saving the economy. According to Fuentes, the main objectives of the plan were to improve and transform various parts of the economy, and also to make sure that the burden of the crisis was

spread fairly by creating a more just society.[9] The particular
sacrifice required of the Left was its acceptance, over the coming
year, of wage increases not exceeding the expected rate of
inflation. As wages had run far ahead of inflation for several years,
it did not seem a high price for the opposition to pay. In addition,
there were a considerable number of benefits offered as a reward
for its collaboration. These included higher pensions and unemployment benefit, improvements in education, the health service
and housing programmes, and tax reforms aimed at the wealthy.
In particular, indirect taxes were to be reduced in favour of a
progressive income tax.

The crucial figure in the negotiations was Carrillo, whose
enthusiasm for the plan made it difficult for the socialists to reject
it. The communist leader hailed the Moncloa Pacts as 'the most
serious progressive agreement made in this country between
working-class and bourgeois forces since the thirties'.[10] Camacho,
the communist leader of the CCOO, argued that it was necessary
to support the government in order to preserve democracy. The
comisiones and the PCE backed the agreement no doubt partly
because they considered it to be in the national interest. But it also
fitted in conveniently with their own strategy. The party had only
enjoyed seven months of legality (and only nine years of legal
existence since its foundation in 1921) and it desperately needed to
become respectable. The Moncloa Pacts provided an opportunity
for the communists to play some role, however small, in the
running of the country, and to demonstrate their sense of
responsibility.

Neither the PSOE not the socialist union liked the Moncloa
Pacts, although they signed them in the end. They were suspicious
of Suárez's conversion to social democracy, and they resented his
adoption of their policies. Moreover, they were sceptical of his
ability to carry out the proposed social reforms. But the main
reason for their reluctance to become associated with the plan was
political. Their party was in a very different position from the
PCE and it had a good chance of winning the next elections. There
appeared to be no advantage for the PSOE in supporting a policy
which, if successful, would be of electoral benefit to the
government. Suárez was offering the Left responsibility without
power, and the communists had good reason to accept the offer.
But the socialists knew that it contained little for them. Besides,

they realized that a 'responsible' Communist Party and a 'social democratic' Suárez were a threat to their own electoral prospects. That the socialists did sign the agreement in spite of its disadvantages is a measure of *their* sense of responsibility.

The Moncloa Pacts, combined with other measures taken by Fuentes such as the devaluation of the peseta, could claim several achievements. Strikes became less frequent, so that by 1978 the number of hours lost in labour disputes was only 45 per cent of the 1976 figure.[11] Inflation fell rapidly from 27.4 per cent in October 1977 to 16.3 per cent twelve months later, which was slightly lower than the rate recorded during Franco's last year.[12] There was also an improvement in the trade balance, brought about mainly by devaluation. In 1978 exports grew by more than 27 per cent, and imports by only 4 per cent. For the first time since 1973, Spain's balance of payments showed a surplus.[13]

In spite of these successes, however, there was little increase in economic activity. The steel industry was dramatically in debt, two of its greatest firms on the edge of bankruptcy. The credit squeeze had led to a decline in investment, and many companies managed to survive only by refusing to pay the heavy social security payments which were required of them.[14] Meanwhile, unemployment increased during the year by another quarter of a million to reach 1,083,000, or 8.2 per cent of the active population.[15]

The rapid growth in unemployment convinced the Left that it had made a poor bargain over the Moncloa Pacts. The PSOE and the UGT refused to renew them the following year, arguing that such agreements should be made between unions and employers. By February 1978 even Carrillo was saying that the pacts were virtually dead. Besides the rise in unemployment, the Left also resented the fact that those parts of the pacts which they had liked remained largely unimplemented. The government was simply not prepared to spend enough money to make significant improvements in housing and the social services. Public expenditure in Spain accounted for a much smaller proportion of the national income than in France or Italy, and government spending on the social services amounted to only 12 per cent of Spain's GDP, as opposed to an average of 25 per cent in the EEC.[16] Admittedly, Fernández Ordóñez managed to make the tax system more equitable by increasing direct taxation. But even after his much-vaunted fiscal reform, Spaniards remained very under-taxed by comparison with other European countries. In 1979 taxes were still taking a smaller proportion of their incomes than in any other OECD country except Turkey.[17]

Tax reform did not bring about a significant redistribution of wealth, but it greatly annoyed conservatives who for years had been accustomed to paying very little tax at all.* Many of them had voted for Suárez because he had seemed more likely to defeat the Left than Fraga, and they were horrified to see the government carrying out 'left-wing' policies. The powerful businessmen's association, the *Confederación Española de Organizaciones Empresariales* (CEOE), criticized the Moncloa Pacts and the rest of Fuentes Quintana's policies. It particularly disliked a proposal that unions should participate in company decisions, and campaigned success-fully to get the idea removed from the new labour legislation. Perhaps Suárez felt he had gone too far in alienating the Right, or perhaps he was merely bored by economics once the euphoria of the Moncloa Pacts had passed. Fuentes soon realized that he was not receiving the support necessary to complete his projects, and he resigned from the government in February 1978. Taking advantage of the opportunity to appease his conservative critics, Suárez then replaced a number of other ministers, including the minister of labour who, because his brother was a 'worker-priest' and a leader of the CCOO, was regarded as being sympathetic to the communist trade union. Rodríguez Sahagún, the vice-president of the CEOE, became minister of industry, while Abril Martorell, the vice-president for political affairs, added Fuentes's position to his own. While conservatives were relieved by the disappearance of Fuentes and the appointment of Rodríguez Sahagún, no one was impressed by the emergence of Fernando Abril Martorell as the key figure in the government. Abril was an unpopular figure and the closest associate of Suárez who, as civil governor of Segovia, had given him his first job. An agricultural engineer by training, he had little knowledge of economics, and in the critical circumstances of the moment, he seemed an inept choice to take charge of the economy.

The UCD lacked an overall majority in the *Congreso* and so was forced to come to an agreement with one or more of the other

*As a result of the tax reforms, the number of Spanish taxpayers increased by nearly three times, from 1.8 million in 1977 to 5.3 million in 1979.[18]

parties. With the support of *Alianza Popular*, the government
would have had enough votes to push its legislation through. But
Suárez did not wish to make concessions to Fraga. Besides, he felt
that it was not the right moment to govern by small majorities; he
should try instead to find as much common ground as possible,
and govern through consensus. Before the elections, he had
justified his candidature by saying that he wanted to prevent Spain
from being polarized between Left and Right. Thus it was logical
that afterwards he should have looked for collaboration not from
Alianza Popular, which would have led to a clear ideological
division, but from the socialists. It was a wise decision, and it
fitted in well with his personal inclinations. Suárez was never a
parliamentarian. Devoid of strong convictions himself, he had a
horror of ideological confrontation. He disliked all kinds of debate
and visited the *Congreso* as seldom as possible. Under Suárez,
government became a matter of arranging things quietly behind
the scenes, in the corridors of the *Congreso*, or late at night in the
restaurants of Madrid. During Suárez's second government, the
PSOE behaved in public as a normal opposition, loudly denouncing the government and its policies, but in private its leaders were
often co-operating closely with the UCD. For most of the time
the government was run according to a set of compromises
worked out, after much bargaining, by the two main parties.

The spirit of compromise, even if it did not last, had been
present during the negotiations over the Moncloa Pacts. Its
presence was more obvious, and also longer-lasting, in the
difficult negotiations over the constitution.

Spain had had an unfortunate constitutional history. Discount-
ing various constitutional reforms and constitutions not put into
practice, the country received no less than eight constitutions
between 1812 and 1975.* Five of them lasted for eight years or
less, and the average was seventeen. Only one of them, Cánovas's
constitution of 1876, was designed to be acceptable to most shades
of political opinion; and it was the most successful, lasting until
Alfonso XIII turned to a dictator in 1923. The other constitutions
failed principally because successive governments wrote them to

---

*There were new constitutions in 1812, 1834 (technically known as a royal
statute), 1837, 1845, 1869, 1876 and 1931. Franco's seven Fundamental Laws,
promulgated between 1938 and 1967, can probably be regarded as a constitution,
although a rather strange one.

suit themselves and their supporters rather than the country as a whole. When they were overthrown, their constitutions went with them.

The UCD saw the need to break with historical tradition and produce a constitution which all the main political forces could accept. In July 1977 a constitutional committee was set up, consisting of 36 deputies of the *Congreso*, which in turn appointed a sub-committee of seven to produce a draft constitution. The sub-committee completed its work in December, and at the beginning of January the first draft was published by the *Cortes*. This was studied by the deputies, who suggested over a thousand amendments, and then handed back to the sub-committee. Over the following two months, the seven politicians worked their way carefully through the amendments. The consensus began to break down over the issues of education and the Church, and the government had to rely on the support of *Alianza Popular* to get its way. The PSOE reacted angrily to this development and withdrew its representative, Gregorio Peces-Barba, from the sub-committee. As the co-operation of the socialists was essential for the success of the constitution, the two main parties agreed to compromise again. In late May, Abril Martorell, the vice-president of the government, and Alfonso Guerra, the deputy leader of the PSOE, sat up all night in a Madrid restaurant to sort out their disagreements. After hours of haggling, they worked out a series of compromises, and in the following session the constitutional committee approved a string of articles almost without debate. The inter-party bargaining infuriated *Alianza Popular*, which withdrew in protest from the committee, arguing that constitutional matters should be decided in parliamentary committee and not in restaurants.*[19]

In July, a year after the formation of the constitutional committee, the text finally reached the *Congreso*. The debates were of little interest, because nearly everything of importance had already been decided, and the text was passed with only two negative votes and 14 abstentions (most of them from *Alianza Popular*). It then went to the *Senado*, where a further 1,200 amendments were suggested. These were examined by another

*Fraga was in the United States when Silva Muñoz announced that *Alianza Popular* would withdraw on 23 May. On his return he promtly reversed Silva's decision.

constitutional committee, and a number of changes were made. The senators discussed the text at the end of September and, after more uninspiring debates, passed it. Since the text approved by the *Senado* contained some important differences from the one passed by the *Congreso*, however, it was left to yet another committee, this time composed of both senators and deputies, to reconcile the two. On 31 October the amended text was at last approved overwhelmingly by both chambers. In the *Congreso* it received 325 votes, including those of the UCD, the PSOE, the PCE and all but one of the Catalan nationalists. Six deputies voted against and 14, including the Basque Nationalist Party, abstained. Of all the political parties, only *Alianza Popular* was unable to adopt a firm position. Half of its 16 deputies voted affirmatively with Fraga, but 3 abstained and 5, including Silva Muñoz and Fernández de la Mora, voted against.*

The new constitution was the longest of all the Spanish constitutions, even longer than the Constitution of Cádiz or the Fundamental Laws, and two or three times as long as the others. It also took a very long time to produce: while the Second Republic's constitution of 1931 was passed in less than six months, the 1978 text took more than fifteen. Even allowing for the importance of finding a consensus, it was an excessively long period to spend on the task. As Fraga warned, the population was becoming disillusioned by the sight of politicians endlessly discussing abstract points while terrorism increased and the economic situation remained critical.[20]

The constitution was not an original document. It borrowed freely from previous Spanish constitutions and from some modern European ones. In the preamble the nation announced its objective of establishing an 'advanced democratic society'. Article 1 defined Spain as 'a social and democratic State of Law', whose 'higher values' were liberty, justice, equality and political pluralism. It declared that sovereignty resided in the Spanish people and that the political form of the state was a parliamentary monarchy.

The monarchy did not become a serious issue because the communists refrained from making it one. Carrillo had promised Suárez in the spring of 1977 that his party would accept the

*In the upper house, 226 senators voted in favour, 5 voted against, and 8 abstained.

monarchy on condition that Juan Carlos led the country to democracy. A year later he declared before the constitutional committee that the king had played a vital role in the transition, and that therefore the Communist Party would vote for Article 1: '. . . as long as the monarchy respects the constitution and popular sovereignty,' he said, 'we will respect the monarchy'.[21] The Socialist Party, however, decided to contest the matter, and introduced an amendment which, if successful, would have made Spain a republic. In the constitutional committee its representatives claimed that the monarchy was incompatible with democracy because it implied that the king and not the people was sovereign. 'In Spain', one of them dramatically declared, 'liberty and democracy have come to have only one name: Republic!'[22]

The socialist stance was supported by none of the other parties and the amendment was easily defeated. The PSOE accepted the decision and did not raise the point again. The amendment had been a half-hearted gesture in any case, designed to appeal to the party's republican members, rather than a serious attempt to change the nature of the state. The socialists knew that they had no chance of imposing their will, and that it would be disastrous if they had. They therefore used the issue for internal party reasons and as a bargaining counter to exchange for concessions on other matters.

The most controversial articles in the constitution were those dealing with education, the Church and regional autonomy. In 1931 the republicans had stated bluntly that Spain had no official religion and that no church or religious institution would receive any financial help from the state.[23] The harshness of the government's anticlericalism, and the refusal to concede that the Catholic Church had a special role in national life, had been largely responsible for the great division in Spanish society during the thirties. As Carrillo reminded the deputies in 1978, the attacks on the Church had given Franco an ideological basis for his 'crusade'. Even though the religious question was no longer such a controversial issue, he warned the Left not to repeat its mistakes.[24]

On both the religious and the educational articles, the Communist Party took more moderate positions than the socialists. There was general agreement that the Church should be disestablished, and that the privileges granted by Franco should be rescinded. But the UCD (and, of course, the Church) wanted to include some reference to the historic role of the Catholic Church. To Carrillo this seemed a very minor concession, and he was happy to make it. But once again the socialists decided to oppose the government. Only after the Abril-Guerra dinner, and in exchange for concessions on other things, did the PSOE accept Article 16:3, which stated that, although there would be no state religion, 'the authorities will take into account the religious beliefs of Spanish society and will therefore maintain relations with the Catholic Church and other confessions'.

The wording of Article 16 was apparently one of the reasons for the PSOE's withdrawal from the constitutional subcommittee in March 1978. Another was the question of private education, which was supported strongly by *Alianza Popular* and the UCD. Again the communists swallowed their political principles and again the socialists refused. They did not like private education (which in Spain usually means schools run by the Church or the religious orders) and they were opposed to providing it with public funds. Again the matter was resolved by an Abril-Guerra compromise. Article 27 would guarantee freedom of education and bind the government to give some financial assistance to private schools; it would also ensure that children in state schools could receive religious teaching if their parents so wished. On the other hand, the article gave the state some control over the institutions it helped to finance by giving it the authority to inspect and license them. Furthermore, teachers, parents and in some cases pupils would be given the right to participate in the administration of any institution receiving public funds.

Alianza Popular, which was excluded from the restaurant bargaining, complained bitterly about these compromises. To give the state any control over private education, argued its spokesmen, negated the principle of freedom of education. Another compromise they opposed was Article 32:5 which, as they recognized, plainly opened the way for a divorce law. Fraga felt that the family was insufficiently protected by the constitution, but he was proud of his successful amendment to Article 15, which in its final form began, 'All have the right to life . . .' The use of the word 'all' convinced him that the future legalization of abortion was now impossible.[25]*

* This seems questionable. The original draft stated that '*las personas tienen derecho*

In Fraga's view the most important task for the authors of the constitution was to define the relationship between the regions and the state. The success or failure of the constitution, he believed, depended on the development of an autonomous system that safeguarded the unity of the nation.[27]

Spain has been ruled by heavily centralized governments for most of the last 300 years, and, as we have seen, Franco's regime carried this trend to an extreme. The least centralized governments were the two short-lived republics, and for that reason the Basque country, like Catalonia, remained loyal in 1936. During the dictatorship, Basque and Catalan nationalists were prominent in the *antifranquista* opposition, and their claims were eventually adopted by the Left. In March 1976 *Coordinación Democrática* called for the recognition of 'the rights and political liberties of the different *nationalities** and regions of the Spanish state (emphasis added). When the political parties began to consider the constitution, there was widespread agreement on the need for regional autonomy. Even *Alianza Popular*, whose *franquista* leaders had helped to impose a rigid centralist policy on the country, declared itself in favour of regionalism. For Article 2 of the constitution, it proposed a text which stated that Spain would 'recognize and encourage regional, provincial and local autonomy' and 'take into account the principles of autonomy and decentralization in all its legislation'.[29]

But the Left and the nationalists required stronger language. They wanted a text which recognized not only regional differences in Spain but 'national' differences as well. A confusing draft

---

a la vida', but AP replaced *las personas* by *todos* (all). The substitution was made specifically to preclude the possibility of legalizing abortion, but it is doubtful whether *todos* can include the foetus. In its widest sense, *todos* can mean 'all creatures' (not only human), in which case the constitution prescribes vegetarianism! But in the sense used in the rest of the constitution it simply means 'all people'. And whatever arguments are made about life beginning at conception, a foetus is not legally a person.[26]

*Nationalists in Catalonia, the Basque country and Galicia had, of course, long regarded their regions as nations, but the *national* parties, even of the Left, had not accepted this definition. In 1918 the PSOE called for the establishment of a 'republican confederation of the Iberian nationalities', but later dropped the demand.[28] The word nationality, used in this sense, does not appear in the 1931 constitution.

was produced referring to the 'peoples' and 'nationalities' of Spain, which seemed to imply that there was no Spanish people as such but only a collection of different peoples living in Spain. Herribert Barrera, the radical Catalan deputy, even claimed that Spain was not a nation but a state consisting of a group of nations. Nor was it a fatherland, he argued, because a people cannot have more than one of these, and the only fatherland of the Catalans was Catalonia.[30]

The final text for Article 2 was a compromise, leaving out the word 'peoples' but retaining the reference to 'nationalities': 'the Constitution is based on the indissoluble unity of the Spanish Nation, the common and indivisible homeland of all Spaniards, and recognizes and guarantees the right to autonomy of the nationalities and regions which compose it.' The following article established Castilian as the official language of the state but recognized that in the autonomous communities the local language would also be official.* Similarly, while the red and yellow flag would be the national flag, the autonomous communities would be allowed to use their own flags and symbols as well. Article 4 stated that on public buildings and at official occasions, the national and local flags should fly together. Towards the end of the text, the constitution dealt with the autonomy statutes and their limitations.

The constitution's provisions for autonomy were too little for the Basques, good enough for the Catalans, and too much for the Right. Fraga had strenuously opposed the use of the word 'nationalities', pointing out that *nación* and *nacionalidad* mean the same thing, and that a nation cannot consist of other nations. The acceptance of the concept of nationalities, he believed, would be a time-bomb for the unity of Spain.[31] Fernández de la Mora went further, predicting that it would lead to a 'national disaster',[32] while Silva Muñoz argued that the constitution would culminate in the break-up of Spain.[33] In the short run, however, it merely led to the break-up of *Alianza Popular*. Silva and Fernández de la Mora could not stomach the constitution, left the party and tried to found something even further to the Right called *Derecha*

---

*Article 3:2 does not define 'the other Spanish languages [which] will also be official in the respective autonomous communities', but they are presumably limited to the more obvious ones (Galician, Catalan, Basque) and do not include the scores of dialects in Spain.

Democrática Española (Spanish Democratic Right). It was the third party Silva had attempted to set up in under four years.*

Five weeks after the constitution had been passed by both chambers of the *Cortes*, it was submitted to the country through a referendum. The campaign leading up to the vote was uninteresting because all the main parties were on the same side. In favour of the constitution were the UCD, the PSOE, the PCE, the major part of AP and the main Catalan nationalist party. Between them, these and allied parties had won over 90 per cent of the votes in the election the previous year.

Among the parties campaigning for abstention were the stalinists of Enrique Líster, radical nationalist groups in the Basque country and Catalonia, and the Basque Nationalist Party itself. Those who rejected the constitution entirely included an ultra-nationalist Basque group called *Herri Batasuna* and a collection of extreme right-wing parties. Together with the largely imaginary parties of Silva and Fernández de la Mora, the *Falange*, *Fuerza Nueva* and a carlist group all urged a negative vote. The constitution was denounced by the *Falange* as 'anti-national, anti-social, anti-catholic and anti-family',[35] and a handful of bishops, led by the cardinal-archbishop of Toledo, agreed. They claimed it was an agnostic constitution which would lead to permissiveness. The Church as a whole, however, did not take a position on the constitution.

Predictably, a large majority of the Spanish people accepted the constitution, 87.9 per cent of those voting recording a 'yes' vote, 7.8 per cent voting 'no', and the remainder casting null or blank votes. Nevertheless, the abstention rate was higher than had been expected: barely two-thirds of the population bothered to go out to vote. The results indicated that in most of Spain, including Catalonia, people were content with the constitution, but not over-enthusiastic about it. Abstention was well above the national average only in Galicia, where it has long been a tradition, and in the Basque country, the only region where the constitution

---

*The first was *Unión Democrática Española*, which he founded in 1975. Finding himself in a minority on the party's executive committee, he left to form *Acción Democrática Española*, which he brought into the coalition of *Alianza Popular*. Silva and Fernández de la Mora apparently discussed the formation of an alliance with the neo-fascists of *Fuerza Nueva*, but it never came off, and *Derecha Democrática Española* disappeared from sight.[34]

encountered concentrated opposition. Less than half the Basques voted, and of those who did, a fifth cast negative votes.

There was considerable disappointment about the low turn-out, but it was not very surprising. The electorate was being asked to vote on a long and complicated document which few people had read. Besides, as there was no danger of its defeat, there was little incentive to make the journey to the polling-booth. The apathy, however, probably had other causes as well. Within a few months of the elections, political commentators had begun to talk about *desencanto*, or disenchantment, with the political process. 'This country likes bulls and blood', wrote one of them. 'When consensus is reached, people are disappointed.'[36] The facile cliché does not help to explain the *desencanto*, but people were undeniably disillusioned by the behaviour of politicians during the first year of democratic government. They had expected a great deal from democracy – open government, political morality, the participation of all – and they discovered political reality: the incompetence of government, the low standard of public debate, the midnight pacts in smoke-filled rooms. Just as *franquistas* had believed that democracy would lead to disaster and the break-up of Spain, many Spaniards had expected it to cure their economic, political and social problems. And of course it did not.

On 27 December the king signed the constitution, and two days later the prime minister announced that national elections would be held in the spring. The previous year Suárez had promised to hold municipal elections, but he had later postponed them, presumably because he realized that the government would lose in each of Spain's large cities. He now declared that they would take place on 3 April 1979, *after* general elections had been held on 1st March. The government reasoned that a defeat in the local polls after a victory in the national contest would be of little consequence. A local government defeat before the elections, however, might damage the UCD's credibility and lead to a further reverse at national level.

The *Cortes* elected in 1977 was not a parliament equipped with the authority to control the executive or to introduce major legislative initiatives. It was in effect a constituent *Cortes* whose task was to write a constitution under which the new democratic regime could be nurtured. It was a temporary body needed to oversee a certain phase of the transition, and Suárez was right not to take advantage of his party's position in the *Congreso* by attempting to govern for a full term. In June 1977 he had acquired a mandate to complete the transition he had begun the previous year. He now needed a further one to govern the country.

The UCD could go to the electorate with a reasonably successful record. Its twenty months in office had seen the making of the constitution and the Moncloa agreements on the economy. Although all the main parties had made important contributions to each of these developments, the government inevitably received most of the credit. The economic situation was still bad, with unemployment growing rapidly, but the government could not be held wholly responsible for this since its policy had been endorsed by both the unions and the parliamentary opposition. One area in which the UCD had achieved very little was the Basque country. In spite of generous amnesties in 1977, and the autonomy envisaged by the constitution, political violence had escalated and in 1978 ETA killed 68 people. The organization had become increasingly ambitious and among its latest victims were a number of senior army officers.

The political forces of the Right were particularly critical of the government's failure to combat terrorism. Fraga argued that the policy of amnesty coupled with political concessions was folly, and the results seemed to support his contention: terrorism increased rather than diminished, while the police and the armed forces became gradually more resentful. When reproached in the *Congreso* for the ominous manner in which he discussed terrorism, Fraga replied that the statistics for 1978 for political violence were higher in every respect, except for the burning of churches, than those of 1936.[37] For the Right, the UCD's weakness over terrorism was typical of its incapacity to deal with the problems of the country. 'Dictatorship and civil war will return,' warned Fraga, 'if we continue with a government that does not govern.'[38]

Many people inside *Alianza Popular*, and many others to its Right, believed not only that the government was wrong but, more fundamentally, that the system was wrong too. The *desencanto* was far more pronounced on the Right than on the Left. In the opinion of many conservatives, democracy was a disaster, and almost all the country's problems could be attributed to its failings: strikes, inflation, pornography,* terrorism and so on.

*The increase in pornography was the only one of these that could be attributed

Fernández de la Mora doubted whether the transition could possibly have been carried out worse.[40] Antonio Carro, another of Franco's ministers who was now an AP deputy, claimed that none of Spain's problems – 'separatist nationalism, relentless terrorism, frightening unemployment and a decaying economy' – had existed during the dictatorship.[41] The remark, typical of the sentiments of many who went around saying that life was better under Franco, suggests ignorance or bad faith on the part of its author. Separatism and political terrorism were present through much of the dictatorship and increased towards the end. The economic crisis was caused largely by the international recession of the middle seventies. Besides, the main economic problems which Suárez had to deal with had their roots in the *franquista* epoch. Inflation and unemployment both tripled during the last five years of Franco's life;[42] the balance of payments deficit was at its highest during the years either side of his death.[43]

Fraga was the voice of the *franquista* Right. He articulated its fears, its resentments and its criticisms. But he did not really belong to it. At the same time that he was hammering the government for its weakness and its failure to deal with ETA and other problems, he was moving his party towards the political centre. The attempt to set up a *franquista* party, headed by ministers of the old regime, had been a mistake, although Fraga never formally admitted it. What the country needed, he now believed, was a liberal-conservative party, similar to that formed by Cánovas a century earlier,[44] a kind of Spanish Tory party. Such a party, a 'moderate and progressive Right', should become one of the pillars of the new democracy; the other would be a 'realistic, non-revolutionary Left'. If, he argued, Spain achieved a two-party system along these lines, parliamentary government could flourish as in Britain, France or Germany. But if the present situation continued, the country would end up with a system like Italy or Portugal.[45]

During 1978 *Alianza Popular* shed its leading *franquista* names. One by one they left, either because they had been disappointed

---

to the change of regime. There had been a similar situation during the Second Republic, when the relaxation of censorship led to a rash of erotic publications.[39] In 1974 Spaniards were crossing the Pyrenees to watch films such as *Last Tango in Paris*. Four years later films that had been cut in Britain and France could be seen in their entirety in Spain.

by the election results or because they disagreed with Fraga. The last to go, López Rodó, departed in January of the following year, leaving Fraga free to build the sort of party that Areilza had been urging on him in the summer of 1976. One of the first things he did was to renew his links with the former minister of foreign affairs. Areilza had originally wished to rejoin the UCD but, as Suárez refused to accept him, he formed a new group called *Acción Ciudadana Liberal* (Liberal Citizens' Action). Calling for a new majority of the liberal, 'civilized' Right, he then joined Fraga in an alliance called *Coalición Democrática* (CD). Another important recruit was Osorio, who had refused to remain in the cabinet in June 1977; he later resigned as adviser to Suárez because he was 'fed up with giving advice to someone who hears it without listening to it'. Much of 1978 he had spent writing a book to prove that the transition had not been achieved by only one man.[46]

Since the elections, the parties of the Left had also been gravitating towards the centre. At its national conference in Madrid in April 1978, the Communist Party formally abandoned leninism, accepting democratic means of attaining power and renouncing the concept of the dictatorship of the proletariat. The 'eurocommunist' positions adopted by the party, together with the moderate role it played during the Moncloa Pacts and the constitutional process, were part of Carrillo's search for respectability. Not all of the PCE liked these developments, and a considerable number of militants in Asturias and Catalonia left the party in protest at the betrayal of Lenin's teachings. La Pasionaria, the frail and elderly president of the PCE, was also uncomfortable about any move away from the Soviet Union, but she was effectively prevented from voicing her doubts to the press. When a persistent American journalist tried to obtain an interview with La Pasionaria, she was told that she could submit a series of questions so long as they did not include one on eurocommunism. When she finally did gain access to the civil war leader, she was forced to hold the interview in the presence of a 'comrade' who interrupted whenever the conversation touched on controversial issues.[47]

Despite internal unrest over Carrillo's eurocommunism, the morale of the party was generally high. Within a few months of its legalization, the party could claim a membership of over 200,000, far more than any other party in Spain.[48] There had been some disappointment about the meagre scale of the results obtained in the elections, but most people believed that the party's real strength was much higher. They reasoned that many pro-communist electors had not dared to vote for the PCE so early in the transition, and had voted socialist instead. Once parliamentary government had been successfully installed – with the co-operation of a respectable Communist Party – they would return to their natural allegiance. There was some tangible evidence to support this argument. The first trade union elections, held early in 1978, resulted in a major victory for the *comisiones obreras* over the socialist UGT and other unions. If workers who voted for the communist-dominated trade union subsequently voted for the PCE itself, the party would make extensive gains in the elections. Furthermore, two by-elections held in May at opposite ends of the country – Asturias and Alicante – saw the communists doubling their share of the poll. In 1977 the PCE's support in Asturias was only one-third of the UCD's; eleven months later both parties received 23 per cent of the vote.

The PSOE, confirmed as the predominant force of the Spanish Left, spent much of 1978 mopping up the remaining socialist groups in the country. The Catalan socialists (PSC) were formally brought into the party, and they were followed by Galician and Aragonese groups. The most important development was the incorporation of Tierno Galván's PSP. The 'old professor', still, in spite of his electoral defeat, one of the most popular politicians in the country, had little alternative but to concede to the PSOE. The party he had formed a decade earlier was heavily in debt; his closest associates had resigned or were threatening to do so. At the PSP's last conference in April, he therefore recommended a merger with the PSOE, and the delegates accepted his advice. The PSP disappeared, but its leader became honorary president of the PSOE and the party's candidate as mayor of Madrid. With the extinction of Tierno's party, the PSOE's rivals were reduced to the *histórico* remnant, which presented no threat whatsoever, and the *Partido Socialista de Andalucía* (PSA), led by a Sevillian, Alejandro Rojas Marcos. González and Guerra, who were also socialists and Sevillians, were irritated by the appearance of a specifically Andalusian socialist party. Distrusting Rojas Marcos, whom they regarded as a bogus socialist, they had earlier decided to ignore his party and to refuse to allow it to join them.★

Unlike *Alianza Popular* or the Communist Party, the PSOE did not undergo ideological changes between the end of 1977 and 1979. The party remained saddled with the radical, marxist programme of 1976, the moderate, social democratic manifesto of 1977, and a leader who in May 1978 said that at the next conference (May 1979) he would propose the removal of the word 'marxism' from the party's programme.[50] This failure to define itself caused the socialists considerable problems in the election campaign. While the UCD claimed that the PSOE was at heart a left-wing party pretending to be social democratic, the PCE attacked it as a centre party pretending to be radical. Carrillo argued, with some justification, that the PSOE's radicalism – evident in the early opposition to the Moncloa Pacts, the republican amendment to the constitution, and the inflammatory speeches of Alfonso Guerra – was merely a facade.[51] Apart from being irresponsible, these performances were being put on, he claimed, in order to deceive left-wing voters.

The electoral campaign, which began early in February 1979, was of a generally low standard. Unemployment was the electorate's chief preoccupation, and all the parties talked confidently about combating it. But there was little depth to their arguments on this or other subjects. The party programmes were almost uniformly vague and gave little indication of what the opposition parties would do if they found themselves in government. They all fought aggressive campaigns, with a high content of personal abuse, based on moderate programmes. All of them were converging towards the centre and were hoping to capture 'moderate' votes: Carrillo had sloughed off leninism, Fraga had got rid of francoism, González had said he would jettison marxism. The four main parties were going for the votes of the centre-left and the centre-right, and thus most of the criticism was directed against the PSOE and the UCD. The government party was attacked by all the others – especially CD (AP plus Areilza and Osorio) and the PSOE – for being weak and incompetent; the PSOE was attacked by all the others – especially the UCD and the PCE – for the contradictions between its programme and its manifesto.

The PSOE went into the elections expecting to emerge from

---

*This is according to the evidence of Felipe González. Rojas Marcos has denied that he ever suggested joining the PSOE.[49]

them as the largest party in the *Congreso*. It therefore adopted an astonishingly moderate programme bereft of socialist proposals. It called for firm government, liberty and security, a modern army and so on, but it did not propose nationalization – except for a part of the electricity grid – or other radical measures. Felipe González acquired a new image, appropriate to one about to form a government. He started appearing in a tie and suit, instead of shirt sleeves, and the photograph on his posters made him look older and more serious.

The PSOE's moderation gave Carrillo the opportunity to make inroads among the party's left-wing supporters. The old communist leader knew that in these elections the PCE had its last chance to become a major force in Spanish politics, and he made an intense effort to capture the working class vote. He claimed repeatedly that the 'social democratic' PSOE had betrayed the working class and that true socialists should vote communist. The PSOE was no longer the party of Pablo Iglesias,* but the party of Willy Brandt and Helmut Schmidt.[52] Its leader was a handsome fellow, he admitted, but politics were not a beauty contest and the elections should not be, as in 1977, 'a plebiscite between two pretty boys'.[53] González refused to answer this criticism, stating that he would do nothing to damage the Left's chances in the election. Displaying remarkable restraint, he even advised people to vote communist rather than for a party of the Right.[54]

The communists' attacks on the PSOE were matched by Fraga's criticism of the UCD. His *Coalición Democrática* did not bother to elaborate on its own programme or ideological beliefs, but concentrated on hammering the government for its weakness and broken promises. Areilza criticized the 'frivolity' of the UCD, while Fraga dwelt on the incapacity of Suárez and Abril, describing their party as a 'great national swindle'. The violence of their language concealed the fact that CD's economic ideas were similar to the government's. Areilza admitted that fiscal reform had been necessary, if badly carried out, while Osorio even suggested that the election could lead to a coalition government of CD and the socialists.[55]

Suárez and González were less aggressive than the other leaders, but their followers did not show similar restraint. Probably the

*Pablo Iglesias (1850–1925) was one of the principal founders of the PSOE in 1879. He later became leader both of the party and of the UGT.

worst language in the campaign was used by the PSOE's deputy leader, Alfonso Guerra, who had a habit of labelling his opponents fascists or nazis. The UCD fought a cleverer campaign than in 1977, its leaders advising the electorate not to vote socialist because of its marxist programme, or to waste its vote by choosing the CD. On the last day of the campaign Suárez went on television to warn voters of the socialist threat. Abandoning the moderation he had shown earlier, he told them that they had to choose between marxism and a free and christian society. Although he denied it, he was playing intelligently on conservative fears, advising the Right to vote for the Centre to stop the Left.

Opinion polls during the campaign gave the socialists a slight edge over the UCD, and put both parties well ahead of the others. Observers expected the two to finish with a similar number of seats in the *Congreso*, and much time was spent speculating on the nature of the coalition that this would necessitate. The polls also indicated that Spaniards were less interested in the result than in 1977, and that there would be a high abstention rate. On 1st March they were proved right: only two-thirds of the electorate bothered to go to the polling stations. Although the voting age had been reduced from 21 to 18, and the electorate had therefore expanded by more than three million, fewer votes were cast in the second elections than in the first.

None of the main national parties received a significant increase in support, except for the communists who won 300,000 more votes and three extra seats, though they had hoped for a much greater improvement on their 1977 result. The UCD won almost the same number of votes but three new seats, leaving them only seven short of an overall majority. The PSOE also gained three more seats than in 1977 but, as it had been reinforced by the PSP's six seats in the meantime, it suffered a net loss. As for *Coalición Democrática*, Fraga's new formation lost nearly a third of the support of his old one, and began the new parliament with just nine deputies.

The socialists lost partly because the Right rallied to Suárez, and partly because of the strength of the regional vote in two of their strongholds. The advance of local parties was the most notable – and, as far as the Basque country was concerned, most disturbing – aspect of the election. Three seats in the *Congreso* and one in the

Senado were won by *Herri Batasuna*, the Basque extremist coalition which acted as ETA's political front. In the PSOE's heartland of Andalusia, the party suffered its worst defeat, losing much of its support to the local socialist party, the PSA.

After 1st March the Spanish Right found itself totally unrepresented in 90 per cent of the country. It won no seats in the two Castiles (not counting Madrid), Andalusia, Extremadura, the Levante and Aragon. Outside Galicia and the capital, it elected only two deputies. Suárez's tactics had worked. By telling Spaniards not to split the anti-socialist vote, he had gained the support of people who disliked and distrusted him. One natural supporter of Fraga in Seville said that he voted for Suárez 'holding his nose'.[56]

As in 1977, it was very much a personal victory for the prime minister. The UCD was still less of a party than its rivals, and its other leaders had made little impact on the nation. The electorate did not vote for the UCD but for Suárez and his record over the previous two years. His appearances on television (which once more was used shamelessly to support the government) again made a vital contribution to the victory.* Suárez's famous charm, which was so pervasive that one politician had to tell him that he was not a snake and therefore there was no point trying to charm him,[58] still worked on the Spanish people.

---

*According to research done by the German Social Democratic Party, Suárez's final television appearance won him nearly a million floating votes.[57]

PART THREE

Reactions to the Transition

11
Catalonia and the Basque Country

The first task of the restored monarchy was to establish parliamentary democracy. Its second was to dismantle Franco's centralized administration and set up an alternative system acceptable to the country's regions. The experience of the previous three regimes seemed to demonstrate that democracy and centralized government were incompatible in Spain.

Decentralization ought to have been a priority. The violence in the Basque country should have made it clear to the government that long delays in tackling the issue would only strengthen the position of the extremists. In Catalonia the political forces were less strident, but almost all of them opposed the policy of Arias. The Catalans had never liked the Borbóns, ever since the first one had removed their *fueros* in 1714. In 1931 they had voted overwhelmingly to get rid of Juan Carlos's grand-father. Their attitude towards the new king was at best sceptical, and they required some rapid encouragement if they were to be persuaded to accept his regime.

The Catalan *antifranquistas* were remarkably united. By 1976 twenty political parties and more than eighty other groups belonged to the 'Assembly of Catalonia', set up five years earlier. Their political colouring ranged from trotskyism to christian democracy, but the assembly's components agreed on two fundamental demands: the restoration of the autonomy statute of 1932, and the appointment of Josep Tarradellas as their negotiator with the government.[1]

Tarradellas, a veteran politician of the republic, was a dignified old man living frugally in exile in a small village by the Loire. He had no power, no organized following, and he was not involved

213

in party politics. His only firm political asset was the fact that in 1954 the exiled deputies of the *Generalitat* had elected him as their president. To many Catalans who had never seen him, he was thus their legitimate leader, a symbol both of their autonomous past and their present aspirations. In the middle seventies he became a sort of De Gaulle figure to them. Prominent Catalans flocked to his home in France, and returned to Spain demanding his reinstatement as president of an autonomous Catalonia. Tarradellas relished the role accorded him. He wanted to go back to Catalonia as a national hero, like his father-in-law, the legendary Colonel Macià, who had returned from France in 1931 to become the first president of the Catalan government. So he sent messages to the Madrid government announcing his co-operation on condition that it accepted his position as president of the *Generalitat*. In the meantime he warned both the government and his fellow Catalans that he alone had the right to negotiate Catalonia's immediate future.

In the autumn of 1976, three months after the formation of Suárez's first government, a Catalan businessman told Osorio that the way to solve his region's problem was 'to re-establish the *Generalitat*, to invite Tarradellas to Madrid to visit the king, to persuade him to accept the monarchy and the unity of Spain, then to name him president of the *Generalitat*, whose functions he would negotiate with the government'.[2] The vice-president thought it a good idea and recommended the scheme to Suárez. But the prime minister was not, at that time, enthusiastic. He sent an emissary to France, but did nothing else to follow up the idea. Tarradellas, he told Osorio, was too old for the part.[3]

The following year, Suárez changed his mind. In June 1977, largely as a result of his failure to deal with the Catalan question, the UCD was badly beaten in the elections in Catalonia. A coalition between local socialists, led by Joan Reventós, and the regional branch of the PSOE, won a decisive victory. The government party came fourth, after the local communist party, which scored heavily in Barcelona, and a nationalist coalition led by Jordi Pujol. The return of Tarradellas – though eagerly demanded by Reventós and by the Assembly of Catalan Representatives – was Suárez's attempt to establish some personal credibility in Catalonia. Tarradellas, like other elderly politicians such as Carrillo and Gutiérrez Mellado, admired the youthful prime minister, and the details of his return were quickly worked out by the two men. On 23 October, after an absence of thirty-eight years, Tarradellas came home to Barcelona. The following day, in an event presided over by Suárez, he was installed as president of the *Generalitat*.

The manoeuvre was highly successful. In 1932 public opinion had been angrily divided over the question of Catalan autonomy, but forty-five years later Spaniards accepted it as logical and necessary. Only the extreme Right regarded the re-establishment of the *Generalitat* as an outrage.[4] The Catalans themselves were aware that the reconstituted *Generalitat* was largely powerless, little more than a symbol, but they regarded it as an assurance that after the constitution they would acquire real autonomy. Catalan politicians co-operated in the drafting of Spain's constitution, which in December 1978 was overwhelmingly approved by the Catalan electorate. In none of the four provinces did the negative vote reach 5 per cent, and the abstention rate was lower than the Spanish average.

The establishment of autonomy was a lengthy process, and Catalans became increasingly restive at the delays and prevarications of the government. In April 1979, four months after the Catalan deputies had approved a draft statute of autonomy, there was a massive demonstration in Barcelona to demand a quick restoration of home rule. Suárez was in no hurry to comply, and nor was Tarradellas. The old man was evidently enjoying his time in the *Generalitat*, and seemed to be trying to delay progress towards a statute and elections which would inevitably turn him out. In the summer, the *Congreso* finally approved a statute giving Catalonia its own parliament and a considerable measure of home rule. According to the articles of the document, the *Generalitat* would have far-reaching powers over education, the economy, the social services, and much else besides. A referendum on the statute was held the following October, and a huge majority of those who went to the polls voted in favour. Abstention was high (40 per cent) but this may have been partly caused by the heavy rains on the day, and by the indifference of the Murcian and Andalusian immigrant workers to the question of Catalan nationalism. In addition, the Catalans had already been asked to vote three times over the previous ten months – general elections, municipal elections and the constitution – and this probably contributed to the widespread apathy.

Those parties which regarded themselves as Catalan nationalist before anything else, had fared badly in both general elections, chiefly because their main aims were shared by the leading 'national' parties. The *Esquerra*, descendant of the party which Macià, Companys and Tarradellas had all belonged to in the thirties, won on each occasion a solitary seat in Barcelona. Pujol's party, which underwent a series of metamorphoses and ended up as *Convergència i Unió* ('Convergence and Union'), could manage only fourth place in the 1979 elections, behind the three principal 'national' parties. In some ways *Convergència* resembled the old *Lliga* of Cambó. It was regionalist, liberal and, although more to the Left on social issues than the *Lliga*, it appealed to the same section of society: the liberal-minded, nationalist middle classes. But whereas the *Lliga*'s rivals were anti-nationalist, *Convergència*'s competitors broadly shared Pujol's views on the regional question. When Catalans went to vote in the general elections, they had the choice of several parties which differed on many things, yet most of the manifestoes appealed to their nationalist sentiment. Not surprisingly, many people decided to vote for a party which might come to power in Madrid.

In the autonomous elections of 1980, however, the situation was very different. Catalans were voting for a Catalan parliament and the politics of the rest of the peninsula did not affect them. Consequently, they voted for their own nationalist parties, and all the 'national' parties, except the communists (who were in any case largely autonomous of the PCE), suffered defeats. The socialists lost a large chunk of their votes to the *Esquerra*, while the UCD lost nearly half of its support to Pujol. *Convergència* won an unexpected victory, and was able, with support from the UCD and the *Esquerra*, to form a government.* Shortly afterwards, Tarradellas, now in his eighties, reluctantly stepped down and handed over the *Generalitat* to Jordi Pujol. The Catalan question

---

*Four years later Pujol won an even more impressive victory. Several months before the autonomous elections in April 1984, it seemed almost certain that he would be defeated by the socialists. In the event, *Convergència* increased its share of the poll from 28 per cent to 48 per cent and won an overall majority in parliament. The socialists came a distant second; the communists and the *Esquerra* were practically obliterated, losing between them nearly three-quarters of their seats.

was no longer a serious political issue.

There were problems and quarrels during the restoration of Catalan autonomy, and there were problems and quarrels afterwards, over the slow transfer of powers from Madrid. But considering the historical dimensions of the question, and the centuries of antagonism between Castile and Catalonia, it is remarkable how easily and peacefully the matter was resolved. Most of the credit was due to the Catalans themselves, who combined moderation with unity and a sense of purpose. In contrast to the rest of Spain, Catalonia's leaders during the transition had been prominent and courageous opponents of Franco. They were not ex-ministers or former officials of the *Movimiento* suddenly claiming to be democrats. Tarradellas had spent the entire dictatorship in exile, Pujol had been tortured and imprisoned by the regime, and they were accepted by Catalans as men who had proved their fitness to govern.

Tarradellas was a difficult and autocratic man, but he did Spain and Catalonia a great service. He wanted to see a democratic Spain and an autonomous Catalonia; and he realized that they depended upon each other. The fragile regime, beset by violent enemies in other corners of the peninsula, could not have survived a rupture with Catalonia. Tarradellas's intention, like Cambó's, was to use Catalan nationalism to help the democratization and modernization of Spain; and to manage it he had first to satisfy the nationalist aspirations of the Catalans. Tarradellas, backed by men with such prestige as Pujol and Reventós, and assisted by talented younger politicians like Miquel Roca and Eduard Punset, had the strength to get his own way. Radical nationalism was smothered in Catalonia because no one could successfully dispute his authority.

Adolfo Suárez also deserved credit for the success of the venture, and he received it when his party increased its vote and representation in Catalonia in the 1979 elections. He had various Catalan friends and advisers, and, unlike many of his colleagues, he possessed an intuitive feeling for the region and its problems. Understanding Catalonia's relationship to the rest of Spain, he realized that the success of the constitutional monarchy depended upon a satisfactory resolution of the Catalan question. On one occasion he remarked that those who believed the monarchy could only be consolidated by a socialist government, could see no further than their noses. The reconstruction of the state, he said perceptively, would be complete the day a Catalan became prime minister.[5]

Unfortunately, Suárez did not have a similar understanding of the Basque country, an area which required even more urgent treatment than Catalonia. He succeeded a government which regarded the Basque problem as a problem of order. You have to kill terrorists, Franco had argued, or they will kill you,[6] and Arias's government had stuck faithfully to this view. Fraga, apparently oblivious of the events of the previous eight years, believed that the Basque problem could be settled by sending in the army, setting up military courts, and shooting the terrorists.[7]

If the Basques had to choose between ETA and a government in which the Franco/Fraga 'reasoning' predominated, it clearly was going to side with ETA. In the summer of 1976, therefore, Suárez should have moved quickly to assure Basques that his government was radically different from its predecessors not only in its attitude to democratic reform but also in its attitude to the Basque country. Some early concessions, as gestures of good will, might have won Basque confidence. But, fatally, he delayed. He did make the concessions, but too late and under pressure, and public opinion had already turned against him.

When Suárez was appointed prime minister, the Basque people had two immediate demands: the legalization of its flag, the *ikurriña*, and an amnesty for political prisoners. It also pressed strongly for the repeal of the notorious decree of June 1937 which referred to Vizcaya and Guipúzcoa as the 'traitor provinces' and abolished their fiscal privileges. The offensive phrases had in fact been removed some years earlier, but the financial clauses remained. Their rapid repeal, argued several officials in the summer of 1976, would be a gesture that would cost the government little and mollify the Basques a lot. Among those who recommended this course of action were the presidents of the councils of Vizcaya and Guipúzcoa, and the leadership of the *Guardia Civil*.[8]

Suárez did not appear to realize that he was waging a battle with ETA for Basque public opinion. He waited until the last days of October before repealing the decree, and by that time ETA had assassinated the president of the Guipúzcoan council. (His Vizcayan colleague was killed a year later.) There was an even longer delay over the *ikurriña*, which was not legalized until the following January. The Law for Political Reform, submitted to the country the previous month, was thus considered without enthusiasm. The abstention rates in Vizcaya (47 per cent) and Guipúzcoa (55 per cent) were much the highest in Spain.

The problem with Suárez's Basque policy was that it was invariably overtaken by events. By the time he had conceded one thing, the Basques were demanding another. His policy was that of an opportunist, acting only in reaction to pressures and events. His decisions, made usually in response to disorders and demonstrations, appeared always to be dictated by tactical considerations, not by conviction or by principle. The amnesty conceded shortly before the 1977 elections was plainly intended as a measure to restrict violence during the campaign. Had it been conceded earlier, as part of a coherent policy, it would have had a much greater effect.

The government announced a 'pre-autonomy' statute for the Basque country in December 1977, but no other progress towards a political settlement of the problem was made while discussions over the constitution were taking place. The Basques' resentment at this failure, and their lack of faith in the government, were reflected in the unco-operative attitude of the nationalist deputies in the constitutional debates. As we have seen, the constitution provided for the decentralization of government and autonomy for all Spain's regions. But it did not satisfy the Basques, who demanded recognition of their foral traditions.

Alfonso Osorio understood the magic which the word 'foral' has for the Basques and suggested an amendment re-establishing 'the historic rights of the foral territories' abolished by the laws of 1876 and 1939. But the government refused to accept it. Osorio, by then a strong critic of Suárez, claimed that it was a great opportunity wasted, and he was probably right. The Basque Nationalist Party (PNV) wanted express recognition of the foral rights, but apparently it would have agreed to Osorio's suggestion.[9] The party's acceptance of the constitution would have been an immense advantage to the government in its attempt to pacify the Basque country, but Suárez, and especially his vice-president Abril, were not prepared to make that extra concession. The PNV representatives consequently abstained in the votes in the *Cortes* and, declaring that 'our *fueros* are our constitution', recommended an abstention in the subsequent referendum. The fact that less than a third of the Basque electorate voted in favour of the constitution indicated the extent of the government's failure to understand the Basque problem.

In July 1979, three years after Suárez had become prime minister, the government and the PNV finally reached agreement on the contents of an autonomy statute for the Basque country. Suárez had tardily recognized that the only chance of bringing peace to the region lay in the creation of an effective autonomous government controlled by Basque nationalists. He thus agreed to a statute which, at least in theory, gave the Basques a substantial measure of self-government, more indeed than they had received through the statute of 1936. The Basques were defined as 'an autonomous community within the Spanish state', and given their own parliament in Guernica. The Basque statute, like the Catalan, listed an impressive range of subjects over which the local government would have control. Among other things, the Basques were given the right to their own radio and television stations, and to set up their own police force.

The agreement between Suárez and the PNV leader, Carlos Garaikoetxea, was a major breakthrough for both sides. Left to themselves, the two men would have continued to co-operate, and the provisions of the statute might have been put smoothly into practice. But unfortunately both of them were constricted by other factors and the co-operation soon ceased. Suárez was accused by conservative politicians of selling out to the Basques, and Garaikoetxea was accused by fellow Basques of selling out to Madrid. The three main obstacles to the attainment and consolidation of autonomy were the opposition of the Spanish Right, the equivocal attitude of Garaikoetxea's own party, and the terrorist campaigns of ETA.

Spanish right-wingers believed a firm hand was necessary in the Basque country, not a string of concessions which would lead to 'the break-up of Spain'. Silva railed against the decision to give the Basques control of their own schools so that they could 'teach children how to hate Spain'.[10] Fraga ranted on about order, obsessed by the sight of Spanish flags being burnt by Basque demonstrators.[11] The weakness of the government, he insisted, permitted ETA to act almost with impunity. It was partly in deference to protests from the Right and from the armed forces, which were losing increasing numbers of men in terrorist attacks, that the government began to slow down the transfer of powers to the new Basque government in Guernia. In response, the PNV announced in January 1980 that it was boycotting the Madrid parliament until devolution was speeded up.

At the time of Franco's death, Catalan politicians of all colours were in general agreement on a solution for their regional problem. In the Basque country there was no such consensus. There were nationalists who favoured outright separatism, nationalists who genuinely accepted autonomy, and nationalists who were prepared to accept autonomy as a tactical move, a half-way stage before eventual independence. What the Basque country lacked was a Tarradellas with the authority and the will to unite the disparate tendancies. The PNV, the historic nationalist party and principal component of the Basque government in exile, should have played the decisive role. But its leaders were not prepared, or not able, to accept political responsibility.

The difficulty with the PNV was that it was still divided – as it had been ever since the end of the nineteenth century – into moderate regionalists and extreme nationalists. The leadership remained in moderate hands but it was unable to unite the party behind it. The PNV may have been a member of the Christian Democratic Union, but ideologically and structurally it was a party of the distant past. The influence of Sabino Arana still hung heavily over the behaviour of its members. When its leader, Juan Ajuriaguerra, suggested accepting the constitution and getting rid of Arana's old motto, *Jaungoikoa eta Lagizarra* (see above p.113), he was howled down by the pure *sabiniano* nationalists. He died shortly afterwards, in 1978, and was succeeded by Garaikoetxea, who resigned after a brief period to become president of the Basque government, and then by Xabier Arzallus. Arzallus, a former Jesuit, also set about modernizing the party, and provoked a similar reaction. The party did not want to be modernized, claimed the radical nationalists; it wished to remain an old-fashioned popular movement which respected its traditions.

By 1980 the two wings of the PNV disliked each other so much that it seemed illogical for them to remain in the same party. But the *sabinianos*, who hated Arzallus and regarded him as 'an incompetent and machiavellian impostor',[12] refused to leave. In the Basque country the PNV is regarded not just as a party but as the chief national institution, and to leave it is considered almost sacrilegious. Arzallus was eventually reduced to expelling several hundred *sabinianos* who, in the spring of 1982, formed a collective called *Euzkotarrak*. Accusing Arzallus of betraying the Basques, and of trying to 'hispanicize' the PNV,[13] its members complained that he was planning to convert Basque nationalism into mere *'folklorismo'*.[14]

The PNV leadership was hampered all along by the attitude of the party's radicals. The *sabinianos* opposed the decision to participate in the constitutional discussions, they opposed the negotiations over the statute and they opposed the statute itself because it did not restore the foral system. On nationalist questions there was very little difference between this group of highly reactionary people and the 'maoist', 'third world' leaders of ETA. This is a point which is seldom recognized by right-wing Spaniards who maintain that ETA is simply a small marxist group controlled by the KGB. ETA may have maoist leaders and receive Russian backing, but at its core it is a *sabiniano* organization, and its supporters owe far less to Marx or Mao than they do to Sabino Arana. ETA's intolerance and fanaticism come from carlism via Arana, not from *Das Kapital* or the Long March. Many of its most effective gunmen come from those same areas which provided carlism with its best fighting-men.

The intransigence of the *sabiniano* group in the PNV made it practically impossible for the party to take an unambiguous stance on anything other than police brutality. Arzallus was a fine orator and an able man, but he did not have the character, and perhaps not the will, to fashion a coherent programme for his party. Throughout the critical period of the transition, the PNV leadership lacked the courage to state unambiguously where it stood on the vital issues of terrorism and eventual independence. It remained ambivalent on a solution to the crisis – except to call repeatedly for more autonomy – ambivalent on its long-term aims, and ambivalent on ETA. If the Basque Nationalist Party had accepted the constitution and categorically condemned ETA's violence during the early years of the transition, a solution to the Basque problem might have been possible. Its equivocation on these issues left the PNV open to the accusation of complicity: as Madrid's leading paper put it, the party was 'consciously or unconsciously, following a policy that in the final analysis gives moral support to terrorism'.[15]

Since the autumn of 1974, ETA had been divided into two organizations, a 'political-military' wing (ETA-*pm*) and a military wing (ETA-*militar*) which split away in protest against the main group's decision to dilute violence with political activity. Eduardo Moreno Bergareche, the ETA-*pm* leader known as 'Pertur', wanted to transform his group into a Basque nationalist workers' party. He was fed up with the gunmen of ETA, who he said were now running a police state in which they simply liquidated their rivals, and he now wished to concentrate on the political struggle.[16] He did not get far. In July 1976 he disappeared in France, almost certainly murdered by ETA's Berezi comandos on the orders of their leader, Miguel Angel Apalategui.

Pertur's followers did, however, set up the party that he envisaged, and in 1977 it contested the elections under the name of *Euskadiko Ezkerra* (Basque Left). Unfortunately, its sole deputy in the *Congreso* was a flamboyant fanatic, Francisco Letamendía, who did nothing for the reasonable and responsible image which the party was trying to put forward. However, Letamendía soon resigned and the leadership revolved around a San Sebastian lawyer, Juan María Bandrés, and a former member of ETA, one of those sentenced to death at Burgos, Mario Onaindía. Later they were joined by another ex-ETA member, Roberto Lertxundi, who brought with him the bulk of the Basque Communist Party. Under their collective leadership, *Euskadiko Ezkerra* evolved into a serious and comparatively moderate force, although it never received as much support as its rivals. Since it did not possess a fanatical *sabiniano* element, it could take clear decisions without breaking the party. Rejecting the tactics of ETA, which Lertxundi compared to the Sicilian mafia,[17] *Euskadiko Ezkerra* encouraged the negotiations between Suárez and Garaikoetxea, and accepted the eventual statute. The party believed that the only solution for the Basque country was full autonomy within the Spanish state.

The various political groups which supported ETA-*militar* did not contest the 1977 elections. But shortly afterwards they formed a coalition, *Herri Batasuna* (Popular Unity) which, to almost universal surprise and dismay, won 172,000 votes (15 per cent of the Basque poll) in 1979, electing three deputies and a senator. It owed its success largely to the number of well-known figures it paraded as candidates, in particular to the presence of Telesforo Monzón.

Monzón, a former minister of the 1936 Basque government who broke with the PNV in the 1950s because it continued to collaborate with Spanish republicans, was one of the legendary figures of the Basque country, a national hero for thousands, an irresponsible opportunist for thousands more. Descended from a noble family, and the owner of two medieval houses in Vergara, Telesforo Monzón personified many of the bewildering contradictions of Basque nationalism. Both anti-marxist and anti-capitalist, he had a simple, carlist approach to politics, although his family had originally been liberals. He once told a Spanish court that he refused to recognize it, because the only courts he recognized were those of God and Euskadi.[18] A poet and a romantic, he was also a defender of ETA terrorism. He was bigoted and intransigent, yet he was capable of inspiring Basques of all creeds and classes. At his funeral in 1981, the vast crowd was divided between those crossing themselves and those with clenched fists.

Herri Batasuna was a rejection front more than a political party. It fought elections but then refused to send its representatives to the parliaments of Guernica and Madrid. It was a pure nationalist movement – though, like ETA, some of its leaders were marxists – and it stood only for a united, independent Basque country which included the Pays Basque and Navarre. It was inconceivable that Navarre – 'mother of Euskadi, heart of Euskadi, soul of Euskadi, spirit of Euskadi', wrote Monzón[19] – would not be part of the Basque country. Navarre should join Euskadi even if its inhabitants chose otherwise, asserted *Herri Batasuna*, because of their ancient historical association. 'Euskadi,' announced one of its leaders, 'is a nation which has rights that cannot be forfeited or decided by voting.'[20] In its rigid fanaticism and sweeping intolerance, its refusal to compromise and its incapacity for self-criticism, *Herri Batasuna* proved a worthy descendant of carlism and Sabino Arana.*

Apart from its demand for independence, *Herri Batasuna* did not have a political programme. It was simply opposed to every measure which the government had taken: anti the constitution,

---

*I was once watching the news on Spanish television with a Basque friend who is a socialist and a nationalist, though not a member of a political party. The programme included a report on Iran, and when we saw scenes of Ayatollah Khomeini's supporters yelling slogans and rampaging through Tehran, he turned and said, 'this is the nearest thing the rest of the world has to *Herri Batasuna*.'

anti the statute, anti the Basque government. In 1982 *Herri Batasuna* was still demanding a *ruptura* with the previous regime. Its leaders still talked about 'the fascist regime in Madrid', and argued that they could not have been expected to stop fighting after Franco's death merely because Madrid pretended to change its political system. One of them even suggested that only a *ruptura* could save Spain, and therefore ETA was doing Spaniards a favour by carrying on the struggle![21]

ETA's most ruthless commander, Miguel Angel Apalategui was released, after a brief period in a French prison, in 1977, and shortly afterwards he organized ETA's most bloodthirsty and sustained offensive. After a comparatively mild year in 1977, during which the organization could claim only twelve victims, it assassinated 68 people in 1978, half of them policemen. As its successes increased, it became more ambitious, and its targets included colonels and generals. Between the summers of 1978 and 1979, its gunmen murdered ten high-ranking officers. In June 1979 it extended its operations to Spain's Mediterranean beaches, so as to dissuade tourists from bringing much-needed foreign exchange into the economy. The deaths ETA inflicted in 1979 totalled 78, while the following year it broke a new record, murdering more than ninety people.[22]

Although both ETA and *Herri Batasuna* denied that they were hoping to provoke an army coup, this is obviously what they were trying to do. They knew they had more chance of waging a successful guerrilla war against a repressive military dictatorship than against a democratic regime based on overwhelming popular support. ETA often timed its assassinations to coincide with particularly difficult moments of the transition, such as the debate on the Law for Political Reform. After it had helped to provoke the attempted coup of 1981, it concentrated its attacks on army officers, presumably so as to 'encourage' them to try again.

Shortly after the agreement between Suárez and Garaikoetxea in the summer of 1979, ETA announced that it would carry on the struggle until the Basques had a real democracy instead of 'the military dictatorship of Juan Carlos'.[23] Two months later, Monzón declared that ETA would not lay down its arms unless the 'government agrees to a parliamentary amnesty, withdraws the forces of occupation (*sic*) and recognizes the unity of the Basque country and its right to self-determination'. 'Until the sovereignty of the Basque people is recognized,' he added, 'I will never publicly criticize the actions of ETA-*militar*.'[24]

The Basque electorate voted in favour of the autonomy statute in October 1979 and abstained in no greater numbers than the Catalans voting in their simultaneous referendum. The elections to the Basque parliament in Guernica the following March also had similarities with those in Catalonia. The UCD and the PSOE were punished for the delays in reaching autonomy, while the nationalist parties increased their vote. The PNV predictably gained the most seats while *Herri Batasuna* unexpectedly took second place in front of the socialists. The *Herri Batasuna* deputies then refused to take their seats, a decision which left the PNV with a bare overall majority. Garaikoetxea was thus elected *lendakari*, or president, of a government of PNV members.

On his election, Garaikoetxea announced that his objectives were peace, the development of autonomy, and a solution to the economic crisis.★ His intention, supported by Arzallus, was to set up a strong nationalist government with sufficient autonomy to attract Basques away from ETA. The difficulty was that both ETA and the Spanish government seemed determined to make his task as difficult as possible. Devolution had been a slow process under Suárez, but after his resignation in January 1981 and the attempted coup a month later, it became slower still. Nevertheless, there were some real advances. Among Suárez's last actions were a decision to give the Basques authority to raise their own taxes, and a move to encourage the formation of an autonomous Basque police force.

During 1980, the worst year of terrorist violence, public opinion in the Basque country finally began to turn against ETA. In May a number of intellectuals denounced political violence, and later in the year the PNV began to adopt a less equivocal stance. In November, after the assassination of two local UCD leaders, the party took part in an anti-ETA demonstration in San Sebastian. (ETA's response was to attack a bar in Zarauz a few hours later

---

★The economic crisis, severe in any case in the Basque country, was exacerbated by ETA's activities, which discouraged investment and terrified industrialists. Various members of the Neguri oligarchy were assassinated, and many others left the region, with their companies, to avoid a similar fate. Those who remained often survived only because they agreed to pay the 'revolutionary taxes' which ETA extorted from them.

and kill four policemen and a civilian.) Arzallus remained provocative and ambiguous, criticizing Madrid and the police in intemperate language, but he also criticized ETA. 'We want no tyrants, not even Basque ones,' he announced on Basque national day in 1982.[25] To the ETA/*Herri Batasuna* claim that nothing had changed since Franco, he retorted: 'the only thing that has not changed is that you go on killing in a country which has abolished the death penalty.'[26]

One of the obstacles to a full-hearted condemnation of ETA by moderate nationalists was the behaviour of the police force. Members of the *Guardia Civil* had acted with extreme brutality during the dictatorship, and their behaviour did not improve substantially under the new regime. The long list of Basques, often quite unconnected with terrorism, who emerged from the cells bearing clear marks of torture – a few did not emerge, having died in custody – reinforced the belief of many that they were a people under military occupation. On occasion, when Basque opinion had been outraged by some ETA atrocity, the effect was offset by an ugly piece of police brutality. In February 1981 ETA murdered José María Ryan, a man whose only 'crime' was that he was the chief engineer at a nuclear power station of which ETA disapproved. The socialists, the communists, *Euskadiko Ezkerra* – every party except *Herri Batasuna* – organized a massive demonstration to protest against the 'fascist fanatics' of ETA. A few days later, José Arregui, a member of ETA, died in police custody in Madrid, his corpse revealing that he had been subjected to long and intense torture. The Basque country went on strike, and the effect of Ryan's death was nullified. As *Deia*, a Basque paper close to the PNV, commented more than a year later: 'if the murder of Ryan had not been followed a few days afterwards by the dramatic death of the ETA militant José Arregui, while in police custody, ETA's cause would probably now have less support. ETA is nourished by the mistakes of the security forces.'[27]

ETA's campaign reached its zenith in 1980, the organization attacking indiscriminately the representatives of parties and organizations which did not share its views: by the autumn an opponent was being murdered on average every two days. Apart from soldiers, policemen and businessmen who refused to give it money, ETA's targets included socialist, communist and trade union offices in Pamplona, UCD leaders in Guipúzcoa, and various people in Navarre who opposed the forcible unification of their region to the Basque country which the extremists demanded. In the following year, the number of ETA's victims dropped, not because the terrorists had changed their ideas, but because they themselves had taken heavy casualties and did not have enough gunmen. The killings and kidnappings continued, however, during subsequent years, without any indication that they might ever stop. In 1984 even Federico Krutwig – a leading ETA figure of the sixties and the man largely responsible for setting the organization on its violent path – admitted that ETA was becoming a band of gangsters whose policy bordered on fascism.[28]

Basque separatism was, and remains, the most intractable of the problems of contemporary Spain. A policy of repression failed to solve it, and a policy of concessions and liberalization also failed to solve it – though the latter would have had a better chance had it not been preceded by the former. The results indicated that those who argued for more concessions were as mistaken as those who demanded repression. The amnesties did not reduce terrorism, nor did democracy, nor the statute, nor the Guernica parliament. As Fraga and the Right were constantly pointing out, concessions and violence seemed to go together. However, this is too simple a view. Had the concessions been made at the right time and for the right reasons, the Basque people as a whole might possibly have been converted to Suárez's programme of democracy.

The government made a number of mistakes. Osorio claimed that Suárez did not understand the Basque problem – very few people in Madrid did – and thought that the Basques were just obstinate.[29] Certainly he displayed a curious insensitivity towards the Basque country, which he did not visit until a month before his resignation. In October 1980, an accident in the Vizcayan village of Ortuella, which killed fifty schoolchildren, preceded the murder of the two prominent Guipúzcoans in the UCD. Within hours of the Ortuella tragedy, the Queen was in the town, visiting the wounded and the bereaved. But Suárez did not go. He did not react publicly in any way. He did not go to the *Congreso* and make a statement about Ortuella or the ETA killings. He did not even go to the funerals of the murdered men of his own party.

Suárez's Basque policy failed, but few other politicians in Madrid had any better solutions to offer. In spite of the delays in producing and then implementing it, the autonomy agreement provided the only possible chance of a peaceful settlement. Suárez cannot really be blamed for the persistence of the Basque problem, because he received little help either in Madrid or from the Basques. The qualitative difference between the politicians of the Basque country and Catalonia was a crucial factor in the success of one regional policy and the failure of another. The Basque country produced no statesman such as Tarradellas, no politician with the skills of Pujol, no spokesman as articulate as Roca. But behind the Basques' failure to lead, there was a failure of will. The PNV could not decide whether, in the final analysis, it wanted the transition to succeed.

Yet behind the failures and limitations of contemporary politicians lies the historical inheritance. Liberalism, the great Basque anthropologist, Julio Caro Baroja, once remarked, had never entered the Basque countryside, which remained a place of dogmatism and absolutism.[30] Elsewhere, he said that 'to be a liberal in the Basque country is to be a lunatic; it is like talking to yourself in the street'.[31] A hundred years ago, Sabino Arana made a few converts to his fanatical ideology, and these have multiplied so that they now encompass a large and powerful section of the community. ETA is not a Basque edition of the Red Brigades but the violent wing of an intolerant nationalist movement which stretches across the political spectrum.* This movement – which, if the votes of *Herri Batasuna* are added to an estimated number of *sabinianos* in the PNV, probably represents a fifth of all Basques – is powerful enough to veto any other group's programme for the Basque country, but not powerful enough to impose its own. Only if it is decisively defeated, which is not likely, or if it decides to compromise, which is less likely still, will the Basque problem be solved.

---

*An example of this was provided by the position of the collective *Euzkotarrak* in the 1982 elections. During the campaign, this right-wing, highly reactionary body, which regarded Arzallus as too liberal and too modern, advised people to vote for ETA's political front.[32]

12
The Role of the Military

Between 1976 and 1980 Spaniards were given the opportunity to rid themselves of much of General Franco's legacy. In various elections and referenda, they had the chance to do away with the regime's laws, its politicians, and its system of national and local administration. The only institution of Franco's they were not allowed to touch was the one which put him there in the first place: the army. The *Caudillo* had made the army the chief bulwark of his regime, and he ensured that it would remain a bastion of *franquismo* after his death. He had reinforced the traditional political role of the armed forces to such an extent that they found it impossible to relinquish once he had gone. They demanded a right of veto over the political changes after 1975 and, when this was not conceded by the government, a number of senior officers devoted themselves to one of the oldest traditions in the Spanish army: the art of military conspiracy. Between 1978 and 1982, they plotted at least five coups d'état against the democratic regime.

Since France's defeat in the Peninsular War, the Spanish army has spent more time and energy interfering in its country's politics than in defending Spain or Spanish possessions from external threats. The military role of an army, which in the sixteenth century had been the best in Europe, had been reduced, by the end of the nineteenth century, to garrisoning its own country and to launching minor, often unsuccessful, raids against the Moroccans. Its political role was far more exciting: between the Constitution of Cádiz (1812) and the uprising of 1936, parts of the army rebelled on more than fifty occasions with the intention of changing Spain's form of government. For much of the nineteenth century – especially between the two carlist wars – the army was in effect *the* government. After the restoration of the monarchy in 1876, the army's power declined, and since that date, only two of the many coups have been successful: Primo de Rivera's in 1923, and Franco's in 1936.

Franco restored the army to its self-appointed position as guardian of the nation's values and exterminator of imported heresies. He gave it the first place among the institutions, showering it with parades and decorations, and fortifying its sense of political responsibility. During the dictatorship, the armed forces provided 40 of Franco's 114 ministers and nearly a thousand *procuradores* of the *Cortes*.[1]

Franco kept the armed forces happy by pandering to their sense of importance, not by paying them good salaries or buying them decent equipment. Spain's military budget was surprisingly low for what was at least partly a military dictatorship. In 1966 the government's expenditure per member of the armed forces was a third of Italy's and less than a sixth of what Britain or France was spending.[2] A derisory sum – 6.5 per cent[3] – of the army's budget was spent on new equipment, with the obvious result that the soldiers had to put up with almost obsolete weaponry, which they received, second-hand, from the United States.*

The huge proportion of military expenditure devoted to personnel – 82 per cent of the army's budget[4] – did not mean that officers had high salaries.† It was simply an indication of the

---

*By contrast, the navy spent a quarter and the airforce nearly a third of their budgets on equipment, and were thus able to buy some boats and aeroplanes that were reasonably modern. All the same, the Phantoms which the air force was flying during the seventies were aeroplanes which the Americans had already used and discarded.

†Throughout the dictatorship, military salaries remained far lower than their civilian equivalents. 'For a long time now,' noted Gerald Brenan in 1950, 'it has been almost impossible for a Spanish officer or NCO to live on his pay. As the hours in which they are employed are few, they nearly always take on other jobs in commerce or business, or supplement their earnings on the Black Market. This is not generally regarded as dishonest. The rations provided are deliberately far larger than can be consumed, and every officer and NCO has the privilege of selling his share of what is left.'[5] There was in fact a law which forbade the practice of *pluriempleo* (multi-employment) but the regime did not enforce it, or even encourage its observation. During the 1960s, more than three-quarters of the officers on the general staff either had jobs – often as teachers or businessmen – or were looking for them.[6]

chronic problem of overmanning – a problem which has a long history. For generations, Spain's military efficiency has been sacrificed by governments which – except in the early thirties – have refused to contemplate a major reduction in the country's vast and largely superfluous officer class. Even Franco recognized that the excessive number of people in the army made it expensive to keep up as well as incapable of fighting a modern war.[7] But he refused to make more than minor alterations to its structure because he was not prepared to wound the susceptibilities of his principal supporters by getting rid of dozens of redundant generals.

Franco's army shared the conservative, traditional, 'Castilian' views of its commander-in-chief.* After the civil war, its officer corps consisted of the most conservative section of the republican army (those who had rebelled with Franco) and those newcomers (often carlists or falangists) who had joined out of enthusiasm for the 'crusade'. There was no room for liberalism or republicanism within its ranks, then or later. Subsequent generations of officers were educated by the civil war victors and inculcated with their ideals. As Spain itself began to shake off the crusade mentality, the army remained faithful to the 1936 mission. An opinion poll published recently revealed remarkably old-fashioned views among applicants to the military academy in Zaragoza. Three-quarters of those interviewed replied that their principal preoccupation was 'territorial integrity' and 'the unity of the fatherland'. Among the things they particularly disapproved of were materialism, ungodliness, 'anarchical liberty', conscientious objection and pornography.[9]

In the sixties an officer of the Spanish army, Julio Busquets, conducted a sociological survey of his companions, and in his subsequent book he listed the reasons for the military's isolation from the rest of society. These included the high rate of 'self-recruitment' (four-fifths of officer cadets were the sons of military men†) and the large number of marriages between officers and the daughters of officers, the education cadets received

*Army officers came overwhelmingly from Castile, and from mainly rural regions such as Andalusia and Galicia. Very few were Basque or Catalan. During the sixties, the Castilian town of Burgos provided almost as many candidates for the *Academia General Militar* as the whole of Catalonia and the Basque country put together.[8]

at military schools and at the academy, the work they did which gave them little contact with the civilian population,★ the existence of special military housing, separate hospitals, chemists and so on, the frequency of new postings which made it difficult, even for those who wished to, to become familiar with the local society, and an intellectual life often limited to reading extreme right-wing newspapers.[13] It was perhaps not surprising that this background should produce men such as General García Rebull, a man who saw the hand of freemasonry behind everything that went wrong. 'Political parties,' he once declared, 'are the opium of the people, and politicians are its vampires.'[14]

The army which Juan Carlos inherited was thus overmanned, underpaid, inefficient, reactionary, and loyal to his predecessor. It was also, as the senior defence minister recognized in 1976, the oldest in Europe.[15] The promotion ladder was so blocked that officers usually spent twenty-seven years between leaving the military academy at Zaragoza and becoming lieutenant-colonels; full colonels were often in their sixties, fifteen years older than their equivalents in other European armies. In 1980 there were over 400 generals in active service, in an army which contained only 3 divisions and 28 brigades. The military budget was still very small. Spain's armed forces contained a total of 342,000 men, about 70 per cent of the number maintained by France and Germany, yet their budget was only a quarter the size of the French and one eighth the size of the German. The small budget and the over-manning had the same effect as in Franco's time. The state was unable to pay its armed forces properly – a Phantom pilot could have earned three times his salary if he flew for *Iberia* – and it could not afford to provide them with proper equipment.[16]

The army was not worried by Suárez's appointment as premier, because there was nothing in his background which suggested he

†By 1979 the level of army 'self-recruitment' was down to 64 per cent. Conversely, the figure for the navy was up from 66.7 per cent in 1969 to 81 per cent ten years later. The air force remained much the same, slightly more than half the entrants to the *Academia General del Aire* being sons of military men.[10] Significantly, less than one per cent of those cadets with civilian backgrounds were of working-class families.[11]

★*Pluriempleo* did something to increase contact with civilian life but, according to Busquets, its effect was often wasted because those officers who got on best in their civilian jobs often abandoned the army altogether.[12]

might be a dangerous liberal. The generals' first lengthy encounter with him – at the famous meeting in September 1976 – had been reassuring. One of the participants allegedly stood up at the end of it and exclaimed to the prime minister, 'Long live the mother who bore you!'[17] Many officers did not care for Suárez's reform programme – 15 of the 53 *procuradores* who voted against the Law for Political Reform were military men – but their relations with Suárez did not deteriorate until the legalization of the Communist Party in the following spring. After that decision, significant sections of the armed forces regarded Suárez with intense hostility. That a man of the *Movimiento* should legalize the Communist Party, after assuring them that he would not do so, was to them an act of treason. The event reinforced their anti-democratic instincts and led them to hinder the remainder of the transitional process.

Military pressure on the government became apparent shortly after the general elections in 1977. In October of that year, the army forced the government to exclude from its proposed amnesty members of the old republican army★ and the more recent *Unión Militar Democrática* (UMD).† General Gutiérrez Mellado, the vice-president for defence matters, told a UCD leader that if the amnesty was conceded to these groups, he would not be able to maintain discipline in the army and would resign from his post.[20] Military pressure was also applied during the debates on the constitution, and a number of modifications were consequently made.[21] The constitution as a whole was widely disapproved of in military circles, and the three military senators

★There were several thousand soldiers of the republican army still in Spain. Many of them had been maimed in the civil war, and could neither work nor receive social security.

†The UMD was founded in August 1974 by a handful of officers in Barcelona. Its aim, in the words of one of its founders, was 'to struggle for the transformation of the country into a democratic regime'.[18] At its height, the organization had about 300 members, most of them army captains. In March 1976, nine of the UMD's leaders were convicted of 'plotting military rebellion', expelled from the army and given gaol sentences of up to eight years. Four months later, following Suárez's appointment, they were released from prison, but not allowed to return to their posts. Gutiérrez Mellado clearly had some sympathy with them,[19] although, as they had infringed the law, he refused to have them back in the army. He also realized that their reinstatement would have provoked the fury of a large number of generals and other officers.

appointed by Juan Carlos were among the tiny number of
representatives who did not vote in its favour. At the referendum
two months later – in which the nation voted affirmatively by a
ratio of eleven to one – it has been estimated that the armed forces
supported the constitution by barely two to one.[22]

When Gutiérrez Mellado joined the government in 1976, a
massive task awaited him. He had to persuade an army, for which
'democracy' was a dirty word, to accept a democratic regime. He
had to persuade an army, which had enjoyed a political role for
nearly two centuries, that it must not interfere in politics. And he
had to do something about bringing it up to date. Yet any
fundamental changes he made had to be slow ones: he could not
suddenly accelerate promotion without either causing a still
greater blockage at the top or retiring prematurely a large number
of senior officers. Many of his changes were structural ones –
setting up a ministry of defence instead of keeping the three
separate ministries, reorganizing the general staff, establishing a
new intelligence organization – which were important in themselves, but did little to tackle the real problems. The Law of Active
Reserve, however, which was finally approved in 1981, was a
measure designed to remove some of the congestion in the senior
ranks.

It was impossible to 'de-politicize' in a short time an army
which had accepted political responsibilities for so many generations. Gutiérrez Mellado made a number of changes that,
superficially, made the army appear less political, although there is
no evidence that they made it *feel* less political. He banned
members of the armed forces from taking part in political
activities, from joining political parties and trade unions, and from
expressing political views in public. He substituted the victory
parade, held to commemorate the end of the civil war, by 'the day
of the armed forces'. And he appointed a number of generals,
whom he trusted, to important positions around the country.

There was a tradition in the Spanish army that promotions
should be made according to strict seniority, which meant that the
best officers reached the top in old age, and the worst were assured
of becoming colonels. Gutiérrez Mellado reasoned that, at a time
of radical political change, it made no sense to give sensitive posts
to generals who openly disapproved of that change. He therefore
promoted a number of liberal-minded generals above the heads of

their comrades to positions such as captain-general of Madrid or commander of the *Guardia Civil*. He also decided to remove several generals, whose opposition to the regime was well-known, to posts outside Madrid. In the months following a meeting near Valencia in September 1977, in which nine leading generals (five of them ex-ministers) discussed their complaints of the government, Gutiérrez Mellado transfered a number of senior officers. Among them was General Milans del Bosch, who was removed from the command of the Brunete armoured division (stationed just outside Madrid) and sent as captain-general to Valencia.

The promotions, 'out of turn', of the more liberal generals aroused great indignation among the others. The appointment of Ibáñez Freire, first as commander of the *Guardia Civil* and later as captain-general of Catalonia, provoked immense anger and was probably the principal cause of the resignation of the chief of staff in May 1978. A year later, the appointment of General Gabeiras to the most senior army post caused still greater resentment. The new chief of staff was only a divisional commander, and his appointment meant that he had to be promoted to lieutenant-general, and then to overtake all the other lieutenant-generals who were senior to him. The supreme army council had apparently recommended Milans del Bosch for the post, and the choice of Gabeiras came as a surprise. Several generals reacted by expressing their anger to the press and by boycotting the lunches to which Gabeiras invited them.[23]

In the course of 1977, Suárez and Gutiérrez Mellado became the two principal hate-figures of the most reactionary sections of the armed forces. The Bunker had long regarded the vice-president as suspect because he was a friend of Díez-Alegría, the liberal chief of staff dismissed by Arias in 1974. In December 1975 it had campaigned vigorously against the suggestion that he might join the government, and allegedly compiled a defamatory dossier on him.[24] After he had become a cabinet minister the following year, members of the armed forces claimed that he did not properly represent them, and often showed him disrespect. A campaign of denigration was launched by the right-wing press, which mocked him and persistently referred to him as 'señor Gutiérrez' or 'el Guti'. Aspersions were cast, quite unjustifiably, on his war record and his service with the army.

As the democratic reforms progressed – and political terrorism simultaneously increased – the discipline of the police and the armed forces steadily declined. In July 1978, the police were involved in several disgraceful incidents in which units rampaged around towns in Navarre and the Basque country. The following month, the police federation issued a statement criticizing the government and accusing it of exploiting the police for political purposes. Indiscipline in the army was a more individual matter, frequently displayed at the funerals of policemen or soldiers murdered by ETA. The emergence of coffins from Madrid churches repeatedly provoked cries – from both civilians and officers – of 'Franco! Franco!', 'the army to power', 'Guti – traitor and freemason!' The funeral of General Ortín Gil, the military governor of Madrid, was turned into a demonstration against the government in which members of the armed forces gave the fascist salute and insulted Gutiérrez Mellado.

One of the most notorious incidents took place in November 1978 in Cartagena, at a meeting of several hundred officers in the presence of the vice-president. During question time, the local *Guardia Civil* commander, General Atarés, became very over-excited and attacked both the government and the constitution. Gutiérrez Mellado ordered him to leave the room, which he did, yelling 'traitor' on the way. A few minutes later, Atarés returned and shouted once more at the defence minister, calling him, among other things, a freemason, a coward and a spy. At his court-martial six months later, Atarés – whose defence lawyer claimed the incident was an emotional outburst between two Spanish patriots with different views – was acquitted of the charge of insulting his superior.[25]

Military attitudes towards the government were undoubtedly influenced by the shrill and often hysterical campaign conducted against it by extremists of the civilian Right. Officers' reading tastes, as Busquets had pointed out, were often limited to falangist or neo-fascist newspapers which devoted much space to sneering at Suárez and Gutiérrez Mellado. Day after day papers such as *El Alcázar, Fuerza Nueva, El Imparcial* or *El Heraldo Español*, attacked the 'mediocre' prime minister and his 'treacherous' and 'cowardly' government'. They reported in detail the frequent speeches of Girón, Blas Piñar and Fernández Cuesta, their rantings about 'chaos' and 'disorder', their appeals 'to safeguard the unity of the fatherland'. Other extremists such as Sánchez-Covisa, the leader of the *Guerrilleros de Cristo Rey*, or the fanatical Duke of Tovar, openly exhorted the army to 'do its duty' and topple the 'traitors'.

One officer who witnessed the path to democracy with growing frustration was an excitable Andalusian in the *Guardia Civil*, Lieutenant-Colonel Antonio Tejero. With his massive moustache and his large, droopy eyes, he looked – and behaved – like a foreigner's caricature of a Spanish policeman. He seemed such a buffoon that even the authorities did not take him seriously, and his repeated infractions were punished by either a mild reproof or a few days under arrest. In October 1977 he nearly provoked a massacre in Málaga by ordering his armed subordinates to stop a perfectly legal demonstration. The following August he wrote an impertinent letter to the king in which he attacked the constitution. After the first incident, he was arrested for a month and after the second for two weeks. But his career survived undamaged.

In the autumn of 1978, when Tejero was stationed in Madrid, he conceived his first plot to overthrow the government. On 11 November he invited four officers from the army and the armed police to the Cafe Galaxia, and explained his plan. He would assault the Moncloa Palace on 17 November and capture the government ministers during a cabinet meeting, while his confederate, Captain Saenz de Ynestrillas, would take over various strategic places in Madrid. Holding the entire cabinet hostage, Tejero would then demand a government of 'national unity', presumably headed by the military. The crucial factor in his calculations was the power vacuum there would be in the capital on that day: the king would be in Mexico, and most of the senior generals, including Gutiérrez Mellado, would be outside Madrid.

Two days after the cafe meeting, one of those present informed his superior officer of the conspiracy. Suárez, however, was not told of the plot for another three days. No doubt some of the intelligence officers who knew, simply did not think Tejero capable of executing such a plan, but there appear to have been others who, for more dubious reasons, deliberately kept their knowledge from the government. In any case, on the evening before the coup was due to take place, Tejero and Saenz de Ynestrillas were arrested. To the liberal paper *El País*, which uncovered details of the plot, and to most other commentators, it seemed clear that a serious military coup had been planned. To the Right, and to many in the army, this view was greatly exaggerated: the affair was not a plot at all, they claimed, but merely 'a chat in a cafe'. The military court which tried them seemed to agree: Tejero received a sentence of seven months and Saenz de Ynestrillas one of six months and a day.

A year after the discovery of 'Operation Galaxia', another plot was uncovered. This one would have involved two of the best units in the army, the armoured division stationed a few miles west of Madrid, and the parachute brigade, stationed a few miles east, which would seize simultaneously the Moncloa Palace and other parts of the capital. The chief conspirator, General Torres Rojas, was not tried or even arrested; he was simply transferred while on holiday to La Coruña. The government tried hard to pretend that no conspiracy existed, and even made the ridiculous claim that the general's transfer – after only six months as commander of the armoured division – had been planned long beforehand. When the newspaper *Diario 16* revealed the real reason for the removal of Torres Rojas, such pressure – both political and military – was put on the paper that the editor was forced to resign.

By 1980 the government's attitude towards the military had become absurd. Officers who had belonged to a peaceful political organization had lost their careers, while others who had tried to overthrow the state retained theirs. Members of a theatre group which had allegedly insulted the armed forces went to prison, but soldiers who plotted a coup d'état were free to try again. The government had rightly set out to conciliate the armed forces, to try to persuade them to accept democracy, but it took this policy too far. Its weakness and leniency towards the conspirators had the opposite effect of what was intended. Instead of mollifying the army, this policy of appeasement merely encouraged dissidents to become more daring. After all, they had little to lose. How could a few months in prison be a deterrent to a man who hated democracy as much as Antonio Tejero?

In the autumn of 1980, after the army had come to power in Turkey, Madrid was full of rumours of new conspiracies. As ETA's offensive reached its peak, Girón and his friends renewed their litany: 'we can't go on like this,' 'the hour for action,' 'the fatherland in danger,' 'Spain must be saved'. Right-wing papers discussed 'the lesson of Ankara', while Fraga declared that 'the Turkish solution seemed inevitable'.[26] After a further round of ETA killings in November, Felipe González privately said that he thought a military coup was likely.[27] Even in left-wing circles, it was suggested that a solution to the crisis might be a government of national unity presided over by a general. People began to talk about an 'Operation De Gaulle' to bring to power a strong leader. To many, such a plan seemed perhaps the only way to forestall a violent coup and the establishment of a military junta.

By the New Year, at least two military coups were being plotted. Tejero, who was still, amazingly enough, in Madrid at the head of a transport unit, planned to capture the *Congreso* and thus precipitate a military dictatorship. He would be supported by Milans del Bosch, a general with great prestige in the army, who would stage a *pronunciamiento*. Once this had received the support of the other captain-generals and the army was in control of the situation, Milans would come forward as the Spanish Pinochet.

The second plot had a comparatively mild objective: the establishment of a government of national unity presided over by a general. The man who saw himself in this role was Alfonso Armada, an aristocratic general who had held posts close to Juan Carlos almost continuously since 1955. Armada was a strong conservative with little respect for Gutiérrez Mellado or his reforms; he admitted that his ideas were so far apart from the vice-president's that they could never agree.[28] In 1977 he left his position as secretary of the royal household, claiming that he wished to resume his military career.[29] It is fairly certain, however, that he was removed after pressure from Suárez, who discovered that he had been writing letters in support of *Alianza Popular* on royal household notepaper. Armada subsequently took up a post at Lérida, and returned to Madrid, as Gabeiras's deputy, shortly before the coup. According to one of Spain's most experienced journalists, Armada's rebellion was based on motives of personal ambition and his hatred of Suárez.[30]

The crucial figure in both these plans was Jaime Milans del Bosch, captain-general of Valencia. Tejero believed rightly that he could capture the *Congreso*. Armada believed wrongly that he could persuade both the deputies and the king to accept his solution. But only Milans had the charisma and the strength to swing the armed forces behind them. A bluff, powerful man, Milans del Bosch was the sixth general his family had produced in direct descent. His grandfather had been chief of the military household of Alfonso XIII, and a more distant ancestor had staged an unsuccessful *pronunciamiento* in 1817. Milans was an outspoken, disgruntled man who complained that he was being ignored by Juan Carlos. He had a low view of politicians and of democracy. 'The balance of the transition,' he had declared in a newspaper interview, 'does not seem to be positive: terrorism, insecurity, inflation, economic crisis, pornography and, above all, a crisis of authority.'[31]

In a flat in Madrid, on 18 January, Milans del Bosch discussed his plans with eighteen other conspirators.[32] His personal preference would clearly have been for Tejero's plot, but he needed Armada because of his influence with the king. He decided, therefore, to use Tejero's scheme to pave the way for Armada's solution.* According to Milans, Armada had told him that the king was fed up with the politicians and would look favourably – although he could not support it openly – upon a quick, clean coup.† Milans suggested that Tejero should take the *Congreso*, the armoured division would seize strategic points in the capital, and he would persuade the other captain-generals to support the coup. After that, Armada would go to the *Congreso*, with the king's mute approval, and put himself forward as leader of a government of national unity. (Milans reserved for himself the position of

---

*Armada was not at the meeting and claimed later he knew nothing of any plot. 'The Armada solution was not a conspiracy,' he declared, but a means, conceived after the assault on the *Congreso*, to solve the crisis.[33] To the astonishment and disgust of the other conspirators, Armada insisted throughout the trial and afterwards that he was entirely innocent – although several officers, including Milans and Tejero, claimed to have discussed the plot with him personally. Either Armada was lying to save himself, or everybody else was lying for no good reason. Although there is still some ignorance about the precise nature of Armada's role, all available evidence suggests that he was guilty.

†Milans was hoping to emulate the efficient coup of General Primo de Rivera, which Alfonso XIII had accepted in 1923. Juan Carlos, however, refused to play the role of his grandfather. 'The king is not a devourer of books,' a member of his staff later remarked, 'but there are two historical episodes which he has studied well: that of his grandfather, Alfonso XIII, and that of his brother-in-law, Constantine [ex-king of Greece].'[34]

president of the junta of the chiefs of staff.) The new government would modify but not overturn the constitution, it would 'freeze' marxism, combat terrorism and shear the autonomous regions of most of their powers.

Tejero was not enthusiastic about this programme. He wanted to see marxism destroyed not put on ice, to have the autonomy statutes revoked not amended, to get rid of democracy in all its forms unless it were the 'organic democracy' of General Franco. He wanted the new government to be headed by Milans and a military junta, not by Armada and various politicians. Either Tejero was deliberately deceived, or he simply misunderstood what was eventually decided, because on the night of the coup he still thought he would get his junta. He agreed to storm and hold the *Congreso* – while Milans and the armoured division played their respective parts – until a senior general arrived to take charge of the situation.

The coup, or coups, had been planned for the spring, but Suárez's unexpected resignation persuaded the conspirators to bring their plans forward. It was decided to assault the *Congreso* on the evening of 23 February, when all the deputies would be voting for a new prime minister. That afternoon Tejero assembled about 200 members of the *Guardia Civil*. A few were his accomplices, but most of them had no idea what they were meant to be doing: some were told they were to undertake an operation against ETA. At just after twenty past six, Tejero and his subordinates burst into the *Congreso*. He shouted 'Everyone on the floor', and one of the policemen began firing his gun into the ceiling. Every deputy disappeared under the seats except Suárez, who remained immobile, Gutiérrez Mellado, who remonstrated, and Carrillo. The vice-president told Tejero to hand over his pistol and get out. The conspirators became angry and forced the elderly general – and Suárez who had got up to help – back to their seats. Within a short time, Tejero was in full control of the building and announcing that he would take orders from no one save General Milans. He is reported to have warned that if the *Congreso* was assaulted, he was 'ready to build barricades with the corpses of the deputies'.[35]

Milans del Bosch listened to the assault on his radio and quickly telephoned Tejero to make sure it had gone according to plan. He then issued a manifesto in the name of the king, declared martial law in Valencia, and began telephoning his fellow captain-generals. He told Armada later during the night that he was supported by four of them.

The third stage of the plan was not as successful as the first two. The armoured division of Brunete was supposed to be the main military force behind the coup, leaving its barracks after the seizure of the *Congreso* to take over key positions in Madrid. Two small units did go out to take over and 'protect' the main radio and television buildings; about an hour and a half after Tejero's assault, soldiers arrived in the office of the director of television and ordered him to play martial music. But they did not stay long and the armoured division fulfilled little else of its allotted role. Torres Rojas had come from La Coruña to take over his former troops if their present commander, General Juste, refused to join the plot. But his nerve seems to have failed, like that of the other leading conspirator in the division, Colonel San Martín. The captain-general of Madrid, Quintana Lacaci, learnt of Torres Rojas's presence in the capital and arranged for him to be ordered back to Galicia. Quintana was also responsible for preventing other units of the armoured division from leaving their barracks. After a hesitant start, in which he was either bewildered or undecided as to which side he should back, Juste came down against the conspirators. But he failed to prevent a handful of his younger officers from going out in the small hours to join Tejero.

The coup was lost on the telephone. Within half an hour of the *Guardia Civil*'s attack, Milans and the king were both calling up the country's military leaders. Milans was asking for their support 'in the name of the king', Juan Carlos was telling them that he was on the other side. General after general was telephoned by the king, informed that his name was being used in vain, and told to accept no orders unless they came from the chiefs of the general staff. Juan Carlos encountered hesitations and evasions. The success of Tejero's manoeuvre, the backing of Milans, the involvement of Armada, made some of them feel that to oppose the coup would be to waste a fine opportunity to get rid of the obnoxious democracy. But the king's authority brought them into line. Juan Carlos was, after all, a military man and their commander-in-chief. He was perhaps the only part of the regime for which some of them had any respect. They remembered his years of education in the armed forces, and his constant attention to them since then. They remembered the occasion when, with

Franco on his death bed, Juan Carlos had flown to the Spanish Sahara to show solidarity with troops who were demoralized and uncertain how to react to Morocco's 'Green March'. They may have been dismayed, and perhaps surprised, that the king refused to back Milans, but they accepted his decision.

After three hours of telephone calls, Juan Carlos asked for a television crew to come to the Zarzuela to film a broadcast he wished to make to the Spanish people. The crew took an hour and forty minutes to assemble and drive the few miles to the palace; it then took an hour and fifty minutes to film the short broadcast, take it back to the studios, and put it on the air. It was not until after one o'clock, when Spaniards had been waiting anxiously for nearly seven hours, that they heard the king assure them that the Crown would not tolerate any attempts which 'aimed at interrupting by force the democratic process determined by the Constitution and approved by the Spanish people by means of a referendum'.

The king's message was broadcast at almost the same time as Milans del Bosch's attempt to combine the two conspiracies finally failed. General Armada went to the *Congreso* shortly after midnight. He had suggested to Gabeiras that he should offer Tejero a means of escape *and* offer himself to the deputies as the next prime minister. Armada was given permission by Gabeiras to tell Tejero that he could leave the country by aeroplane, and *not* given permission by either the chief of staff or the king to put himself forward as head of a national government. Nevertheless, he decided that he would go ahead with the plan: 'for the good of Spain,' he told Milans on the telephone, 'I would be prepared to sacrifice myself.'[36]

So Armada went to the *Congreso*, intent on convincing people that he was behaving like a martyr and following no premeditated plan. The *guardias* let him in, and he went to Tejero to explain his proposal. The colonel would withdraw the *Guardia Civil* while Armada entered the chamber, addressed the deputies, and convinced them to choose him as prime minister. Tejero was horrified both by the plan and by the suggestion that he should get in an aeroplane and leave the country. He said furiously that he had not risked his life and career so that Armada could preside over a constitutional government, and refused to allow him into the chamber. The two of them then went off to telephone Milans, who advised Tejero to accept Armada's solution. Tejero replied that he would accept nothing other than a military junta headed by Milans, and Armada left the *Congreso*. Milans had blundered. The two coups he had planned to combine proved incompatible.

Earlier in the night, the king had spoken to Milans and ordered him to withdraw his troops. He would neither abdicate, he said, nor leave the country, and he would rather be shot than accept the conspiracy. At some stage during the small hours, Milans realized that he had failed and called his troops off the streets of Valencia. Shortly before four in the morning, he withdrew his manifesto and went to bed.

Tejero had been told that two hours after he had stormed the *Congreso*, he would be relieved by reinforcements and by a senior general. He waited for eighteen hours and received no reinforcements except Armada, whom he did not want, a naval officer who was an old friend, and a bizarre column of fourteen landrovers containing 113 military police led by a major of the Brunete division. An officer with charisma, and much admired by his subordinates, Major Pardo Zancada was one of the few 'heroes' among the conspirators. When he left the division's barracks under the nose of General Juste, he knew that the coup was going badly. But he felt so ashamed that Tejero had been abandoned in the *Congreso* that he was determined to share his fate. Pardo's honour and his conscience told him to go, and so he went, followed by four loyal captains and the police unit. When he was inside the Congreso, he was offered a safe conduct for himself and his men. But even though he knew that Milans had withdrawn his tanks, he refused the offer. So did the captains. They had to stay for the same reasons that they had to come: because their honour and sense of duty told them to.[37]

As the night wore on, Tejero felt increasingly betrayed and abandoned. At one stage he threatened to kill the director-general of the *Guardia Civil* who had come to talk to him in the courtyard. By dawn he was finding it difficult to keep order among the *guardias*. He tried to raise their morale by reminding them of heroic events such as the siege of the Alcázar de Toledo. But his hold was loosening: some of his subordinates escaped from the building by climbing out of a window. Tejero became desperate, and seemed capable of anything. Realizing that all was lost, he was thinking of some 'heroic' and bloodthirsty end, a sort of Samson

finale in which he would kill himself and his enemies. Later he had
another idea. He would humiliate the deputies by making them
take their trousers off and leave the *Congreso* in their underpants.
But when the time came to surrender, neither he nor Pardo
demanded difficult conditions. Both of them insisted that only
they should be considered responsible for what had happened.
Everybody else should be absolved because they had only obeyed
orders. When it was pointed out to him that his captains could
hardly be regarded as innocent since they had followed him
voluntarily, Pardo conceded that they too could be arrested.
Before midday the terms were agreed, and shortly afterwards the
deputies were allowed to leave. On his arrest, Tejero is alleged to
have said: 'today I am going to have a long siesta, because for
several nights I have not slept a wink. But tomorrow . . .
tomorrow I will start preparing the next coup.'[38]

Thirty-three people were tried for their part in the coup, all but
one of them military men, the civilian a well-known falangist who
had co-ordinated some of Tejero's telephone calls on the night.
Yet these thirty-three were only a small proportion of those
involved. Some civilians and many more soldiers knew about the
conspiracies, but only those most publicly involved were tried. At
the vital conspiratorial meeting on 18 January, nineteen people
were present, but only five of them went on trial. From Valencia,
a city under martial law with tanks on the streets, only three
people faced prosecution. Among those who did not have to stand
trial was the colonel who ordered the armoured unit to 'protect'
the radio and television buildings. None of the lieutenants or lesser
ranks who followed Pardo Zancada were taken to court, and the
lieutenants of the *Guardia Civil* who assaulted the *Congreso* and
manhandled Gutiérrez Mellado were later acquitted.

For the thirty-three people who were tried, the prosecutor
asked for sentences totalling 287½ years. Fifteen months after the
attempted coup, at the beginning of June 1982, the military court
gave its verdict: a total of 122½ years for the defendants. Only
Milans and Tejero received the thirty year sentences which the
prosecutor had asked for. The others, except for the lieutenants
who went free, were given much shorter terms. Armada, for
whom the prosecutor had requested a sentence of thirty years, was
given six years. The prosecution appealed against the sentences,
and the Supreme Court later handed out much sterner ones. It

over-ruled most of the acquittals, increased most of the prison terms, and recognized Armada as one of the chief conspirators by sentencing him to thirty years.

Gutiérrez Mellado later recognized that the conspirators had planned their coups as a reaction to the terrorist offensive and to the government's policy on regional autonomy. He also said that the personal ambitions of certain people, and the encouragement of certain civilians, were important factors.[39] But what did the plotters really want? Nostalgia for the old days was obviously a motive, but which old days? *Franquista* Spain of 1939 or *franquista* Spain of 1975? These reactionary officers and their civilian allies talked endlessly about their country's 'eternal values', but the values – often sexual – which they were referring to, had long since disappeared. In 1975 the main difference between Spain and Italy was not social, nor sexual nor economic, but political. How then could a new dictatorship restore the values which the old one had lost? Spain's urbanized and relatively sophisticated society of the eighties could not have swallowed the crusading doctrines of the thirties.[40]

If it is difficult to see what the plotters wanted, it is even harder to know who – apart from *El Alcázar* and its readership – would have supported them. In 1936 Franco could count on about a third of the population, as well as powerful forces such as the Church, the landowners and the great industrialists. In 1981 none of the country's principal forces would have backed the coup because they had nothing to gain from a South American type of dictatorship. An opinion poll taken a few weeks after the event indicated that the coup would have been supported by only four per cent of the population.[41] In 1936 Spanish conservatives felt threatened, rightly or wrongly, by a left-wing government, and so supported the uprising. The situation in 1981 was entirely different. The coup took place while the *Congreso* was in the middle of voting for a new prime minister, Leopoldo Calvo-Sotelo, who was not a communist, or an anarchist, or even a republican, but a conservative from a well-known conservative family.

In the months following the coup, right-wing Spaniards claimed that its significance had been exaggerated. It was a minor affair, they said, just an incident involving an impetuous general, a lunatic colonel and a handful of extremists. But it was much more than that. The army was divided between those who supported the coup, those who hesitated, and those who remained loyal. On the night, the last two categories outweighed the first, but only because the king and two senior generals put their weight behind them. The vital loyalty of Quintana and Gabeiras vindicated Gutiérrez Mellado's policy of promoting 'liberal' generals out of turn. But the vice-president had little other compensation. His labour of four years had been compromised. He knew that if the king had not been there, or had been out of the country, or had not stood full-square behind the constitution, then Milans would have won.

In the end only one man saved the achievements of the previous five years. But in doing so, he revealed the fragility of the new democracy. The great constitutional structure, erected so laboriously in recent years, could be blown over in minutes by a ridiculous colonel. The day after the coup, the king invited the political leaders to the Zarzuela and, in effect, told them to grow up. The system could not survive, he said, if the monarch was required to intervene directly in the affairs of government. The politicians had to govern the country, and to do so properly they must avoid the endless bickering between parties.

The king's role on the night of 23 February won him the respect and adulation of millions of people who had always considered themselves republicans. 'If one is a Spanish patriot now,' said Claudio Sánchez Albornoz some time after the coup, 'one can only be a monarchist.'[42] Sánchez Albornoz had once headed the republican government in exile.

13
The Collapse of the Centre (1979–82)

The electoral triumph of March 1979 marked the high point of Suárez's career. During the previous three years almost everything had gone right; over the following two years almost everything went wrong. His Gallup poll rating, which had averaged about 60 per cent, dropped remorselessly: by the summer of 1980, less than a quarter of the Spanish electorate approved of the prime minister's policies.[1] On all sides, even from Suárez's own party, people were demanding his replacement. 'The political class,' he was told by a leading journalist, 'seems convinced that you were the right man for the transition, but that you are not the right man for democracy.'[2]

Luck, boldness and inspired improvisation had been the chief ingredients of Suárez's success. But his luck ran out and his audacity deserted him. Faced by the perennial problems of terrorism and economic failure, Suárez found that he could no longer produce the quick, imaginative answers with which he had solved difficulties in the past. In 1980 Spain suffered its worst year of terrorism (nearly a hundred victims of ETA), its highest unemployment figure yet (nearly 1.5 million, or 11.5 per cent of the working population) and its largest balance of payments deficit.[3] The country needed leadership, but Suárez failed to lead. He remained in the Moncloa Palace, nervous, silent and brooding, working by himself far into the night, depending heavily on coffee, sleeping pills and amphetamines.[4] Intensely sensitive to criticism, he met fewer and fewer people. He provoked the hostility of the press by refusing to talk to journalists, and he scandalized the country by failing to attend the funerals of UCD leaders murdered in the Basque country. At a time of national crisis, he did not appear on television and he only rarely visited the *Congreso*. In the twelve months after 1979, he failed to take part in over three-quarters of the parliamentary votes.[5] His lack of leadership was criticized by all parties and prompted the socialists to table a motion of censure in the *Congreso*. 'Suárez has reached the highest level of democracy he is capable of administering,' declared Guerra in May 1980. 'Suárez cannot stand any more democracy, and democracy cannot stand any more of Suárez.'[6] The debate on the censure motion produced some fine oratory, notably from Fraga and González, and a humble admission from Suárez that he had made some mistakes. Although the motion was defeated, not a single deputy outside the UCD supported the government.

Suárez was hurt by all kinds of criticism, but particularly that emanating from his own party. He had taken charge of the *Centro Democrático* in the spring of 1977, turned it into an electoral force, and won two elections for it. But he did not convert the UCD into a proper party. It remained a coalition of disparate groups, held together by the attraction of power. The first conference was held in October 1978, when the UCD claimed to have 80,000 members. Its statutes gave wide powers to the presidency – to which Suárez was easily elected – with control of much of the policy-making and the drawing up of electoral lists. Suárez was determined to reduce the power of the UCD's factional leaders – dubbed the 'barons' – and to set up a monolithic party firmly under his control. After his electoral victory in March 1979, he felt strong enough to leave most of the barons out of his new cabinet – the leaders of christian democrat, liberal, and social democrat groups, as well as Cabanillas of the *Partido Popular* and Martín Villa, were all excluded – and to form a government of people he could count on to support him.

The exclusion of the barons, the shortcomings of the government, and the increasingly autocratic behaviour of Suárez, helped to foster a powerful dissident movement inside the UCD. Most of the opposition came from liberals such as Joaquín Garrigues – the only baron with the charm and charisma to compare with Suárez – and from young, right-wing christian democrats such as Oscar Alzaga and Miguel Herrero de Miñón. They complained of the absence of internal debate in the party, and criticized Suárez's secretive and authoritarian leadership. They also claimed that the prime minister's policies were improvised and opportunist. The government, they contended, had abandoned its voters on the centre-right, to carry out social democratic policies in collusion with the PSOE.*

In the summer of 1980 Garrigues delivered an ultimatum to Suárez: the prime minister must share control of the UCD with the factions and bring them back into government, or he would leave the party. The liberal leader, whom many considered as a possible successor to Suárez, died only a few weeks later from leukaemia, but his ultimatum had its effect. In September Suárez formed a new cabinet, promising a fresh approach and more open government. The principal barons were brought back, with the exception of Lavilla, the hostile christian democrat, who remained speaker of the *Congreso*. Suárez then asked for a vote of confidence, which he received (with the support of Catalan and Andalusian nationalists) and even went to a press conference. But the fresh approach was not forthcoming. Suárez retreated to the Moncloa and the criticisms returned. In October he suffered a severe setback when the 'official' candidate for the post of UCD parliamentary spokesman received the votes of barely a quarter of the party's deputies. Worse still, the victor was Miguel Herrero, the most passionate and flamboyant of Suárez's critics.

At the beginning of 1981, shortly after the dissidents had published a manifesto, Suárez decided to resign from the presidency of both the government and the party. He had been in power for four and a half years, and he was physically and mentally exhausted. He felt that the constant criticism of journalists and politicians had destroyed his image and his credibility. With the support of his own party, he might have been

---

*It is tempting to see the conflict inside the UCD in class and cultural terms. The critics frequently came from privileged, 'establishment' backgrounds. They were well-educated, sophisticated and often linked to institutions of the Church. Suárez and his closest associates – Abril, Martín Villa, Calvo Ortega – were usually self-made men whose careers had begun in the *franquista* bureaucracy. One might justly say of them that they had passed from *franquismo* to a type of social democracy without having become democrats. Suárez's advisers may have been disliked often for snobbish reasons, but the tenacity with which they clung to power was certainly unattractive.[7]

able to carry on, but he believed it was impossible to remain as prime minister while under attack from such a sizeable section of the UCD. He felt bitter, betrayed and alone. Old allies such as Osorio and Fernández Miranda had long since left him, and the country's most powerful institutions – the army,* the Church and the banks were all hostile. It was impossible, he believed, to recover his standing in the country; his continuation in power, he told his associates, would lead only to an electoral disaster.[9]

At the end of January, Suárez announced his intention of resigning. A few days later the UCD, celebrating its second party conference in Majorca, chose its new leaders. Had Suárez's resignation been a genuine renunciation of power, performed in the interests of the UCD, he would presumably have done something to promote party unity at the conference. Instead, he went out of his way to exacerbate the differences between his supporters and the dissidents. His behaviour suggested that his resignation was not a selfless gesture of personal sacrifice, but a tactical move designed to take the pressure off his shoulders while leaving him in effective control of the party. Suárez was resigning as the UCD's president, but he was determined to ensure that the post and the other important positions in the party would be held by his supporters.

Nearly 2,000 delegates went to Palma for the conference, of whom about a third were liberals or christian democrats belonging to the 'critical sector'. Another third were supporters of Suárez, and the remainder were divided between social democrats and followers of Martín Villa, who also supported Suárez. Landelino Lavilla, the most prominent member of the 'critical sector', suggested that the executive should be elected by proportional representation to ensure a fair distribution of seats between the factions. But Suárez refused to accept the idea, and in the subsequent contest only seven of the thirty-nine places on the committee were won by his critics. Moreover, the crucial positions of president and secretary-general were each won by unconditional supporters of Suárez. By the end of the conference, the UCD was firmly under the control of the departing prime

*There were many rumours then and since that pressure from the armed forces persuaded Suárez to resign, but no evidence has been produced to support the theory. Suárez himself roundly denies it.[8]

minister, while the 'critical sector', which could count on strong support both among the parliamentary party and the membership in the country, found itself virtually excluded from the apparatus.

Suárez's resignation and his courage in the *Congreso* during the attempted coup, were applauded by many people, including his opponents. Had he left power quietly, and done what he could to assist the new government, his prestige might have recovered. Had he retired gracefully, he might have returned triumphantly at a later date as the saviour of the centre. But Suárez lived for politics and power, and he could not relinquish them voluntarily. He could not go into business, or retire and write his memoirs, because these things did not interest him. So he stayed in politics, determined to keep the party in his own hands and to prevent the new prime minister from tampering with it. In the process, he damaged his own credibility still further, and contributed significantly to the destruction of the UCD.

One of the few things that Suárez and the barons were able to agree on was the choice of a successor. Every possible candidate was regarded as suffering from some insuperable drawback except for Leopoldo Calvo-Sotelo, the vice-president for economic affairs. In character, Calvo-Sotelo was almost the reverse of Suárez. He was a serious, somewhat lugubrious figure, entirely lacking in popular appeal. He presented a rather staid image to both the press and the public, and made no effort to improve it. A quiet, aloof man, who enjoyed reading and playing the piano, he was untypical of the politicians of his age. One of the qualities people admired in him was his aversion to political manoeuvring and his distaste for late-night scheming in Madrid restaurants.

On 25 February, two days after the attempted coup, Calvo-Sotelo received an overall majority in the *Congreso*, and shortly afterwards he formed a government. From the beginning he was beset by problems: terrorism, which claimed the lives of several senior officers during his first weeks in power; unemployment, which was mounting swiftly towards the two million mark; the chaotic state of the autonomies, which was highly damaging to the ruling party; and the appalling 'rape-seed scandal', in which some 400 people died apparently after being poisoned by adulterated oil. Meanwhile, the internal squabbling of the UCD became shriller and more violent, never ceasing until all the factions ran like lemmings over the cliff in the elections of 1982.

Calvo-Sotelo's twenty months in office cannot be described as successful although the government did negotiate Spain's entry into NATO in May 1982. The fault was partly his own, since as prime minister he displayed a certain timidity and lack of leadership, but more the result of the circumstances in which he came to power. In the aftermath of the unsuccessful coup, the democratic system virtually ceased to function. Astonishing though it seemed, the coup's failure led to an increase, not to a weakening, of the army's influence in the country. Instead of castigating the military for the degrading and embarrassing spectacle in the *Congreso*, the public and the politicians became immensely respectful. At the end of May, barely three months after the coup, the armed forces held their annual celebrations in Barcelona, and were cheered enthusiastically by tens of thousands of Catalans. Each day of the event, the national press devoted several pages to uncritical reports on the state of the army, the *Guardia Civil*, the navy and the air force. To the unwary foreigner, it must have seemed as if the armed forces were returning from a glorious victory.*

In the summer of 1981, Spain's political classes were paralysed by fear of another coup. While rumours of new conspiracies circulated around the capital, the political parties seemed to have entered into a pact not to do anything that might offend the army. Socialist politicians began making respectful remarks about the military, acknowledging its importance and mentioning its 'historic role'. When one of them, unable to digest this hypocrisy, broke ranks, he was instantly reprimanded: a senator who declared in a debate that the army had been abusing its power for years, was contradicted by a senior colleague who assured the chamber that the PSOE knew that 'the immense majority of the'

---

*The army seemed impenitent for its performance on the 23 February, and its courts martial continued to penalize minor infractions by democratic-minded officers more heavily than indiscipline from extremists. In October 1981 the same court-martial had to deal with Captain Juan Milans del Bosch (a son of the coup leader) who in the Club de Campo in Madrid had loudly voiced his opinion that the king was a 'useless pig'; and Colonel Alvaro Graíño, an officer who had written to a newspaper denouncing the presence of right-wing extremists in the army. The colonel's 'crime' led to his detention for two months, while the insult to the monarch cost Captain Milans only one month. After an outcry from the press, the captain-general of Madrid later doubled the captain's penalty.

armed forces are democrats'.[10] It was an extraordinary claim, which everyone knew to be untrue, but the circumstances were thought to justify such humbug.

Fear of the army effectively prevented the exercise of democratic government. Calvo-Sotelo's policies were determined by what he thought the army would permit, while the PSOE practically relinquished its role as the parliamentary opposition. Some socialist leaders even admitted in private that they hoped to lose the next elections, since a socialist victory would be bound to provoke another coup. That the main opposition party, which had already lost two elections, was hoping to lose a third, said much about the health of the democratic regime.

One measure clearly designed to placate the military and assure them that the unity of Spain was not threatened, was the LOAPA, a law intended to 'harmonize' and sort out the autonomy process. By the summer of 1981, the development of 'the state of autonomies' envisaged by the constitution was in a desperate muddle. Catalonia and the Basque country had their own governments, but were arguing with Madrid over the devolution of powers, Galicia and Andalusia had each held a referendum which embarrassed the government, and all the other regions were moving slowly towards obtaining their statutes. At the end of the process, Spain would be faced by a bewildering array of referenda and elections, all taking place at different times: in diverse parts of the country, the political parties would be campaigning against each other every few weeks. The government and the PSOE agreed, therefore, to try to standardize the autonomy process, and the LOAPA was introduced in the summer of 1981. Some measure was plainly necessary to unravel the chaos, but the main effect of the LOAPA was to antagonize Catalonia and the Basque country. Nationalist parties in both regions condemned the law, arguing that it infringed their autonomy statutes, and complaining that their historic national rights were being reduced to the significance of all the other regions'.

The UCD had lost credibility over the autonomy process long before the LOAPA controversy. The construction of 'the state of autonomies' was the most ambitious enterprise undertaken by the constitutional monarchy. It was a comprehensive attempt to solve a problem which had bedevilled the country for the whole of the

century. Unfortunately, the plan was marred from the beginning
by ambiguity. In order to satisy Basque and Catalan aspirations,
the constitution employed the word 'nationalities', but it did not
specify which parts of the country were nationalities and which
were regions. The idea of being a nationality was very fashionable
just then, and regions which had previously experienced no
nationalist feelings suddenly claimed to be nationalities. The
government, anxious to provide a general framework for its
policy, offered autonomy to all, but subsequently regretted it.
Having embarked upon an ambitious path via the constitution and
the Basque and Catalan statutes, Suárez felt that the process was
going too fast and decided to slow it down. The discontent of the
military and the hostility of the Right played an important part in
his decision to place restrictions on how regions would achieve
autonomy, and on how they would exercise it.

The constitution contained two articles outlining different
methods for the attainment of autonomy. A fairly rapid route was
designed for the historic nationalities – Catalonia, the Basque
country and Galicia★ – and a slower, more complicated one for the
rest. It was not, in general, difficult to distinguish between a
historic nationality such as Catalonia and a region such as
Extremadura. But there was one doubtful case. Andalusia had a
nationalist party, which had five seats in the *Congreso*, and many

---

★Galicia is probably a nationality as much as any other part of Spain. It has its
own language (*gallego*), its own culture, a clearly defined geographical area, and
an economy largely cut off from the rest of Spain. Alfonso Castelao, the 'apostle'
of Galician nationalism, described *gallego* as a 'son of Latin, brother of Castilian,
and father of Portuguese'.[11]

Galician nationalism goes back to the nineteenth century and was a
considerable force during the Second Republic. It had a strong home-rule party,
the ORGA, which espoused moderate policies and demanded autonomy rather
than independence. Salvador de Madariaga, who admitted he was 'not an
out-and-out home-ruler', joined the party in 1931 and was relieved to discover
that its leaders were equally moderate.[12]

In recent years Galician nationalism has been more of a cultural than a political
movement. It is difficult to find visible expressions of it in Galicia, except on road
signs which local extremists have methodically disfigured, crossing out Castilian
names and substituting *gallego* spelling. There are a number of Galician
nationalist parties, but all of them are small and have done badly even in
municipal and autonomous elections. The Galician People's National Bloc,
which is the largest, has never gained as much as 7 per cent of the vote in any
election.

Andalusians, even though they did not support this party, thought they should obtain autonomy in line with the historic nationalities.* The government's decision to treat Andalusia as an ordinary

*Andalusia is such a large and important part of Spain that the idea of it having a regional, let alone a nationalist, outlook seems strange. There is no historical justification, based on ancient rights or medieval customs, for Andalusian nationalism. The region is not, and never has been, a single entity or even a confederation of different units. Since the Reconquest it has been an extension of Castile populated mainly by Castilians. Andalusia's western provinces, heavily romanized and centred on Seville, have little in common with the eastern areas, where Moorish influence was stronger and lasted much longer. Seville had close historical ties with Cádiz and Huelva, and to a lesser extent with Córdoba, but it had practically none with Granada. Communications between the two greatest Andalusian cities are still virtually non-existent.

Andalusian nationalism has employed folkloric and historical symbols, but it is less of a nationalist movement than a protest against economic exploitation by the rest of Spain. Andalusia has mineral wealth and potential agricultural wealth – in the early Middle Ages it was the most prosperous region in Europe – yet it also has the highest unemployment and the most widespread poverty in Spain. The principal reason for this is that Andalusia has little industry, and the products which it grows or extracts are processed outside the region. Since the collapse of its iron industry in the 1860s, Andalusia's contribution to Spain's GNP has steadily dwindled.

A small nationalist movement, largely inspired by the poet Blas Infante, emerged in the early part of the twentieth century. A couple of conferences were held, a green and white flag was designed, and a poem written by Infante became the Andalusian anthem. In 1936 Infante was shot by Franco's men and might have been forgotten had he not been 'discovered' many years later by Antonio Burgos, a Sevillian journalist with regionalist sympathies.[13] Infante quickly became the patron saint of a local movement, which in 1976 became the *Partido Socialista de Andalucía* (PSA). After a dismal showing in the 1977 elections, the party received encouragement from the UCD which saw in it a means of taking votes away from the PSOE. Led by Alejandro Rojas Marcos, the PSA won five seats in the general elections of 1979, and took charge of a number of town councils after local elections in the following month.

The PSA was not the only nationalist group in Andalusia. To its right there was Andalusian Unity, a small party formed by the ex-UCD minister Clavero; to its left, the United Andalusian People's Party, a breakaway from the extreme left-wing Workers' Party. The nationalist movement was also supported by a radical trade union in the anarchist tradition, the *Sindicato de Obreros del Campo* (Union of Rural Workers). Andalusian nationalism collapsed in 1982, with crushing defeats for the PSA in both elections. The PSA was a casualty of the UCD's Andalusian policy, which it misguidedly supported. An additional reason for its failure may have been the electorate's realization that Andalusia is not, after all, a nationality, and therefore does not need a nationalist movement.

region provoked an uproar and caused Manuel Clavero Arévalo, the minister of culture, to resign in protest. With the benefit of hindsight, one can point to the Andalusian muddle as the first stage in the collapse of the UCD.

Suárez decided that Andalusia should obtain autonomy by the slower route laid out in the constitution unless a majority of the electorate in each of the eight provinces voted for the faster route. If this condition had been demanded of the Catalans, Catalonia would also have had to travel the longer road, and the government presumably calculated that the Andalusians would not come near to fulfilling it. Suárez therefore called a referendum for February 1980, recommended that the electorate should abstain, and prevented the state media from giving time or space to those who disagreed with him. He miscalculated disastrously. The angry Andalusians turned out in larger numbers than either the Basques or the Catalans had done, and voted overwhelmingly in favour of rapid autonomy. However, one province – Almería – failed to meet the requirement that half its electorate must vote positively, and according to the stipulations of the government, this result invalidated all the rest. It was a ridiculous situation, and made the Andalusians even angrier. They could not proceed to elections and the establishment of an autonomous government – even though nearly two-thirds of them had gone to the polls – but in Galicia, where later in the year only 28 per cent of the electorate voted in the referendum, the autonomy process could go smoothly ahead.*

The Andalusian fiasco was followed by further setbacks for the government in the autonomous elections to the Basque and Catalan parliaments. In Catalonia the UCD lost nearly half its share of the poll and limped home in fourth place; in the Basque country it came fifth, winning only six seats in an assembly of sixty-one. Yet its real electoral disaster did not come until the Galician elections of October 1981. In the Basque country it had been defeated by regionalist and left-wing parties, but there was as yet no threat to its hold on the centre-right. In Galicia, however,

*During the autumn the UCD and the PSOE came to an agreement on how to resolve the problem caused by the referendum. Two new laws were passed which gave Andalusia the right to obtain autonomy by the faster route, except for Almería which had to go the slower way, although it could join up later on. Andalusians approved of their autonomy statute in a referendum in October 1981, and elections were held the following May.

the government was defeated by *Alianza Popular*, a party it had annihilated in every single contest until then. Fraga's supporters more than doubled their vote, and were able to form the regional government.

Worse was to come. UCD optimists pointed out that Fraga was Galician and that the region had produced four of his nine deputies in 1979. In Andalusia, by contrast. AP had never won a single seat, while the UCD had won 26 in 1977 and 24 two years later. Surely, they reasoned, the government could defeat Fraga in the Andalusian elections of May 1982. They were wrong. By the summer of 1982, the UCD had discredited itself in the eyes of the country by its incessant feuding, and it had alienated most of its former supporters in Andalusia by its autonomy policy. In the elections the PSOE gained an overall majority (52 per cent of the vote) while AP quadrupled its 1979 share of the poll to come second (17 per cent). The UCD, which in the two general elections had gained an equivalent number of seats to the PSOE, came a poor third, winning only a quarter as many votes as the socialists.

Apart from their implications for local politics (the nationalists did very well in Catalonia and the Basque country, and very badly in Galicia and Andalusia), the autonomous elections had a major impact on the state of national politics. The results revealed the remarkable rise of two of the main four parties, and the no less remarkable collapse of the other two. They indicated that Spain was abandoning the French model and advancing rapidly towards a two-party system.

The principal beneficiary of these developments was the PSOE. In spite of its defeat in the first three autonomous elections (coming a well-beaten third in two of them), the impressive victory in Andalusia left little doubt that it would win the next general elections. After the party's unexpectedly poor showing in the 1979 elections, there had been some discontent among its members: the leadership was considered to be too moderate, the organization to be undemocratic. To the indignation of the party's left wing, Felipe González had announced in May 1978 that he would like to see the word 'marxism' removed from the party's resolutions. A year later, at the PSOE's conference, he encountered strong opposition to his proposal and decided to resign. The decision was greeted with consternation by the delegates, even by those who opposed his policies, and the conference broke up in confusion.

Felipe González was the party's greatest electoral asset, a fact which his socialist critics fully recognized. Apart from the elderly Tierno, there was no other figure in the party who enjoyed any popular support whatever. The success of the Spanish Socialist Party between 1977 and 1982 can be ascribed above all else to the image of its secretary-general. Spaniards are usually very critical of their politicians, but during the transition it was difficult to meet anyone who really disapproved of González. Even the most rabid anti-socialists usually exempted him from their denunciations of the Left. González undoubtedly had an attractive personality: he was honest, *simpático*, moderate and convincing. Yet it is not easy to see why these qualities should have secured him immunity from criticism. The press, which attacked Carrillo, lambasted Fraga, and helped to destroy Suárez, seldom had a harsh word to say about González. Spain's affection for its socialist leader, who was known universally as Felipe, was a unique phenomenon. No other leader was ever referred to by his christian name: Fraga was never Manolo (though supporters talked respectfully of Don Manuel), Suárez was never Adolfo, Carrillo never Santiago. But they were merely politicians, legitimate targets for abuse. Felipe was different: he was treated as an inviolable part of the national patrimony, a sort of modern José Antonio.

Four months after González's resignation, another conference was arranged to elect a secretary-general and a new executive committee. The Left put up a list of candidates to contest the election, but there was never much doubt that Felipe and a moderate executive would be elected without difficulty. The controversy which had begun the crisis was settled by a compromise. The word 'marxism' did appear in the programme, but not in a prominent position. It was merely recognized that marxism was 'a theoretical instrument' for analysing social problems.

At the 1981 conference, González consolidated his hold on the party by personally winning 100 per cent of the delegates' votes. The Left was excluded from all positions of influence, and a moderate social democratic programme was adopted. The resolutions made a vague reference to the possible nationalization of the 'energy sector and a part of the financial sector', but it was ambiguous and not, in any case, binding on a future socialist government. González himself made it clear that his priorities were not nationalization but administrative reform, safeguarding civil liberties, and combating unemployment.[14]

All Spain's leaders suffered in comparison with Felipe González, but none so much as Santiago Carrillo. The communist leader played an important and responsible role during the transition, and in the process showed himself to be a better patriot and a worse politician than many had expected. His moderate pragmatic policies were good for Spain but bad for the party. His insistence on competing with González for the same votes led to the reverse in Andalusia (the PCE's share of the poll dropped from 13.4 per cent to 8 per cent) and to total collapse in the general elections a few months later. Given that their party programmes were similar, why should anyone, in a country trying hard to forget the past, reject Felipe for an elderly veteran of the thirties implicated in one of the worst atrocities of the civil war?

Returning to Spain after nearly forty years of exile, Carrillo discovered a very different PCE from the one he had left behind in 1939. Some of the 'pro-soviet' old guard were still around, chiefly in Barcelona, but there was also a younger, larger, more modern group, particularly strong in Madrid. Its members had joined the party during the dictatorship, often as students or teachers, because to be a militant of the Communist Party seemed the best way of opposing Franco. In the absence of a visible socialist party, they joined the PCE with the intention of making it the predominant force of the Left in the post-Franco years. But in order to achieve this, they needed an up-to-date party with creative, open leadership. Carrillo came back from exile and brought with him a stolid and unregenerate bureaucracy. His own autocratic leadership, and his refusal to modernize the PCE's structure, drove the best intellectuals out of the party. Ramón Tamames, one of Spain's most talented economists, left in May 1981 because of the party's refusal 'to dynamize, debureaucratize and democratize itself'.[15]

At the party's tenth conference in July 1981, the remaining reformists in the party were defeated in their attempts to promote modernization and internal debate inside the party. During the following months, those who did not leave voluntarily were often purged by Carrillo. In the autumn the Basque Communist Party, which had flopped in the autonomous elections, decided to merge with *Euskadiko Ezkerra*. This decision, heretical to orthodox communists, was welcomed by the reformists, who organized a public meeting of support in Madrid. Carrillo's reaction was typical of his behaviour during the long years of his leadership. He dissolved the central committee of the Basque party, and expelled those in the PCE who sympathized with it. Among those purged were various councillors in Madrid, as well as six prominent members of the party's central committee. Following the expulsions, the Communist Party virtually ceased to exist in the Basque country, while in Madrid it lost a large chunk of its membership. Between 1978 and 1981, 14,000 militants from the capital deserted the party.[16]

Carrillo's repeated purges – these included Catalonia where a number of 'pro-soviets' were thrown out – naturally had a demoralizing effect on the party. The communist leader was offering the membership a stark choice: get out or conform. But conform to what? To the viewpoint of a man who – in spite of his eurocommunist views – was treating the party as if the stalinist era had never ended? Carrillo managed to alienate almost everybody in the PCE except those who, for whatever reason, remained unconditionally loyal to his person. He abandoned leninism and angered the hardliners, but failed to reform the party, and thus drove out the moderates. He destroyed the party's traditions without offering anything new to replace them. In the general elections of 1982, both the 'pro-soviets' and the reformists abandoned him, and the PCE lost two-thirds of its support.

The only party that was enlarging its membership in 1982 was *Alianza Popular*. In the fortnight following the Andalusian elections, it acquired 5,000 new members, and by the beginning of July the total stood at 60,000.[17] In spite of its disastrous performance in the 1979 elections, the party had continued its evolution from *franquismo* to modern conservatism. Fraga guessed correctly that the UCD was an artificial creation which would sooner or later break up. He therefore encouraged it to disintegrate in the belief that he would be able to pick up most of the pieces. From 1980 he was calling for the formation of a 'new majority', by which he meant a great alliance of the country's liberal and conservative forces. His objectives were the destruction of the UCD and the setting-up of a two-party system, aims that were shared by the powerful businessmen's association, the CEOE. Abandoning the government party, which it claimed had been carrying out social democratic policies, the CEOE began pouring funds into *Alianza Popular*.[18] The Spanish Right, convinced that it had been cheated of its rightful representation during the previous five years, was at last rallying to Manuel Fraga.

The realignment of forces which Fraga was promoting, was assisted – in some cases consciously – by the UCD politicians. In 1981 there were two principal conflicts going on inside the UCD: one over the control of the apparatus, which was eventually won by Calvo-Sotelo, and the other over the ideology, or lack of it, of the party. A crucial issue which helped to divide the party (christian democrats on one side, social democrats and Suárez's followers on the other) was the divorce bill introduced by Fernández Ordóñez, the social democrat minister of justice. Fernández Ordóñez's reliance on socialist votes to secure a majority to defeat conservative amendments to the bill, so enraged the party's christian democrats that one of their leaders called for his resignation.[19] In reaction to the social democrats' behaviour over divorce, their opponents in the party promoted the so-called 'moderate platform' sponsored by 70 parliamentarians. The christian democrats in the UCD were hoping to pull the party to its 'natural' position in the centre-right, and Oscar Alzaga, one of their most prominent leaders, called publicly for a coalition between the UCD and *Alianza Popular*.[20] In response to the rightward drift of the party, Fernández Ordóñez resigned from the cabinet at the end of August. A few weeks later, he and nine other deputies left the UCD to set up a social democratic party.

The exodus of the social democrats was the beginning of the party's disintegration. The next to go were three right-wing deputies who crossed the floor and joined Fraga. They included Ricardo de La Cierva, an 'official' historian of *franquismo* during the dictatorship who was in any case out of place in a centre party, and Miguel Herrero de Miñón, the party's parliamentary spokesman. It is difficult to explain Herrero's move except as the unprincipled action of an opportunist. A gifted demagogic speaker, Herrero described himself as a 'radical Tory',[21] but sounded more like a reactionary conservative of the 1930s. He had devoted the past two years to a single-minded campaign against

Suárez and his followers. He had fought tirelessly to force Suárez's resignation and subsequently to eject the *suaristas* from their posts in the party hierarchy. By the end of 1981, he had contributed to the attainment of both objectives. Weeks later, when his fellow conservatives in the UCD were now in the ascendancy, he defected to AP. The only likely explanation for his behaviour is that he was trying to ingratiate himself with Fraga by inflicting as much damage as possible on the UCD.

After Herrero's departure, there was a short lull in the disintegrating process before the Andalusian defeat set it going again. In July 1982 UCD deputies formed no less than three new parties: a liberal party, based on the newly-formed 'Liberal Clubs' containing people from outside as well as inside the UCD; a christian democrat party headed by Alzaga which intended to contest the next elections in coalition with Fraga; and a party set up by Suárez, the *Centro Democrático y Social*, which appeared to have no purpose other than to re-elect Suárez and his friends.

In less than nine months, the UCD deputies had scattered to seven different parties, ranging from the socialists (in whose lists Fernández Ordóñez and some of his companions fought the general election) to *Alianza Popular*. It was a bewildering display of frivolity, irresponsibility, and unbridled opportunism. Many of the people who abandoned the UCD did so because they calculated they had better chances of remaining deputies if they joined another party. There was thus some poetic justice in the fact that a majority failed to get re-elected. Neither AP nor the PSOE gave the deserters much of a welcome. Fraga's men had spent years in the political wilderness, and were understandably reluctant to sacrifice their own ambitions for people who had been in power for two legislatures and would do anything to hang on to it. In spite of the much-trumpeted alliance between AP and the christian democrats, several prominent followers of Alzaga failed to get on the electoral lists. Similarly, a number of social democrats were not included among the PSOE's candidates, while the liberals, who in September announced an electoral pact with the UCD, had to break the agreement a few days later on discovering that they also had been left out.

By August 1982 the UCD had been reduced to little more than a remnant of the *Partido Popular* and the followers of Martín Villa. Calvo-Sotelo realized that he no longer had the authority to govern and decided to call a general election. The loyalists of the UCD, under their new president Landelino Lavilla, fought a courageous campaign, but nobody could take them seriously. The party which had governed alone throughout the transition had destroyed itself. As Emilio Attard, the retiring deputy for Valencia, commented: 'Our electorate, the entire Spanish electorate, was scandalized by something it could only interpret as the product of our limitless ambitions. It could not understand how, after having demonstrated tolerance, mutual respect and peaceful coexistence between politicians and political parties . . . we practised a ferocious cannibalism among ourselves, our offices turned into places for internecine struggles, personal threats, insults and rivalry . . .'[22]

The 1982 campaign was much duller than the previous two. There was no doubt that the socialists would win, and speculation merely centred on how easily they would do so. The one uncertain result was which party would do worst: the UCD, the Communist Party, or the new group of Suárez? The only drama of the campaign was provided by the army and the extreme Right. On 2 October, Colonel Muñoz Gutiérrez was arrested along with two other officers; discovered in his flat were the details of a coup d'état planned for 27 October, the day before the elections. There appeared to be close links between the conspirators and the extreme Right, but no civilians were charged. Muñoz Gutiérrez was a close friend of Blas Piñar, and his wife was a candidate in the lists of *Fuerza Nueva*. Among the candidates of Piñar's party were the wives of at least ten other officers.[23]

Blas Piñar had been elected to the *Congreso* in 1979 because most of the extreme Right had united behind him. In 1982, however, *Fuerza Nueva* had to compete with three separate falangist groups as well as a new 'party' set up by the adulators of Lieutenant-Colonel Tejero. The candidacy of Tejero was undoubtedly the most bizarre aspect of the election. Since being sentenced to thirty years' imprisonment for seizing the *Congreso*, the 'Guy Fawkes' of Spanish politics had been living under guard in a luxury apartment in the outskirts of Madrid. He was waited on by a servant and received gifts of wine, flowers and sea-food from middle-class ladies of the Salamanca district.[24] As there were no restrictions on his visitors, he was able to organize a political party, *Solidaridad Española*, without interference. A programme* was produced and a list of candidates drawn up: Tejero himself headed the list in Madrid, his son was the first candidate in Valencia and his daughter the first in Seville. Although the government tried hard to have him excluded from the election, the Spanish courts declared Tejero's candidacy to be legitimate. His supporters' chief campaign tactic was to drive up and down Madrid's Castellana in a lorry draped with Spanish flags, shouting through loud-hailers.

Extremist antics aside, the campaign developed predictably enough. Fraga stumped the country, eyes bulging, banging rostrums and losing his temper with journalists. There was a certain American flavour to *Alianza Popular*'s campaign. At public meetings, attractive girls in red and white uniforms ushered the audience to its seats; when the speeches finished, balloons were let down from the ceiling and the campaign song – 'It's time for solutions' – was blared over the loud-speakers.

In a desperate attempt to close the gap with the socialists, Fraga was prepared to take votes from anywhere. While he demanded the allegiance of former UCD voters in the centre, he was taking out full pages of advertisements in *El Alcázar*. He courted

---

*This consisted of an anodyne leaflet about the right to work and the importance of a just agrarian policy. There was no mention of the type of government Tejero was proposing. Angel López Montero, who was Tejero's lawyer as well as the vice-president of *Solidaridad Española*, said in all seriousness that the party favoured 'a presidential system with a parliament and political parties'. He also claimed that the party supported freedom of expression, although he admitted he was not in favour of unrestricted freedoms but of 'liberty with responsibility'.[25]

The quality of Tejero's propaganda was almost unbelievable. One poster read:

Tu Apellido nos dice
*E*spaña
*J*usticia
*E*speranza
*R*evolución
*O*rgullo
(Your name spells for us Spain, Justice, Hope, Revolution, Pride)

A leaflet circulating around Madrid the previous year contained the message: 'Spaniard, if you do not wish your wife and daughters to be raped in the street, if you do not wish your sons to be sold drugs and pornography; if you want bread and work for yourself and your family; if you do not want to be torn away from God, demand the liberty of Tejero and Milans. They will save us.'[26]

unreconstructed *franquistas* by declaring himself in favour of capital punishment, and by remarking that he 'understood', although he did not 'excuse', the officers implicated in the recent conspiracy.

As usual, the PSOE fought a moderate campaign based on a social democratic programme: their most radical schemes were to nationalize the electricity grid and propose a referendum on Spain's continued membership of NATO. González's only mistake was to make a rash and unnecessary promise to create 800,000 new jobs in four years. Although he talked about reducing working hours and lowering the retirement age, he was not able to give a convincing explanation as to how his promise would be fulfilled.

The turn-out on 28 October was 78 per cent, more than ten percentage points higher than in the previous election. The results were largely as predicted: neither Tejero nor Blas Piñar came near to being elected, Tejero winning only a tenth of the votes necessary to gain a seat and parliamentary immunity. Of the main national parties, Suárez's CDS did worst, electing only two deputies, Suárez himself in Madrid, and Rodríguez Sahagún in Avila. The Communist Party was humiliated, losing all but four of its twenty-three seats, while the UCD was reduced from 168 deputies (before the desertions) to twelve. More than three-quarters of its 1979 voters abandoned the party, most of them gravitating to Fraga, a good many choosing the PSOE, and a few opting for Suárez. *Alianza Popular* multiplied its support by more than five times, winning nearly 5.5 million votes and 106 seats. The Socialist Party increased its vote from 5.47 millions in 1979 to 10.1 millions, and its 202 new deputies assured it of a large overall majority.

The socialist victory was a sober occasion. González had warned his supporters not to be provocative, so they did not go dancing in the streets chanting victory slogans. Socialists were naturally pleased with the result, but so were a lot of other people. As in 1977, many Spaniards who were not supporters of the winning party were nonetheless glad that it had won. There was a widespread feeling among the uncommitted that, for the health of the country, a socialist victory was necessary. Many liberal-minded people, who had voted for the UCD in 1979, supported the PSOE in 1982. In doing so, they knew they were voting not for socialism but for democracy and the consolidation of the regime. In the third elections of the monarchy, González's party was, in the truest sense of the word, the *liberal* option.

Epilogue

The distinguished philosopher, Julián Marías, once tried to imagine himself as an historian in the year 2000, studying the transition to democracy from contemporary newspapers.[1] His research would be divided into two parts: to begin with, he would read about the events themselves, then he would look at the press comments. His reaction, after completing the first stage, would be one of astonishment that so much had been achieved in so short a time. In just forty months – from the death of Franco to Suárez's second electoral triumph – Spain had been transformed radically but peacefully, with scarcely any interruption in the lives of its inhabitants. Political liberty had been restored, parties and trade unions had been legalized, human freedoms and the rights of regional minorities had been recognized. Above all, sovereignty had been restored to the people, whom the government had consulted regularly about the changes.

The historian, having noted the achievement, would then turn to the editorial pages, expecting no doubt to discover evidence of exuberance and national pride. Instead, he would find almost invariably: 'a) sarcastic contempt for Spain as a whole – though not for each of its 'wonderful' regions; b) limitless disdain for those who had presided over and carried out the transition, people considered to be reactionary, mediocre and often mentally deficient; c) total disenchantment with democracy, the monarchy, elections, the parliamentary system . . . etc.; and d) complete scepticism regarding the future of Spain and the community of Spanish peoples.'

Marías's eulogies of the transition were perhaps excessive, and so were his strictures on the press, but there was much truth in his argument. Some of the press played an important and usually positive role during the development of democracy. Newspapers such as *El País* and *Diario 16*, or magazines such as *Cambio 16* and *Cuadernos para el diálogo*, did a lot to promote political debate and inform people of what was really happening. But much of the press (not including *El País*, one of the most impressive papers in Europe) contributed also to a certain trivialization of politics. It disliked and frequently despised politicians, but at the same time it was fascinated by them. No doubt this was partly a reaction to decades of censorship, but it hardly excuses the exorbitant amount of time spent discussing politicians, their preoccupations, and even their hobbies: *Cambio 16*, an otherwise excellent magazine, regularly tracked down politicians during the summer holidays and photographed them in bathing-shorts. The correspondents of different papers used to give their verdicts on the performances of the cabinet, and 'league tables' of ministers were drawn up.[2] If a politician without ideas set up a party without ideology, he would receive pages of press coverage. As long as it had a title containing at least two of the vogue adjectives – social, liberal, christian, popular and, of course, democratic – the party was assured of lengthy analyses.

By 1979 the press had become generally dismissive about both Suárez and the UCD: the eventual downfall of each can be attributed at least partly to its hostility. Suárez and his party were disliked less for what they were than for what they had been. Because he had a *franquista* past, the prime minister could not be an honest politician (according to the right-wing press) or a true democrat (according to left-wing papers). For Juan Luis Cebrián, the editor of *El País*, the UCD was merely *franquismo* in disguise: 'the Right made a pretence of embracing the new democratic faith by adopting a borrowed name . . . Suárez and his UCD offered a policy of continuity barely disguised as change . . .'[3] The obsession with 'democratic purity' was absurd in a country where, a few years before his death, Franco's active opponents had numbered a few thousand. Nor did it come well from Cebrián, whose career had begun in the press of the *Movimiento*.

Many of the problems associated with the transition were a natural consequence of there being no break with the past. Reform rather than *ruptura* meant that *franquista* attitudes lingered on in many areas of public life. It meant that vital changes could not be carried out, or else had to be done very slowly. It meant that the government did not dare to reform the army or the *Guardia Civil* (though the Armed Police was altered and converted into the National Police). Reform of the civil service, like reform of the judiciary, had to wait for the consolidation of the regime. Not until the socialists came to power was anything done to make the bureaucracy more efficient; not until January 1983 were civil servants told to get to work on time, to give up siestas and to reduce the hours spent chatting in cafes.

The attempt to reform *franquismo* was bound to make the transformation imperfect. But even an imperfect transformation was preferable to a more thorough and radical change that could have been achieved only by violence and probably would not have been achieved at all. A *ruptura* would have led to civil war or a military take-over. If the army could rise against Calvo-Sotelo, it would certainly have risen against a government which proposed the repudiation of the past.

In a country with a notoriously violent political tradition, the peaceful implementation of far-reaching political reform was a remarkable achievement. It owed its success primarily to the restraint shown by so many Spaniards during the transition, to the restraint of the Church which, while it took a stance on moral issues subjected to political debate, refused to become an active supporter of the Right, to the restraint of Carrillo and his communists, who put their country before the dogmas to which they had sacrificed their lives, to the restraint of millions of workers who, after forty years of repression, allowed Franco's inheritors to assume power.

Many people contributed actively to the success of the venture: politicians, trade unionists, journalists, businessmen, academics, some generals. But without the king it would not have been possible. The institution of the monarchy gave the country stability, and the person of Juan Carlos gave it direction. His dignified yet completely unpompous behaviour, his courage and his common sense, and his innate political wisdom, saved the regime from the fate of the Second Republic. After the king, the most important figure was his second prime minister. Adolfo Suárez had many faults and made many mistakes, but when all these have been listed and added up, the achievement still stands. He accomplished more than any other prime minister in the history of Spain, and he reduced the high and often dangerous level of confrontation in public life. His speeches contained no threats, no aggression, no demagoguery; unlike many of his colleagues, he was not forever denouncing his opponents. In 1977 he did Spain a great service by preventing the country from dividing into ideological blocs; when, after his overthrow, polarization occurred, the moment was no longer dangerous.

Visitors to Spain in recent years must have been often surprised by Spanish attitudes to the new democracy. They are likely to have met people who claim that too much has changed – and inevitably for the worse – or those who complain that nothing has changed and say that Spain is still a *franquista* state. Since 1979, Suárez's achievement has been endlessly belittled: people who had believed that it was impossible to reform *franquismo*, later declared that it had in fact been very simple. What should have been a straightforward exercise, they argued, had been disastrously mishandled.

Spaniards may seem excessively casual and indifferent to their democracy, yet their scepticism and lack of confidence are not wholly unjustified. The transition was an extraordinary and almost a miraculous process, and that must be admitted before any criticism is made. Yet it was a flawed miracle, and the people's disenchantment was to some extent caused by the failures of politicians.

It is almost impossible to exaggerate the importance of the post-Franco period in the context of Spanish history. For four hundred years Spain had rejected Europe. The greatest power in christendom had turned inwards at the end of the sixteenth century, disdaining almost all of the non-Spanish-speaking world. Since then, small groups of people – the reformers of the Enlightenment, the liberals of Cádiz, the republicans of the thirties – had tried to open up Spain's closed and unregenerate society.[4] Their intentions had been good, but they were too weak, too divided, and they did not understand the forces of Spanish history. In 1975, in much easier circumstances, when Spanish society was richer and more mature than ever before, another opportunity presented itself.

Between 1976 and 1979, Spain's politicians skilfully erected the structure of democracy. Avoiding the mistakes of the Second Republic, they built on solid foundations, insisting that their laws and institutions should be those which a large majority of the Spanish people wanted. Suárez was repeatedly and sometimes rightly criticized for his transparent pragmatism. Yet in the circumstances of 1976, a pragmatist – not a statesman of immutable principles – was what the country needed. Spain has suffered too much from people who pay attention to nobody's principles but their own.

During his resignation broadcast, Suárez said that he was stepping down because he did not wish 'the democratic system of co-existence to be once again a parenthesis in the history of Spain'. A month later, army officers tried and failed to undo his achievement. Yet even if the coup had been militarily successful, it is doubtful whether the army's return to power would itself have been more than a parenthesis. Democracy may not have fulfilled the hopes of many Spaniards, but it was recognized as being infinitely preferable to dictatorship. The lack of popular support for the coup showed how successful Suárez had been in overcoming the divisions in Spanish society. People were no longer prepared to back rebellion simply because they did not like what the government was doing.

The leaders of the transition had neither the faults nor the virtues of their predecessors of the Second Republic. They aroused neither enthusiasm nor hatred. They built a system which did not inspire devotion but neither did it provoke alienation. Compared to the republican politicians, Suárez's men were a grey and mediocre team. But they succeeded where the republicans failed, chiefly because they sought agreement with other political parties before carrying out their policies.

Spanish democracy was for many people a disappointment. They expected too much of it, just as they expected too much of politicians. Inevitably, they became disenchanted. The UCD was not a great political party: it possessed no orators, no intellectuals and no statesmen; its policies frequently failed; the behaviour of its deputies was often frivolous and self-seeking. In 1982 the sterility of centrist politics impelled people to search for an alternative; some turned nostalgically to the past, others turned hopefully for a new beginning.

The UCD collapsed in the 1982 elections largely as a consequence of internal bickering. Yet perhaps its role was by then over. The UCD was more, as well as less, than a political party. It was indeed a hastily-assembled coalition of discordant factions, and for that reason it died. But it was also an organization which embodied much of post-Franco Spain. The UCD, with its strange array of liberals, social democrats, *franquista* officials and others, represented a huge section of modern Spanish society. Its values, politics and aspirations were shared by millions of Spaniards who wanted to change the country, fundamentally, peacefully, and without losing the social and economic gains achieved under the dictatorship. In government the UCD often failed. But in its primary tasks – the reunification of Spanish society and the transformation of the political system – it could claim an outstanding achievement.

Glossary of Political and Other Organizations in Spain

Alianza Popular Conservative coalition set up under Manuel Fraga's leadership in 1976. Fought 1979 elections as principal component of *Coalición Democrática*, but returned to its original name before becoming principal opposition party in 1982.

CCOO (*comisiones obreras*) Workers' commissions set up in the late fifties to deal with labour grievances in the Basque country and Asturias. Dominated by the Communist Party, it is now one of the two main trade union forces in Spain.

CDS (*Centro Democrático y Social*) Political party formed by Adolfo Suárez and supporters who broke away from the UCD in the summer of 1982.

CEDA (*Confederación Española de Derechas Autónomas*) Coalition of conservative Catholic parties, led by José María Gil Robles, which emerged as the largest party in the *Cortes* after the 1933 elections.

CEOE (*Confederación Española de Organizaciones Empresariales*) Powerful businessmen's association led by Carlos Ferrer Salat.

CNT (*Confederación Nacional del Trabajo*) Anarcho-syndicalist trade union founded in 1910. Enjoyed enormous influence before 1939 in Catalonia, Andalusia and the Levante.

Coalición Democrática Conservative coalition organized around *Alianza Popular* to contest 1979 elections.

Confederación de Ex-Combatientes Extreme right-wing organization of falangist civil war veterans and younger supporters led by José Antonio Girón de Velasco.

Convergència i Unió Liberal-conservative party led by Jordi Pujol and Miquel Roca Junyent. Main representative of Catalan nationalism and largest party in the Catalan parliament.

275

Coordinación Democrática United opposition force set up in March 1976 to demand a break with the regime. Result of a merger between the communist-led *Junta Democrática* and the socialist-dominated *Plataforma de Convergencia Democrática*.

Esquerra The party of left-wing Catalan nationalism. Dominated the *Generalitat* in the thirties but played a much smaller role in the post-Franco years.

ETA (*Euskadi ta Askatasuna* – Basque Homeland and Liberty) Extremist Basque nationalist organization set up in 1959. Initiated campaign of violence in 1968 and has been responsible for about 400 assassinations since then.

Euskadiko Ezkerra Left-wing Basque nationalist party, which campaigns for full autonomy for the Basque provinces within the Spanish state.

Falange Española Fascist party set up by José Antonio Primo de Rivera in 1933. Numerically insignificant until the civil war, it was then 'adopted' by Franco and became the sole party tolerated by the regime. Later known as the *Movimento Nacional*.

Federación de Partidos Democráticos y Liberales Liberal group set up by Joaquín Garrigues Walker. Became main liberal component of the UCD in 1977.

FRAP (*Frente revolucionario anti-fascista patriotico*) Extreme left-wing terrorist organization.

Fuerza Nueva 'New Force', a neo-fascist party grouped around the magazine of the same name. Led by Blas Piñar, it gained one seat in the 1979 elections but lost it in 1982.

Generalitat The autonomous Catalan government set up in 1932. Abolished by Franco, it was restored by Suárez's government in 1977, which appointed the exiled leader Josep Tarradellas as president.

GRAPO (*Grupo revolucionario antifascista primero de Octubre*) Shadowy terrorist group, allegedly of the extreme Left, suspected by many of being financed by the extreme Right.

Guardia Civil Special police force set up in the 19th century to deal with bandits. Later used for more political purposes, it was regarded by his opponents as one of the chief instruments of Franco's repression.

Guerrilleros de Cristo Rey Band of right-wing fanatics and hooligans led by Mariano Sánchez-Covisa.

Herri Batasuna (Popular Unity) Coalition of militant Basque nationalist groups which acts as ETA's political front.

Izquierda Democrática Left-wing christian democratic group set up by Joaquín Ruiz Giménez. Disbanded after its failure to win a seat in the 1977 elections.

JONS (*Juntas de Ofensiva Nacional Sindicalista*) Small fascist party set up in the early thirties which merged with the *Falange* in 1934.

Junta Democrática Opposition front dominated by the Communist Party which was set up in Paris in 1974.

Lliga Regionalista Conservative Catalan nationalist party founded in 1901 to work for home rule for Catalonia.

Movimiento Nacional See *Falange Española*.

Partido Demócrata Cristiano The main christian democratic group inside the UCD. Formed from splits in *Izquierda Democrática* and the UDE.

Partido Popular Liberal, centre-right group set up at the end of 1976 under the leadership of Pio Cabanillas and José María de Areilza. Later became one of the principal components of the UCD.

PCE (*Partido Comunista Español*) The Spanish Communist Party.

Plataforma de Convergencia Democrática Opposition front set up in 1975 as rival to the *Junta Democrática*. Included the PSOE and *Izquierda Democrática*.

PNV (*Partido Nacionalista Vasco*) Basque Nationalist Party founded by Sabino Arana in 1895. Largest party in the Basque parliament.

PSA (*Partido Socialista de Andalucía*) Andalusian nationalist party which enjoyed some success in the 1979 elections before collapsing in 1982.

PSAD (*Partido Social de Acción Democrática*) Social democratic group formed around Dionisio Ridruejo in the late fifties.

PSI (*Partido Socialista del Interior*) Socialist party set up by Tierno Galván in 1968 after his explusion from the PSOE. Known as the PSP (*Partido Socialista Popular*) after 1974, it merged with the PSOE in 1978.

PSOE (*Partido Socialista Obrero Español*) The Spanish socialist party. Provided the main parliamentary opposition during the transition, and won the 1982 elections with a large overall majority.

PSP see PSI.

Tácito Group of young christian democrats who in the early seventies pressed for political reforms from inside the Franco- regime.

UCD (*Unión de Centro Democrático*) Coalition of small parties of the centre-right set up by Adolfo Suárez before the 1977 elections. Formed minority governments between 1977 and 1982. Divisions inside the party and numerous defections caused its collapse in the 1982 elections and its disbandment soon afterwards.

UGT (*Unión General de Trabajadores*) Socialist trade union with close links to the PSOE. With the CCOO, the leading union in the country.

Unión Demócrata Cristiana (at one time known as *Izquierda Demócrata Cristiana*) Left-wing christian democratic group set up in the fifties by the former CEDA minister Manuel Giménez Fernández.

Unión Democrática Espanõla (UDE) Association formed by Federico Silva Muñoz in 1975. Silva later left to join *Alianza Popular* and the rest of the group set up the *Partido Demócrata Cristiano*.

Unión Española Liberal–conservative monarchist group which opposed the Franco regime during the sixties.

Notes

Chapter 1: In Search of Franquismo *(p. 3–18)*

1. George Orwell, *Homage to Catalonia* (1938) p.49.
2. From UN General Assembly resolution passed on 12 December 1946 by 34 votes to 6 with 13 abstentions.
3. Adolf Hitler, *Table Talk 1941–1944*, (ed. Trevor-Roper) (1953) p.520.
4. Quoted in Stanley Payne, *Falange: A History of Spanish Fascism* (1962) p.261.
5. José Antonio Girón de Velasco. Quoted in Angel Bayod (ed.), *Franco visto por sus ministros* (1981) p.46.
6. See Vicente Pozuelo Escudero, *Los últimos 476 días de Franco* (1980) pp.64–5.
7. *Ibid.* pp.39,46.
8. This has been quoted in a number of books about Franco, e.g. S.F.A. Coles, *Franco of Spain* (1955) p.30, and Herbert Matthews, *The Yoke and the Arrows* (1958) p.60.
9. See Hugh Thomas, *The Spanish Civil War* (3rd ed. 1977) p.689.
10. Matthews, *op.cit.* pp.47–8.
11. Sir Samuel Hoare (Viscount Templewood), *Ambassador on Special Mission* (1946).
12. *Ibid.* p.222.
13. Quoted in Brian Crozier, *Franco* (1967) p.11.
14. Pozuelo, *op.cit.* p.154.
15. F. Franco Salgado-Araujo, *Mis conversaciones privadas con Franco* (1976) p.23.
16. Gregorio López Bravo. Quoted in Jesus Ynfante, *La prodigiosa aventura del Opus Dei* (1970) p.194.
17. Pozuelo, *op.cit.* between pp.176 and 177.
18. Crozier, *op.cit.,* p.297.
19. Denis Mack Smith, *Mussolini* (1981) p.145.
20. Benjamin Welles, *Spain: The Gentle Anarchy* (1965) p.26.
21. See Raymond Carr, *Spain: 1808–1939* (2nd ed. 1982) p.692. Carr calls Franco 'the Haig of the Civil War'.

22. 200,000 is the figure calculated by the American historian, Gabriel Jackson, in *The Spanish Republic and the Civil War, 1931–1939* (1965) pp. 526–40. An official in the ministry of justice gave an American journalist in 1944 the total of 193,000 (See Charles Foltz, *The Masquerade in Spain* 1948 p.97). Others, such as Hugh Thomas, *op.cit.* and George Hills, *Spain* (1970), give much smaller figures.

23. Thomas, *op.cit.* p.514.

24. See Hoare, *op.cit.* p.72. General Muñoz Grandes, Franco's vice-president, was treated in similar fashion. See Max Gallo, *Spain under Franco* (1973) p.359.

25. F. Franco Salgado-Araujo, *op.cit.* p.176.

26. A.R. Vilaplana, *Burgos Justice* (1938) pp.17,22–3. See also Thomas, *op.cit.* pp.280–1.

27. Pozuelo, *op.cit.* p.49.

28. Raimundo Fernández Cuesta in Bayod (ed.), *op.cit.* p.21.

29. This speech is reproduced in Ian Gibson, *En Busca de José Antonio* (1980) pp.313–7.

30. From a speech delivered on 2 February 1939. Quoted in Matthews, *op.cit.* p.142.

31. In a letter to Churchill of 18 October 1944. Quoted in Hoare, *op.cit.* p.142.

32. This was part of Franco's victory prayer in the Church of Santa Barbara in Madrid. It is quoted in Crozier, *op.cit.* p.294.

33. See Gibson, *op.cit.* p.36.

34. This is quoted from a text book published in 1945 with the approval of the ministry of education: José Luis Asián, *Elementos de Geografía Regional e Historia de España* (1945) p.176.

35. Quoted in Max Gallo, *op.cit.* pp.134–5.

36. See Matthews, *op.cit.* p.9.

37. From a speech in Valencia in May 1939. Quoted in Coles, *op.cit.* p.32.

38. Quoted in Raymond Carr and Juan Pablo Fusi, *Spain: Dictatorship to Democracy* (1979) p.109.

39. Cited in Jacques Georgel, *El Franquismo: Historia y Balance 1939–1969* (1971) p.201.

40. See the remarks by Luis González Vicén, a member of the National Council, in Georgel, *op.cit.*, pp.149–50.

41. Georgel, *op.cit.* p.149.

42. From an interview with the correspondent of *United States News and World Report*, 20 May 1955. Quoted in Georgel, *op.cit.* p.122.

43. From remarks made to the journalist Christopher Buckley. Quoted in Coles, *op.cit.* p.148.

44. See Georgel, *op.cit.* p.122.

45. See Richard Herr, *Modern Spain* (1974) pp.28–34.

46. José Antonio Primo de Rivera. Quoted in Payne, *op.cit.* p.40.

47. *Ibid.* p.44.

48. *Ibid.* pp.126–7.

49. See Gibson, *op.cit.* p.37.

50. Payne, *op.cit.* p.14.

51. *Ibid.* p.79.

52. *Ibid.* p.222.

53. José Luis de Arrese in Bayod (ed.), *op.cit.* p.61.

54. Matthews, *op.cit.* p.73.

55. Carlton Hayes, *Wartime Mission in Spain* (1945) pp.71,242. Franco later denied that he had ever had a photograph of Mussolini on his desk, see Franco Salgado-Araujo, *op.cit.* p.255, but Hayes's account is corroborated by Hoare, *op.cit.* p.284.

56. See Antonio Garrigues y Díaz Cañabate, *Diálogos conmigo mismo* (1978) p.59.

57. Cited in Hills, *op.cit.* pp.235,249.

58. Quoted in Payne, *op.cit.* pp.259–60.

59. Amando de Miguel, *Sociología del Franquismo* (1975) p.71.

60. Juan J. Linz, 'An Authoritarian Regime in Spain', first published in E. Allardt and Y. Littunen (eds), *Cleavages, Ideologies and Party Systems* (1964) and reproduced in Stanley Payne (ed.), *Politics and Society in Twentieth-Century Spain* (1976).

61. This is the title (*El Crepúsculo de las Ideologías*) of a book by Gonzalo Fernández de la Mora (1961).

62. See the comments by Alberto Ullastres, minister of commerce, in Amando de Miguel, *op.cit.* pp.224–5.

63. *Ibid.* pp.227–8.

64. *Revista de Opinión Pública* (January–March 1969) p.278. Cited in José Amodia, *Franco's Political Legacy* (1977) p.285.

65. See Ynfante, *op.cit.* p.329.

66. Quoted in Raymond Carr, *The Spanish Tragedy* (1977) p.269.

67. In an interview in Salvador Pániker, *Conversaciones en Madrid* (1969) p.330.

68. Quoted in Miguel, *op.cit.* p.363.

Chapter 2: The Structure of the Dictatorship (pp. 19–33)

1. From Article XII of the Statutes of the *Falange*.

2. Charles W. Anderson, *The Political Economy of Modern Spain* (1970) p.243.

3. These remarks are from an interview which Franco gave to a correspondent of *United States News and World Report*, 20 May 1955. Quoted in Jacques Georgel, *El Franquismo: Historia y balance 1939–1969* (1971) p.122.

4. *Ibid.*

5. From a speech made by José Antonio Primo de Rivera on 29 October 1933. Quoted in Stanley Payne, *Falange: A History of Spanish Fascism* (1962) pp.38–41.

6. See José Amodia, *Franco's Political Legacy* (1977) p.102.

7. *Ibid.* pp.153–4.

8. See Kenneth Medhurst, *Government in Spain* (1973) p.34.

9. See Payne, *op.cit.* pp.216–20.

10. See Medhurst, *op.cit.* p.214.

11. Quoted in Herbert Matthews, *The Yoke and the Arrows* (1958) pp.79–80.

12. *Ibid.*

13. Salvador de Madariaga, *Spain: A Modern History* (1958) p.596.

14. Georgel, *op.cit.* p.158.

15. See note 22 to Chapter 1.

16. Law of Political Responsibilities, February 1939.

17. Amodia, *op.cit.* p.173.

18. Emmet John Hughes, *Report from Spain* (1947) p.142.

19. Julio Busquets Bragulat, *Pronunciamientos y golpes de Estado en España* (1982) pp.179–80.

20. See the chapter by Norman Cooper, 'The Church: From Crusade to Christianity', in Paul Preston (ed.), *Spain in Crisis* (1976) p.50.

21. *Ibid.*

22. See Amando de Miguel, *Sociología del Franquismo* (1975) pp.117–20.

Chapter 3: Non-Political Revolutions (1959–75) (pp. 34–50)

1. See the article by Solís in Angel Bayod (ed.), *Franco visto por sus ministros* (1981) p.104.

2. Edward E. Malefakis, *Agrarian Reform and Peasant Revolution in Spain* (1970) p.11. See also Banco de Bilbao, *Informe Económico 1979* pp.142–3.

3. Malefakis, *op.cit.* p.12.

4. Manuel Fraga Iribarne, Juan Velarde Fuertes, Salustiano del Campo Urbano (eds), *La España de los años 70*, Vol.2 (1973) pp.946–7.

5. See Joseph Harrison, *An Economic History of Modern Spain* (1978) p.150. See also Raymond Carr and Juan Pablo Fusi, *Spain: Dictatorship to Democracy* (1979) p.66.

6. Calculated from figures given by the Banco de Bilbao, *op.cit.* pp.142–3, and the *Instituto nacional de estadística* (INE), *España, Anuario Estadístico 1982* p.329. INE has slightly higher figures for the creation of new jobs than the Banco de Bilbao.

7. INE, *op.cit.* p.57. See also United Nations, *Demographic Yearbook 1981*.

8. Harrison, *op.cit.*, p.151.

9. See John Naylon, *Andalusia* (1975) p.23.

10. *El disputado voto del señor Cayo* (1978).

11. See, for example, Miguel Delibes, *Castilla, lo Castellano y los castellanos* (1979).

12. Stanley Payne, *Falange* (1961) pp.89–90.

13. Harrison, *op.cit.* p.160. See also Juan Martínez-Alier, *Labourers and Landowners in Southern Spain* (1971) p.107.

14. Martínez-Alier, *op.cit.* p.106.

15. Eduardo Sevilla-Guzmán, 'The Peasantry and the Franco Regime' in Paul Preston (ed.), *Spain in Crisis* (1975) p.115.

16. Comisaría del Plan de Desarrollo, *III Plan de Desarrollo 1972–5: Económico y Social* (1971) p.177.

17. Malefakis, *op.cit.* p.418.

18. INE, *op.cit.* p.107.

19. Malefakis, *op.cit.* pp.29,94.

20. Harrison, *op.cit.* p.160.

21. Malefakis, *op.cit.* p.83.

22. Julian Pitt-Rivers, *The People of the Sierra* (1954) pp.16,203. Ronald Fraser found a similar situation in another Andalusian village at the beginning of the

seventies. Only one large landowning family was still living in the village where he was doing research for *The Pueblo* (1973).

23. Banco de Bilbao, *Renta nacional de España* (1973) p.104.

24. Sima Lieberman, *The Contemporary Spanish Economy* (1982) pp.127–8, 132–44. See also Raymond Carr, *Modern Spain* (1980) p.28.

25. Raymond Carr, *The Spanish Tragedy* (1977) p.255.

26. Brian Crozier, *Franco* (1967) p.445.

27. Stanley Payne, *Politics and the Military in Modern Spain* (1967) pp.439–40. See also Ramón Tamames, *La República, La Era de Franco* (1980) p.426, and Harrison, *op.cit.* pp.153–4.

28. Manuel-Jesús González, *La Economía Política del Franquismo* (1979) p.31.

29. *Ibid.* p.197.

30. *Ibid.* p.200.

31. See Wolfgang Wipplinger, 'Spain's Economic Progress since 1960' in Salisbury and Theberge (eds), *Spain in the 1970s* (1976) p.7.

32. James D. Theberge, 'Spanish Industrial Development Policy in the Twentieth Century' in Salisbury and Theberge (eds), *op.cit.*, p.29.

33. Alison Wright, *The Spanish Economy 1959–1976* (1977) pp.30,84.

34. Harrison, *op.cit.* pp.152,156.

35. Gerald Brenan, *The Spanish Labyrinth* (1960) p.11.

36. Marqués de Villavieja, *Life has been Good* (1938).

37. Pablo Neruda, *Memoirs* (1976) p.249.

38. Villavieja, *op.cit.* from the foreword.

39. For information on Spanish pupils at Stonyhurst, I am grateful to Mr Macadam, the Registrar for Old Boys. See also Villavieja, *op.cit.* p.46.

40. Quoted in Amando de Miguel, *Sociología del Franquismo* (1975) p.97.

41. See *Cambio 16* 22 June 1981, p.35.

42. Banco de Bilbao, *Renta nacional de España* (1973) p.33.

43. *Marketing Potentials of Europe's Regions* (1973). Cited in Naylon, *op.cit.* pp.9,17.

44. See Melveena McKendrick, *Cervantes* (1980) pp.17–18.

45. Jorge de Esteban and Luis López Guerra, *La crisis del Estado franquista* (1977) p.174.

46. William T. Salisbury, 'Spain and Europe: the Economic Realities' in Salisbury and Theberge (eds), *op.cit.* p.36.

47. José Maravall, *The Transition to Democracy in Spain* (1982).

48. Quoted in Carr, *op.cit.* p.284.

Chapter 4: Inside the Regime (pp.51–80)

1. Quoted in Sergio Vilar, *Protagonistas de la España Democrática: La oposición a la dictadura 1939–1969* p.507.

2. Reproduced in Laureano López Rodó, *La larga marcha hacia la monarquía* (1977) pp.37–8.

3. Claude Bowers, *My mission to Spain* (1954) pp.351–2.

4. *Ibid.*

5. Quoted in Raymond Carr, *The Spanish Tragedy* (1977) pp.125–6.

6. Norman Cooper, 'The Church: From Crusade to Christianity' in Paul Preston (ed.), *Spain in Crisis* (1975) p.50.

7. Quoted in Emmet John Hughes, *Report from Spain* (1947) pp.63–4.

8. Article 2 of the *Ley de Principios del Movimiento Nacional* 17 May 1958.

9. Jacques Georgel, *El Franquismo: Historia y balance 1939–69* (1971) p.235.

10. *Ibid.* p.190.

11. Cooper, *op.cit.* p.55.

12. Georgel, *op.cit.* p.206.

13. Cited in Jorge de Esteban and Luis López Guerra, *La crisis del Estado franquista* (1977) p.62.

14. Reproduced in Georgel, *op.cit.* p.209.

15. Tad Szulc, 'The politics of Church-State relations in Spain' in Salisbury and Theberge (eds), *Spain in the 1970s* (1979) p.73.

16. Cooper, *op.cit.* pp.75–6.

17. Such was the opinion of one of his ministers, José María Sánchez-Ventura y Pascual. See Angel Bayod (ed.), *Franco visto por sus ministros* (1981) p.424.

18. Quoted in Juan J. Linz, 'An Authoritarian Regime: Spain' in Stanley G. Payne (ed.) *Politics and Society in Twentieth-Century Spain* (1976) p.190.

19. From an interview with the author in Madrid, October 1982. See also Vilar, *op.cit.* pp.447–66, and Salvador Pániker, *Conversaciones en Madrid* (1971) pp.332–4.

20. Jesus Ynfante, *La prodigiosa aventura del Opus Dei: genesis y desarrollo de la Santa Mafia* (1970).

21. Gonzalo Fernández de la Mora, *Pensamiento español 1967* (1968) p.112. It is discussed in Amando de Miguel, *Sociología del Franquismo* (1975) p.338.

22. See Miguel, *op.cit.* p.338.

23. Pániker, *op.cit.* p.330.

24. Quoted in Paul Preston (ed.), *op.cit..* From the introduction.

25. Miguel, *op.cit.* p.228.

26. *Ibid.* p.227.

27. Manuel Fraga Iribarne, *El cañón giratorio* (1982) pp.47,50.

28. Miguel, *op.cit.* p.99.

29. Manuel Fraga Iribarne, *How Spain is Governed* (1952, 2nd English ed.) p.33.

30. Vilar, *op.cit.* p.584.

31. Quoted in Georgel, *op.cit.* p.161.

32. See Hughes, *op.cit.* pp.103–4.

33. Xavier Tusell, *La oposición democrática al franquismo* (1977) pp.84–7.

34. Pedro Sainz Rodríguez, *Un reinado en la sombra* (1981) pp.133,183–6.

35. Ramón Tamames, *La República, La Era de Franco* (1980) p.566.

36. Quoted in Arnold Hottinger, *Spain in Transition: Franco's Regime* (1974) p.41.

37. For the *Madrid* episode, see Rafael Calvo Serer, *La dictadura de los franquistas* (1973) and *Mis enfrentamientos con el poder* (1978).

38. See Georgel, *op.cit.* p.219.

39. Bernard Crick, *George Orwell: A Life* (1980) p.219.

40. See *Blanco y Negro*, 16 March 1974.

41. 2 April 1970.

42. See López Rodó, *op.cit.* pp.387–95.

43. *Ibid.* p.446.

44. Quoted in Ynfante, *op.cit.* p.175.

45. López Rodó, *op.cit.* p.32.

46. H.K. Southworth, *Antifalange* (1976) pp.37–8.

47. Emilio Romero, 'Entrevista con Carrero Blanco' in *Pueblo*, 7 February 1968. Quoted in Ynfante, *op.cit.* p.314.

48. López Rodó. *op.cit.*, pp.419, 435.

49. *Ibid.* p.445.

50. *Ibid.* p.458.

51. See the anecdote told by Fraga, *op.cit.* p.66.

52. FO371/39742.

53. See Bayod, *op.cit.* p.310.

54. Miguel, *op.cit.* pp.351–5.

55. 28 April 1974.

56. Reported in *The Times*, 23 May 1974.

57. 27 September 1974.

58. For an amusing description of this event, see *Cambio 16*, 30 December 1974.

59. From an interview reproduced in the *International Herald Tribune* 20 February 1975.

60. *Cambio 16*, 23 December 1974.

61. *Cambio 16*, 31 March 1975.

62. *Le Monde*, 17 April 1975.

63. *International Herald Tribune*, 17 December 1974.

64. *Cambio 16*, 23 December 1974.

65. *Cambio 16*, 3 February 1975.

66. Raymond Carr, *Spain 1808–1939* (1966) p.504.

67. *New York Times*, 3 March 1975.

68. *The Times*, 4 November 1974.

69. *Le Monde*, 31 January 1975.

70. *Cambio 16*, 31 March 1975.

71. Quoted in Raymond Carr and Juan Pablo Fusi, *Spain: Dictatorship to Democracy* (1979) p.205.

72. *The Times*, 2 October 1975.

73. See Bayod (ed.) *op.cit.* p.392.

74. Vicente Pozuelo Escudero, *Los últimos 476 días de Franco* (1980) pp.126–7, 158.

75. José Yglesias, *The Franco Years* (1977) p.220.

Chapter 5: The Opposition (pp. 81–104)

1. Samuel Hoare, *Ambassador on Special Mission* (1946) p.293.

2. *La Velada en Benicarló* (1939).

3. See Antonio Tellez, *Sabate: Guerrilla Extraordinary* (1974).

4. Quoted in Xavier Tusell, *La oposición democrática al franquismo* (1977) p.276.

5. Salvador de Madariaga, *Spain* (1958) p.455.

6. Tusell, *op.cit.* p.176.

7. *Ibid.* p.94.

8. *Ibid.* pp.212,262–3.

9. *Ibid.* p.154.

10. Pedro Sainz Rodríguez, *Un reinado en la sombra* (1981) p.178.

11. Laureano López Rodó, *La larga marcha hacia la monarquía* (1978) p.15.

12. Tusell, *op.cit.* p.33.

13. López Rodó, *op.cit.* p.15.

14. *Ibid.* pp.17–18.

15. José María Gil Robles. Quoted in Xavier Tusell, *op.cit.* p.61.

16. Quoted in López Rodó, *op.cit.* pp.48–50.

17. *Ibid.*

18. Madariaga, *op.cit.*, p.449. Gil Robles's anti-fascist opinions are quoted in Richard A.H. Robinson, *The Origins of Franco's Spain* (1970) pp.134–5,140,171. Paul Preston argues that if Gil Robles was not theoretically a fascist, in practice he was close to being one. See Preston, *The Coming of the Spanish Civil War* (1983) pp.44,47–8,88,92,155,194–5.

19. Conversation with the author in London, September 1980.

20. Sainz Rodríguez, *op.cit.* p.39.

21. Tusell, *op.cit.* p.71.

22. *Ibid.*

23. Sainz Rodríguez, *op.cit.* pp.178–80.

24. López Rodó, *op.cit.* p.229.

25. Tusell, *op.cit.* p.292. For an account of the affair, see José Maravall, *Dictatorship and Political Dissent* (1978) pp.102–3.

26. Tusell, *op.cit.* p.294.

27. Jacques Georgel, *El Franquismo: Historia y balance 1939–69* (1970) p.110.

28. Julián Ariza, *Comisiones Obreras* (1976) p.23.

29. Sergio Vilar, *Protagonistas de la España democrática: la oposición a la dictadura 1939–1969* p.322.

30. José Yglesias, *The Franco Years* (1971) p.240.

31. Madariaga, *op.cit.* p.630.

32. Ian Gibson, *Paracuellos: como fue* (1983) and Carlos Fernández, *Paracuellos: Carrillo culpable?* (1983). In *Cambio 16*, 21 February 1983, the two authors accuse each other of inadequate research.

33. Arnold Hottinger, *Spain in Transition: Prospects and Policies* (1974) p.36.

34. Guy Hermet, *The Communists in Spain* (1974) pp.78–9.

35. Recorded in Dionisio Ridruejo, *Escrito en España* (1964) p.29.

36. Vilar, *op.cit.* p.177.

37. *Ibid.* pp.504–8.

38. Benjamin Welles, *Spain: the Gentle Anarchy* (1965) p.198.

39. Tusell, *op.cit.* pp.335–6.

40. Salvador Pániker, *Conversaciones en Madrid* (1971) p.338. See also Vilar, *op.cit.* pp.463–4.

41. Pániker, *op.cit.* p.336.

42. Luis García San Miguel, *Teoría de la Transición* (1981) p.126.

43. Tusell, *op.cit.* p.389.
44. *Ibid.* p.394.
45. *ABC*, 9 June 1962.
46. 10 June 1962. Quoted in Tusell, *op.cit.* pp.399–400.
47. *Ibid.*
48. *Ibid.* p.406.
49. Rafael Calvo Serer, *Mis enfrentamientos con el poder* (1978) p.29.
50. *Observer*, 26 October 1975.
51. See José Maravall, *The Transition to Democracy in Spain* (1982) p.145. For the early career of González, see Eduardo Chamorro, *Felipe González: un hombre a la espera* (1980).
52. *Cambio 16*, 9 December 1974.
53. *The Times*, 21 October 1975.
54. Ridruejo, *op.cit.* (1964) p.31.

Chapter 6: The Resurgence of Local Nationalism (pp. 105–30)

1. Quoted in Ian Gibson, *En busca de José Antonio* (1980) p.24.
2. Gerald Brenan, *The Spanish Labyrinth* (1960) p.311.
3. Cited in Gregorio Morán, *Los españoles que dejaron de serlo* (1982) p.30.
4. Quoted in Vicente Pozuelo Escudero, *Los últimos 476 días de Franco* (1980) p.252.
5. José Ortega y Gasset, *España Invertebrada* (1964) p.48.
6. *Ibid.* p.62.
7. From 'A orillas del Duero', reproduced in *Poesías Completas* (1981) pp.137–9.
8. Ortega, *op.cit.* pp.58,64,70.
9. Gibson, *op.cit.* p.18.
10. José Pemartín, quoted in Jaume Rossinyol, *Le problème national catalan* (1974) p.146.
11. See J.H. Elliot, *Imperial Spain 1469–1716* (1978) pp.30,82–4,124–6.
12. Brenan, *op.cit.* p.25.
13. Jaime Vicens Vives, *An Economic History of Spain* (1969), parts of which are reproduced in Roger Highfield (ed.), *Spain in the Fifteenth Century (1369–1516)* (1972). See pp.273–5.
14. Raymond Carr, *Spain 1808–1939* (1966) p.30–1.
15. Pierre Vilar, *Spain: a brief history* (1980) p.72.
16. Josep Benet. Quoted in Sergio Vilar, *Protagonistas de la España democrática: la oposición a la dictadura 1939–1969* p.426.
17. Quoted in Eduard Punset, *España: sociedad cerrada, sociedad abierta* (1983) p.228–9.
18. Jordi Solé-Tura, *Catalanismo y revolución burguesa* (1970) pp.28–9,192.
19. Luis Suárez Fernández, *Navegación y comercio en el golfo de Vizcaya: un estudio sobre la política marinera de la Casa de Trastámara* (1958) p.106. See also Jean-Claude Larronde, *El nacionalismo vasco: su origen y su ideología en la obra de Sabino Arana-Goïri* (1977) pp.9–11, and Javier Corcuera Atienza, *Orígenes, ideología y organización del nacionalismo vasco (1876–1904)* (1979) p.23.

20. Brenan, *op.cit.* p.210.

21. Telesforo Monzón, *Herri Baten Oihua* pp.78,95.

22. Fernando García de Cortázar and Manuel Montero, *Historia de Vizcaya* (1980) p.114.

23. Larronde, *op.cit.* p.76.

24. *Ibid.* p.146.

25. In particular, see Alfonso de Otazu, *El igualtarismo vasco: mito y realidad* (1973). See also Corcuera, *op.cit.* pp.25,357,581.

26. Larronde, *op.cit.* pp.108–11,139,143–7.

27. See Jacques Allières, *Les Basques* (1977) p.53, and Salvador de Madariaga, *Spain* (1930) pp.306–8.

28. Felix Ducha Arrizabalaga in *Muga*, No. 21, Año 4 (no date) pp.68–73.

29. Larronde, *op.cit.* pp.120,130,141–2.

30. Allières, *op.cit.* p.73.

31. García de Cortázar and Montero, *op.cit.* p.71.

32. Pierre Lafitte, *Grammaire Basque* (1962) p.27. Quoted in Larronde, *op.cit.* p.121.

33. Larronde, *op.cit.* pp.71,89,120–1,134.

34. From the *Fuero de Vizcaya*, cited in Corcuera, *op.cit.* p.23.

35. Larronde, *op.cit.* pp.217–8.

36. *Ibid.* p.208, and Corcuera, *op.cit.* p.70.

37. *Muga, op.cit.* p.62.

38. Larronde, *op.cit.* pp.333–4. See also Juan Pablo Fusi, *Política obrera en el País Vasco (1880–1923)* (1975) pp.199–202.

39. Quoted by Norman L. Jones in 'The Catalan Question since the Civil War' in Paul Preston (ed.), *Spain in Crisis* (1975) p.236.

40. Gibson, *op.cit.* p.25.

41. García de Cortázar and Montero, *op.cit.* pp.138–40.

42. Quoted from Elliot, *op.cit.* p.262.

43. Cited in Morán, *op.cit.* p.123.

44. From a speech delivered in Bilbao on 8 July 1937. Quoted in García de Cortázar and Montero, *op.cit.* p.148.

45. José Yglesias, *The Franco Years* (1977) p.225.

46. Pablo Casals, *Joy and Sorrows* (1981) p.73.

47. Dionisio Ridruejo, *Escrito en España* (1964) pp.18,177. Sergio Villar, *op.cit.* pp.485,489.

48. Gurutz Jaúregui Bereciartu, *Ideología y estrategia política de ETA* (1981) p.207.

49. The former street names of Baracaldo are listed in *Plano y Guía del Gran Bilbao* (1981) pp.27–9.

50. See the remark by Franco cited in Rossinyol, *op.cit.* p.590.

51. See Norman Jones, *op.cit.* p.238.

52. Elena de la Souchère, *Explication de l'Espagne* (1962) p.299.

53. Ridruejo, *op.cit.* p.177.

54. Casals, *op.cit.* p.85–6.

55. Jacques Georgel, *El franquismo: Historia y balance 1939–1969* (1970) pp.208–10.

56. Rossinyol, *op.cit.* p.432.

57. Sergio Vilar, *op.cit.* pp.411–3.

58. Benjamin Welles, *Spain: The Gentle Anarchy* (1965) pp.151–2.

59. Georgel, *op.cit.* p.176.

60. Edward C. Hansen, *Rural Catalonia under the Franco Regime* (1977) p.137.

61. Quoted in Fusi, *op.cit.* p.203.

62. Monzón, *op.cit.* p.75.

63. *Ibid.* pp.35,44. This view was confirmed to me in interviews with Monzón's widow and his brother Isidro in 1981 and 1982.

64. Jaúregui, *op.cit.* pp.101–2.

65. See the interview in *Cambio 16*, 23 January 1984.

66. Fernando Sarrailh de Ihartza, *Vasconia* (1963) pp.15,250.

67. Quoted in Jaúregui, *op.cit.* p.413.

68. *Ibid.* pp.209–10.

69. Sarrailh de Ihartza, *op.cit.* p.30.

70. See Morán, *op.cit.* pp.272–4. Also Jaúregui, *op.cit.* pp.127,199. ETA's admiration for zionism was described to me by Isidro Monzón in November 1981.

71. Jaúregui, *op.cit.* pp.309,437–8,447–8.

72. Herbert Southworth, *Guernica! Guernica!* (1977) pp.272–5,308–9.

73. Morán, *op.cit.* pp.351–2.

Chapter 7: The Return of the Monarchy (pp. 133–48)

1. Letter from Franco to Don Juan, 12 May 1942. Reproduced in Pedro Sainz Rodríguez, *Un reinado en la sombra* (1981) pp.351–3.

2. *ABC*, 23 August 1969. Quoted in Richard Herr, *Modern Spain* (1974) p.287.

3. Letter from Carrero to Franco, August 1944. Quoted in Laureano López Rodó, *La larga marcha hacia la Monarquía* (1978) p.47.

4. See F. Franco Salgado-Araujo, *Mis conversaciones privadas con Franco* (1976) pp.9,18,38,54,94,99,146,224,238,255,311,353,488.

5. Letter from Franco to Don Juan, 7 February 1944. Reproduced in Sainz Rodríguez, *op.cit.* pp.363–4.

6. See, for example, López Rodó, *op.cit.* p.17.

7. Sainz Rodríguez, *op.cit.* pp.221–2.

8. *Ibid.* p.76.

9. López Rodó, *op.cit.* pp.289–90.

10. *Ibid.* pp.331–2,339,350–4.

11. *Le Monde*, 29 January 1974.

12. Vicente Pozuelo Escudero, *Los últimos 476 días de Franco* (1980) p.136.

13. See, for example, the suggestion put forward by J. de Esteban and L. López Guerra in *Informaciones*, 1 May 1976, and by the same authors in *Posible*, 17 June 1976. Reproduced in J. de Esteban and L. López Guerra in *De la Dictadura a la Democracia* (1979) pp.96–8,140.

14. See Antonio Garrigues y Díaz-Cañabate, *Diálogos conmigo mismo* (1978)

p.163, and José María de Areilza, *Diario de un ministro de la Monarquía* (1977) pp.13–14.

15. Alfonso Osorio, *Trayectoria política de un ministro de la Corona* (1980) p.54.

16. Gregorio Morán, *Adolfo Suárez: Historia de una ambición* (1979) p.20.

17. Areilza, *op.cit.* p.53.

18. *Ibid.* p.13.

19. Osorio, *op.cit.* p.123.

20. Areilza, *op.cit.* p.173.

21. *Ibid.* p.52.

22. *Ibid.* p.104.

23. *Ibid.* p.84.

24. Osorio, *op.cit.* p.100. Areilza, *op.cit.* pp.81,96,100,113.

25. From an interview with Fraga on American television, 24 February 1976. Quoted in the *Financial Times* and the *Daily Telegraph* 25 February 1976.

26. Areilza, *op.cit.* p.76.

27. Reported in the *Guardian* 30 March 1976.

28. Osorio, *op.cit.* p.80–1.

29. Areilza, *op.cit.* p.200.

30. Esteban and López Guerra, *op.cit.* p.139.

31. Constantine Christopher Menges, *Spain: The Struggle for Democracy Today* (1978) pp.32–3. See also José Maravall, *The Transition to Democracy in Spain* (1982) pp.12–13.

32. See, for example, Osorio, *op.cit.* pp.52,101.

33. Manuel Fraga Iribarne, *Después de la Constitución, y hacia los años 80* (1979) p.200.

34. See Areilza, *op.cit.* pp.110,113,124.

35. *Ibid.* p.153.

36. Osorio, *op.cit.* pp.91–4.

37. Europa interview in *The Times* 4 May 1976.

38. Areilza, *op.cit.* p.113.

39. *Cambio 16*, 18 March 1976.

40. Sainz Rodríguez, *op.cit.* p.318.

41. Areilza, *op.cit.* pp.106–7,133,178.

42. *Ibid.* p.157.

Chapter 8: Suárez and the Defeat of the Right (pp. 149–61)

1. For the election of the *terna* see Gregorio Morán, *Adolfo Suárez: Historia de una ambición* (1979) pp.56–61, and Alfonso Osorio, *Trayectoria política de un ministro de la Corona* (1980) p.129.

2. See, for example, Osorio, *op.cit.* p.146.

3. Morán, *op.cit.* p.346. This claim is repeated by José Oneto in *Los últimos días de un presidente* (1981) p.82.

4. Josep Melià, *Asi cayó Adolfo Suárez* (1981) p.131.

5. See Morán, *op.cit.* pp.169–70,254–5.

6. José María de Areilza, *Diario de un ministro de la Monarquía* (1977) p.182.

7. See, for example, the comments of General Francisco Coloma Gallegos in

Angel Bayod (ed.), *Franco visto por sus ministros* (1981) p.306.

8. Osorio, *op.cit.* pp.137,328.

9. From conversations with José María de Areilza and Antonio Garrigues y Díaz-Cañabate in Madrid, October 1983.

10. Osorio, *op.cit.* pp.134–5.

11. *El País*, 8 July 1976.

12. Antonio Senillosa, who headed Suárez's electoral list in Barcelona in 1982; Francisco Fernández Ordóñez, who was subsequently minister of finance; and Josep Melià, who became one of Suárez's closest aides and was appointed civil governor of Catalonia. See Osorio, *op.cit.* p.136.

13. *Ibid.* p.150.

14. *Ibid.* p.184. Morán, *op.cit.* p.310.

15. Manuel Gutiérrez Mellado, *Un soldado de España* (1983) pp.148–9.

16. José María de Areilza, *Cuadernos de la transición* (1983) p.67.

17. Osorio, *op.cit.* p.149.

18. J.L. Guinea, *Los movimientos obreros y sindicales en España* (1978) p.167.

19. The letter is reproduced in *Blanco y Negro*, 9 October 1976.

20. *El Alcázar*, 27 September 1976.

21. In declarations to *La Vanguardia*, 24 October 1976. Reproduced in Osorio, *op.cit.* p.232.

22. Quoted in *The Times*, 8 September 1976.

23. Osorio, *op.cit.* pp.232–3.

24. *Ibid.* pp.238–9.

25. *Blanco y Negro*, 13 November 1976.

26. *El Alcázar*, 16 December 1976.

27. Osorio, *op.cit.* pp.248–9. See also Alfonso Armada, *Al Servico de la Corona* (1983) p.150.

Chapter 9: 1977: the General Elections (pp.162–86)

1. Alfonso Osorio, *Trayectoria política de un ministro de la Corona* (1980) pp.92–4.

2. José María de Areilza, *Diario de un ministro de la Monarquía* (1977) p.126.

3. Eduardo Chamorro, *Felipe González* (1980) pp.132–3.

4. Osorio, *op.cit.* p.155.

5. *The Times*, 12 August 1976.

6. Osorio, *op.cit.* p.162.

7. Francisco Fernández Ordóñez, *La España necesaria* (1980) p.66.

8. See the article by Amando de Miguel, 'Spanish political attitudes, 1970' in Stanley G. Payne (ed.) *Politics and Society in Twentieth Century Spain* (1976) pp.208–232. See also José Amodia, *Franco's Political Legacy* (1977) p.285.

9. See, for example, *Diario de Barcelona*, 25 April 1976.

10. José María de Areilza, *Cuadernos de la transición* (1983) p.40.

11. Areilza, *op.cit.* (1977) pp.122,156.

12. Luis García San Miguel, *Teoría de la transición* (1981) p.124. See also J. de Esteban and L. López Guerra, *Los partidos políticos en la España actual* (1982) p.120.

13. Osorio, *op.cit.* p.195.

14. Areilza, *op.cit.*(1983) p.30.

15. Manuel Fraga Iribarne, *El cañón giratorio* (1982) p.75.

16. Areilza, *op.cit.* (1983) p.43.

17. Amando de Miguel, *Sociología del Franquismo* (1975) pp.228.

18. Fraga, *op.cit.* p.61.

19. Josep Melià, *Asi cayó Adolfo Suárez* (1981) p.136.

20. José Jiménez Blanco, *De Franco a las elecciones generales* (1978) p.247.

21. Areilza, *op.cit.* (1983) p.86.

22. Santiago Carrillo, *Memoria de la transición* (1983) pp.40–3.

23. Areilza, *op.cit.* (1977) pp.195–6.

24. In an interview with the *New York Times*, 19 June 1976.

25. Osorio, *op.cit.* p.206.

26. See Simón Sánchez Montero in *Le Monde*, 1 January 1977.

27. Osorio, *op.cit.* p.277.

28. Carrillo, *op.cit.* p.46.

29. *Ya*, 31 March 1977.

30. For a full account of the legalization of the PCE see Osorio, *op.cit.* pp.280–91.

31. *Ibid.* p.289.

32. *Ibid.* pp.289–90.

33. Manuel Gutiérrez Mellado, *Un Soldado de España* (1983) p.150.

34. Osorio, *op.cit.* p.146.

35. *Ibid.* p.301.

36. For an account of these events see Areilza, *op.cit.* (1983) pp.108–14; Osorio, *op.cit.* pp.301–2, and Eduardo Chamorro, *Viaje al centro de UCD* (1981) pp.159–62.

37. Osorio, *op.cit.* p.302. Areilza, *op.cit.*(1983) p.114.

38. Gregorio Morán, *Adolfo Suárez: Historia de una ambición* (1979) p.340. See also *Interviu*, 14 May 1981.

39. Areilza, *op.cit.* (1983) pp.92–5. See also Emilio Attard, *Vida y muerte de UCD* (1983) p.42.

40. Fraga, *op.cit.* p.76.

41. J. de Esteban in *El País*, 11 May 1977.

42. See Osorio, *op.cit.* pp.262–3.

43. Chamorro, *op.cit.* (1981) p.89.

44. José Luis Aranguren, *La democracia establecida* (1979) p.151.

45. Chamorro, *op.cit.* (1981) p.168.

46. See Marino Gómez-Santos, *Conversaciones con Leopoldo Calvo-Sotelo* (1982) pp.171–6.

47. Fernández Ordóñez, *op.cit.* p.78.

48. Osorio, *op.cit.* p.311.

49. Chamorro, *op.cit.* (1981) p.168.

50. *Ya*, 11 May 1977.

51. *Cambio 16*, 9 May 1977.

52. *Guardian*, 2 May 1977.

53. Attard, *op.cit.* p.57.

54. See the article by Julián Marías in *El País*, 18 September 1977.

55. *ABC*, 24 May 1977.
56. *ABC*, 25 May 1977.
57. *ABC*, 22 April 1977.
58. Osorio, *op.cit.* p.315.
59. *Ibid.* pp.316–8.
60. Aranguren, *op.cit.* p.151.
61. The point is well made in J. de Esteban and L. López Guerra, *El régimen constitucional español* Vol.1 (1980) pp.19–20.

Chapter 10: Consensus and the Constitution (pp. 187–210)

1. See Alfonso Osorio, *Trayectoria política de un ministro de la Corona* (1980) p.328.
2. *Ibid.*
3. See the report of the Banco de España of 2 June 1981, and the article in *El País* discussing the report on the following day.
4. See José Maravall, *The Transition to Democracy in Spain* (1982) pp.12–13, 53,60.
5. Banco Urquijo, *La Economía española ante la década de los 80* (1980) pp.63–4. It is difficult to establish an accurate figure for unemployment because the main banks and INE usually produce very different statistics. In its annual report of 1982, the Banco de España points out that the figures it gives for the increase in unemployment during that year are only an indication of 'the attitude of the jobless towards registering themselves at the local unemployment office, which often has little or nothing to do with the real level of unemployment.' This explanation suggests that the Banco de España and INE, which always gives a lower figure than the large banks, invariably underestimate the jobless total.
6. Banco de España, *Informe Anual*, p.478.
7. Ministerios de Comercio y de Economía, and the Banco de España. Reproduced in Banco Urquijo, *op.cit.* p.127.
8. J. de Esteban and L. López Guerra, *De la Dictadura a la Democracia* (1979) p.317. See also John F. Coverdale, *The Political Transformation of Spain after Franco* (1979) p.89.
9. See Emilio Attard, *Vida y muerte de UCD* (1983) p.67.
10. Santiago Carrillo, *Memoria de la transición* (1983) p.53.
11. Maravall, *op.cit.* p.13.
12. Banco Urquijo, *op.cit.* pp.86–7, and Banco de España, *op.cit.* p.478.
13. Banco Urquijo, *op.cit.* pp.126–8.
14. The employers' social security contribution – 80 per cent of the total contribution in 1977 – was considerably higher in Spain than in the rest of Europe. See OECD Economic Surveys, *Spain* (1982) p.33. For the state of Spanish industry at that time see the article by James Markham in the *International Herald Tribune*, 6 March 1978, and Sima Lieberman, *The Contemporary Spanish Economy* (1982) p.323.
15. Banco Urquijo, *op.cit.* p.64.
16. Maravall, *op.cit.* pp.126–7.
17. *Ibid.* pp.124–6.

18. Robert Graham, *Spain: Change of a Nation* (1984) p.291.

19. For descriptions of the drafting of the constitution, see J. de Esteban and L. López Guerra, *El régimen constitucional español* Vol. 1 (1980) pp.23–7, and Manuel Fraga Iribarne, *Después de la Constitución, y hacia los años 80* (1979) pp.22–33.

20. Manuel Fraga Iribarne, *La Constitución y otras cuestiones fundamentales* (1978) p.178.

21. Richard P. Gunther, 'Political evolution towards democracy: political parties' in J.L. Cacigao *et al.* (eds.), *Spain 1975–1980* (1982) pp.166–7.

22. *Ibid.* pp.167–8.

23. Articles 3 and 26 of the 1931 constitution. They are reproduced in J. de Esteban (ed.), *Las Constituciones de España* (1981) pp.191,197–8.

24. See Gunther, *op.cit.* pp.175–6.

25. Fraga, *op.cit.* (1979) p.27.

26. See the argument in Esteban and López Guerra, *op.cit.* (1980) pp.141–2.

27. Fraga, *op.cit.* (1978) p.23.

28. Alfonso Castelao, *Sempre en Galiza (versión castellana* 1977) pp.420–1.

29. Fraga, *op.cit.* (1979) p.25.

30. *La Vanguardia*, 9 May 1978. Quoted in Julián Marías, *Cinco años de España* (1981) p.206.

31. Fraga, *op.cit.* (1978) p.151.

32. See Angel Bayod (ed.), *Franco visto por sus ministros* (1981) p.298.

33. Federico Silva Muñoz, *La transición inacabada* (1980) pp.64–6,91–2.

34. Luis García San Miguel, *Teoría de la transición* (1981) p.157.

35. This was the message on the party's wall-posters in Toledo and elsewhere, October 1978.

36. Quoted in the *International Herald Tribune*, 27 June 1978.

37. Speech in the *Congreso*, 8 November 1978. Reproduced in Fraga, *op.cit.* (1979) pp.34–85.

38. This remark was widely criticized at the time. See the article by Josep Melià in *Blanco y Negro*, 13–19 September 1978.

39. See Gerald Brenan, *Personal Record* (1974) p.279.

40. See Bayod, *op.cit.* p.298.

41. *Ibid.* p.349.

42. Banco Urquijo, *op.cit.* pp.63–4,86–7.

43. *Ibid.* p.127.

44. Manuel Fraga Iribarne, *El cañón giratorio* (1982) p.145.

45. Fraga, *op.cit.* (1979) pp.183–4.

46. *Cambio 16*, 24 September 1978.

47. The interview was conducted by Merle Woolin for the New York magazine *Viva*. It is reproduced in *Cambio 16*, 1 October 1978, pp.22–3.

48. J. de Esteban and L. López Guerra, *Los partidos políticos en la España actual* (1982) p.144.

49. Eduardo Chamorro, *Felipe González* (1980) pp.117–8.

50. *Informaciones*, 9 May 1978.

51. Carrillo, *op.cit.* pp.54–5.

52. Chamorro, *op.cit.* pp.164–6.

53. From extracts of Carrillo's campaign speeches, quoted in Asociación

independiente, *España, a las urnas* (1979) pp.71–7.

54. *Ibid.* p.75–6.
55. *Ibid.* pp.26–8,42,44,82–7.
56. From a conversation with the author in Seville, November 1980.
57. Cited in Josep Melià, *Asi cayó Adolfo Suárez* (1981) p.29.
58. Attard, *op.cit.* p.76.

Chapter 11: Catalonia and the Basque Country (pp. 213–29)

1. See *Blanco y Negro*, 9 October 1976.
2. Alfonso Osorio, *Trayectoria política de un ministro de la Corona* (1980) p.320.
3. *Ibid.* p.323.
4. See the comments of *El Alcázar*, 30 September 1977.
5. Quoted in Josep Melià, *Asi cayó Adolfo Suárez* (1981) p.123.
6. Vicente Pozuelo Escudero, *Los últimos 476 días de Franco* (1980) p.112.
7. Jose María de Areilza, *Diario de un ministro de la Monarquía* (1977) p.153. This view was repeated to me in an interview with Manuel Fraga in October 1983.
8. Osorio, *op.cit.* pp.209–13.
9. *Ibid.* p.213.
10. Federico Silva Muñoz, *La transición inacabada* (1980) p.103.
11. Fraga repeatedly mentioned this in his speeches and articles. See the numerous references in his *La Constitución y otras cuestiones fundamentales* (1978).
12. This was one of many similar descriptions I heard from members of the *sabiniano* wing in Bilbao in 1982.
13. *El País*, 30 March 1982.
14. From interviews in Bilbao, April 1982.
15. *El País*, 26 September 1978.
16. Gregorio Morán, *Los españoles que dejaron de serlo* (1982) pp.363–6.
17. *Observer*, 18 February 1979.
18. Reported in *El País*, 7 November 1980.
19. Telesforo Monzón, *Herri Baten Oihua* p.94.
20. *New York Times*, 4 November 1979.
21. In an interview with Miguel Castells, *Herri Batasuna*'s senator for Guipúzcoa, April 1982.
22. No two analysts agree on the number of ETA victims during these years, but reliable statistics are given in *Cambio 16*, 30 March 1981 and Robert P. Clark, *The Basque Insurgents: ETA, 1952–1980* (1984) pp.125–6,133.
23. *Le Monde*, 26 July 1979.
24. *Le Monde*, 27 September 1979.
25. *Diario 16*, 12 April 1982.
26. *El País*, 17 October 1983.
27. *Deia*, 22 April 1982.
28. *Cambio 16*, 23 January 1984.
29. Osorio, *op.cit.* p.213.
30. *New York Times*, 18 July 1980.
31. Morán, *op.cit.* pp.325–6.

32. See *El País*, 17 October 1982.

Chapter 12: The Role of the Military (pp. 230–48)

1. Rafael Bañón Martínez, *Poder de la burocracia y Cortes franquistas (1943–1971)* (1978) p.266. Cited in Julio Busquets, *Pronunciamientos y golpes de Estado en España* (1982) pp.178–9.
2. Amando de Miguel, *Sociología del Franquismo* (1975) p.161.
3. Ramón Tamames, *La República, La Era de Franco* (1980) p.340.
4. *Ibid.*
5. Gerald Brenan, *The Face of Spain* (1950) p.117.
6. Julio Busquets, *El militar de carrera en España* (1971) pp.270–1.
7. F. Franco Salgado-Araujo, *Mis conversaciones privadas con Franco* (1976) p.396.
8. Busquets, *op.cit.* (1971)) p.214.
9. Jesús M. Paricio, *Para conocer a nuestros militares* (1983) pp.127,136.
10. *Ibid.* p.60.
11. Francisco Caparrós, *La UMD: militares rebeldes* (1983) p.25.
12. Busquets, *op.cit.* (1971) p.273.
13. This list was originally published in Busquets *op.cit.* (1971) pp.272–3. It was subsequently reproduced, with some modifications, in Julio Busquets, Miguel A. Aguilar and Ignacio Puche, *El Golpe: anatomía y claves del asalto al Congreso* (1981) pp.15–16, and in Busquets, *op.cit.* (1982) pp.187–91.
14. Quoted in Carlos Fernández, *Los militares en la transición política* (1982) p.24.
15. General Gutiérrez Mellado, cited in *Cambio 16*, 31 August 1981.
16. See *Cambio 16* of 1 June 1981 and 31 August 1981.
17. Fernández, *op.cit.* pp.105–6.
18. *Ibid.* pp.45–6. See also Caparrós, *op.cit.*
19. See Manuel Gutiérrez Mellado, *Un soldado de España* (1983) pp.132–8.
20. Busquets, *op.cit.* (1982) pp.36–7.
21. *Ibid.* pp.156–7.
22. From a survey carried out by one of the UMD leaders and published in *La Calle* No.38, December 1978. See Fernández, *op.cit.* p.302.
23. Alfonso Armada, *Al servicio de la Corona* (1983) p.215.
24. José María de Areilza, *Diario de un ministro de la Monarquía* (1977) pp.76–7. See also Gutiérrez Mellado, *op.cit.* p.40.
25. For descriptions of this incident, see Fernández, *op.cit.* pp.257–8, and Pilar Urbano, *Con la venia . . . yo indagué el 23–F* (1982) p.19.
26. See the interview in *Cambio 16*, 24 November 1980.
27. Urbano, *op.cit.* p.42.
28. Armada, *op.cit.* p.154.
29. *Ibid.* pp.209–12.
30. José Oneto, *La verdad sobre el caso Tejero* (1982). See also the same author's *La noche de Tejero* (1981).
31. *New York Times*, 25 November 1979.
32. For an account of this meeting, see Urbano, *op.cit.* pp.61–6.
33. Armada, *op.cit.* pp.230–1.

34. Urbano, *op.cit.* p.272.
35. *Ibid.* p.169.
36. *Ibid.* p.210.
37. *Ibid.* pp.248–56.
38. *Ibid.* p.300.
39. Gutiérrez Mellado, *op.cit.* p.120.
40. For an interesting discussion of these points, see the early chapters of Víctor Alba, *La soledad del Rey* (1981).
41. *Cambio 16*, 6 April 1981.
42. Quoted in Urbano, *op.cit.* p.287.

Chapter 13: The Collapse of the Centre 1979–82 (pp.249–68)

1. *Cambio 16*, 8 June 1981.
2. José Oneto in *Cambio 16*, 19 October 1980.
3. Banco de España, *Informe anual*, 1981 and 1982.
4. For descriptions of Suárez's life in the Moncloa, see Josep Melià, *Asi cayó Adolfo Suárez* (1981) and José Oneto, *Los últimos días de un presidente* (1981).
5. Emilo Attard, *Vida y muerte de UCD* (1983) p.179.
6. *New York Times*, 1 June 1980.
7. For comparisons between the backgrounds of the two groups, see Eduardo Chamorro, *Viaje al centro de UCD* (1981) p.22, and Melià, *op.cit.* p.86.
8. *El País*, 20 November 1983.
9. See Melià, *op.cit.* pp.67–76, and Oneto, *op.cit.*
10. See the report in *El País*, 15 May 1981.
11. Alfonso Castelao, *Sempre en Galiza* (1977) p.43.
12. Salvador de Madariaga, *Spain* (1958) p.677.
13. For the rediscovery of Blas Infante, see Juan Teba, *La Sevilla de Rojas Marcos* (1981) pp.261–77.
14. See Felipe González, *Un estilo ético* (1982).
15. *El País*, 12 May 1981. Tamames was particularly critical of Carrillo's personal rule. See also Manuel Azcárate, *Crisis del Eurocomunismo* (1982) especially pp.21–4.
16. J. de Esteban and L. López Guerra, *Los partidos políticos en la España actual* (1982) p.154.
17. *Cambio 16*, 19 July 1982.
18. See the interview with Carlos Ferrer Salat, president of the CEOE, in *Cambio 16*, 13 September 1982.
19. Oscar Alzaga. See Attard, *op.cit.* p.229.
20. From a speech delivered at the Club Siglo XXI. Reported in *Diario 16*, 26 May 1981.
21. In conversation with the author, February 1982.
22. Attard, *op.cit.* p.296.
23. *Cambio 16*, 18 October 1982.
24. *Cambio 16*, 11 October 1982.
25. From an interview with the author in October 1982.
26. Reproduced in an article by Vicent Ventura in *El País*, 21 May 1981.

Epilogue (pp. 269–74)

1. Julián Marías, *Cinco años de Espana* (1981) pp.137–40.
2. See *El nuevo lunes*, 16 February 1981 and 1 June 1981.
3. Juan Luis Cebrián, 'The pre-constitutional experiment' in J.L. Cacigao and others (eds) *Spain 1975–1980: the conflicts and achievements of democracy* (1982) pp.16–17.
4. For an interesting view on this point, see Eduard Punset, *España: sociedad cerrada, sociedad abierta* (1983) pp.39–42.

Bibliography

List of Books Cited in the Notes

Alba, Victor, *La soledad del Rey*, Planeta, Barcelona 1981.

Allardt, E. and Littunen, Y. (eds.), *Cleavages, Ideologies and Party Systems*, Transactions of the Westermark Society, Vol 10, Helsinki 1964.

Allières, Jacques, *Les Basques*, Presses Universitaires de France, 1977.

Amodia, José, *Franco's Political Legacy*, Allen Lane, London 1977.

Anderson, Charles W., *The Political Economy of Modern Spain*, University of Wisconsin Press, Milwaukee 1970.

Aranguren, José Luis, *La democracia establecida*, Taurus, Madrid 1979.

Areilza, José María de, *Cuadernos de la transición*, Planeta, Barcelona 1983.

Areilza, José María de, *Diario de un ministro de la Monarquía*, Planeta, Barcelona 1977.

Ariza, Julián, *Comisiones Obreras*, Avance, Barcelona 1976.

Armada, Alfonso, *Al servicio de la Corona*, Planeta, Barcelona 1983.

Asián, José Luis, *Elementos de Geografía Regional e Historia de España* Bosch, Barcelona 1945.

Attard, Emilio, *Vida y muerte de UCD*, Planeta, Barcelona 1983.

Azaña, Manuel, *La Velada en Benicarló*, Castalia, Madrid 1974.

Azaña, Manuel, *Obras completas* (4 Vols) Oasis, Mexico 1966–8.

Azcárate, Manuel, *Crisis del Eurocomunismo*, Argos Vergara, Barcelona 1982.

Banco de Bilbao, *Informe Económico 1979*.

Banco de Bilbao, *Renta nacional de España 1973*.

Banco de España, *Informe Anual 1981 and 1982*.

Banco Urquijo, *La Economía española ante la década de los 80 1980*.

Bañón Martínez, Rafael, *Poder de la burocracia y Cortes franquistas (1943–1971)*, Estudios Administrativos, Madrid 1978.

Bayod, Angel (ed.), *Franco visto por sus ministros*, Planeta, Barcelona 1981.

Bowers, Claude, *My Mission to Spain*, Gollancz, London 1954.

Brenan, Gerald, *Personal Record: 1920–1972*, Cambridge University Press,

.bridge, 1974.

.an, Gerald, *The Face of Spain*, Turnstile Press, London 1950.

.enan, Gerald, *The Spanish Labyrinth*, Cambridge University Press, Cambridge, 1974.

Busquets Bragulat, Julio, *El militar de carrera en España*, Ariel, Barcelona 1981.

Busquets Bragulat, Julio, *Pronunciamientos y golpes de estado en Espana*, Planeta, Barcelona, 1982.

Busquets Bragulat, Julio, *El Golpe: anatomía y claves del asalto al Congreso*, Ariel, Barcelona 1981.

Cacigao, J.L. *et al.* (eds.) *Spain 1975–1980,* José Porrua Turanzas, Madrid 1982.

Calvo Serer, Rafael, *La dictadura de los franquistas*, Calvo Serer, Paris 1973.

Calvo Serer, Rafael, *Mis enfentamientos con el poder*, Plaza & Janes, Barcelona 1978.

Caparrós, Francisco, *La UMD: militares rebeldes*, Argos Vergara, Barcelona 1983.

Carr, Raymond, *Modern Spain*, Oxford University Press, London 1980.

Carr, Raymond, and Fusi, Juan Pablo, *Spain: Dictatorship to Democracy,* George Allen & Unwin, London 1979.

Carr, Raymond, *The Spanish Tragedy*, Weidenfeld & Nicolson, London 1977.

Carr, Raymond, *Spain 1808–1939*, Clarendon Press, Oxford 1966.

Carrillo, Santiago, *Memoria de la transición*, Grijalbo, Barcelona 1983.

Casals, Pablo, *Joy and Sorrows*, Eel Pie, London 1981.

Castelao, Alfonso, *Sempre en Galiza*, Akal, Madrid 1977.

Chamorro, Eduardo, *Felipe González: un hombre a la espera*, Planeta, Barcelona 1980.

Chamorro, Eduardo, *Viaje al centro de UCD*, Planeta, Barcelona 1981.

Clark, Robert P., *The Basque Insurgents: ETA 1952–1980*, University of Wisconsin Press, Milwaukee 1984.

Coles, S.F.A., *Franco of Spain*, Neville Spearman, London 1955.

Comisaría del Plan de Desarrollo, III Plan de Desarrollo 1972–5: Económico y Social 1971.

Corcuera Atienza, Javier, *Orígenes, ideología y organización del nacionalismo vasco 1876–1904*, Siglo XXI, Madrid 1979.

Coverdale, John F., *The Political Transformation of Spain after Franco*, Praeger, New York 1979.

Crick, Bernard, *George Orwell: A Life*, Secker & Warburg, London 1980.

Crozier, Brian, *Franco*, Eyre and Spottiswood, London 1967.

Delibes, Miguel, *Castilla, lo castellano y los castellanos*, Planeta, Barcelona 1979.

Delibes, Miguel, *El disputado voto del señor Cayo*, Destino, Barcelona 1978.

Eaton, Samuel, D., *The Forces of Freedom in Spain 1974–1979*, Hoover Institution Press, Stanford 1981.

Elliott, John H., *Imperial Spain 1469–1716*, Penguin, London 1978.

España, a las urnas, Asociación independiente, Madrid 1979.

Esteban, J.L. (ed.), *Las constituciones de España*, Taurus, Madrid 1981.

Esteban, Jorge de, and López Guerra, Luis, *De la Dictadura a la Democracia*, Universidad Complutense, Madrid 1979.

Esteban, Jorge de, and López Guerra, Luis, *El régimen constitucional español*, (2 Vols) Labor, Barcelona 1980.

Esteban, Jorge de, and López Guerra, Luis, *La crisis del Estado franquista, Labor, Barcelona 1977.*

Esteban, Jorge de, and López Guerra, Luis, *Los partidos políticos en la España actual*, Planeta, Barcelona 1982.

Fernández, Carlos, *Los militares en la transición política*, Argos Vergara Barcelona 1982.

Fernández, Carlos, *Paracuellos: Carrillo culpable?* Argos Vergara, Barcelona 1983.

Fernández de la Mora, Gonzalo, *El Crepúsculo de las Ideologías*, Rialp, Madrid 1965.

Fernández de la Mora, Gonzalo, *Pensamiento español 1967*, Rialp, Madrid 1968.

Fernández Ordóñez, Francisco, *La España necesaria*, Taurus, Madrid 1980.

Foltz, Charles, *The Masquerade in Spain*, Houghton Mifflin, Boston 1948.

Fraga Iribarne, Manuel, *Después de la Constitución, y hacia los años 80*, Planeta, Barcelona 1979.

Fraga Iribarne, Manuel, *El cañón giratorio*, Argos Vergara, Barcelona 1982.

Fraga Iribarne, Manuel, *How Spain is Governed*, Diplomatic Information Office, Madrid 1952.

Fraga Iribarne, Manuel, *La Constitución y otras cuestiones fundamentales*, Planeta, Barcelona 1978.

Fraga Iribarne, Manuel *et al.* (eds.), *La España de los años 70 (Vol 2)*, Editorial Moneda y Crédito, Madrid 1973.

Franco Salgado-Araujo, Francisco, *Mis conversaciones privadas con Franco*, Planeta, Barcelona 1976.

Fraser, Ronald, *The Pueblo*, Allen Lane, London 1973.

Fusi, Juan Pablo, *Política obrera en el País Vasco 1880–1923*, Turner, Madrid 1975.

Gallo, Max, *Spain under Franco*, George Allen & Unwin, London 1973.

García de Cortázar, Fernando, and Montero, Manuel, *Historia de Vizcaya*, Txertoa, San Sebastian 1980.

García San Miguel, Luis, *Teoría de la Transición*, Nacional, Madrid 1981.

Garrigues y Díaz-Cañabate, Antonio, *Diálogos conmigo mismo*, Planeta, Barcelona 1978.

Georgel, Jacques, *El Franquismo: Historia y balance 1939–1969*, Ruedo Ibérico, Paris 1971

Gibson, Ian, *En Busca de José Antonio*, Planeta, Barcelona 1980.

Gibson, Ian, *Paracuellos: como fue*, Argos Vergara, Barcelona 1983.

Gómez-Santos, Marino, *Conversaciones con Leopoldo Calvo-Sotelo*, Planeta, Barcelona 1982.

González, Felipe, *Un estilo ético*, Argos Vergara, Barcelona 1982.

González, Manuel-Jesús, *La Economía Política del Franquismo*, Tecnos, Madrid 1979.

Graham, Robert, *Spain: Change of a Nation*, Michael Joseph, London 1984.

Guinea, J.L., *Los movimientos obreros y sindicales en España*, Ibérico Europea de Ediciones, Madrid 1978.

Gutiérrez Mellado, Manuel, *Un soldado de España*, Argos Vergara, Barcelona 1983.

Hansen, Edward, *Rural Catalonia under the Franco Regime*, Cambridge University Press, Cambridge 1977.

Harrison, Joseph, *An Economic History of Modern Spain*, Manchester University Press, 1978.

Hayes, Carlton, *Wartime Mission in Spain*, Macmillan, London 1945.

Hermet, Guy, *The Communists in Spain,* Saxon House, Farnborough 1974.

Herr, Richard, *Modern Spain*, University of California Press, 1974.

Highfield, Roger (ed.), *Spain in the Fifteenth Century (1369–1516)*, Macmillan, London 1972.

Hills, George, *Franco: the Man and His Nation*, Robert Hale, London 1967.

Hills, George, *Spain*, Ernest Benn, London 1970.

Hitler, Adolf, *Table Talk 1941–1944* (ed. H. Trevor-Roper), Weidenfeld & Nicolson, London 1953.

Hoare, Samuel, *Ambassador on Special Mission*, Collins, London 1946.

Hottinger, Arnold, *Spain in Transition: Franco's Regime*, Sage Publications, London 1974.

Hottinger, Arnold, *Spain in Transition: Prospects and Policies*, Sage Publications, London 1974.

Hughes, Emmet John, *Report from Spain*, Latimer House, London 1947.

Instituto Nacional de Estadística, *España, Anuario Estadístico 1982*.

Jackson, Gabriel, *The Spanish Republic and the Civil War*, Princeton

University Press, Princeton, 1965.

Jaúregui Bereciartu, Gurutz, *Ideología y estrategia política de ETA*, Siglo XXI, Madrid 1981.

Jiménez Blanco, José, *De Franco a las elecciones generales*, Tecnos, Madrid 1978.

Keyserling, Count, *Europe*, Jonathan Cape, London 1928.

Lafitte, Pierre, *Grammaire Basque*, Bayonne 1962.

Larronde, Jean-Claude, *El nacionalismo vasco: su origen y su ideología en la obra de Sabino Arana Goïri*, Txertoa, San Sebastian 1977.

Lieberman, Sima, *The Contemporary Spanish Economy*, George Allen & Unwin, London 1977.

López Rodó, Laureano, *La larga marcha hacia la monarquía*, Noguer, Barcelona 1977.

Machado, Antonia, *Poesías Completas*, Espasa-Calpe, Madrid 1981.

Mack Smith, Denis, *Mussolini*, Weidenfeld & Nicholson, London 1981.

Madariaga, Salvador de, *Spain*, Ernest Benn, London 1930.

Madariaga, Salvador de, *Spain: a modern history*, Praeger, New York 1958.

Malefakis, Edward, *Agrarian Reform and Peasant Revolution in Spain*, Yale University Press, Newhaven 1970.

Maravall, José, *Dictatorship and Political Dissent*, Tavistock Publications, London 1978.

Maravall, José, *The Transition to Democracy in Spain*, Croom Helm, London 1982.

Marías, Julián, *Cinco años de España*, Espasa-Calpe, Madrid 1981.

Marketing Potentials of Europe's Regions, Euro-Potentials and Planning, London 1973.

Martínez-Alier, Juan, *Labourers and Landowners in Southern Spain*, George Allen & Unwin, London 1977.

Matthews, Herbert, *The Yoke and the Arrows*, Heinemann, London 1958.

McKendrick, Melveena, *Cervantes*, Little, Brown & Co, Boston 1980.

Medhurst, Kenneth, *Government in Spain*, Pergamon Press, Oxford 1973.

Melià, Josep, *Asi cayó Adolfo Suárez*, Planeta, Barcelona 1981.

Menges, Constantine Christopher, *Spain: the struggle for democracy today*, Sage Publications, London 1978.

Miguel, Amando de, *Sociología del Franquismo*, Euros, Barcelona 1975.

Monzón, Telesforo, *Herri Baten Oihua*, Mesa nacional de Herri Batasuna (n.d.).

Morán, Gregorio, *Adolfo Suárez: Historia de una ambición*, Planeta, Barcelona 1979.

Morán, Gregorio, *Los españoles que dejaron de serlo*, Planeta, Barcelona 1982.

Naylon, John, *Andalusia*, Oxford University Press, London 1975.

Neruda, Pablo, *Memoirs*, Souvenir Press, London 1976.

OECD Economic Surveys, *Spain*, Paris 1982.

Oneto, José, *La noche de Tejero*, Planeta, Barcelona 1981.

Oneto, José, *La verdad sobre el caso Tejero*, Planeta, Barcelona 1982.

Oneto, José, *Los últimos días de un presidente*, Planeta, Barcelona 1981.

Ortega y Gasset, José, *España invertebrada*, Espasa-Calpe, Madrid 1964.

Orwell, George, *Homage to Catalonia*, Secker & Warburg, London 1938.

Osorio, Alfonso, *Trayectoria política de un ministro de la Corona*, Planeta, Barcelona 1980.

Otazu, Alfonso de, *El igualtarismo vasco: mito y realidad*, Txertoa, San Sebastian 1973.

Pániker, Salvador, *Conversaciones en Madrid*, Kairos, Barcelona 1969.

Paricio, Jesús M., *Para conocer a nuestros militares*, Tecnos, Madrid 1983.

Payne, Stanley, *Falange: a History of Spanish Fascism*, Oxford University Press, London 1962.

Payne, Stanley (ed.), *Politics and Society in Twentieth-Century Spain*, New Viewpoints, New York 1976.

Payne, Stanley, *Politics and the Military in Modern Spain*, Oxford University Press, London 1967.

Pitt-Rivers, Julian, *The People of the Sierra*, University of Chicago Press, 1954.

Pozuelo Escudero, Vicente, *Los últimos 476 días de Franco*, Planeta, Barcelona 1980.

Preston, Paul (ed.), *Spain in Crisis*, Harvester Press, Hassocks, Sussex 1976.

Preston, Paul, *The Coming of the Spanish Civil War*, Methuen, London 1983.

Prieto, Indalecio, *Palabras de ayer y hoy*, Ercilla, Santiago (Chile) 1938.

Punset, Eduard, *España: sociedad cerrada, sociedad abierta*, Grijalbo, Barcelona 1983.

Ridruejo, Dionisio, *Escrito en España*, Losada, Buenos Aires 1964.

Robinson, Richard A.H., *The Origins of Franco's Spain*, David & Charles, Newton Abbot 1970.

Rossinyol, Jaume, *Le problème national catalan*, Mouton, Paris 1974.

Sainz Rodríguez, Pedro, *Un reinado en la sombra*, Planeta, Barcelona 1981.

Salisbury, William T. and Theberge, James D. (eds.), *Spain in the 1970s: Economics, Social Structure, Foreign Policy*, Praeger, London 1976.

Sarrailh de Ihartza, Fernando (pseudonym of Federico Krutwig), *Vasconia*, Norbait, Buenos Aires 1963.

Silva Muñoz, Federico, *La transición inacabada*, Planeta, Barcelona 1980.

Solé-Tura, Jordi, *Catalanismo y revolución burguesa*, Edicusa, Madrid 1974.

Souchère, Elena de la, *Explication de l'Espagne*, Grasset, Paris 1962.

Southworth, H.K., *Antifalange*, Ruedo Ibérico, Paris 1967.

Southworth, H.K., *Guernica! Guernica!*, Univ. of California Press, Los Angeles 1967.

Suárez Fernández, Luis, *Navegación y comercio en el golfo de Vizcaya: un estudio sobre la política marinera de la Casa de Trastámara*, Escuela de Estudios Medievales del Consejo Superior de Investigaciones Científicas, Madrid 1958.

Tamames, Ramón, *La República, La Era de Franco*, Alianza, Madrid 1980.

Teba, Juan, *La Sevilla de Rojas Marcos*, Planeta, Barcelona 1981.

Tellez, Antonio, *Sabate: Guerrilla Extraordinary*, Davis-Poynter, London 1974.

Thomas, Hugh, *The Spanish Civil War*, Hamish Hamilton, London 1977.

Tusell, Xavier, *La oposición democrática al franquismo*, Planeta, Barcelona 1977.

United Nations, *Demographic Yearbook 1981*.

Urbano, Pilar, *Con la venia . . . yo indagué el 23–F*, Argos Vergara, Barcelona 1982.

Vicens Vives, Jaime, *An Economic History of Spain*, Princeton University Press, Princeton 1969.

Vilaplana, A.R., *Burgos Justice*, Constable, London 1938.

Vilar, Pierre, *Spain: a brief history*, Pergamon Press, Oxford 1980.

Vilar, Sergio, *Protagonistas de la España democrática: la oposición a la dictadura 1939–1969*, Ediciones Sociales, Paris (n.d.)

Villavieja, Marqués de, *Life has been Good*, Chatto & Windus, London 1938.

Welles, Benjamin, *Spain: The Gentle Anarchy*, Pall Mall, London 1965.

Wright, Alison, *The Spanish Economy 1959–1976*, Macmillan, London 1977.

Yglesias, Jose, *The Franco Years*, Bobbs-Merrill, Indianapolis 1977.

Ynfante, Jesús, *La prodigiosa aventura del Opus Dei*, Ruedo ibérico, Paris 1970.

List of Newspapers and Periodicals Cited in the Notes

ABC Seville and Madrid
El Alcázar Madrid
Arriba Madrid
Blanco y Negro Madrid
La Calle Madrid
Cambio 16 Madrid
Cuadernos para el diálogo Madrid
Daily Telegraph London
Deia Bilbao
Diario 16 Madrid
Diario de Barcelona Barcelona
Financial Times London
Fuerza Nueva Madrid
Guardian London
Informaciones Madrid
International Herald Tribune Paris

Interviu Barcelona
Le Monde Paris
Madrid Madrid
Muga Bilbao
El Nuevo Lunes Madrid
New York Times New York
Observer London
El País Madrid
Posible Madrid
Pueblo Madrid
Revista de Opinión Pública Madrid
The Times London
La Vanguardia Barcelona
Viva New York
Ya Madrid

Index

320

Index

Salvador Merino, Gerardo, failure to establish national syndicalism, 22
Sánchez Albornoz, Claudio, 248
Sánchez-Covisa, Mariano, 70, 238
San Martín, Colonel José Ignacio, 243
San Sebastian, 119
Santiago, General Fernando de, 140; resignation of, 155–6
Santiago de Compostela, 48
Sarrailh de Ihartza, Fernando (pseudonym of Federico Krutwig Sagredo), see Krutwig
Sartorius, Nicolás, 93
Satrústegui, Joaquín, opposition to Franco, 99–101
Schmidt, Helmut, 208
Second Republic, 37, 116, 133, 186, 204, 256, 272–3
Second Vatican Council, 55–9
Segorbe, Ignacio Medina, Duke of, 49
Segura, Cardinal Pedro, criticism of falangists, 15
Senado, 158, 210; 1977 elections to, 185; debates constitution, 195–6
Serrano Suñer, Ramón, 66
Serrat, Joan Manuel, 125
Servicio Nacional de Concentración Parcelaria (SNCP), activities of, 38–9
Seville, 257; spoliation of, 48–9
Silva Muñoz, Federico, 57–8, 76, 150, 153, 165, 171, 220; formation of UDE, 75; leaves UDE, 169; opposes constitution, 196, 200; leaves AP, 200–1
Sindicato de Obreros del Campo, 257
Sindicato Español Universitario (SEU), 91–2
social democrats, 171, 182, 188; opposition to Franco, 97–8; divisions among, 165; join UCD, 180–1; role in UCD disputes, 250–2, 263–4
Socialist International, supports González, 103, 165–7
Socialist Party, see PSOE
Sociedad Euskalerria, 116–17
Sofia, Princess (later Queen), 63, 228
Solchaga, Carlos, 73
Solidaridad Española, defeat in 1982

elections, 265–7
Solís, José, 136, 140, 157; on Franco's achievement, 34; the Solís Statute, 65; dismissed by Franco, 66; reinstatement of, 75
Soria, 172,184
Sos del Rey Católico, 36
Sota, Sir Ramón de la, support for Basque nationalism, 116–17, 120
Soviet Union, 42, 82, 95, 105, 205; PCE attitude towards, 96–7
Spanish Sahara, 144
Spinola, General Antonio, 72
Stabilization Plan, success of, 44–6, 59
Stonyhurst, 47
Suárez, Adolfo, 60, 75, 162, 164, 165, 167, 169, 205, 238, 240, 260, 263, 265, 269; joins Arias government, 140; speech on political reform, 143–4; appointed prime minister, 150; early career of, 150–2; forms government, 152–3; political programme of, 154; passes Law for Political Reform, 156–8; referendum victory, 159–60; popularity of, 161; attitude to left-wing opposition, 163; rivalry with Fraga, 170; and legalization of PCE, 174–7; takes charge of UCD, 177–80; electoral victory of, 182–6; forms 2nd government, 187–8; economic policy of, 189–93; favours consensus politics, 194–5; calls new elections, 202; criticized by Fraga, 208; in 1979 elections, 209; victory of, 210; policy towards Catalonia, 214–18; policy towards Basque country, 218–29 passim; and Basque statute, 220–1; armed forces' attitude to, 233–4, 236–7; during attempted coup, 242; decline in popularity, 249–50; UCD criticism of, 250–1; resignation of, 251–3; autonomy policy of, 256–8; sets up CDS, 264; defeat in 1982 elections, 267; hostility of press to, 270; achievements of, 271–3
Suárez, Fernando, 157
Supreme Court, 171; refuses to